Modernism was made to be annotated. Amanda Golden shows how it was made by *being* annotated—in the hands of midcentury moderns who encountered and then taught Joyce, Eliot, and the rest, in college. Opening doors on the classrooms, faculty offices, and personal libraries of Plath, Berryman, and Sexton, this attentive, innovative, and surprisingly lively book shows that the marginal is central to the story of modernism in postwar America.

—*Langdon Hammer,*
Niel Gray, Jr. Professor of English,
Yale University

Amanda Golden's meticulously researched *Annotating Modernism* broadens not only our understanding of midcentury poetry's relationship to modernism, but our understanding of literary influence itself. By focusing on the "untapped resources" of midcentury poets' marginalia on modernist works, and their teaching notes on modernist authors, Golden makes a compelling case that modernism is an ongoing social and literary construction, both contested and promoted by the academy and the midcentury poets—Plath, Hughes, Sexton, and Berryman—who taught within it. This is a timely and necessary study that brings materialist discourse and theories of influence together in original and innovative ways.

—*Heather Clark,*
Professor of Contemporary Poetry,
University of Huddersfield,
author of Red Comet: The Short Life and
Blazing Art of Sylvia Plath *(Knopf, 2020)*

Annotating Modernism

Making extensive use of archival materials by Sylvia Plath, John Berryman, and Anne Sexton, Amanda Golden reframes the relationship between modernism and midcentury poetry. While Golden situates her book among other materialist histories of modernism, she moves beyond the examination of published works to address poets' annotations in their personal copies of modernist texts. A consideration of the dynamics of literary influence, *Annotating Modernism* analyzes the teaching strategies of midcentury poets and the ways they read modernists like T. S. Eliot, James Joyce, Ezra Pound, Virginia Woolf, and W. B. Yeats. Situated within a larger rethinking of modernism, Golden's study illustrates the role of midcentury poets in shaping modernist discourse.

Amanda Golden is Associate Professor of English at New York Institute of Technology.

Annotating Modernism
Marginalia and Pedagogy from Virginia Woolf to the Confessional Poets

Amanda Golden

Frontispiece: Sylvia Plath, "Smith Dorm Room," 1955, "Smith Scrapbook," oversize box 8, LMC 1862, folder 36, Plath mss. II, Lilly Library, Indiana University, Bloomington, Indiana.

Routledge
Taylor & Francis Group

LONDON AND NEW YORK

First published 2020
by Routledge
2 Park Square, Milton Park, Abingdon, Oxon OX14 4RN

and by Routledge
52 Vanderbilt Avenue, New York, NY 10017

*Routledge is an imprint of the Taylor & Francis Group, an informa
business*

© 2020 Amanda Golden

British Library Cataloguing-in-Publication Data
A catalogue record for this book is available from the British
Library

Library of Congress Cataloging-in-Publication Data
A catalog record has been requested for this book

ISBN: 978-1-4724-1076-4 (hbk)
ISBN: 978-1-315-56723-5 (ebk)

Typeset in Sabon
by codeMantra

For my family and in memory of my grandfathers.

Contents

Figures

Acknowledgments

Marks in the margin and notes prepared for teaching often comment on published texts but have not been published themselves. In publishing *Annotating Modernism*, I have had extraordinary support from permissions holders, literary estates, and editors. For their generous permission, I thank Kate Donohue, Adam Fisher, Carol Hughes, Frieda Hughes, Linda Gray Sexton, Faber and Faber, and Sterling Lord, Litteristic, LLC. At *Modernism/modernity*, which published a portion of Chapter 2, I thank Nick Wolterman and Lawrence Rainey. I cannot express enough gratitude to Ann Donohue for acquiring this book and Michelle Salyga and Bryony Reece for seeing it through to publication.

Annotating Modernism is the result of research and archives, courses and mentors. This project began at the University of Washington under the direction of Brian M. Reed, an unparalleled poetry scholar and teacher, joined by outstanding committee members, Sydney Kaplan and the late John Coldewey. I began reading Sylvia Plath, Anne Sexton, and John Berryman in Peter Balakian's Contemporary American Poetry class at Colgate University. The class met in the same room where Sexton had taught her "Anne on Anne" course on her own poetry in 1972. At Colgate, I am grateful to Peter, the late Bruce Berlind, Susan Cerasano, Michael Coyle, Jane Pinchin, Lynn Staley, and Sarah Wider. I also thank Sexton's former students, particularly Craig Carlson, Richard D. Enemark, Nancy Flanagan Kinsella, and Lydia Woodward, who generously gave interviews and sent copies of materials, including their notes in the books of Sexton's poetry that they read for the course. After graduating from Colgate, I moved to Amherst, Massachusetts and started working with Plath's manuscripts and personal library in the Mortimer Rare Book Room at Smith College. For nearly 20 years, Smith has been a vital part of my life. I thank Martin Antonetti, Barbara Blumenthal, Amanda Ferrara, Mary Irwin, the late Enid and Eugene Mark, the late Mark Morford, Ellen Nodelman, Shannon Supple, and Nanci Young.

I am fortunate to have fantastic colleagues and students at New York Institute of Technology. I thank Elizabeth J. Donaldson and Jonathan Goldman for providing generous feedback on portions of the manuscript.

For supporting my research, I have the deepest gratitude for President Henry C. Foley, Provost Junius J. Gonzales, Dean of the College of Arts and Sciences Daniel Quigley, and English Department Chair Elaine Brown. It has also been a joy to work with Nada Anid, Hal Burton, Anthony DiMatteo, Holly Fils-Aime, Edward Giuliano, Francine Glazer, Jennifer Griffiths, Lori Jirousek-Falls, Kevin LaGrandeur, Lissi Athanasiou-Krikelis, Loraine Lazarus, John Misak, Christopher Moylan, Maryse Prezeau, Michael Schiavi, Katherine Williams, Karen Wolff, and Roger Yu. In addition, I thank my students, particularly Rebekah Geevarghese, Uzma Patel, and Savina Ruppaner.

Generous fellowships have supported my research. For inviting me to Emory University's Bill and Carol Fox Center for Humanistic Inquiry as a N. E. H. Post-Doctoral Fellow in Poetics, I will always be grateful to Martine Brownley, Keith Anthony, Colette Barlow, and Amy Erbil. I am also indebted to Emory's Stuart A. Rose Manuscript, Archives, and Rare Book Library, for a Research Fellowship and for the years I have spent in the archives. I thank Julie Phillips Brown, Elizabeth Chase, Amy Hildreth Chen, Bryan Chitwood, Sumita Chakraborty, Margaret Greaves, Kerry Higgins-Wendt, Walter Kalaidjian, Barbara Ladd, Amy Li, Benjamin Reiss, Ronald Schuchard, Kathy Shoemaker, and Kevin Young. As a graduate student, I received an Everett Helm Fellowship from Indiana University's Lilly Library that allowed me to work with Plath's teaching materials. For their support, I thank Rebecca Cape and the Lilly Library staff. A Dissertation Fellowship from the University of Texas at Austin's Harry Ransom Humanities Research Center also enabled my research with Anne Sexton's archive and the Ransom Center's Authors' Libraries Collection, and I thank Richard Oram, Molly Schwartzburg, and Jennifer Tisdale.

Archivists, curators, and library staff members have been instrumental in my completion of *Annotating Modernism*. I thank, at the British Library, Helen Broderick; at the University of Minnesota, Barbara Bezat, Richard Kelly, and Kathryn Hujda; at the University of Virginia, Jean Cooper; and at Colgate, Sarah Keen. I am also grateful to the staff of the Rare Book and Manuscript Library at Columbia University, Seeley G. Mudd Library at Princeton University, the Schlesinger Library at the Radcliffe Institute for Advanced Study, Harvard University Archives, and Isaac Gewirtz and the staff of the Berg Collection of the New York Public Library. Since arriving in New York, the Wertheim Study and the Allen Room at the New York Public Library have provided spaces for contemplation and revision, and I thank Melanie Locay.

While writing this book, I have learned from phenomenal scholars. Peter K. Steinberg's precision has raised the bar immeasurably for Plath scholarship. Anita Helle's friendship and collaboration have been a source of inspiration for over a decade. Mark Hussey has taught me to be a vigilant editor and a discerning critic. Agnes Scott College's Works-in-Progress Group and the New York Modernism Seminar hosted energetic, productive discussions of portions of the manuscript. I am also indebted to Jo Gill for generously reading the Sexton chapter. For their years of inspiring conversations and sharp feedback, my gratitude to Amy E. Elkins, Emily James, Margaret Konkol, and Sarah Terry is immeasurable. At a pivotal moment, Randi Saloman read the entire manuscript, lending invaluable insights. Dennis Duncan not only provided astute, careful commentary, but also invited me to discuss *Annotating Modernism* for his Paratexts Podcast and at Oxford University's Bodleian Library for the Material Texts Working Group.

Friends and colleagues have provided unfailing intellectual energy and support. I am grateful to Jane L. Anderson, Danielle Apfelbaum, Sally Bayley, Emily Bloom, Tracy Brain, Rebecca Burnett, Sarah-Jane Burton, Laura Butler, Marsha Bryant, Lynda K. Bundtzen, Wayne Chapman, the late Nephie Christodoulides, Kathleen Connors, Heather Clark, Debra Rae Cohen, Dianna Coppolo, Stephen Coppolo, Deirdre Coyle, Christine Cozzens, Anna Creadick, Anthony Cuda, Luke Ferretter, Adrienne Forgette, J. Ashley Foster, John Golden, Suzanne Golden, Terry Gifford, Christopher Grobe, Gillian Groszewski, John Haffenden, Langdon Hammer, the late Mark Hinchcliffe, Hilary Holladay, Kamran Javadizadeh, Judith Kroll, Cassandra Laity, Richard Larschan, Dorothea Lasky, Melissa Maday, Naomi Mercer, Megan Miller, the late Sidney Monas, Paige Morgan, John Morgenstern, Maeve O'Brien, Robin Peel, Shanna Perkins, Siobhan Phillips, Judith Raymo, Shawna Ross, Bess Rous, Emily Setina, Rahmat Shoureshi, James Simon, Dawn Skorczewski, Carrie Smith, Peggy Thompson, Rachel Trousdale, Janine Utell, Richard Utz, Susan Van Dyne, Victoria Van Hyning, Linda Wagner-Martin, Kelly Walsh, Laura Webb, and Kristina Zimbakova.

This project benefits most from its earliest supporters. I am honored to have worked with Karen V. Kukil, a scholar and curator for whom I have the deepest respect. Annotating would not mean as much to me as it does without Dr. Terry Kidner, who taught me that I could pursue a career that I had never imagined possible.

Finally, *Annotating Modernism* could not have become a reality without my family: Shirley Goldfine and Vickie, Andrew, Louise, Ben, Molly, Jack, and Kate Golden.

Permissions

Previous versions or portions of *Annotating Modernism* were published as

"Anne Sexton's Modern Library." In *Collecting, Curating, and Researching Writers' Libraries: A Handbook*, edited by Richard W. Oram and Joseph Nicholson, 65–76. Lanham, MD: Rowman & Littlefield, 2014.

"'A Brief Note in the Margin': Virginia Woolf and Annotating." In *Contradictory Woolf: Selected Papers from the Twenty-First Annual Conference on Virginia Woolf*, edited by Derek Ryan and Stella Bolaki, 209–214. Clemson University Press, 2012.

"Introduction: Reassessing Anne Sexton." In *This Business of Words: Reassessing Anne Sexton*, edited by Amanda Golden, 1–16. Gainesville: University Press of Florida, 2016.

"John Berryman at Midcentury: Annotating Ezra Pound and Teaching Modernism." *Modernism/modernity* 21, no. 2 (April 2014): 507–528.

"Sylvia Plath's Teaching Syllabus: A Chronology." *Plath Profiles: An Interdisciplinary Journal of Sylvia Plath Studies* 2 (August 2009): 209–220. Accessed 20 March 2020. http://scholarworks.iu.edu/journals/index.php/plath/article/viewFile/4746/4381

"Ted Hughes and the Midcentury American Academy." *The Ted Hughes Society Journal* 3 (2013): 47–52.

Introduction
Annotating literary history

An annotation is part of a story. A note in the margin is a clue, a detail. And yet, even as marginalia may provide pieces to a puzzle, we rarely attempt to understand annotating as a genre, let alone what annotations can tell us about literary and institutional histories.[1] Part of marginalia's allure lies in the fact that we can never know what a reader was thinking as he or she read. But the markings, annotations, and other records that writers leave behind become part of a larger set of texts. The contours of these artifacts matter. Textures elicit different responses; an alignment of words catches the eye. We see one writer reading another, one generation reading another. And when we turn to the twentieth century, the material history of reading shapes the version of modernism that midcentury readers encounter.[2]

Interpreting marginalia and teaching notes means, to borrow Stephen Orgel's phrase, "finding evidence in the hitherto irrelevant."[3] With regard to early modern texts, Orgel points out that in bibliographic study, "the habits of reading, manifested in various marks and marginalia, have become as central to the nature of the book as format and typography, watermarks and chain lines" (2). Not all evidence is legible. Orgel finds that investigating "individual acts of reading . . . has been possible only because reading in early modern culture sometimes left traces, and sometimes those traces are decipherable" (2). In a similar fashion, *Annotating Modernism* seeks to understand writers' reading practices in their own time, broadening our sense of the influence of the New Criticism, the reading of modernism, and the development of literary history following World War II.

Margins remain largely untapped spaces in modernist studies. Authors' libraries and teaching notes present an exemplary but overlooked resource for tracing the history and reception of Anglo-American modernism. Considering midcentury poets' marginalia and underlining in their personal copies of modernist texts, *Annotating Modernism* illustrates that modernism is not a discrete literary period but a discourse that is the result of institutionally situated processes. The chapters that follow demonstrate that modernism is an ongoing and contested social project and that the university is integral to the formation and redefinition of modernist discourse.[4]

For over a decade, historical approaches have flourished in modernist studies. In its attention to writers' and readers' annotations, this book redefines the parameters of what Douglas Mao and Rebecca Walkowitz refer to as "the media of modernism."[5] Such materials, they suggest, present the opportunity "to encounter ambitions for literary art that might otherwise be lost to historical memory" (Mao and Walkowitz, 744). Ann Ardis has added that "the production of richer, thicker histories of modernism is a hallmark of the new modernist studies."[6] Moving from the significance of lines and markings to larger midcentury cultural and social issues, *Annotating Modernism* sheds new light on modernism's history in postwar academic institutions.

By interpreting the materials that record and shape writers' reading practices, *Annotating Modernism* broadens the scope of existing material histories of modernism. In *Material Modernism: The Politics of the Page* (2001), George Bornstein interprets versions of texts from the first half of the twentieth-century in order to argue that modernist texts are not static, fixed entities.[7] In their reconsiderations of modernism, Bornstein and Lawrence Rainey, in *Institutions of Modernism: Literary Elites and Public Culture* (1998) and *Revisiting* The Waste Land (2005), have addressed the publication history of modernist texts.[8] Unlike the versions of published texts that Bornstein and Rainey consider, *Annotating Modernism*'s focus on the unpublished contents of personal libraries, teaching materials, and other forms of archival fragments enables a new material history of modernism. Interventions in print culture studies have made it no longer possible to ignore the impact of the production and publication of texts. *Annotating Modernism* turns to what readers' handling of these texts can teach us about materiality and reading practices.[9] Interpretations of material culture can be wide ranging.[10] In *The Death of the Book: Modernist Novels and the Time of Reading* (2016), John Lurz addresses what he calls "the physical relationship we have with our so-called reading material" (15).[11] While his consideration of "materiality" emphasizes the production, publication, and circulation of books (10), annotating and underlining can also make reading a physical process, adding layers to the pages of texts.

In its treatment of marginalia, *Annotating Modernism* historicizes the artifacts that readers create. Genetic criticism has also addressed these fragments, what Dirk Van Hulle poetically calls "paper fossils," as one of many records of writers' thought processes.[12] Van Hulle captures well the fragmentary and disparate record of writers' encounters with ideas. With regard to Charles Darwin, Van Hulle insists that

> it is necessary to try and retrace all the paths and dead ends in the maze of Darwin's reading traces. Again, mapping the labyrinth gives the false impression of a chaotic mind at work, but it is clear that the creation of this mess was an integral part of, perhaps even a precondition for, the written invention which resulted in *On the Origin of Species.*

(54)

Van Hulle is less invested in the history of modernism, however, than in interpreting the ways that modern writers' notes may inform their characters' thoughts, particularly in the work of Virginia Woolf and James Joyce. *Annotating Modernism* begins with both writers, but shifts its focus to the ways that pedagogical and institutional contexts shaped their fictional representations of marginalia, anticipating the underlining and annotating that readers would come to add as they made their way through Woolf's and Joyce's fiction.

Academic institutions anchor *Annotating Modernism*'s attention to midcentury writers' reading of modernism. David M. Earle has noted that there has not been sufficient attention to "how modernism was defined and canonized by academia."[13] Rachel Sagner Buurma and Laura Heffernan have since approached this question more broadly, collecting syllabi for their digital project, "The Teaching Archive: A New History of Literary Study."[14] Drawing on these materials, Buurma and Heffernan have argued that T. S. Eliot's teaching in Extension School courses provided the groundwork for the style and content of his essays in his influential collection, *The Sacred Wood* (1920).[15] They demonstrate that Eliot's pedagogy in teaching working-class students provided a foundation for his essays, and, in turn, its subsequent impact on close reading for generations of college students (Buurma and Heffernan, 265). Giving critical attention to less widely known classrooms, Buurma and Heffernan insist, "does more than supplement or diversify existing stories of the discipline of English literary studies; it requires a radical rewriting of them" (265). The poets in *Annotating Modernism* experienced reverberations of *The Sacred Wood*'s influence, and the particularity of their encounters with it underscores the necessity of further archival research that engages the intersection of pedagogy and literary history.

Examining mid- to late-twentieth-century academic reading strategies, *Annotating Modernism* considers the history of modernism's introduction into curricula and the extent to which close reading strategies developed in response to texts from the first half of the twentieth-century.[16] Robert Scholes has reflected that "attending Yale just before the midcentury, I was more or less indoctrinated into the New Critical account of aesthetic value, which I see now as a distinctly Modernist account."[17] Scholes is not alone in this impression, and *Annotating Modernism* considers the extent to which the critical discourse that developed in response to modernist texts also informed postwar poets' private and public negotiations with literary texts.

Shifting from what Rainey calls modernism's "shared institutional structures" to postwar academic institutions allows us to see the ways that universities created the modernism we have inherited (*Institutions*, 6). While critics were part of this process, academia was where their ideas circulated, deployed by teachers and transformed by students. Poets in particular provide the focus of this book because, as they returned to universities to teach writing and literature, they created troves of materials that blend close reading and research with images and ideas they admired. In doing so, they expanded the role of the "poet-critic" or "poet-teacher," teaching across genres and reading widely in criticism.[18] Moving outward from the locations where postwar poets studied and taught modernist texts, this book also considers the ways that the contents of poets' annotated books and teaching notes respond to larger cultural, historical, and political trajectories.[19]

Margins preserve words, terms, and ideas. Concepts that writers identify as they annotate may be among those that they learned as students.[20] Mark McGurl and Amy Hungerford have respectively argued in *The Program Era: Postwar Fiction and the Rise of Creative Writing* (2009) and *Postmodern Belief: American Literature and Religion Since 1960* (2010) that creative writing courses were sites where writers encountered the modes of reading that modernist critics demonstrated, altering the structure of postwar literature.[21] As Hungerford has proposed elsewhere, "the second half of the twentieth century sees not a departure from modernism's aesthetic but its triumph in the institution of the university and in the literary culture more generally."[22] Modernism thrived in universities, and as writers read and taught, they documented aspects of its impact. Given that annotation is a learned strategy and its content changes with the academic climate, marginalia allow us to see some of the ways that writers' material practices and interpretative strategies were both institutionally and individually informed.[23]

As students and teachers of literature, postwar poets' treatment of modernism intersected with—and at times was inseparable from—the language of midcentury academic institutions. During his final poetry lecture at the University of Cincinnati in 1952, John Berryman paused to note the following,

> I must say something about the famous difficulty of modern poetry. Most first-rate modern painting, architecture, music, is difficult. The difficulty of modern poetry is not isolated. What Matthew Arnold predicted has now taken place: modern art, including poetry, has to carry the job once done by religion and philosophy . . . This makes the poet a priest. . . . Priests have . . . made themselves clear . . . Oracles are obscure. Human personality is obscure. The audience imagines that the poet writes for the audience. This is not even economically the case. Universities, foundations, publishing houses, support the poet. . . . Milton's <u>Lycidas</u> describes a blind fury—really a fate called a fury in anger. It takes knowledge and wit to know it is a fate. But less knowledge is to be found in the modern audience, and this causes a reaction in the artist.[24]

By returning to Milton's subtlety, Berryman emphasized not only that recent critical approaches had overlooked this kind of attention but also that readers were losing the ability to understand modern poetry and what preceded it. For Berryman, this level of perception was also the result of careful study. When he taught Milton on a different occasion, Berryman showed his students the copy he had annotated.[25] In this book and throughout his library, part of the process of reading meant making impressions on a page, creating a record of thoughts, definitions, and interpretations.

Reading materials

The reading experience is not limited to printed words. In *The Textual Condition* (1991), Jerome McGann argued that the physical and aesthetic properties of texts inform reading practices.[26] Books include what Gerard Genette has categorized as paratexts, aspects that are separate from the body of the text, including chapter headings, footnotes, and appendices.[27] The materials that *Annotating Modernism* considers often lie outside of Genette's rubric, particularly as they include writers' markings in published texts.[28] To this end, they reflect Jacques Derrida's description of annotations as "parasitic and grafted," added with skill and feeding on the thoughts of others.[29]

Annotating Modernism analyzes the following types of responses: marginal notes, textual markings, writing inside covers, notes on pages inserted within books, and teaching materials. Marginal notes comprise words or phrases that readers have inscribed in texts. Textual markings include lines in the margin, asterisks, stars, brackets, and check marks. Writing in texts takes the form of inscriptions on the front and back covers, flyleaves, or endpapers of books in addition to lists of page numbers or writing on pages that are kept with books, slipped between the pages or appended by archivists. The shape that notes and markings take becomes inseparable from their contents, distinguishing their role in the archive as artifacts and impressions of reading.

Annotations, teaching notes, and other records of reading are literary and cultural artifacts. In *Practicing New Historicism* (2000), Stephen Greenblatt urges literary critics to emulate the strategies of anthropologists, interpreting "a much broader and less familiar range of texts."[30] Annotated books, textual fragments, and teaching notes fulfill and complicate Greenblatt's recommendation that literary critics investigate "unfamiliar cultural texts" that are "often odd, fragmentary, [and] unexpected" (28). Many of the objects that *Annotating Modernism* considers are mundane in their construction, yet rare in their singularity, condition, and significance.[31] By asking new questions about the historical, political, and cultural implications of writers' reading, underlining, and marginalia, this book also responds to Cary Nelson's call for further treatment of "the relations between poetry and the rest of social life."[32] As he clarifies, "[n]o single story can be told about modern poetry and its varied audiences that is even marginally adequate" (*Repression and Recovery*, 7). Nelson's point is not limited to poetry; it applies to other genres, including modernist fiction, which was a subject of study for midcentury poets. As a result, readers' notes and marginalia become invaluable histories of literary modernism.[33]

Modernist writers' underlining and annotating present a physical record, one that builds upon existing forms of commentary, some examples of which are included in modernist texts. Turning to the ways that modernist writers handled and altered the texts that they read, we will see that their doing so shaped not only their writing but also readers' interpretation of it.

Modernist reading

Students and professors of literature are familiar with the types of annotation that this book considers. Readers may have already underlined passages or added notes in the margins.[34] Teachers inscribe texts with commentary, explications, and definitions; their notes, in turn, inform the material they present to students. Students subsequently inscribe in blank texts the contents of their observations in addition to the information that their teachers provide.[35]

As Richard Poirier has argued, readers' texts are emblematic of a larger tension in writers' and readers' annotation of modernist texts:

> The kinds of clues supplied by Eliot's famous notes, Joyce's handouts, [and] Yeats's system . . . all tended to nullify a reading experience which in itself meant to mock the efficacy of such schematizations. As a result, there have been for most readers at least two texts of works like *The Waste Land* or *Ulysses*. One is full of marginalia by which the work is translated into something orderly, fit for class discussion, lectures, and articles, while the other is remembered with fondness for all kinds of fragmentary pleasure.[36]

Readers cannot explain in margins the elements that comprise a text's difficulty, or, in Poirier's terms, the enjoyment of reading it. While annotations necessarily differ from one's thoughts while reading, the notes also provide a textual record. As we will see in the texts that this study considers, each reader's copy of *The Waste Land* or *Ulysses* is a different document.[37]

Eliot's *Waste Land* presents a paradigmatic example for modernist considerations of annotation because of the endnotes it includes.[38] As readers may know, Eliot added the endnotes to fill pages for his publisher, Boni and Liveright. The notes present a peculiar form of commentary as they identify sources that Eliot and subsequent readers have considered futile. As Berryman points out in a lecture he gave at Cincinnati in 1952,

> [t]he substance of the poem is not found in Eliot's notes which are stuffy and misleading. They were forced on him by his American publisher who would not take the poem unless he could stretch it to the length of a book.[39]

(Ames)

The impact that Eliot's sources had for the midcentury reading popula-
tion, however, is emblematic of the extent to which academic close reading
strategies developed in response to modernist texts.[40] While, like Berry-
man, critics have been wary of Eliot's notes, they also shaped interpreta-
tions of his poem.[41] As William Carlos Williams put it in 1951, *The Waste
Land* "[gave] the poem back to the academics."[42] Sources that Eliot iden-
tified, such as Jessie Weston's *From Ritual to Romance* (1920), informed
such midcentury readings of *The Waste Land* as Elizabeth Drew's inter-
pretation in *T. S. Eliot: The Design of His Poetry* (1949).[43] In the notes
that Sylvia Plath prepared to teach the poem in 1958, she advised that her
students consult Eliot's endnotes and, when she annotated her copy of the
poem, she inscribed their contents and excerpts from Drew's close read-
ings in the margins.[44]

Since midcentury, *Waste Land* readers have had access to a wealth of
annotations. In 2015, Christopher Ricks and Jim McCue published *The
Poems of T. S. Eliot*, a 1500-page volume with extensive annotations, some
elaborating on the contents and origins of Eliot's endnotes.[45] This treat-
ment adds to Lawrence Rainey's publication of *The Annotated* Waste Land
in 2006, which follows Eliot's notes with 51 pages of annotations.[46] The
point of considering *The Waste Land* notes, however, is not to address ob-
fuscation or elitism. These notes are part of a more interesting phenomenon
of modernists' consideration of the materiality of texts.

While *The Waste Land* arrives with Eliot's notes, it could be argued that
Ezra Pound's densely packed *Cantos*, with what Edmund Wilson called
its "cargo of erudition," invite annotations.[47] Readers like Berryman took
a pencil to Pound's poetry, and Pound himself was not averse to writing
in books. James Laughlin remembers in his poem "Ezra (Pound)," "[t]he
books you loaned me / Were full of caustic marginalia" (lines 21–2).[48]
Pound's library in the University of Texas at Austin's Harry Ransom Center
reflects his idiosyncrasies, like the instructions that *Instigations of Ezra
Pound: Together with "An Essay on the Chinese Written Character" by
Ernest Fenollosa* (1920) was a "[d]esk copy not to be leant."[49] Pound's
character emerges in different ways here; in some cases, we see him or-
ganizing and ordering others' possible use of his books, and in others, we
can see his textual emendations, correcting what were likely typographical
errors following publication.

As Pound notes in a letter to Williams: "It is not necessary . . . to read
everything in a book in order to speak intelligently of it. Don't tell every-
body I said so."[50] Pound's observation also speaks to annotation, in that it
is often the result of readers' making their way through texts, perhaps se-
lectively. Possibly to this end, Pound marked texts and listed page numbers
inside the back covers of books like Henry Adams's *History of the United
States of America*.[51] Pound's library also includes his copies of his con-
temporaries' books, which teach us about the state in which he may have
encountered and sought to preserve these texts.

Examining volumes from different writers' libraries together presents new material links that can alter our sense of modernist networks and institutions. Several modernist writers' personal libraries in the Authors' Libraries Collection at the Ransom Center enable the reconstruction of books' circulation and writers' exchanges of each other's publications.[52] Pound, for instance, saved the issues of what began as Wyndham Lewis's "Serial Story" *Tarr* (1916) in *The Egoist*.[53] The pile of what Pound called "a much-handled file of EGOISTS" remains in an envelope with a hole punched at the top of the first copy. On it, Pound indicated in blue pencil, "TARR – / NOT TO BE REMOVED."[54] While he was fighting in World War I, Lewis had entrusted Pound with the task of preparing *Tarr* for publication in the United States, and it appears that Pound worked with the serialized versions to do so.[55] Similarly piecemeal, the unbound pages that comprise Lewis's *Ulysses* are enclosed in manila cardboard and begin on page 115. This sheaf, which contains Lewis's annotations, begins in the "Aeolus" episode and ends during the play in "Circe."[56] By contrast, Evelyn Waugh's fine edition of Joyce's novel is bound in brown leather, with white marbled boards and a gold printed title on the spine.[57] As these examples demonstrate, the appearance and condition of books, whether decorative or fragmentary, have the potential to inflect writers' engagement with their contents.

Nineteenth- and early twentieth-century writers' references to annotation reveal a sense of marking and writing in books as informed, yet instinctive, practices.[58] Marginalia provide different kinds of evidence, taking on a life beyond the pages on which they remain. Cristanne Miller points out that

> many nineteenth-century Americans exchanged books with marked passages and kept scrapbooks with cut-out articles and written-in items. [Emily] Dickinson writes: "A Book I have – a friend gave – / Whose Pencil – here and there – / Had notched the place that pleased Him –."[59]

In this instance, markings provide an extension of their author's presence, and another can share in the aftermath of the experience, imagining what may have prompted it. Such impressions can also document more sinister presences. In Robert Louis Stevenson's *The Strange Case of Dr. Jekyll and Mr. Hyde* (1886), Hyde defaced "a pious work, for which Jekyll had several times expressed a great esteem, [and] annotated [it], in his own hand, with startling blasphemies."[60] This evidence helps to unravel what had occurred.[61] Jekyll calls it one of Hyde's "apelike tricks . . . scrawling in my own hand blasphemies on the pages of my books" (Stevenson, 1719). Marginalia can also be cryptic. Early in the twentieth-century, Joseph Conrad's unnamed narrator of *Heart of Darkness* (1902) recounts Marlow's discovery of "notes penciled in the margins and plainly referring to the text. I couldn't believe my eyes! They were in cipher!"[62] While marginal glosses typically clarify texts, here the notes' inscrutability is emblematic of the codes that annotators use.

Near the close of the first half of the twentieth-century, modernist writers' reflections on the materiality of texts and reading practices record not only their own strategies but also the impact of modernism. In their fiction, E. M. Forster, Woolf, and Joyce address and critique the physicality of books, annotation, and marginal commentary.[63] Forster's survey of his books in his late piece, "In My Library" (1949), speaks to the range of texts and contexts that informed his work. Forster's relationship to his library may have influenced the images of books in such novels as *Howards End* (1910). Readers remember, for instance, the murderous effect of a provoked "shower" of books at the novel's close.[64] Leonard Bast's "familiarity with the outsides of books" shapes Margaret Schlegel's sense that one must "only connect the prose and the passion," which teachers of modernism so frequently introduce (*HE*, 105, 170).[65] Critics also know the reading of Forster's contemporary, Virginia Woolf; her essays and reading notebooks have presented not only a focus of criticism devoted to her work but also modernist writers' reading. As we will see at the end of this segment, in her late novel *The Years* (1937), Woolf provides insight into the process of annotating and its role as an institutional practice.

In his essay, "In My Library," Forster introduces readers to the disorder of his books:

> my library, so far as I have created it, is rather a muddle. Here's one sort of book, there's another, and there is not enough of any sort of book to strike a dominant note. Books about India and by Indians, modern poetry, ancient history, American novels, travel books, books on the state of the world, and on the world-state, books on individual liberty, art-albums, Dante and books about him[.] . . . The absence of the collector's instinct in me, the absence of deliberate choice, have combined with a commendable variety of interests.[66]

The "muddle" of Forster's library not only records the historical and literary sources that captured his interest but also is itself modernist in its rendering of the disorganized present. Writing almost four decades after *Howards End*, Forster is also applying its terms to his own library. Knowing that his characters understood Leonard to be limited to the exterior of texts, Forster distinguishes himself as "a lover of the interiors of books, of the words in them" ("In My Library," 294). While his books might form a haphazard arrangement, Forster suggests that he, unlike Leonard, is not "a muddle of a man" (*HE*, 135). Near the close of the novel, Helen desires to stay with her library at Howards End because "the presence of all the books . . . soothes her" (*HE*, 278). When writing "In My Library," Forster updates this sentiment, drawing a connection between the materiality of books and literary history:

> at night . . . they come into their own, and attain a collective dignity. It is very pleasant to sit with them . . . not reading, not even thinking,

but aware that they, with their accumulated wisdom and charm, are
waiting to be used, and that my library, in its tiny imperfect way, is a
successor to the great private libraries of the past.

("In My Library," 294–5)

Despite Forster's romantic image, he is aware that the books in his library
grapple with modernity's incomprehensible realities.

Forster gestures toward this paradox in an anecdote about encountering
one of his own books. At the beginning of his preface to Mulk Raj Anand's
Untouchable (1935), Forster recounts finding a reader's annotation in the
novel he had published over a decade earlier, *A Passage to India* (1924):

> Some years ago, I came across a copy of a book by myself, *A Passage
> to India*, which had apparently been read by an indignant Colonel. He
> had not concealed his emotions. On the front page, he had written,
> "burn when done", and lower down: "Has a dirty mind, see page 215".
> I turned to page 215 with pardonable haste. There I found the words:
> "The sweepers of Chandrapur had just struck, and half the commodes
> remained desolate in consequence."[67]

(v)

With this introduction, Forster is able to shift to larger issues at stake
in Anand's novel of Colonial India.[68] Readers who inscribe books do so
knowing that someone may encounter their comments. Citing a response
to William Blake, H. J. Jackson has pointed out that "marginalia are
always invasive."[69] Returning Forster's book to the club library for read-
ers to find, the Colonel certainly wanted his remark to have a political
effect. In his choice of anecdote, however, Forster subverts the Colonel's
attempt to diminish the significance of the worlds that Forster and Anand
depict.[70]

Woolf was similarly intrigued with the impact of handling books and
reflects the unpredictability of doing so in her essay, "The Love of Reading"
(1929–32):

> At this late hour of the world's history books are to be found in every
> room of the house—in the nursery, in the drawing room, in the din-
> ing room, in the kitchen. And in some houses they have collected so
> that they have to be accommodated with a room of their own. Nov-
> els, poems, histories, memoirs, valuable books in leather, cheap books
> in paper—one stops sometimes before them and asks in a transient
> amazement what is the pleasure I get, or the good I create, from passing
> my eyes up and down these innumerable lines of print?[71]

Beginning with the "world's history books," Woolf captures the scope
and significance of the texts that fill homes by the late twenties. Readers'

libraries, she illustrates, combine order and disorder. Some libraries, as Woolf notes, alluding to the well-known essay that she had completed in the year that she started "The Love of Reading," are fortunate to have "a room of their own."[72] Lingering over the appearance of books, Woolf imagines joy in their pages. As a publisher herself, Woolf was familiar with the construction of books, from the significance of covers to typesetting.[73]

Woolf maintained a contradictory relationship to academic institutions. Critics are familiar with her childhood freedom to read throughout her father's library and her arguments for women's education in *A Room of One's Own* (1929) and *Three Guineas* (1938).[74] As Jackson teaches us in *Marginalia* (2002), writing in books is a technique that students have learned in school.[75] While Woolf rarely annotated her personal library, academic institutions informed her responses to marginalia.

As she put it in her 1923 diary, Woolf's usual strategy was "reading with pen & notebook."[76] Hermione Lee has argued that Woolf "hardly ever marked her books, and was satirical about people who did."[77] Lee is referring to Woolf's response to marginalia in a three-page manuscript in Woolf's Monks House Papers at the University of Sussex. In this sketch, Woolf proposes that a "student of character" should consider readers' tendency to write "in the margins of books" ("Woolf's Marginalia," 113). It is significant that Woolf selects a student, as annotating is often a student practice and several different types of academic and institutional contexts informed the composition of her manuscript.[78]

In Woolf's novels *To the Lighthouse* (1927) and *The Waves* (1931), Mr. Ramsay and Bernard both envision different forms of annotating, without writing in the margins of books. Mr. Ramsay imagines "scraps of paper on which one scribbles notes in the rush of reading."[79] While writing *To the Lighthouse,* as Jane De Gay has noted, Woolf would have also returned to the image of herself behind her parents as they read that remains in her father's photograph album.[80] Unlike Mr. Ramsay, Bernard in *The Waves* gestures toward more conventional forms of marginalia. He proposes, "let us turn over these scenes as children turn over the pages of a picture-book . . . I will add, for your amusement, a comment in the margin."[81] Bernard also characterizes mental notes as "making marks in the margin of my mind" (*W*, 189).

The Years presents a detailed image of late nineteenth-century annotating in an academic context. In the first segment of the novel depicting 1880, Woolf envisions Edward Pargiter at Oxford annotating his Greek text, rapt with excitement as he prepares to translate. He

> read; and made a note; then he read again. . . . He caught phrase after phrase exactly, firmly, more exactly, he noted, making a brief note in the margin, than the night before. Little negligible words now revealed shades of meaning, which altered the meaning. He made another note; *that* was the meaning. His own dexterity in catching the phrase plumb

in the middle gave him a thrill of excitement. There it was, clean and entire. But he must be precise; exact; even his little scribbled notes must be clear as print.[82]

Woolf here captures the proximity of Edward's note taking to his thought process. The speed of this passage with its short, punctuated segments also mirrors Edward's experience of thinking, writing, and returning to his text. Woolf's account of his response here is closer to the act of reading than the notes in Edward's text that would remain. Her reference to his notes as "scribbled" possesses an echo of Mr. Ramsay's effort to respond to his reading. Woolf's choice of phrasing captures the imprecision of writing responses while reading, maneuvering in small spaces, afraid of losing one's notion, despite efforts otherwise.[83]

As we have seen in Woolf's depiction of annotating practices, creative thought and institutional practice are intertwined in a fashion that remains at the core of modernism to the present. Edward's annotating also recalls the techniques that readers have brought to Woolf's novels, particularly those that preceded *The Years*. As their careers progressed, Woolf and Joyce imagined their relationship to academia in different ways.[84] Woolf, as a publisher, had a different proximity to the physicality of pages than her contemporaries did, but neither she nor Joyce were as copious annotators as their postwar readers would become. With regard to *Ulysses*, Joyce famously remarked, "I've put in so many enigmas and puzzles that it will keep the professors busy for centuries."[85] The next segment will illustrate the ways that Joyce's rendering of marginalia in his "Night Lessons" episode of *Finnegans Wake* (1939) resembles the responses that his fiction engendered.

Schoolroom annotating

Annotation is not only commentary on past texts. *The Waste Land* illustrates that annotation can accompany new work. In the "Night Lessons" episode, *Finnegans Wake* II.2, twin brothers Shem and Shaun write in the margins of a mock schoolbook while their sister Issy comments in the footnotes.[86] Unlike *The Waste Land*, in which the notes follow the poem, Joyce's annotations comment upon the narrative in this episode as they continue it.[87]

The school setting of "Night Lessons" critiques the academic context often informing readers' acquisition of annotating strategies. While visually the annotations and footnotes allow for a form of clarity in interpretation, Joyce referred to the episode as "[t]he part of *F.W.* accepted as . . . the most difficult of all . . . the technique here is the reproduction of a schoolboy's (and schoolgirl's) old classbook complete with marginalia by the twins, who change sides at half time."[88] Luca Crispi has observed that "this pedagogical theme was not the chapter's rationale for the first eight years of its gestation: it had its own specific 'plot' long before the chapter's form took precedence over its content."[89] After composing the content of his chapter's textbook, Joyce subsequently annotated it himself, filling in the fictional glosses and footnotes.[90] As John Whittier-Ferguson has pointed out, the children "join Joyce's readers who in the very act of reading . . . join the annotating author himself."[91]

Joyce was not a copious annotator; his invention of the marginalia for *Finnegans Wake* represents his response to the genre.[92] His brother, Stanislaus, recorded in an entry of his *Dublin Diary* (1903) that Joyce's

> intellect is precise and subtle, but not comprehensive. He is no student. His artistic sympathy and judgment are such as would be expected in one of his kind of intellect—if he were not more than a critic, I believe, he would be as good a critic of what interests him as any using English today.[93]

Stanislaus also recalled in *My Brother's Keeper* (1958) that Joyce

> devoured books . . . my brother remembered little or nothing of most of the books he read so voraciously and that at need he could make use of the one or two things he did remember from his reading. He read quickly[.] . . . If a book did . . . make some impression on him, he tried to read as many by the same writer as he could lay his hands on.[94]

Joyce's tendencies suggest those of a reader who annotates not out of a desire for scholarly mastery, but with selective interests.[95]

Among the books Joyce annotated most, his inscriptions in Jonathan Swift's *Gulliver's Travels* present a contrast to the type of reading that "Night Lessons" critiques.[96] Annotating *Gulliver's Travels* in his copy of Swift's *Works*, Joyce indicated several passages with short pencil lines in the margin.[97] Emphasizing some passages with up to three lines, Joyce stresses particular points in the text; unlike his characters in the "Night Lessons" episode, Joyce does not indicate in words the significance of his markings.[98] The difference between Joyce's own strategies and those that he depicts in his novel reflects the extent to which, like Woolf, he rendered the practice of annotating that readers had brought to his texts.

The appearance of Joyce's "Night Lessons" pages is visible in Figures I.1 and I.2. These images are from the copy of Alfred Young Fisher, professor at Smith College from the late thirties to the sixties (*UJ*, 684 note).[99] His colleague Daniel Aaron remembered that Fisher "annotated the texts of *Ulysses* and *Finnegans Wake* with the zeal of a medieval grammarian."[100] Fisher added his responses to those of Joyce's characters, which on the left side of the page are in italics and on the right side of the page are in capital letters, resembling different writers' handwriting (Figure I.1). Lawrence

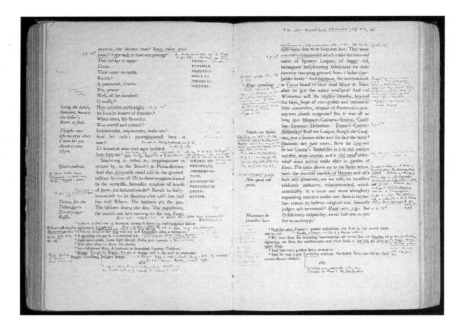

Figure I.1 Alfred Young Fisher's annotations in James Joyce's *Finnegans Wake* II.2, page 262, Alfred Young Fisher papers, Mortimer Rare Book Collection, MRBC-MS-0031, Smith College Special Collections, Northampton, MA.

Lipking has characterized annotations as definition and commentary, or marginal glosses and marginalia, which he argues can be present in the same note.[101] On the right side of page 262, the note, "PROBA- POSSILBLE PROLOGO- MENA TO IDEAREAL HISTORY," plays in childlike spelling with the speculation of a reader drawing larger connections to the term.[102] This annotation and the one beneath it critique the language of marginal glosses, including words that readers need to interpret. The main text, by contrast, is playful. The comment on the left side of the page echoes this sentiment with such phrases as *"Swing the banjo"* and *"Tickets for the Tailwaggers Terrierpuppy Raffle."*

Joyce's twins mimic readers' annotating habits (Figure I.2). For instance, on the right side of page 281, the note, "EXCLAMATION," punctuates the unpunctuated, resembling the exclamation points with which readers often fill their books. Identifying the references in Issy's footnotes on the bottom of page 281, Fisher also continues the procedure of identification to which Joyce is responding. In addition, the incoherent question on the left side of page 280, *"How matches metroosters?"* (which Roland McHugh translates as, "how much is my trousers?"), mimics the ways that readers ask questions in the margins.[103]

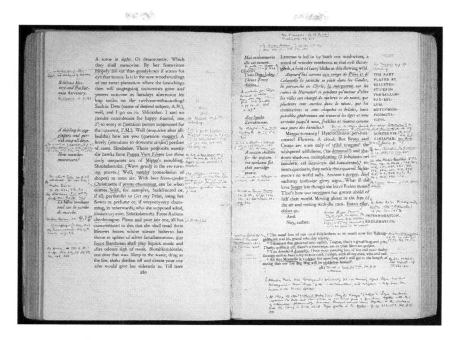

Figure I.2 Fisher's annotations in *Finnegans Wake* II.2, pages 280–1, Fisher Papers.

Joyce's incorporation of marginalia presents one example of the ways that his late modernist novel expanded the boundaries of what a text could include. In one of the most aesthetically adventurous moments in Western art history, he integrated text and commentary in a form that is both creative and lucid. The annotations in *Finnegans Wake* prefigure midcentury extensions of modernism in which teaching, reading, and writing are inseparable. Modernism has the reputation of concerning itself with the autonomous, free-standing artwork. In fact, as we will see in the following chapters, the intimacy of texts and surrounding texts is integral to modernism, and margins and edges present a meeting ground.

Annotating modernism

During her final term at Smith College in the spring of 1955, Sylvia Plath studied poetry writing with Alfred Young Fisher.[104] On Plath's typescript of "Two Lovers and a Beachcomber by the Real Sea," Fisher suggested in the margin that she "note passage in Ulysses p. 375."[105] She closed the poem: "Water will run by rule; the actual sun / will scrupulously rise and set; / . . . / and that is that, is that, is that."[106] On page 375 in Fisher's personal copy of *Ulysses*, his underlining suggests that Plath's final line recalls Joyce's repetitive phrasing: "showed me her <u>next year</u> in drawers return <u>next in her next her next</u>."[107] In the margin, Fisher added: "fig. of Passover <u>Seder</u> catechism expressing exciting hope of return."[108] The aphorism to which Fisher alluded, "next year in Jerusalem," extends the circularity to which Plath's poem had referred.[109] While, as a student, Plath presented an ideal case, the fact that Fisher could refer to Joyce so readily in his feedback reflects the scope of the novel's circulation in academia at midcentury.[110]

Over the next two decades, John Berryman's poetry comes to critique the academic culture that shaped Fisher's annotating of *Finnegans Wake* and the dexterity with which he referred to *Ulysses*. When Berryman came to write his life poem, *The Dream Songs* (1969), he crafted Henry, a protagonist who had traversed the literary, critical, and academic contexts that Berryman had.[111] In Dream Song 35, titled "*MLA*," Berryman's speaker tells the "—assistant professors, full, / associates, —instructors—others—any—" to "forget your footnotes" (*DS*, 39; lines 1–2, line 17). Later, in Dream Song 245, "A Wake-Song," Berryman adapts both Joyce's form in the "Night Lessons" chapter of *Finnegans Wake* and Eliot's notes to *The Waste Land*. In addition to Joyce and Eliot, by alluding to "K," the protagonist of Franz Kafka's *The Trial*, Berryman broadens his treatment of modernism in "A Wake-Song," incorporating writers he had studied and taught. In his course called "Humanities 54" at the University of Minnesota from the mid-fifties to the mid-sixties, Berryman taught *The Trial* with such texts as Eliot's *Waste Land* and Joyce's *Ulysses*. In a parenthetical combination of epigraph and stage direction, Berryman informs readers that the poem will present "K's first administration seen in the light of the relevant history." Early in the poem, he mimics Joyce's playful speech in Henry's request for a "sur-vivid fool" (*DS*, 264; line 1). Berryman's footnotes to Dream Song 245 add his satiric feedback to that of other nineteenth- and twentieth-century American writers and critics beyond the landscape of Kafka's novel that motivates the body of the poem: "Our contempt for our government is mildly traditional, as represented by the communistic fascists Mark Twain, Stephen Crane, Edmund Wilson, and other maddogs" (*DS*, 264).[112] Like Joyce, Berryman's humor mocked the genre of academic and poetic commentary while contributing to it, incorporating references of a wide scope with the tone and juxtaposition of terms that is in concert with previous Dream Songs.

As Anne Sexton's career progressed, like Berryman, so too did her gestures to modernist figures, particularly as she prepared to teach her own poetry. In retrospect, it seems fitting that Molly Bloom would appear in Sexton's work. In poems like "Her Kind" (1959), Sexton speaks for women whose passions have not been given prominent literary treatment.[113] It is less expected that Sexton would have known to allude to Molly Bloom, and in doing so, Sexton reflects her literary range and attention to the surrounding field. She mentioned Molly Bloom in the sixth lecture she composed for her "Anne on Anne" course on her own poetry at Colgate University in 1972. In her teaching notes, Sexton prepared questions (with answers in parentheses) that guided her students through close readings of her poems. Teaching her poem "Knee Song" (1969), Sexton asked her students, "What other work of art uses 'yes, oh yes, yes' (Molly Bloom- Ulysses)."[114] In appearance, the single stanza lyric's lowercase words that lack punctuation until the final line are not unlike Joyce's monologue. The difference, however, is in Sexton's short lines: "yes oh yes yes yes two / little snails at the back / of the knee building bon- / fires something like eye- / lashes something two zippos / striking yes yes yes small" (*Complete Poems*, 205; lines 10–15). Combining enjambment with hyphenated broken words, Sexton works with the form of the poem, calling attention to the syllables as the words and thoughts continue. On the next page of her teaching notes, Sexton asked, "[d]o you think I had read that [*Ulysses*] when I wrote it?" (10). While one does wonder whether Sexton read *Ulysses*, her questions remain as part of the artifact that she created.[115] Within two years, Molly Bloom's final lines provide an epigraph for Sexton's late poem, "The Dead Heart" (1974) (*Complete Poems*, 439).[116] From her teaching materials to her poem, Sexton's response to Joyce reflects one of the ways that she contributes to midcentury modernist discourse.

The purpose of considering the above examples is to demonstrate that each of these poets had a hand in shaping readers' engagement with modernism's midcentury circulation in academic institutions. We also see the value of moving across styles and genres, particularly when addressing what writers taught. While treatments of literary influence often focus on a single genre—interpreting, for instance, the ways that a poet of a later generation responded to a poet of an earlier one—modernism is not confined to one mode. Writers can also be unpredictable readers, becoming intrigued as they encounter words and ideas.

Each chapter of *Annotating Modernism* focuses on a poet who possessed a different kind of relationship to academia. The first chapter, "Reading Modernist Texts: Sylvia Plath's Library and Teaching Notes," argues that Plath was an exemplary student of midcentury modernist criticism. As she prepared to teach, Plath retraced her professors' steps, reading the critics they had introduced and others she had encountered since. By writing in her books and composing teaching materials, Plath preserved some of the interpretations and terminology with which she had become familiar. For instance, Plath refers to "the Jewish question" as she annotates Joyce's *Ulysses* and "death-in-life" as she annotates Eliot's *The Waste Land*. Both concepts are vestiges of larger constellations of ideas at midcentury to which Plath brings new meaning in her work. Ultimately, Plath redefined the modernist discourse that she encountered as a student and teacher as she depicted the post-World War II milieu in her novel *The Bell Jar* (1963) and in such late poems as "Lady Lazarus" (1962).

The second chapter, "John Berryman Annotating Modernism," addresses Berryman as a textual scholar and teacher of modernism in humanities courses. At Princeton University in 1945, Berryman accepted an invitation from James Laughlin to edit Pound's *Selected Poems* for New Directions. After preparing this edition, Berryman developed a humanities pedagogy that was Poundian in its comprehensiveness. His humanities courses at Minnesota enabled interdisciplinary considerations of materials that represented a broad historical and generic scope. In particular, his course called Humanities 54 engaged the literary, cultural, and ethical complexity of modernism from a midcentury perspective. Teaching this course in the aftermath of World War II, Berryman examined the psychological and philosophical significance of Eliot's *Waste Land*, Joyce's *Ulysses*, Anne Frank's *Diary of a Young Girl* (1947), and Hannah Arendt's "Origins of Totalitarianism" (1951). As a result, Berryman's experiments in his humanities courses came to inform his reinvention of modernist discourse in *The Dream Songs*. In doing so, Berryman adapted the lyric and the long poem, reshaping modernism's presence in midcentury poetics.

The final chapter, "Annotating Herself: Anne Sexton's Teaching Notes," argues that Sexton's negotiation of academic contexts informed her self-fashioning as a poet. Sexton's teaching notes for her "Anne on Anne" course at Colgate record the close reading strategies that resulted from her autodidactic career. Unlike Plath and Berryman, Sexton attended a finishing school, but not a university. Instead, Sexton's poetry developed in workshops, public readings, and literature courses at universities. Auditing courses with critics like Philip Rahv broadened her range, and she annotated canonical texts that she came to mention when she discussed her work. The materials in her archive record her responses as a reader of others' texts and her own. As Sexton prepared to teach a course on her own poetry, she composed questions and answers guiding her students through explications. The peculiarity of this course enabled Sexton's redefinition of the roles of poet, teacher, critic, and student. Her teaching notes responded to and reshaped close reading strategies that midcentury critics had defined in relation to modernist texts. As a poet and professor, she not only created new materials but also altered the future interpretation of them.

Following chapters devoted to Plath, Berryman, and Sexton, the Coda, "Ted Hughes and the Midcentury American Academy," turns to Plath's husband, the British poet Ted Hughes. Compared with Sexton, Hughes demonstrated a greater desire to remain outside of the academy and he did not seek teaching posts after leaving the University of Massachusetts, Amherst in the spring of 1958. While critics have assumed that Hughes did not annotate the books in his library, he did write in texts he prepared to teach in his Great Books course at the University of Massachusetts, including a copy of Fyodor Dostoevsky's *Crime and Punishment* that he filled with his own marginalia after Plath annotated it herself to teach at Smith.

Taken in tandem, both sets of notes reflect a material record of Plath's and Hughes's respective pedagogical approaches. After Hughes left academia, his experience teaching provided a background for his later responses to critics as executor of the Plath Estate and critique of academic institutions in *Birthday Letters* (1998).

As teachers, poets left their mark on the academy. Their impressions took hold in the texts they annotated and the students with whom they worked. As a case study, the midcentury reading and teaching of texts from the first half of the twentieth century allows us to chart the emergence of modernism in academic institutions, learning that its formation as a discourse is a process that we continue to annotate.

Notes

1 See H. J. Jackson's *Marginalia* for a historical consideration of annotation practices, including a survey of strategies readers use as they write in library books. Studies of marginalia have focused on literary periods that precede the twentieth century. As Anthony Grafton demonstrates in *The Footnote: A Curious History* (1997), marginal commentary evolved from the marginal gloss and the footnote. Anthony Grafton, *The Footnote: A Curious History* (Cambridge: Harvard University Press, 1997), 30. Regarding functions of marginalia, see Robert Hauptman, *Documentation: A History and Critique of Attribution, Commentary, Glosses, Marginalia, Notes, Bibliographies, Works-Cited Lists, and Citation Indexing and Analysis* (Jefferson: McFarland & Company, Inc., 2008), 74. The *Oxford English Dictionary* (*OED*) dates the definition of margin, referring to a page, to the fourteenth century. s.v. "margin." *n.* 1. a. and s.v. "marginalia" *n. OED*. For medieval and Renaissance marginalia, see *The Edge of the Page*, D. C. Greetham, *The Margins of the Text* (Ann Arbor: University of Michigan Press, 1997) and William H. Sherman, *Used Books: Marking Readers in Renaissance England* (Philadelphia: University of Pennsylvania Press, 2008), respectively.

2 When readers underline part of a word, the whole word will be underlined in transcriptions throughout *Annotating Modernism*.

3 Stephen Orgel, *The Reader in the Book: A Study of Spaces and Traces* (New York: Oxford University Press, 2015), 2; hereafter cited in the text as "Orgel." Focusing on early modern readers, Orgel pursues "an archeology of the use of margins and other blank spaces" (2). See Donald H. Reiman's classification of marginalia as "private documents" in *The Study of Modern Manuscripts: Public, Confidential, and Private* (Baltimore: Johns Hopkins University Press, 1993).

4 The concept of modernist discourse has had a different role in philosophy. See Timothy J. Reiss, *The Discourse of Modernism* (Ithaca, NY: Cornell University Press, 1982).

5 Douglas Mao and Rebecca L. Walkowitz, "The New Modernist Studies," *PMLA* 123, no. 3 (May 2008): 744; hereafter cited in the text as "Mao and Walkowitz."

6 Ann Ardis, "The Feminist Avant-Garde: Transatlantic Encounters of Early Twentieth Century," *Modernism/modernity* 16, no. 3 (September 2009): 628.

7 George Bornstein, *Material Modernism: The Politics of the Page* (New York: Cambridge University Press, 2001); hereafter cited in the text as "Bornstein."

8 Lawrence S. Rainey, *Institutions of Modernism: Literary Elites and Public Culture* (New Haven: Yale University Press, 1998) and *Revisiting The Waste Land* (New Haven: Yale University Press, 2005); hereafter cited in the text as "*Institutions*" and "*Revisiting*."

9 See Faye Hammill and Mark Hussey, *Modernism's Print Cultures* (New York: Bloomsbury, 2016) as well as Lise Jaillant's books *Modernism, Middlebrow and the Literary Canon: The Modern Library Series, 1917–1955* (London: Pickering and Chatto, 2014) and *Cheap Modernism: Expanding Markets, Publishers' Series and the Avant-Garde* (Edinburgh: Edinburgh University Press, 2017).

10 Petra Lange-Berndt points out that "[m]ateriality is one of the most contested concepts in contemporary art." Introduction to *Materiality*, ed. Petra Lange-Berndt (Cambridge, MA: MIT Press, 2015), 12.

11 John Lurz, *The Death of the Book: Modernist Novels and the Time of Reading* (New York: Fordham University Press, 2016).

12 Dirk Van Hulle, *Modern Manuscripts: The Extended Mind and Creative Undoing from Darwin to Beckett and Beyond* (New York: Bloomsbury, 2014), 14; hereafter cited in the text as "Van Hulle."

13 David M. Earle, "MySpace Modernism," *Modernism/modernity* 16, no. 3 (September 2009): 478. In "When Was Modernism?" Raymond Williams points out that "'Modernism' as a title for a whole cultural movement and moment has then been retrospective as a general term since the 1950s" (32). This is partly the case because, he notes later in the piece, "Modernism is canonized . . . by the post-war settlement and its accompanying, complicit academic endorsements" (34). Raymond Williams, *Politics of Modernism* (1989; New York: Verso, 2007). Jessica Berman brought Williams's observations to my attention in *Modernist Commitments: Ethics, Politics, and Transnational Modernism* (New York: Columbia University Press, 2011).

14 Regarding "The Teaching Archive: A New History of Literary Study," see http://rachelsagnerbuurma.org/research/, accessed 23 February 2020.

15 Rachel Sagner Buurma and Laura Heffernan, "The Classroom in the Canon: T. S. Eliot's Modern English Literature Extension Course for Working People and *The Sacred Wood*." *PMLA* 133, no. 2 (2018): 264–81; hereafter cited in the text as "The Classroom in the Canon."

16 Peter Middleton addresses what he calls the "scene of reading" of modernism. Peter Middleton, *Distant Reading: Performance, Readership, and Consumption in Contemporary Poetry* (Tuscaloosa: University of Alabama Press, 2005).

17 Robert E. Scholes, *Paradoxy of Modernism* (New Haven: Yale University Press, 2006), ix–x.

18 Langdon Hammer addresses the phenomenon of the "poet-teacher" in "Plath's Lives: Poetry Professionalism, and the Culture of the School," *Representations* 75 (Summer 2001); hereafter cited in the text as "Plath's Lives." Evan Kindley points out that at midcentury

> literature departments continued to hire poet-critics[.] . . . There was some resistance, on the part of the poet-critics, to the incorporation of modernism and its discursive traditions into the universities, but for the most part they saw academicization as an opportunity, and seized it.
>
> (9)

Hammer makes the distinction that "[t]he hyphenated form poet-critic expressed an addition, a further development: it indicated a poet with the capacity not only to write about poems but to reflect on them, to write about them, and to teach them" (qtd. Kindley 9). Evan Kindley, *Poet-Critics and the Administration of Culture* (Cambridge: Harvard University Press, 2017). Kindley is quoting Langdon Hammer, *Hart Crane and Allen Tate: Janus-Faced Modernism* (Princeton, NJ: Princeton University Press, 1993), 27–8.

19 Regarding the consideration of literature before and after World War II, see also Jennifer Ashton, *From Modernism to Postmodernism: American Poetry and Theory in the Twentieth Century* (New York: Cambridge University Press, 2005), 23, 29.

20 Poets like Robert Lowell and John Berryman taught literature courses and writing workshops. See Paul Mariani, *Lost Puritan: A Life of Robert Lowell* (New York: Norton, 1994), 188 and 263–4; hereafter cited in the text as "*Lost Puritan*" and Helen Vendler's recollection of Lowell's literature course at Boston University from 1955 to 1956 and his 1977 course on nineteenth-century literature at Harvard in "Lowell in the Classroom," in *Robert Lowell: Interviews and Memoirs*, ed. Jeffrey Meyers (Ann Arbor: University Michigan Press, 1988), 288–97.

21 McGurl concludes that "[t]he ways and means of interwar literary modernism have been modified in the postwar period, where they have been codified in the pedagogy of the New Criticism and then disseminated to a range of student populations" (50). In order to understand what this meant, and the extent to which referring to it as "pedagogy of the New Criticism" may limit our understanding of it, the case studies in *Annotating Modernism* examine what professors and students were reading and how they were reading it. Mark McGurl, *The Program Era: Postwar Fiction and the Rise of Creative Writing* (Cambridge: Harvard University Press, 2009); hereafter cited in the text as "McGurl," and Amy Hungerford, *Postmodern Belief: American Literature and Religion since 1960* (Princeton: Princeton University Press, 2010), 17. I thank Benjamin Reiss for bringing *The Program Era* to my attention. See also Hungerford's lecture on Flannery O'Connor's *Wise Blood*, "English 291: The American Novel Since 1945," Spring 2008, *Open Yale Courses*, http://oyc.yale.edu/english/american-novel-since-1945/content/sessions/session-4-flannery-oconnor-wise-blood-cont, accessed 4 September 2011.

22 Amy Hungerford, "On the Period Formerly Known as Contemporary," *American Literary History* 20, no. 1–2 (Spring/Summer 2008): 418.

23 Ronald Schuchard has also argued that Cleanth Brooks and Robert Penn Warren developed their methods of interpretation in response to modernist texts, particularly T. S. Eliot's *The Waste Land*. Lecture, "'The man who suffers and the mind which creates' in *The Waste Land*," T. S. Eliot International Summer School, University of London School for Advanced Studies, London, UK, July 2011.

24 The classicist Van Meter Ames transcribed and typed his notes of Berryman's lectures at the University of Cincinnati in 1952, sending them to his biographer, John Haffenden. The final lecture was on Robert Lowell, Dylan Thomas, and other poets. Letter, Van Meter Ames, 16 June 1974 to John Haffenden [Notes on the Elliston Lectures by John Berryman] Cincinnati, 21 Feb–6 May 1952, box 1, John Haffenden Collection of John Berryman Papers, 1952–1978, Rare Book & Manuscript Library, Columbia University Libraries, New York, NY; hereafter cited in the text as "Ames."

25 John Haffenden, *The Life of John Berryman* (1982; Boston: Routledge, 1983), 204; hereafter cited in the text as "Haffenden."

26 Jerome McGann, *The Textual Condition* (Princeton: Princeton University Press, 1991). See also Catherine Paul, *Poetry in the Museums of Modernism* (Ann Arbor: University of Michigan Press, 2002).

27 Brenda R. Silver quotes the editor of the drafts of *The Waves*, John Graham, "[t]he draft material for a text is . . . an historical document." Brenda R.

Silver, "Textual Criticism as Feminist Practice: Or, Who's Afraid of Virginia Woolf Part II," in *Representing Modernist Texts: Editing as Interpretation*, ed. George Bornstein (Ann Arbor: University of Michigan Press, 1991), 199.

28 Gerard Genette, *Paratexts: Thresholds of Interpretation* (1987; New York: Cambridge University Press, 1997). See also Matthew Bradley, "'Annotation Mapping' and What It Means: Developing the Gladstone Catalogue as a Resource for the History of Reading," *Literature Compass* 6, no. 2 (2009): 503.

29 Jacques Derrida, "This Is Not an Oral Footnote," in *Annotation and Its Texts*, ed. Stephen A. Barney (New York: Oxford University Press, 1991), 204. See H. J. Jackson, "Editing and Auditing Marginalia," regarding annotations' relationship to the texts to which they respond. In *Voice, Text, Hypertext: Emerging Practices in Textual Studies*, ed. Raimonda Modiano and others (Seattle: University of Washington Press, 2004), 72–80.

30 Stephen Greenblatt and Catherine Gallagher, *Practicing New Historicism* (Chicago: University of Chicago Press, 2000), 27; hereafter cited in the text as "Greenblatt and Gallagher." See also Anita Helle, "Lessons from the Archive: Sylvia Plath and the Politics of Memory," *Feminist Studies* 31, no. 3 (Fall 2005): 631–52.

31 See also Stephen Greenblatt, *Shakespearean Negotiations: The Circulation of Social Energy in Renaissance England* (Berkeley: University of California Press, 1988), 8 and *Renaissance Self-Fashioning: From More to Shakespeare* (Chicago: University of Chicago Press, 1984), 1.

32 Cary Nelson, *Repression and Recovery: Modern American Poetry and the Politics of Cultural Memory*, 1910–1945 (Madison: University of Wisconsin Press, 1989), 19; hereafter cited in the text as *"Repression and Recovery."*

33 Critics have addressed different types of midcentury responses to their predecessors. See Alan Filreis's consideration of politics in *Counter-revolution of the Word: The Conservative Attack on Modern Poetry, 1945–1960* (Chapel Hill: University of North Carolina Press, 2008).

34 Similarly, to indicate the way we navigate "things," Bill Brown suggests that his readers may be holding something in their hand as they read. Bill Brown, "The Secret Life of Things (Virginia Woolf and the Matter of Modernism)," *Modernism/modernity* 6, no. 2 (1999): 1–28.

35 Orgel notes an early instance of this practice:

> Erasmus advised students to mark the margins of their books with a set of symbols: they were to 'methodically observe occurrences of striking words, archaic or novel diction, cleverly contrived or well adapted arguments brilliant flashes of style, adages, examples of pithy remarks worth memorizing. Such passages should be marked by an appropriate little sign. [...] They should be employed systematically so that it is clear to what sort of thing they refer.' . . . Erasmus's system has obvious limitations, and though it was widely adopted, it is generally found in combination with other less generalized, more personal, and more intrusive systems like . . . a combination of notes, abbreviations, and an occasional symbol.
>
> (26)

36 Leonard Diepeveen recounts the following anecdote: "an acquaintance, on hearing me describe this book, remarked of *The Waste Land*: 'I didn't even understand the notes.'" Leonard Diepeveen, *The Difficulties of Modernism* (New York: Routledge, 2003), x. Richard Poirier, *The Renewal of Literature: Emersonian Reflections* (New York: Random House, 1987), 104–5; hereafter cited in the text as "Poirier."

37 See Edward L. Bishop, "The 'Garbled History' of the First-edition *Ulysses*," *Joyce Studies Annual* 9 (Summer 1998): 3–36 and "Re: Covering *Ulysses*," *Joyce Studies Annual* 5 (Summer 1994): 22–55. I thank Molly Schwartzburg for bringing Bishop's work to my attention and Charles Rossman for sending me these articles.

38 See John Whittier-Ferguson, *Framing Pieces: Designs of the Gloss in Joyce, Woolf, and Pound* (New York: Oxford University Press, 1996), 5–6.

39 Ames, "First Eliot Lecture by Berryman," page 3. See also Genette, *Paratexts*, 333.

40 See Middleton, *Distant Reading*.

41 Hugh Kenner observed, "we shall do well to discard the notes as much as possible; they have bedeviled discussion for decades." Hugh Kenner, *The Invisible Poet: T. S. Eliot* (New York: McDowell, Obolensky, 1959), 150.

42 Qtd. in James E. B. Breslin, *From Modern to Contemporary: American Poetry, 1945–1965* (Chicago: University of Chicago Press, 1984): 14–15.

43 Jessie Laidlay Weston, *From Ritual to Romance* (1920; Garden City, NY: Doubleday, 1957), former owner Hughes, Emory; hereafter cited in the text as "Weston." Elizabeth Drew, *T. S. Eliot: The Design of His Poetry* (1949; New York: Charles Scribner's Sons, 1950), former owner Plath, Smith; hereafter cited in the text as *T. S. Eliot*. Drew was Plath's professor at Smith.

44 Eliot, *Complete Poems and Plays*, former owner Plath, Smith. For teaching, Plath annotated *Modern American and Modern British Poetry*, ed. Louis Untermeyer (1919; New York: Harcourt Brace, 1955); hereafter cited in the text as "Untermeyer"; in Berg Collection, New York Public Library, New York, NY; hereafter cited in the text as "Berg."

45 T. S. Eliot, *The Poems of T. S. Eliot: Collected and Uncollected Poems* Volume I, ed. Christopher Ricks and Jim McCue (Baltimore: Johns Hopkins University Press, 2015), 569. See Alfred Corn, "A Guide to the Ruins: On T. S. Eliot's Annotations," *The Smart Set*, 2 May 2016, http://thesmartset.com/a-guide-to-the-ruins/#more-10128, accessed 26 June 2018.

46 T. S. Eliot, *The Annotated* Waste Land *with Eliot's Contemporary Prose*, ed. Lawrence Rainey (2005; New Haven: Yale University Press, 2006); hereafter cited in the text as "*The Annotated* Waste Land."

47 Edmund Wilson drew an early distinction in *Axel's Castle: A Study in the Imaginative Literature of 1870–1930*, resolving that, compared to *The Waste Land*, "Pound's work *has* been partially sunk by its cargo of erudition." Annotating her copy of *Axel's Castle*, Plath agreed writing "cf. Pisan Cantos" in the margin of her copy and punctuating it with an exclamation point. Edmund Wilson, *Axel's Castle: A Study in the Imaginative Literature of 1870–1930* (New York: Charles Scribner's Sons, 1950), 111, former owner Plath, Smith; hereafter cited in the text as "Wilson." See Reiman. Noting Bunting's poem, "On the Flyleaf of Pound's Cantos," Jerome McGann tells us, "Pound's work has a substantial *thingness* to it, a kind of hard objective presence" and is "unevadable." My interest lies more in the ways readers navigate its contents, often taking pen or pencil to it. Jerome McGann, *Black Riders: The Visible Language of Modernism* (Princeton: Princeton University Press, 1993), 76.

48 James Laughlin, *Byways*, ed. Peter Glassgold (1993; New York: New Directions, 2005), 83.

49 Ezra Pound and Ernest Fenollosa, *Instigations* of Ezra Pound Together with "An Essay on the Chinese Written Character" by Ernest Fenollosa (New York: Boni and Liveright, [c. 1920]), former owner Ezra Pound. Pound inscribed other books with dates from the thirties when he lived in Rapallo, Italy.

50 William Carlos Williams, "Prologue to *Kora in Hell: Improvisations*," 1918, in *Imaginations*, ed. Webster Schott (1938; New York: New Directions, 1971), 10. Philip Levine brought Williams's piece to my attention. Philip Levine, "Mine Own John Berryman," in *Recovering Berryman: Essays on a Poet*, ed. Richard J. Kelly and Alan K. Lathrop (Ann Arbor: University of Michigan Press, 1993), 17–42.

51 Pound added lists of page numbers, including errors in the text in Henry Adams's *History of the United States of America During the Administration of Thomas Jefferson* 1801–1805 Books I and II 1889, 1930. Henry Adams, *History of the United States of America* (New York: A&C Boni, 1930), former owner Pound, Ransom Center.

52 See "Authors' Libraries," Harry Ransom Center, The University of Texas at Austin, http://www.hrc.utexas.edu/collections/books/holdings/libraries/, accessed 13 July 2019.

53 Wyndham Lewis, "Serial Story—Tarr." *The Egoist* 3, no. 4 (April 1, 1916)–4, no. 3 (April 1917); 12 issues (the story was in 19 issues), library catalogue notes some incomplete, former owner Pound, Ransom Center.

54 Ezra Pound, "James Joyce: At Last the Novel Appears," in *Pound / Joyce: The Letters of Ezra Pound to James Joyce*, ed. Forrest Read (1965; New York: New Directions, 1967), 88. Originally published in *The Egoist* 4, no. 2 (February 1917): 21–2.

55 Paul O'Keefe, *Some Sort of Genius: A Life of Wyndham Lewis* (Berkeley, CA: Counterpoint, 2015), 189. I thank Scott Klein for bringing this reference to my attention.

56 James Joyce, *Ulysses* (Paris, between 1922 and 1926), 544, former owner Wyndham Lewis, Ransom Center.

57 James Joyce, *Ulysses* (Paris: Shakespeare and Company, 1928), former owner Evelyn Waugh, Ransom Center. See also Richard W. Oram, "Cultural Record Keepers: The Evelyn Waugh Library, Harry Ransom Humanities Research Center, University of Texas at Austin," *Libraries & the Cultural Record* 42, no. 3 (2007): 325–8.

58 Regarding *Jekyll and Hyde*, see also Stephen Arata, *Fictions of Loss in the Victorian Fin de Siècle: Identity and Empire* (New York: Cambridge University Press, 1996).

59 Miller is quoting "Death Sets a Thing significant," F640. Cristanne Miller, *Reading in Time: Emily Dickinson in the Nineteenth Century* (Amherst: University of Massachusetts Press, 2012), 5–6.

60 Robert Louis Stevenson, "The Strange Case of Dr. Jekyll and Mr. Hyde," in *The Norton Anthology of English Literature: Volume E: The Victorian Age*, ed. Stephen Greenblatt, et al. (New York: Norton, 2012), 1702–1703; hereafter cited in the text as "Stevenson."

61 An instance where marginalia offers a similar form of clue in a modernist text occurs in Radclyffe Hall's *The Well of Loneliness* (1928). Victoria Rosner argues that "Stephen's marginal gender identity finds a textual mirror in actual marginalia." Victoria Rosner, *Modernism and the Architecture of Private Life* (New York: Columbia University Press, 2005), 113; hereafter cited in the text as "Rosner."

62 Joseph Conrad, *Heart of Darkness*, ed. Paul B. Armstrong (1902; New York: Norton, 2006), 38.

63 Lurz has drawn attention to the role of books in modernist texts; after considering Clarissa Dalloway's reading of *Cymbeline* in a shop window, he argues that the whole of *Mrs. Dalloway* "views the mental world of linguistic deciphering and imagination as bound up with, indeed dependent on the physical or perceptual relationship Clarissa has with that language's material support" (2).

Apart from "the format of the book," however, Lurz focuses on "the book facing the reader," without attending to the ways that readers alter books (7).

64 E. M. Forster, *Howards End* (1910; New York: Modern Library, 1999), 295; hereafter cited in the text as "*HE*."

65 Heather Clark brought this passage to my attention in *The Ulster Renaissance: Poetry in Belfast 1962–1972* (New York: Oxford University Press, 2006), 60.

66 E. M. Forster, "In My Library," in *A Bloomsbury Group Reader*, ed. S. P. Rosenbaum (1949; Oxford: Blackwell, 1993), 294; hereafter cited in the text as "In My Library."

67 E. M. Forster, preface to Mulk Raj Anand, *Untouchable* (1935; New York: Penguin Books, 1940), v.

68 In *Conversations in Bloomsbury*, Anand recounts that Forster told a version of this anecdote to Anand and Leonard Woolf and notes that Forster found this book in the Reform Club. Forster told a similar story, referring to page 242 instead of 215, when he sat with Leonard Woolf and Anand in Tavistock Square a few days later. Mulk Raj Anand, *Conversations in Bloomsbury* (1981; Oxford: Oxford University Press, 1995), 74.

69 H. J. Jackson, *Marginalia: Readers Writing in Books* (New Haven: Yale University Press, 2001), 91; hereafter cited in the text as "*Marginalia*." Thank you to *Modernism/modernity*'s reader for suggesting this reference.

70 Thank you to the members of the New York Modernism Seminar for their suggestions regarding this passage.

71 Virginia Woolf, "The Love of Reading," in *A Bloomsbury Group Reader*, ed. Rosenbaum (Oxford: Blackwell, 1993), 415.

72 Virginia Woolf, *A Room of One's Own*, ed. Susan Gubar (1929; New York: Harcourt, 2005).

73 When the Hogarth Press published *The Waste Land* in England, Woolf helped bind the pages. T. S. Eliot, *The Waste Land* (Richmond: Hogarth Press, 1923). See exhibition by Karen V. Kukil, "Woolf in the World: A Pen and Press of Her Own," accessed 28 March 2018, https://www.smith.edu/libraries/libs/rarebook/exhibitions/penandpress/case3.htm.

74 Virginia Woolf, *Three Guineas* (1938; New York: Harcourt, Inc., 1966).

75 Jackson has observed, "[w]riting notes in response to a text appears to be a habit acquired at school . . . Under instruction, children learn to mark the text conservatively, and to use the endpapers for institutionally approved, standard kinds of note-taking" (21).

76 Diary entry of 28 July 1923. Virginia Woolf, *The Diary of Virginia Woolf: Volume Two 1920–1924*, ed. Anne Olivier Bell, assisted by Andrew McNeillie (New York: Harcourt Brace & Company, 1978), 259.

77 Hermione Lee, *Virginia Woolf* (New York: Random House, 1996), 406; hereafter cited in the text as "Lee." Lee explains that Woolf's "reading notebooks were her system of annotation" (406).

78 Woolf may have composed this manuscript between May 1906 and July 1908. Woolf's manuscript, SxMs18/2/A/A.23/C, is housed at the University of Sussex Library. This manuscript is also included as "(writing in the margin)" in the contents of the Monk's House Papers microfilm, Reel 2. Woolf wrote 22 May at the top of her manuscript. The date on the next manuscript on the Monks House Papers microfilm is 6 July 1908. Subsequent manuscripts from this segment of the microfilm are dated 1906. A facsimile of this manuscript was published in Amanda Golden, "Virginia Woolf's Marginalia Manuscript," *Woolf Studies Annual* 18 (2012): 109–17; hereafter cited in the text as "Marginalia Manuscript." See also Amanda Golden, "'A Brief Note in the Margin:' Virginia Woolf and Annotating," in *Contradictory Woolf: Selected Papers from the Twenty-First Annual Conference on Virginia Woolf,*

ed. Derek Ryan and Stella Bolaki (Clemson, SC: Clemson University Digital Press, 2012): 209–214.

79 Virginia Woolf, *To the Lighthouse* (1927; New York: Oxford University Press, 2008), 37.

80 Jane De Gay, *Virginia Woolf's Novels and the Literary Past* (Edinburgh: Edinburgh University Press, 2006). Leslie Stephen's photograph album, Smith College. https://www.smith.edu/libraries/libs/rarebook/exhibitions/stephen/38h. htm, accessed 29 March 2018.

81 Virginia Woolf, *The Waves* (1931; New York: Harcourt Brace, 1959), 241; hereafter cited in the text as *W*.

82 Virginia Woolf, *The Years*, ed. Eleanor McNees (1937; New York: Harcourt Inc., 2008), 47.

83 Emily James argues that Woolf's use of the word "scribbling" does not tend to be positive: "Scribbling, for Woolf, is an early stage in the writing process, before revising, editing, or published. A publisher herself, Woolf does not glorify this stage of writing; she refers dismissively to the 'scribbling' of female writers." Emily James, "Virginia Woolf and the Child Poet," *Modernist Cultures* 7, no. 2 (2012): 280. In her essay on "The Modernist Inkblot," James discusses how "messy" aspects of writing make an impression on the page as part of the creative process. In doing so, she devotes a section of the article to "Leopold Bloom, scribbler." Emily James, "The Modernist Inkblot," *Twentieth Century Literature* 63, no. 3 (September 2017): 299–328.

84 I thank Mark Hussey for this observation.

85 Quoted in Richard Ellmann, *James Joyce* (1959; New York: Oxford University Press, 1983), 521. Lipking also notes that Shem quotes *Ulysses* (636).

86 Jen Shelton addresses Issy's narrative of incest in her notes in *James Joyce and the Narrative Structure of Incest* (Gainesville: University Press of Florida, 2006).

87 Eliot mentioned in "The Frontiers of Criticism" (1956), "I have sometimes thought of getting rid of these notes; but now they can never be unstuck." T. S. Eliot, *On Poetry and Poets* (New York: Farrar, Straus and Cudahy, 1957), 121. I thank John Whittier-Ferguson for drawing my attention to this passage in *Framing Pieces* (9).

88 James Joyce to Frank Budgen, "End July 1939," in *Letters of James Joyce*, ed. Stuart Gilbert (New York: The Viking Press, 1957), 405–6. See also Lipking, 632.

89 Luca Crispi, "Storiella as She Was Wryt: Chapter II.2," in *How Joyce Wrote Finnegans Wake*, ed. Luca Crispi and Sam Slote (Madison: University of Wisconsin Press, 2007), 214–5; hereafter cited in the text as "Crispi." Crispi also underscores that the chapter undermines the ostensible clarity that marginal notes could bring to a text (214).

90 See also James Joyce, *Finnegans Wake Book II, Chapter 2: A Facsimile of Drafts, Typescripts, & Proofs: Volume I*, ed. Michael Groden (New York: Garland Publishing, Inc., 1978).

91 Whittier-Ferguson, 42.

92 Michael Patrick Gillespie, *James Joyce's Trieste Library: A Catalogue of the Materials at the Harry Ransom Humanities Research Center*, The University of Texas at Austin (Austin: The Harry Ransom Humanities Research Center, 1986), 15; hereafter cited in the text as "*James Joyce's Trieste Library*."

93 Stanislaus Joyce, *The Complete Dublin Diary of Stanislaus Joyce*, ed. George H. Healey (1962; Ithaca: Cornell University Press, 1971), 2.

94 Stanislaus Joyce, *My Brother's Keeper: James Joyce's Early Years* (1958; Cambridge: Da Capo Press, 2003), 79.

95 See also John Bishop, *Joyce's Book of the Dark: Finnegans Wake* (Madison: University of Wisconsin Press, 1986), 27.
96 Gillespie, *James Joyce's Trieste Library*, 231. Joyce's copy of Swift *"The Works*. Carefully selected: with a biography of the author, by D. Laing Purves; and original and authentic notes (Edinburgh: William P. Nimmo, 1869)" (Gillespie, 228). My observations are from Joyce's copy in the Ransom Center. See also Jane Ford, "James Joyce's Trieste Library: Some Notes on Its Use," in *Joyce at Texas: Essays on the James Joyce Materials at the Humanities Research Center*, ed. Dave Oliphant and Thomas Zigal (Austin: The Humanities Research Center, The University of Texas, 1983), 149.
97 See also Gillespie, *James Joyce's Trieste Library*, 16.
98 Shelton, for instance, has argued that in *Finnegans Wake*, Swift presents a version of the protagonist, Earwicker, father of the children who have annotated the "Night Lessons" episode, and a representation of Joyce in *Joyce and the Narrative Structure of Incest* (54). See also 110. See also James S. Atherton, *The Books at the Wake: A Study of Literary Allusions in James Joyce's* Finnegans Wake (London: Faber and Faber, 1959).
99 James Joyce, *Finnegans Wake* (New York: The Viking Press, 1939). Former owner Alfred Young Fisher, Alfred Young Fisher papers, Mortimer Rare Book Collection, MRBC-MS-0031, Smith College Special Collections, Northampton, MA; hereafter cited in the text as "Fisher Papers." Sylvia Plath, *The Unabridged Journals of Sylvia Plath*, ed. Karen V. Kukil (New York: Random House, 2000); hereafter cited in the text as *UJ*.
100 Daniel Aaron, manuscript of "Circle –Northampton, Mass, (1936–1969)," in *The American Scholar*, page 174. Manuscript enclosed with Letter, Daniel Aaron to Anthony Hecht, 26 October 2001, box 8, folder 1, Anthony Hecht Papers, MSS 926, Emory; hereafter cited in the text as "Hecht Papers." I thank Judith Kroll for bringing Aaron's role at Smith to my attention.
101 Lawrence Lipking, "The Marginal Gloss," *Critical Inquiry* 3, no. 4 (Summer 1977): 650; hereafter cited in the text as "Lipking." He distinguishes Shaun's comments as marginal glosses and Shem's contributions as marginalia (635). Lipking also defines marginalia as "traces left in a book . . . wayward in their very nature; they spring up spontaneously around a text unaware of their presence" (612).
102 As Crispi observed, "the visual clues of the text's format . . . mimics and parodies the children's studies" (214).
103 Roland McHugh, *Annotations to Finnegans Wake* (1980; Baltimore: Johns Hopkins University Press, 1991), 280.
104 Sylvia Plath, "Transcript," box 20, folder 25, Sylvia Plath Collection, Mortimer Rare Book Collection, MRBC-MS-00045, Smith College Special Collections, Northampton, MA; hereafter cited in the text as "Plath Collection." In "Plath's Lives," Hammer argues that Fisher's feedback reflects New Critical approaches to poetic form. Hammer finds that Fisher's "brief remarks point up poetic antecedents and analogues. But most of them focus on the 'movement' or 'structure' of the poems" (76–7).
105 Sylvia Plath, "Two Lovers and a Beachcomber by the Real Sea," box 14, folder 271, Plath Collection. The verso of the typescript contains the date, 14 April 1955.
106 Plath, "Two Lovers," Plath Collection. The first "and" in the final line quoted is capitalized in Plath's *Collected Poems* and in a later typescript at Smith, but not in the typescript, in *Mademoiselle* (1955): 62, or in *Granta* 61 (1957): 5. See also Sylvia Plath, *Collected Poems*, ed. Ted Hughes (1981; New York: Harper Perennial, 1992), 327; hereafter cited in the text as "*Collected Poems*."

107 James Joyce, *Ulysses* (New York: The Modern Library, 1942), 375, former owner Fisher, Fisher Papers, Smith.

108 Joyce, *Ulysses*, 375. Fisher Papers, Smith.

109 Plath, "Two Lovers," Plath Collection.

110 "English 41b Poetry." Sylvia Plath, "Transcript," 1955, box 20, folder 25, Plath Collection.

111 John Berryman, *The Dream Songs* (1969; New York: Farrar, Straus and Giroux, 2001); hereafter cited in the text as "*DS*."

112 In the poem, "mad-dogs" is hyphenated because it extends from one line to the next.

113 Anne Sexton, *The Complete Poems* (1981; New York: Houghton Mifflin, 1999), 15–16; hereafter cited in the text as "*Complete Poems*."

114 Anne Sexton, "Lecture Materials for Colgate University," lecture 6, page 9, 1972, box 16, folder 5, Anne Sexton Papers, Ransom Center; hereafter cited in the text as "Sexton Papers." References to Sexton's lecture materials will be in parentheses with the abbreviation *CL* and the lecture and page numbers, i.e., (*CL*, 6; 9).

115 Sexton owned copies of James Joyce's *Exiles* (1918; New York: Viking Press, 1961) and *A Portrait of the Artist as a Young Man* (1916; New York: Viking, 1963), Ransom Center.

116 I thank Kristina Zimbakova for bringing Sexton's reference to Molly Bloom in this poem to my attention.

1   Reading modernist texts
Sylvia Plath's library and teaching notes

By annotating her reading and preparing notes to teach, Sylvia Plath preserved her encounters with modernism at a particular moment. As a result, the books in Plath's personal library and the teaching notes that she composed become vital resources for understanding the extent to which her reading of modernism was inseparable from the critical terminology with which she learned to interpret it.[1] This chapter argues that Plath revised the modernist critical discourse she engaged as a student and teacher as she turned her attention to the post-World War II milieu in her fiction and poetry.[2]

In the spring of 1958, as Plath's year teaching freshman English at Smith College drew to a close, she prepared the following advice for her students: "[T. S.] Eliot said: 'IN MY END IS MY BEGINNING': Begin at this level of work next year."[3] As she did so, Plath was at the end of a year in which she had returned to Smith to teach many of the texts that she once had studied there. Since *The Bell Jar*'s publication under Plath's name in 1966, readers have had a sense of her diligence as a student.[4] Biographies have chronicled Plath's student years alongside those of her fictional likeness, Esther Greenwood.[5] But readers remain less familiar with the more complex ways in which Plath repurposed what she had learned as a student.

This chapter demonstrates the extent to which Plath's reading strategies were integral to her process of self-fashioning as a student and poet.[6] In her marginalia, student notebooks, teaching notes, and other materials, Plath documented sources that informed her study of modernism.[7] Drafting her teaching materials, Plath worked closely from her student notebooks and contemporary criticism.[8] Despite her concern that she was merely "living & teaching on rereadings, on notes of other people" (*UJ*, 346), Plath augmented this archive as she prepared to teach. In doing so, Plath became a student of the criticism of her moment and a teacher who tested its boundaries, engaging the cultural and political implications of texts in ways that anticipated the directions she would pursue in her poetry and prose.[9]

In the decades that have passed since readers encountered Plath's writing of the *Ariel* poems on the reverse sides of her own and Ted Hughes's manuscripts in Susan Van Dyne's *Revising Life: Sylvia Plath's Ariel Poems* (1994), Plath's archives have become vital to critical assessments of her oeuvre.[10] It was while teaching at Smith in the spring of 1958 that Plath removed the "lovely-textured" pink Smith College memorandum paper from the history department supply closet to use for a novel that she was struggling to write (*UJ*, 344). As an instructor, Plath made use of some of these pages to compose her unwieldy sheaf of teaching materials. These notes include passages she collected from critical texts, the result of Plath's reading and preparation as she approached the course texts. Plath drafted and revised her notes, which took on new life in overview materials that framed her classes, including what she referred to as "brief 5 minute lectures on topics."[11] Had she returned home and retrieved these materials, which she left behind before departing for England in late 1959, Plath may have reused them for future teaching or drafted new poems on the versos.[12]

The textures and surfaces of pages altered Plath's handling of them. While teaching at Smith in February 1958, Plath penned an exuberant, reflexive comment on the long, lined pages of the journal in which she was writing: "I love this book, black point of pen skidding over smooth paper" (*UJ*, 322). The pace and feel of underlining and annotating differ from other modes of writing; while underlining, for instance, a reader may register differently the feel of a page or the ink of a pen. The size and shape of Plath's notes range from large letters stretching across the top or along the side of a page, with o's and a's rounded (Henry James's *Portrait of a Lady*), to concise notes and passages from a critical text in the margins (*The Waste Land*), to short paragraphs in open spaces (*Ulysses*).[13] As an annotator and a writer, Plath preferred black ink. She occasionally selected brown or blue ink, at times to accent what she had already underlined.[14] At other moments, she used a red pencil to underline her notes and revisit passages in her books, underlining again what she had previously marked.[15]

As a reader, Plath was possessive of her books; they were part of her intellectual corpus.[16] During her first year as a Fulbright Scholar at Newnham College, Plath loaned some of her books to her Cambridge University classmate, Jane Baltzell. When she had the audacity to mark their pages with pencil, Plath was outraged. In disbelief, she recorded in her journal that Baltzell

> had underlined five of my new books in pencil with notes; evidently she felt that since I'd already underlined them in black, nothing further could harm them; well, I was furious, feeling my children had been raped, or beaten, by an alien.[17]
>
> (*UJ*, 226)

Perhaps unknowingly, Baltzell had altered the terrain that had shaped and documented Plath's thoughts.

Plath's library

Writing in her journal during the summer before she returned to Smith as an instructor, Plath turned her attention to teaching. Paradoxically, "The Beast in the Jungle" provided a source of comfort. Henry James's story, Plath found, "robs me of fear of job because of love of story, always trying to present it in mind, as to a class" (*UJ*, 296). After the term began, Plath reflected that "[t]he material of reading is something I love. I must learn, slowly, how to best present it, managing class discussion" (*UJ*, 619–20). Material becomes a means of preparation, but crafting notes and selecting passages cannot fully prepare one for the unpredictability of teaching, even as, one of her students remembered, Plath did so with book in hand.[18]

In her journal, Plath contemplated the aesthetics of her surroundings. She found it flattering when a visiting college friend recalled that Plath "chose books for the color & texture of their covers" (*UJ*, 316). During the summer after her first year of college, Plath reminisced about the time she had spent in a bookmobile "looking at poetry books and the brightly covered, good clear-printed Modern Library editions" (*UJ*, 124). Teaching later presented sources of material confidence. Plath reflected that her

> 11 o'clock [class was] in the tiny white room which I like most of all simply because of its intimacy, clean whiteness & pleasant lighting. I am sure I teach better in that room, just as I am sure I teach better in certain dresses whose colors & textures war not against my body & my thought.
> (*UJ*, 335)

Plath sustained this sense of contentment in material artifacts as she approached her library.

As Plath collected books for her college courses and purchased related texts, her enjoyment resembled that of Gabriel Conroy, who, Plath underlined in the copy of *Dubliners* that she bought in the spring of her junior year, "loved to feel the covers and turn over the pages of newly printed books."[19] After returning to Smith in the spring of 1954, following the semester she spent recovering from the breakdown that she later depicted in *The Bell Jar*, Plath reported to her friend Phil McCurdy having filled her Lawrence House room with "two bookcases full of my books" (*LV1*, 671). Two months later, she composed another letter to him while "surrounded by literal stacks of new books,—(still smelling faintly and enticingly of printer's ink and sawdust—whatever that ineffable new-book-smell is made up of!)" (*LV1*, 725–6). A lecture for her European Intellectual History course left her "so transfigured that . . . [she] went across the street to buy the collected plays of Ibsen and read them immediately!" (*LV1*, 727). In her excitement, Plath ended up purchasing "TWELVE (12!) books!," her "bookcases . . . overflowing" with them (*LV1*, 727).

At times, such enthusiasm prompted Plath's marking of texts, the resulting annotations presenting potential indications of her immersion and the degree of her response. A diversion from studying, Plath disclosed to McCurdy, led to her uninhibited reading of D. H. Lawrence's *Studies in Classic American Literature* (1923), "from my library of largely unread-but-about-to-be-read-this-summer books" (*LV1*, 725–6).[20] She became overwhelmed after seeking "to read the chapters on Melville. Little did I know what bright blustering, cataclysmic confidences I was plunging into—result; I read the little pamphlet from cover-to-cover, underlining & turning down corners in most enthusiastic abandon" (*LV1*, 725–6). While underlining passages and folding down corners are ostensibly for when one returns to a book, Plath made marking books a part of the reading process.

As closed artifacts and open pages, Plath's books comprise a textual landscape.[21] The arrangement of her student bookshelves records her organization of writers, historical periods, and genres. Before dismantling her final Smith dorm room in the spring of 1955, Plath photographed her bookshelves and desk. She added three images to her Smith scrapbook of "the den where, in [the] midst of books & chianti bottles (empty) thesis on Dostoevsky & about 50 new poems got pounded out" (Frontispiece, Figures 1.1 and 1.2).[22] These photographs not only document the setting

Figure 1.1 Plath, "Smith Dorm Room," 1955, "Smith Scrapbook," oversize box 8, LMC 1862, folder 36, Lilly.

Figure 1.2 Plath, "Smith Dorm Room," 1955, "Smith Scrapbook," oversize box 8, LMC 1862, folder 36, Lilly.

of her creative and critical writing but also the content and organization of her undergraduate library. Among her twentieth-century holdings, for instance, on the second shelf of the bookcase to the left of the chair sit her copies of Pound's *Pisan Cantos*, Eliot's *Complete Poems and Plays*, and Cleanth Brooks's *The Well Wrought Urn* (Frontispiece).[23] Beneath her bulletin board, a second bookcase holds additional modern volumes (Figure 1.1). The third book from the left on the second shelf is Plath's copy of Joyce's *Ulysses*, with a black book jacket that it soon lost.[24] Several of the remaining volumes on the second shelf are by writers from the twentieth-century literature course with Elizabeth Drew that Plath completed during her sophomore year of college, including Woolf, D. H. Lawrence, and Joseph Conrad.[25] On her desk rest recent acquisitions. Against the lamp is Wallace Stevens's *Collected Poems* (1954), which Plath noted on her calendar that she planned to review for her comprehensive exams that spring (Figure 1.2).[26]

Sitting on the bookcase in the photograph that provides a frontispiece for *Annotating Modernism* is a sculpture of Plath's own head. Positioned at a slight angle, its gaze faces the photographer and viewer of the photograph. Its glance is slightly tilted; one can imagine the right eye glancing upward, an eyebrow raised. This look is accentuated further by the characteristic wave in Plath's hair, what Lynda K. Bundtzen has called the "Veronica Lake pageboy" that Plath adopted after returning to Smith in 1954, following her breakdown the previous summer (*The Other* Ariel, 197). Plath's classmate Mary Derr created this work of art, giving it to Plath, who had sat as its subject.[27] After graduating from Smith, she brought it with her to Cambridge in the fall of 1955, abandoning it there. This head would be all but lost were it not for the photograph Plath kept, and, as Langdon Hammer points out, the poem in which it remains.[28]

In "The Lady and the Earthenware Head" (1957), Plath tells the story of leaving this object behind (*Collected Poems*, 69–70).[29] Discarding it was an act that Hammer sees as an attempt to part with her Smith student persona. Hammer cautions that Plath never entirely leaves her student identity behind; she is unable to "release herself from the rules of the classroom" (68). And just as a semblance of it remains standing freely in the photograph before taking on the more functional role of "propping" up books in the poem (*Collected Poems*, 69; line 4), Hammer underscores that "[w]hat she does is change *her relation* to that culture by means of . . . the tools that culture supplied" (81; Hammer's emphasis). In other words, Plath may have started out as one kind of student but becomes a different kind later. The earthenware head also provided an image of Plath to herself, and, in a different way, so did her marginalia and teaching notes, as texts she annotated and created. These materials are visual artifacts and registers of the critical and aesthetic contexts to which Plath responded as she read.

As we will see, Plath's reading of Joyce's *Dubliners, A Portrait of the Artist as a Young Man,* and *Ulysses* engaged their politics and aesthetics. Taking Plath's marginalia in her copy of *Ulysses* as a starting point allows us to untangle her responses to religious, social, and historical strands of Joyce's narrative, their overlap a form of what George Bornstein refers to in *Material Modernism* as "cultural, material, and moral hybridity" (166).[30] And while critics have rightly argued that Plath was immersed in Joyce's creative experiments as she read *Ulysses*, doing so also meant noting the novel's attention to Irish Nationalism and Jewish identity, returning to the latter as she depicted the midcentury cultural climate in her poetry and fiction.[31]

The Jewish question

In his influential essay, "The Plath Celebration: A Partial Dissent" (1973), Irving Howe raised the question of whether it was appropriate for Plath to use material from the Holocaust to describe her personal plight.[32] Compared with the impersonality of the preceding generation, in Howe's terms, confessional poems lack "the mediating presence of imagined event or *persona*" (12–13).[33] Drawing on a personal subject, Plath, as Howe underscored, likened her private tragedy to one of incomprehensible magnitude. It is the presence of Jewish identity, or the gesture toward it, however, that enables a sense of distance in her poems, emulating one of the strategies that Joyce's Bloom modeled. Ultimately, Plath updates Joyce's creative project in "Daddy" (1962) and "Lady Lazarus" (1962), developing personae whose Jewish identity remains unclear.[34]

Plath read Joyce's *Ulysses* during her junior year of college while auditing Elizabeth Drew's "20th Century British Literature" course in the spring of 1953 (*LV1*, 558).[35] A classmate recalled that Plath "could stripsearch *Ulysses* and make all the mythological connections without batting an eye."[36] At the beginning of each episode, Plath inscribed the corresponding *Odyssey* title and identified allusions to Homer's poem in her copy of the novel. Beginning in the fifth episode, she added the attributes from Stuart Gilbert's chart in *James Joyce's Ulysses* (1931).[37] The density of the markings and the size of Plath's copy of *Ulysses* alone are intimidating. Plath responded to the magnitude of Joyce's linguistic *tour de force* in her journal: "i am reading 'ulysses.' god, it is unbelievably semantically big, great, mind cracking, and even webster's is a sterile impotent enuch [sic] as far as conceiving words goes" (*UJ*, 168).[38] Plath admired Joyce's formal and technical experimentation, controversial subject matter, and humor. After reading the novel, she added, "touché," beside Edmund Wilson's remark in *Axel's Castle*, "yet I doubt whether any human memory is capable, on a first reading, of meeting the demands of 'Ulysses'" (210). Similarly, she remarked "poor fools" below Wilson's description of the initial critics' inability to comprehend Joyce's narrative structure (211).

Attentive to what Stephen Dedalus characterizes as the "nets" restraining him in *Portrait of the Artist*, Plath noted Ireland's relation to religious and national institutions in her copy of *Ulysses*. The passages that Plath marked reflect the complex relationship of Irish literature and culture to the British Empire. Early in the novel, for instance, she underlined Joyce's allusion to Oscar Wilde's revision of Shakespeare's Caliban, linking Irish subjectivity and artistic representation: "It is a symbol of Irish art. The cracked lookingglass of a servant" (*U*, 8; Figure 1.3). Plath, likely recording a point Drew made in her lecture, glossed in the margin: "Ireland- servant of England – no true reflection."[39]

As she underlined and annotated her book, Plath revisited Stephen's consideration of national identity. She noted in the margin the "irony: Stephen imprisoned by everything" and underlined the advice of Stephen's former classmate, Haines: "I should think you are able to free yourself. You are your own master" (*U*, 22; Figure 1.4). Stephen responds, "I am the servant of two masters," clarifying, "[t]he imperial British state . . . and the holy Roman catholic and apostolic church." Haines returns to Irish Nationalism, which he had brought to his conversation with Stephen years earlier (in

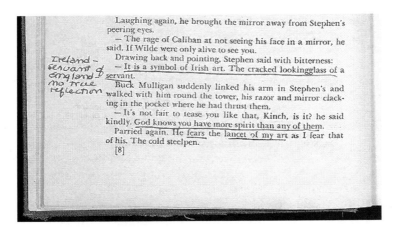

Figure 1.3 Plath's copy of James Joyce's *Ulysses*, page 8, Mortimer Rare Book Collection, MRBC-MS-00045, Smith College Special Collections, Northampton, MA.

Portrait of the Artist), and finds that "history is to blame." Despite the fact that he was determined to distance himself from such influences at the close of *Portrait of the Artist*, as Plath acknowledged in the margin, the "power of church & tradition [is] still strong in Stephen" (Figure 1.4).

Reading *Ulysses* after World War II, Plath's marginalia also reflect the terminology of the world in which she lived. Shifting from art to politics, Plath's note at the bottom of the page clarifying the "English national problem [of] the Jewish question" responds to the following passage: "Of course I'm a Britisher, Haines' voice said . . . I don't want to see my country fall into the hands of German jews either. That's our national problem, I'm afraid, just now" (*U*, 22; Figure 1.4). Plath may have been recalling Drew's point that Joyce's first chapter introduced themes with which the novel as a whole is concerned: "A hint [of a] Gentile-Jew problem—when Haines declares there is such a problem."[40] While the immediate context to which Haines refers is the potential Aliens Bill in March 1904, following the flight of Jews to England from Eastern Europe, the idea of "the Jewish question" would have also had different implications in 1904, 1922, and 1953.[41]

The terms "Jewish question" and "Jewish problem" have a long history, and their comparable ambiguity at midcentury makes the meaning of Plath's annotation in 1953 similarly unclear. Richard J. Bernstein has argued that

> [d]espite the persistent use of the definite article, "the Jewish question" never referred to a single, well-defined determinate issue or question. On the contrary, it was used to designate a whole series of shifting, loosely related, historical, cultural, religious, economic, political, and social issues, ranging from what rights were due to Jews as citizens of nation-states to whether the Jews constituted a distinctive people, race, or nation.[42]

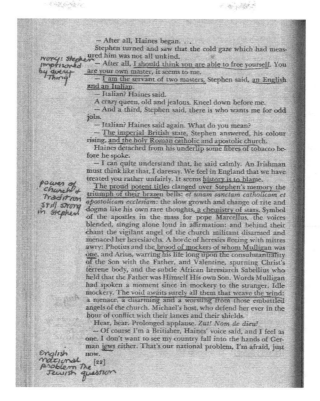

Figure 1.4 Plath's copy of *Ulysses*, page 22, Smith.

Bernstein added that

> "the Jewish question"—an expression that initially gained popularity in the writings of anti-Semites, and was used only later by Jewish intellectuals—takes on a very different shading depending on the specific historical context in which it is used. In the twentieth century, the Jewish question became not only a focal point of concern for Zionists, but also ominous with the Nazi anti-Semitic ideology that demanded a final solution to the Jewish question—the extermination of European Jewry.[43]

A text that Plath studied at Smith refers to both of these senses of the Jewish question as the "Jewish problem."

In the "Religion 14" course that Plath completed during her sophomore year of college, her professor assigned Milton Steinberg's *A Partisan Guide to the Jewish Problem* (1945).[44] Like Bernstein, Steinberg acknowledged that "to many people, anti-Semitism is the Jewish problem. . . . But to take it for the entire Jewish problem is to oversimplify grossly" (11). Steinberg provided a list of concerns the book would address, which Plath recorded in her notes. It included "Problem of Status," which contained, "The rehabilitation of European Jewry and how it is to be effected," "The causes and recent history of anti-Semitism," "Problems of Self-Acceptance," "Problems of the Tradition," and "Problems of Homeland" (13–14). Plath's notes focus on the later chapters, including Chapter Nine, "A Matter of Definitions," which begins with "our key terms 'Jew' and 'Judaism'" (145). It is possible that such an introduction to central issues of concern for the Jewish people, in the past and present, could have informed Plath's consideration of a text like *Ulysses*.[45]

When she read Joyce's "Nestor" episode, Plath encountered Deasy's insults. Writing in the margin, Plath summarized Deasy's sense of "Jews: [as a] cause of England's decay" beside his explanation that "England is in the hands of the jews" (*U*, 34; Figure 1.5). Stephen pointed out that purchasing goods at low price and selling them at a higher one is part of the trade. Plath underlined the question he posed to Deasy: "A merchant, Stephen said, is one who buys cheap and sells dear, jew or gentile, is he not?" (*U*, 34; Figure 1.5). Deasy blames Jews for their rootlessness: "They sinned against the light . . . you can see the darkness in their eyes. And that is why they are wanderers on the earth to this day" (*U*, 34–5). Plath's note in the margin, however, does not share his perspective, taking a longer view of history, and the "fusion of Jews of ages being used by gentiles for source of money then cast aside . . ." (*U*, 35; Figure 1.5).[46]

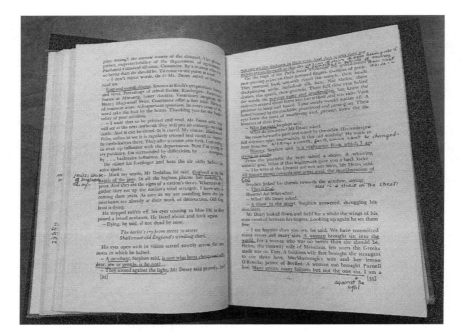

Figure 1.5 Plath's copy of *Ulysses*, pages 34–5, Smith.

In the conclusion of this scene, Joyce critiques the distance from religion in modernity. Following Deasy's accusation, "[t]heir eyes knew the years of wandering and, patient, knew the dishonours of their flesh" (*U*, 35), Plath underscored twice Stephen's response, "Who has not?" (*U*, 35). Shifting perspective, she acknowledged in the margin the significance of "history: events, facts which cannot be changed" (*U*, 35). Plath's comment responds to Stephen's well-known observation that "[h]istory . . . is a nightmare from which I am trying to awake" (*U*, 35). As we have seen, Plath's underlining demonstrated a certain economy. Skipping less significant words and phrases, she placed emphasis on central elements of a text for her own purposes as a student and poet. Near the close of the page, for instance, she remained attentive to Joyce's depiction of religion in modernity. Plath underlined Stephen's pithy statement, "[t]hat is God," and subsequent response, "[a] shout in the street," reiterating in the margin, "God is a shout in the street" (35). Shifting from Stephen to Leopold Bloom, in later portions of the novel, Plath traced Bloom's articulation of his sense of religious and national identity.

Plath's annotations in the "Cyclops" episode of *Ulysses* combine references to the Homeric allusions with attention to Bloom's identity. On the first page, Plath noted the "one-eyed nationalism violent, brutal sub-human nationalists" (287). She observed later in the chapter, "Bloom pretends he doesn't hear anti-semitic [sic] remarks" (318). At a different point, Plath underlined and marked with two lines in the margin Bloom's statement: "And I belong to a race too . . . that is hated and persecuted. Also now. This very moment. This very instant" (326). Plath also noted Joyce's rendering of empathy and distance, underlining Bloom's later question: "why can't a jew love his country like the next fellow?" (331). Bloom's question is one of humanity and the ways that national identity and related boundaries define how others perceive an individual.[47]

Margins are both material and social spaces. When annotating *Ulysses*, Plath used the space of the page to comment on characters' responses to society. Christopher Grobe points out that "[t]he early history of confessionalism in each art form was full of straight, white artists—many of them filled with feelings of 'margin envy,' as they attacked their own straightness and whiteness through acts of 'self-othering.'"[48] A key difference that separates Plath from her midcentury peers and modernist predecessors like Joyce, however, lies in the uncertainty she maintains as to whether her speakers are Jewish.

Plath's poem "Daddy" juggles national and religious identities in the voice of a protagonist who "may well be a Jew" (*Collected Poems*, 223; line 35). Ann Keniston argues that this hesitation reflects a larger separation between the poem's speaker and the vestiges of the Holocaust to which she alludes. In Keniston's view, even as the persona's father

> may resemble a German, the speaker distances herself from this already indirect relation: she is not Daddy's victim but the victim of language

itself. The shift to a more direct equivalence between self and Jew is similarly qualified. Insofar as the speaker is a Jew, the resemblance is limited to particular attributes (she talks like one) or is multiply qualified ("*I think I may* well be a Jew").[49]

Keniston concludes that "the speaker's final statement on the matter is not only tentative ('I may be') but partial: she is not a Jew but 'a bit of a Jew'" (147). In other words, the poem goes to great lengths to convey the insecurity in the speaker's sense of her identity.[50]

Revisiting "Lady Lazarus" in light of the contents of Plath's reading, the seams in the protagonist's relation to Jewish identity become apparent. In her use of comparisons, Plath distances the speaker herself from the Jewish identity that she invokes. Addressing this poem and "Daddy," Keniston argues that

[t]he belated, physically removed speakers of these poems insist that the Holocaust is available only in fragmentary and corrupted form, and Plath's emphasis on the materiality of her poems themselves, on their awkward or obtrusive mechanics, intensifies this sense of distance.

(140)

In the case of "Lady Lazarus," this sense of remove is not only evident in Plath's wording but also in the cloth layer shielding the speaker from her audience. The persona's "face a featureless, fine / Jew linen" (*Collected Poems*, 244; line 8–9) suggests a clean, crisp fabric of high quality.[51] It is possible that speaker's face has been covered with a burial shroud. Calling such a cloth "Jew linen," however, is unclear and reflects a certain awkwardness. Grammatically, it might make sense to refer to "Jewish linen" or "linen Jews use," but neither phrase describes a burial shroud. Plath's choice of "Jew linen," however, is succinct, and presents a pair with "Nazi lampshade" (line 5).

But to be more specific, Plath's reference suggests a *talith*, or prayer shawl. She had learned about this traditional item in her college religion course, recording in notes on Judaism from a book called *The Religions of Democracy*:

"Shema" - Hear O Israel . . .
"Kaddish" – prayer for coming of Kingdom of God.
    language of prayers mostly Hebrew   Exodus
        Tallit- prayer-shawl   Tephillin - 2 boxes - [52]

This was not Plath's only encounter with this ritual. When she read *Ulysses*, she underlined "Talith" in a list of Jewish references that Bloom reads in the "Circe" episode.[53] In both instances, the prayer shawl is among other terms and items that characterize Jewish religious practices, but Plath's underlining of these references also makes them part of a material record that extends from her reading to her writing. The fact that a *talith* is used for prayer and for burial also gives it a function reminiscent of death-in-life, which we will see was a theme Plath emphasized when she taught modernism.[54]

After graduating from Smith, Plath attended David Daiches's Joyce lectures at Cambridge in 1956. Writing to her mother, Plath expressed a new investment in "bringing the larger, social world of other people into my poems" and that these ideas emerged "most interestingly in my series of Seventeen [magazine] stories about social problems: jewish question [sic], sororities, etc." (*LV1*, 1133).[55] In her resolution that "[t]he world and the problems of an individual in this particular civilization are going to be forged into my discipline" (*LV1*, 1133), Plath recalls the close of *Portrait of the Artist*. After teaching the novel, Plath admitted to her brother,

> I must say that in teaching a book one learns it by heart, and gets a really amazing insight. However, this kind of organization and analysis is not the kind I'd use if I were reading the book in light of my own writing: it is much too conscious and analytical.
>
> (*LV2*, 214)

Even as Plath sought to abandon the more deliberate strategies that teaching brings to reading, her experience teaching *Portrait of the Artist* comes to alter the conscience she creates in her own work and the world it depicts.[56]

A Portrait of the Artist

Plath's reading of Joyce's *Portrait of the Artist* presents a vital case study regarding her intellectual development. The novel itself, as Plath underlined in Harry Levin's preface, presents "the record of a developing mind" (*PJJ*, 244). In light of her aspirations as a writer and talent as a visual artist, *Portrait* was a likely choice for Plath. Composing her teaching materials, Plath worked from the Joyce notebook she had kept as a student, supplementing these notes with additional criticism and background information regarding the political contexts to which the novel speaks.[57]

As an undergraduate at Smith, Plath filled a brown, cardboard-backed, spiral bound notebook with notes from Elizabeth Drew's Joyce lectures.[58] The notebook opens with *Portrait of the Artist* and Plath decorated the cover with quotations from the novel, doodling two flowers to their left:

> "artist forging anew in his workshop
> out of the sluggish matter of the
> earth a new soaring impalpable
> imperishable being"[59]

"To live, to err, to fall, to triumph, to
recreate life out of life"[60]

"a priest of the eternal imagination,
transmuting the daily bread of
experience into the radiant body
of everliving life."[61]

Personality of artist: "simplest verbal vesture
                                          of instant of emotion"[62]
1 cry or cadence or mood – Chamber Music
2 Fluid, lambent narrative – Portrait
3 refines self out of existence
    impersonalizes self – Ulysses[63]
  "vitality fills every person
    with vital force so that he assumes
    a proper, intangible esthetic life"[64]

"In the virgin womb of the imagination
the word was made flesh"[65]

Plath's list records a progressive erasure across Joyce's oeuvre, achieving in
Ulysses distance "behind or beyond or above his handiwork, invisible, refined
out of existence, indifferent" (*Portrait*, 168). In doing so, she also adapted a
path Levin charts in *James Joyce: A Critical Introduction* (1941). A key dif-
ference is that Plath attributes to *Ulysses* the culmination that Levin leaves to
Finnegans Wake.[66] After quoting *Portrait of the Artist*—from "[t]he lyrical
form is in fact the simplest verbal vesture of an instant of emotion," to "the
artist . . . paring his fingernails" (Qtd. in *JJ*, 44)—Levin asserts:

> This progress you will see easily in the succession of Joyce's works. The
> cry becomes a cadence in *Chamber Music*[.] . . . The narrative of the
> *Portrait of the Artist* has scarcely emerged from the lyrical stage. . . .
> The shift from the personal to the epic will come in *Ulysses*[.] . . . And
> with *Finnegans Wake*, the artist will have retired within or above or
> beyond his handiwork, refined out of existence.
>
> (*JJ*, 44–5)

The excerpts that Plath featured on the cover of her notebook were drawn
largely from the novel's climax, as Stephen turns from the possibility of
the priesthood to the power of creating art, particularly in language. Plath
later conceded in her teaching notes that Stephen is an "aesthete more than
artist—full of theories of art & language—not a 'maker'—except of a few
verses—" (*TN*).[67] Teaching provided an opportunity to revisit Stephen's
devotion to art, realizing by the end of the term that to be a writer herself,
she needed to leave teaching behind.

As she contemplated teaching *Portrait of the Artist*, Plath grappled with her youthful identification with Stephen Dedalus: "I now go rapidly pace-pace-apace through the book I dreamily campus-wandered with myself, some five years ago, the <u>Portrait of The Artist</u>, word-encanting, descanting" (*UJ*, 321).[68] Near the close of the slim paperback she read as a student, Plath identified in the margin, "[t]he artist," and, turning the page, inscribed horizontally along the margin, "Excellent!" beside Joyce's account of Stephen (which she also underlined) as "<u>a priest of the eternal imagination, transmuting the daily bread of experience into the radiant body of everliving life</u>" (*Portrait*, 172; Figure 1.6). Echoes of passages like this one foregrounded Plath's return to the novel as she contemplated the best way to communicate these ideas to her students and "present, vividly, the act of creation which takes place" (*UJ*, 321).[69]

Developing her teaching materials, it appears that Plath consulted her student notes from Drew's lectures on *Portrait of the Artist* and fleshed out further the ways that Joyce's novel approaches art and its significance.[70] In her Joyce notebook, Plath had recorded that Stephen "[t]urned intensity & passion into Art. Art=Joyce's religion" (*JJN*). Writing her own teaching notes, Plath provided this connection in bold letters that she also underlined: "<u>ART = RELIGION for Joyce</u>. [He draws an] [a]nalogy between

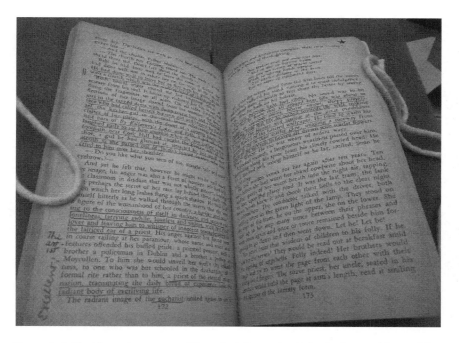

Figure 1.6 Plath's student copy of Joyce's *A Portrait of the Artist as a Young Man*, pages 172–3, Stuart A. Rose Manuscript, Archives, and Rare Book Library, Emory University, Atlanta, GA.

artist and priest: both dedicate lives to vocation, calling. Joyce uses language of religious ritual to describe the role of the artist" (*TN*).[71] As she capitalized and underlined, Plath demonstrated directness and clarity. She defined "<u>ART</u> as <u>EPIPHANY</u>," glossing in parentheses that it means "<u>to show</u>" (*TN*). This process takes a shape that "[i]f not a divine revelation, [is] a moment of sudden <u>illumination</u>" (*TN*). Plath added that Stephen's character is such that "each epiphany" is an "awakening of body," a "literary vocation," and a "farewell to Ireland" (*TN*).[72] She subsequently inquired as to the "[r]<u>aw material of [the] artist</u>" (*TN*), stressing in response: "LIFE, EXPERIENCE" (*TN*).

Preparing to teach *Portrait of the Artist*, Plath annotated a fresh copy of the novel in *The Portable James Joyce*. She underlined the text in black ink and returned to emphasize passages and clarify points using a red pencil. Her teaching notes also contain lists of page numbers and additions in red pencil, perhaps as an extension of her underlining and notes.[73] Annotating the novel, for instance, Plath noted in black ink and red pencil Stephen's explanation of Aquinas's aesthetic theories, and the passage's significance as an epiphany (*PJJ*, 479; Figure 1.7). She similarly underlined and placed in parentheses Stephen's assertion of his independence as an artist: "<u>When the soul of a man is born in this country there are nets flung at it to hold it back from flight. You talk to me of nationality, language, religion. I shall</u>

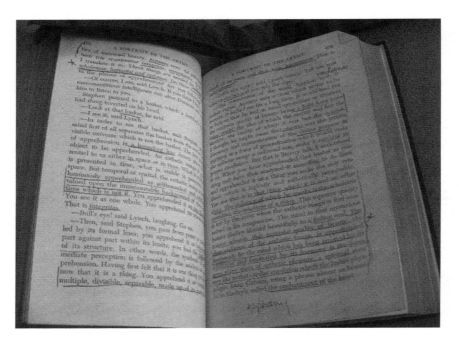

Figure 1.7 Plath's teaching copy of *A Portrait of the Artist* in the *Portable James Joyce*, pages 478–9, Lilly.

try to fly by those nets" (*PJJ*, 468).[74] Plath repeated the previous quotation in her teaching notes, emphasizing that Stephen's "[p]hrases mark complete & final break with old conscience of race – dedication to disciplines of art" (*TN*).[75] Stephen's response to art is inseparable from the political dimensions of his world, and Plath does not shy away from these facets of the novel, expanding upon the materials she prepared to teach Joyce's story "Ivy Day in the Committee Room" earlier in the course.

Introducing "Ivy Day in the Committee Room" in her teaching notes, Plath insisted, "BACKGROUND NEEDED," and clarified that its depiction of "moral paralysis" included the "political scene" (*TN*). She outlined a history of Irish politics that includes the Black and Tans and the "[t]orture-complete political & economic" as well as "hanging and martyred youth," and filled out her introduction of the Fenian brotherhood's resistance by working from sources like *Encyclopedia Americana* (*TN*).[76] Yeats had navigated similar historical terrain in the poems that Plath studied as an undergraduate and would revisit as a teacher. Accordingly, her marginalia in *The Collected Poems of W. B. Yeats* included some of the background informing his poems, drawing on the contents of texts like Thomas Rice Henn's *The Lonely Tower* (1950).[77]

During her junior year of college, Plath prepared a presentation on Yeats's poem "Nineteen Hundred and Nineteen," and it may have been at this time that she recorded in her journal having read "critical books about Yeats all day today" (*UJ*, 174). Plath noted in her copy of Yeats's *Collected Poems* that the poem depicts "England brutally trying to put down violence of nationalists in Ireland with Blacks & tans [sic]."[78] In addition, she underlined the end of Yeats's explanation that "a drunken soldiery / Can leave the mother murdered at her door." Annotating the poem, Plath drew on Henn's explanation in *The Lonely Tower*, adding in the margin that Yeats was referring to "a murder by a burst of a machine gun fire from a passing lorry of Black and tans near Kiltartan" (Yeats, 205).[79] Plath indicated that there was a "hatred of violence resulting from idealism" in a note above the poem's opening lines, which she also underlined: "Many ingenious lovely things are gone / That seemed sheer miracle to the multitude" (Yeats, 204).[80] When Plath came to teach Joyce, Ireland's struggle for independence provided a subject with which she could enrapture her students.

On Sunday, 9 February 1958, Plath wrote to her sister-in-law Olwyn Hughes on pink Smith College memorandum paper. Addressing the letter "To OH" "From SH" "In re shoes, ships, sealing wax," Plath alluded to Lewis Carroll's poem, "The Walrus and the Carpenter," from *Through the Looking Glass* (1872).[81] Carroll's Walrus tells the Carpenter that "[t]he time has come . . . To talk of many things." Doing likewise, Plath discussed her plans to leave teaching, despite the pleasure she ultimately found in it:

> Not writing this year has been the worst of it, & I feel much better now
> that I have shocked the whole English department by saying out-loud

that I am not coming back: this is without doubt the best college to teach at anywhere in America for several reasons: a three to four day week, relative freedom in course books . . . & a lively young faculty.

(*LV2*, 210)

Once she decides to leave teaching

(after a hellish fall spent confronting ghosts of my old student selves in every cranny & coffee shop & teaching from lecture platforms my own professors taught from) one part of me feels sad to leave. I love the power of having 70 girls to teach, & get what is surely a dangerous enjoyment from shocking them into awareness, laughter & even tears, the occasion of the latter being a snowy Saturday spent evoking the bloody & cruel history of the Irish whiteboys, potato famines, mass hangings, etc.

(*LV2*, 210–1)

With stories of strife and uprisings, Plath jolted her students into consciousness as well as conscience, refashioning Stephen's own desire as an artist.

Perhaps while preparing her classes, Plath defined at the top of page 281 in her teaching copy of *Portrait of the Artist*: "white boy: 1761-secret agrarian association." In the novel, readers learn that Stephen's great grandfather was "condemned to death as a whiteboy" (*PJJ*, 281). As Richard Ellmann points out, Joyce's great grandfather had also joined this group of "Catholic agitators against landlords, and was condemned to death, though the sentence was not carried out."[82] While Plath may not have known this element of Joyce's family history, her attention to Irish political history in her teaching materials and marginalia broadens our sense of what Robin Peel has called the "ideological education" that Plath's reading enabled before she returned to England in late 1959.[83] Even as Peel's focus lies mainly outside of Plath's study of literature, we have seen in her handling of Joyce and Yeats an awareness of the political contexts that modernist texts address. Ultimately, Plath tested boundaries as a teacher. Acting both impersonal and dramatic, she adopted a teaching persona that mirrored her approach to modernism. By annotating critical texts, Plath also preserved impressions that informed her development of this perspective.

Practical symbolism: modernist writers in Axel's Castle

During and after the first half of the twentieth century, modernist texts redefined not only the form and content of literature but also the meaning of interpretation.[84] Critics have noted that for readers like Plath, Cleanth Brooks and Robert Penn Warren's *Understanding Poetry* (1938) and Brooks's *The Well Wrought Urn: Studies in the Structure of Poetry* (1947) were formative.[85] A gift from Gordon Lameyer, Edmund Wilson's *Axel's*

Castle was waiting when Plath made a visit home from McLean Hospital for Christmas in 1953. Thanking him, she stressed that *Axel's Castle* was a book she had "always been meaning to read" (*LV1*, 652). Having received her own copy to mark, Plath did so vigorously.[86]

While Eliot's *The Sacred Wood* is among the texts with which a midcentury literature student may have been familiar, the book does not remain in Plath's library. We can find her responses to Eliot's theories of poetic impersonality, however, in her copy of *Axel's Castle*.[87] Her attentiveness captures both enthusiasm and identification, seeing and perhaps celebrating the ideas she had encountered in her coursework. Plath underlined the following sentence, adding a star and writing "good!" in the margin: "<u>Eliot believes that a work of art is not an oracular outpouring, but an object which has been constructed deliberately with the aim of producing a certain effect</u>" (Wilson, 117).[88] The impersonality of poetry elicited a paradoxical response, as Plath added two exclamation points beside Eliot's sense of it as "not a turning loose of emotion, but an escape from emotion; it is not the expression of personality, but an escape from personality" (Wilson, 123; Figure 1.8).[89] Figure 1.8 reveals the possible mark of a formerly turned down corner of the opposite page, the physical impression of her excitement in encountering Eliot's theories and recognizing those she had heard I. A. Richards discuss at Smith in 1954.

Annotating *Axel's Castle* also meant revisiting Richards's clinical approach to poetry. As we can see in Figure 1.8, Plath drew a line beside Wilson's critique of thirties criticism's "detached scientific interest or

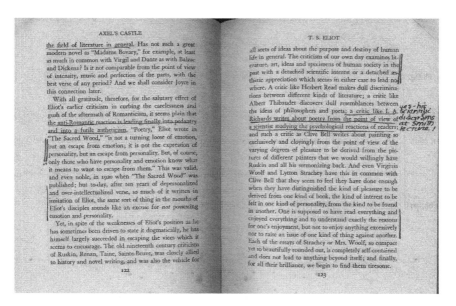

Figure 1.8 Plath's copy of Edmund Wilson's *Axel's Castle*, pages 122–3.

a detached aesthetic appreciation which seems in either case to lead no-where" (123). When he remarked that "a critic like I. A. Richards writes about poetry from the point of view of a scientist studying the psycho-logical reactions of readers," Plath agreed in the right margin, "yes—his scientific diagrams at Smith lecture!"[90] (Figure 1.8). Her response is partly personal, delighted because she had the opportunity to see what Wilson described (*LV2*, 178). At Cambridge, Plath would go on to study "practical criticism," which takes its title from Richards's book.[91] Her enthusiasm, however, subsided by 1962, when, in her interview with the British Coun-cil, Plath noted that "the whole emphasis in England, in universities, on practical criticism . . . [is] almost paralyzing."[92] Her choice of wording is telling, as "paralysis" was a prominent concern to which she attended in Joyce's fiction, drawing on his own admission regarding its centrality to *Dubliners*.[93] Death-in-life and paralysis became part of the critical vocab-ulary that Plath adopted as she taught and recast in her fiction and poetry.

As we have seen, Plath's attention to impersonal and scientific approaches to criticism and poetry was part of her consideration of modernism. Prepar-ing to teach at Smith, Plath returned to *Axel's Castle* and other texts that she had come to know as a student. Plath's annotations and teaching notes record the thematic connections she made among critical texts that alter the shape and trajectory of her course.[94]

Teaching modernist texts

In late September 1957, Plath began teaching English 11 at Smith.[95] She and Hughes had recently settled into an apartment at 337 Elm Street, a 12 minute walk from the campus (*LV2*, 170).[96] Plath taught three sections of the course, meeting in two buildings, Seelye Hall, home of the English De-partment, and what was likely to have been the neighboring Hatfield Hall (*LV2*, 174, n. 2). Plath met approximately 70 first year students in classes at nine and eleven in the morning and at three in the afternoon (*UJ*, 388–9).[97] The morning and afternoon classes operated on two schedules, with the af-ternoon sections meeting on Wednesdays, Thursdays, and Fridays, and the morning sections following on Thursdays, Fridays, and Saturdays. When the term began, Plath saw the Wednesday class as a trial run, refining her lesson when she taught it again the following day (*LV2*, 174).[98] As Mary Ellen Chase, one of the professors who had taught the course during Plath's first year at Smith, told readers of the student newspaper in 1954, it was not an easy course to teach:

> Many years ago, when I was working for my doctorate at the University of Minnesota, Professor E. E. Stoll, whom students of Shakespeare here know as an eminent critic and whom I knew as a friend and teacher, was given to uttering a dark prophecy to all his graduate students about to enter college teaching. His words were to this effect: "You have to be

proof against slings and arrows if you teach Freshman English in any college in the country. You'll not only be blamed for the illiteracy and the bad taste of your students by practically everyone teaching every subject but your own (on the naive assumption that since they *speak* English, they know how it should be taught) but you won't find more than one out of every ten freshmen who will have the faintest notion of what you are trying to do."[99]

Nodding to her Smith students, Chase added, "[n]ow all these slings and arrows in a college happily given to alert criticism and lively, outspoken opinions on most matters are not too disturbing." While visiting Cambridge in the spring of 1956, Chase encouraged Plath to inquire as to whether she could teach at Smith, giving the impression that it was likely she could (*LV1*, 1194). After following Chase's advice, and receiving news of her appointment, Plath prepared for the challenge.[100]

Returning to Smith, what Robert Lowell later called Plath's "brilliant tense presence" was part of her formidable teaching persona.[101] One of her students recalls Mrs. Hughes as

> strict, severe, brisk and to the point. Everyone in the class was scared stiff of her. . . . She rarely cracked a smile. There was little room for discussion. She did the talking. I remember her having many books on the lecturn on top of the desk and, yes, notes, but I don't really remember the extent to which she consulted those notes. She did, however, direct the class in an absolute no-nonsense fashion.
>
> . . . She just walked into the classroom, put her things down on her desk, fixed a steely gaze on us, laid down the law for an hour, gathered up her things and stalked out. . . .
>
> Not only was she strict—stiff might be a better word for her demeanor—but tension is truly the operative term. The tension emanating from her when she walked into the room, when she stood, stiff and straight in front of you, even as she stalked out of the classroom at the end was palpable. I remember having the impression that if she relaxed, she would fall, or, more accurately, explode into a thousand little pieces, right in front of our eyes. . . .
>
> What she was, and even the kids in my class who disliked her thoroughly admitted to this, was a very good teacher. I came into her class without the faintest ideas of what critical reading might be or with even less of a notion as to how to write a coherent critical essay. She taught us all how to do both. She was rigorous, demanding, and thorough in her approach both to her students and to the literature we were reading. And while she never seemed to show great passion and love for that literature, I think it sort of snuck through despite all her efforts to rein herself in.
>
> ("Recollections," 127–30)

Abrupt, yet thorough, Plath's command in the classroom modeled the precision she wanted her students to demonstrate. Combining awkwardness and fragility, Plath pushed the limits of what she may have felt capable of accomplishing.

Drawing on a list that Smith had supplied (*LV2*, 149), Plath opened the course with what she called the "pragmatic syntax of William James" in *Varieties of Religious Experience* (1902) and proceeded to the short fiction of Nathaniel Hawthorne, Henry James, D. H. Lawrence, and Joyce (*LV2*, 163).[102] Plath subsequently utilized her undergraduate study of Fyodor Dostoevsky's fiction to teach *Crime and Punishment*, which she followed with Joyce's *Portrait of the Artist*.[103] She then returned to her Cambridge Tripos reading to teach a tragedy unit beginning with Aristotle's *Poetics* and including *Oedipus Rex*, *Antigone*, and the plays of John Webster and Cyril Tourneur, Henrik Ibsen, and August Strindberg.[104] Plath ended the term with a poetry unit that included predominantly modern poets, and what she once called "the muscular packed verse of Gerard Manley Hopkins" (*UJ*, 164); his poetry, she added in her teaching notes, was "not published until 1918: [and] seems like a contemporary: [a] Modern influence" (*TN*).[105] She followed Hopkins with Yeats, Eliot, Dylan Thomas, W. H. Auden, John Crowe Ransom, e.e. cummings, and Edith Sitwell.

Because Plath left teaching after a year, scholars have hesitated to investigate the content of her course or her pedagogical strategies.[106] As we have already seen her tell her sister-in-law, Plath struggled to find time for creative work during her teaching year. She made this clear in a letter to her friend Ann Davidow-Goodman:

> I was asked back, and also for this year to teach writing, which I would much less like to teach than freshman English (I managed to fit in Dostoevsky and Sophocles along with DH Lawrence and James Joyce). However, although I loved teaching, the great conflict was with writing. I wore my eyes out on 70 student themes every other week and had no energy for writing a thing.[107]
>
> (*LV2*, 312–3)

As an undergraduate at Smith, Plath recorded in notes from a lecture Elizabeth Drew gave on twentieth-century literature that "[t]he Moderns," "Pound, Eliot, Yeats, Joyce, [and] D.H. Lawrence: revealed [a] new & desolating vision of modern civilization—writers [were] angry, horrified, or despairing for [the] past. Yet prose and poetry [was] alive with new dramatic force, vigor[,] & complexity."[108] Preparing to communicate these ideas to her students, Plath revisited the sources that Drew had introduced and complemented them with others. The resulting contents of Plath's teaching materials reflect her own refashioning of the modernism she had inherited.[109]

Now that we have completed a survey of Plath's reading and teaching strategies, the following case study will address her emphasis on the theme of death-in-life in modern literature.[110] The intertextual approach of the following segment also continues a shift in emphasis from critics' attention to Plath's unconscious, psychological motives regarding death to a historically contextualized reading, situated in the materials with which she worked.

Death-in-life

Long before readers became familiar with the gravity of Plath's later poetry and prose, she prepared an explanation for her students on their final day of class regarding the prominence of death in the texts that they had read. Plath's response begins as a statement on poetry and becomes advice for life:

> POETRY: A CREATION, A RECREATION, of worlds: man is god-like, or magnificent . . . insofar as he lives: not numb, dead, insensitive, destructive:
> PEOPLE ASK: why is there so much death, so much living death in the stories, poems, plays & novels that we've read: [from] The Dead to The Wasteland [sic] of death-in-life:
> DEATH IS ONE OF THE MOST MOVING & TROUBLING EX-PERIENCES OF LIFE: DEATH*IN*LIFE emerges AS ONE OF THE MOST TERRIBLE STATES OF EXISTENCE: NEUTRAL-ITY, BOREDOM become worse sins than murder, worse than illicit love affairs: BE RIGHT OR WRONG, don't be indifferent, don't be NOTHING.[111]
>
> (TN)

From her block capitals to the underlining that she added, it hardly seems possible that Plath could emphasize these concepts further. Even as she was concluding a poetry unit, drawing on the texts she taught and the criticism she read, one could also imagine that these were sentiments that she too found sustaining. Advocating the vision of Joyce's artist and warning against the lack of inspiration in Eliot's "Unreal City" (*Complete Poems and Plays*, 39; line 60) Plath's articulation of the extremity and complexity of death and death-in-life underscored the significance that she may have granted to the modernist texts that she selected to teach.[112] In doing so, she clarified that the role of the poet is to represent life, which includes extreme limits of existence.[113]

Adding another layer to her explanation, Plath distinguished living life from depicting it. Her advice suggests the range of experiences that poems depict and the religious significance that readers and writers have granted to poetry and, echoing Stephen Dedalus, art. She clarified that "MANY POETS, MANY READERS live by poetry as people have lived by religion: BOTH ARE RITUALS, PATTERNS, Ordering & giving spe-cial <u>meaning to the most profound experiences</u> of <u>human life</u>" (*TN*).[114] In a later statement, Plath crystallized for students the significance of reading their course texts: "DEATH a main subject because we must live to live more keenly, if necessary more painfully, in order to fully live" (*TN*).[115] Rather than suggesting a morbid fascination, Plath's emphasis on the theme of death-in-life reflects her attention to the ways that modern literature depicts life.

In the texts that Plath taught, the state of death-in-life, in part, describes characters' lack of engagement with their respective modern surroundings. Plath's preparation included returning to the ways that her Smith professors had introduced the texts and writers she had selected to teach. Plath taught using a required English 11 handbook and *Poetic Patterns: A Note on Versification* by Elizabeth Drew (*TN*).[116] Plath's warning to her students on the final day of class echoes Drew's explanation in this pamphlet that Eliot's "The Hollow Men" (1925) depicts a "sense of banishment from human vitality, vitality either for good or evil" and a "condition of meaningless neutrality."[117] Drew's reading of "The Hollow Men" is part of a larger trajectory in critics' readings of Eliot's poems and modern literature at mid-century that Plath's teaching notes reflect. As we will see, Plath returns to Eliot's lines in "The Hollow Men" in her teaching notes, addressing the poem's depiction of death-in-life and paralysis.

In her early book *Chapters in a Mythology: The Poetry of Sylvia Plath* (1976), Judith Kroll argued that the images, symbols, and themes in Plath's creative work form a system that realizes theories in Robert Graves's *The White Goddess: A Historical Grammar of Poetic Myth* (1938).[118] Kroll saw Graves's sense of "death-in-life" and "life-in-death" as integral to this system, elaborating that in Plath's poetry

> the motif of false and true selves derives from the heroine's relation to the male figure from which her true self has been alienated, thus giving rise to a false self. Either the false self or the male (or both) must be killed to allow the rebirth of the true self. . . . [L]ife lived by the false self is death-in-life, while the rebirth of the true self promises life-in-death.
>
> (13)

In Kroll's view, life-in-death is more positive than death-in-life. She adds that

> long before she met Ted Hughes or read *The White Goddess*, Plath had already gone far toward developing intellectual and poetic interests which were entirely consistent, thematically and symbolically, with the Graves material, which is why the material seemed so apt.
>
> (77)

To this end, the texts that Kroll notes Plath had read include Sir James George Frazer's *The Golden Bough*, and Eliot's *The Waste Land* (77). Given the ambiguity of "death-in-life" and "life-in-death," Kroll's readings are valuable. Plath's teaching notes are also part of a material network of texts in which she engaged these concepts and their implications at midcentury.

While death-in-life and life-in-death, which Plath deploys interchangeably earlier, have a literary ancestry that includes Samuel Taylor Coleridge's "Nightmare Life-in-Death" in "The Rime of the Ancient Mariner" (1817), the fact that Plath and the critics whom she read defined the role of paralysis in Joyce's fiction in relation to the presence of death-in-life in Eliot's poetry illustrates a form of collective circulation among these terms, perhaps including subtle colloquial distinctions, at midcentury.[119] Turning to the *Oxford English Dictionary* (OED), beneath the heading of "death" it defines death-in-life as "[a] life that lacks satisfaction or purpose; living death."[120] The definition of "life-in-death," however, incorporates phantasmagoria: "A phantom state, a condition of being or seeming to be neither alive nor dead; something having the form or appearance of the supernatural, an apparition, a spectre. Also, [equals] . . . *death-in-life*."[121] The OED's definition of paralysis includes physical and metaphorical debilitation: "The state of being powerless; a condition of helplessness or inactivity; inability to act or function properly."[122]

Because Plath's references to death-in-life accompany passages in Eliot's poem, her annotations not only teach us how she applied the terms but also allow us to see the ways that marginalia can serve as an index or a point of reference for the use of critical—or with regard to "the Jewish question," cultural—terminology.[123] In his reading of *The Waste Land*, Cleanth Brooks was expanding upon F. O. Matthiessen's use of the term "death-in-life" in *The Achievement of T. S. Eliot* (1935).[124] For Matthiessen, Eliot's *Waste Land*

> is given an additional haunting dimension as a realm of death in life by being linked with Dante's Limbo, the region of those dead who while on earth had "lived without praise or blame," who had not been strong enough in will or passion either to do good or evil, and so were condemned for ever to wander aimlessly, in feverish, useless motion.[125]

Plath's parting advice that her students "be right or wrong" is reminiscent of Matthiessen's sense of Dante. Matthiessen's clarification of the "haunting dimension" also echoes the sense of the paranormal in the OED's definition of "life-in-death." Matthiessen's connections shaped not only Brooks's and Drew's interpretations of Eliot's poem in their respective books *Modern Poetry and the Tradition* (1938) and *T. S. Eliot: The Design of His Poetry*, but also the themes that extended throughout Plath's course.[126]

Brooks's *Modern Poetry and the Tradition* provided a source for Plath's response to "death-in-life" and "living death" in Yeats's poem "Byzantium"

(1932). Yeats closes the poem's second stanza: "I hail the superhuman; / I call it death-in-life and life-in-death." Interpreting these lines, Brooks points out that "'Death-in-life and life-in-death' are of course the dead themselves, who are for Yeats more alive than the living" (196). Probably reading Yeats in Drew's modern poetry course in 1953, Plath added a simplified version of Brooks's explanation beside Yeats's phrase, "death-in-life and life-in-death" in her copy of his *Collected Poems*: "The dead—more alive than the living."[127] Drawing on Matthiessen and Yeats, Brooks's interpretation of death-in-life in Eliot's *Waste Land* was one that also informed Drew's sense of the poem in *T. S. Eliot: The Design of His Poetry*.[128]

As in his reading of "Byzantium," in *Modern Poetry and the Tradition* Brooks addresses the presence of death-in-life in *The Waste Land* and "The Hollow Men": "In Baudelaire's city, dream and reality seem to mix, and . . . Eliot in 'The Hollow Men' refers to this same realm of death-in-life as 'death's dream kingdom'" (143). In her copy of *T. S. Eliot: The Design of His Poetry*, Plath underlined Drew's explanation that "'<u>death's dream king-dom</u>' . . . <u>is the death-in-life of the world of the hollow men</u>" (95). While Brooks associated "death's dream kingdom" with death-in-life, Drew underscored that the hollow men exist within it. Following her teacher, Plath inscribed "death-in-life" beside "<u>death's dream kingdom</u>" in "The Hollow Men" in her copy of Eliot's *Complete Poems and Plays* (57; line 20, underlining Plath).[129] The point of following Plath's steps is not to trace the circulation of death-in-life, though marginalia provide material for doing so, but to demonstrate how her teaching was embedded in the criticism of her time. Teaching Eliot, Plath was building upon her experience teaching Joyce months earlier, which invited her to become acquainted with critics who had connected the themes in his fiction to those of Eliot's poetry.

In her synthesis of death-in-life and paralysis in her teaching notes, Plath was drawing on her reading of Levin's introduction to *The Portable James Joyce* (1946), his *James Joyce: A Critical Introduction*, and Hugh Kenner's *Dublin's Joyce* (1955).[130] Interpreting *The Waste Land*, Brooks clarified that "the hooded hordes are indistinct because completely *unspiritual*— they are the people of the waste land— 'Shape without form, shade without colour, / Paralysed force, gesture without motion—' to take two lines from 'The Hollow Men,' where the people of the waste land once more appear" ("*Modern Poetry*," 160). Kenner subsequently argued that

> [i]t is towards the definition of living death . . . that the entire book is oriented; the first point to grasp about "The Dead" is the universal reference of the title. "I had not thought death had undone so many"; in reading *The Waste Land* aloud Mr. Eliot puts the stress not on "death" but on "undone". That link, through the quotation, with the outer circle of Dante's hell, the souls who lived without blame and without praise, the world of the Hollow Men, is an Eliotic perspective of the utmost relevance to Joyce's story.
>
> (*Dublin's Joyce*, 62)

Kenner's style lays bare Eliot's line—it appears in the text as it may have come to mind. As such, it also lacks interpretation, and he shifts to Eliot's tone while reading to interpret its meaning. Plath, too, preparing to communicate these concepts to her students, reiterated in her teaching notes that, for Kenner, *Dubliners* is the "<u>Definition</u> of living death" and the "[t]itle: THE DEAD: [a] universal reference ('I had not thought death had undone so many')" (*TN*). Even though she would not be teaching Eliot's poetry until later in the term, Plath seized upon this relationship between their work, and her teaching notes introduce the lifelessness that both writers depicted. The connections that critics like Kenner and Levin drew between Joyce and Eliot brought an arc to Plath's course, enabling greater depth when approaching Eliot's poetry, and building upon the class's prior consideration of Joyce's fiction. This sense of lifeless gentility was not limited to Joyce and Eliot; its presence also informed Plath's teaching of James's story, "The Beast in the Jungle" (1903).[131]

James was among the writers whom Plath taught that she had also studied as an undergraduate, reading *The American* (1877), *Portrait of a Lady* (1881), *The Ambassadors* (1903), and his short stories, including "The Beast in the Jungle" and "The Pupil" (1891), in Newton Arvin's American literature course in the spring of 1954.[132] As she prepared to teach "The Beast in the Jungle," Plath underlined and annotated the story in a new copy of James's *Selected Fiction*.[133] Returning to the story, Plath inquired in the upper left hand corner of page 516: "Problem: What is 'the worst?': life—a death—absolute lack of experience."[134] This note responds to a phrase from James's story that Plath underlined, marking it with a star in the left margin: "<u>Then the worst—</u> we haven't faced that. I *could* face it, I believe, if I knew what you think it. I feel" (516). John Marcher is telling May Bartram of his dependence on her to confront the unfathomable. On the following page, Plath wrote "the worst" in the margin beside Marcher's description, which she underlined, of "<u>something that includes all the loss and all the shame that are thinkable</u>" (517). Turning this question over to her students would bring these depths to the classroom, making it a space in which such limits are productively engaged.

When Plath was a student, she recorded in her notebook from Arvin's course that "The Beast in the Jungle" is a "[t]ale of psychological terror with a <u>Gothic quality</u>, pervaded by anxiety, taking form of the <u>terror of 'too later' for life</u>" (*JN*). Marcher's fate became that "<u>no passion had ever touched him</u>," as Plath underscored twice and accentuated with a star in the margin in the copy of "The Beast in the Jungle" that she read as a student.[135] Filled with fear that prevents his connection with others, Marcher anticipates the stalled life in other modernist texts Plath taught.

In Plath's copy of *Axel's Castle*, she underlined Wilson's description of James's heroes'

> <u>regret at situations unexplored</u>[.] . . . T. S. Eliot, in this respect, has much in common with Henry James. <u>Mr. Prufrock</u> and the poet of the "<u>Portrait of a Lady</u>," with <u>their helpless consciousness of having dared too</u>

> The present is more timid than the past: the bourgeois are afraid to let themselves go. The French had been pre-occupied with this idea ever since the first days of Romanticism; but Eliot was to deal with the theme from a somewhat different point of view, a point of view characteristically American. For T. S. Eliot, though born in St. Louis, comes from a New England family and was educated at Harvard; and he is in some ways a typical product of our New England civilization. He is distinguished by that combination of practical prudence with moral idealism which shows itself in its later developments as an excessive fastidiousness and scrupulousness. One of the principal subjects of Eliot's poetry is really that regret at situations unexplored, that dark rankling of passions inhibited, which has figured so conspicuously in the work of the American writers of New England and New York from Hawthorne to Edith Wharton. T. S. Eliot, in this respect, has much in common with Henry James. Mr. Prufrock and the poet of the "Portrait of a Lady," with their helpless consciousness of having dared too little, correspond exactly to the middle-aged heroes of "The Ambassadors" and "The Beast in the Jungle," realizing sadly too late in life that they have been living too cautiously and too poorly. The fear of life, in Henry James, is closely bound up with the fear of vulgarity. And Eliot, too, fears vul-
>
> 102

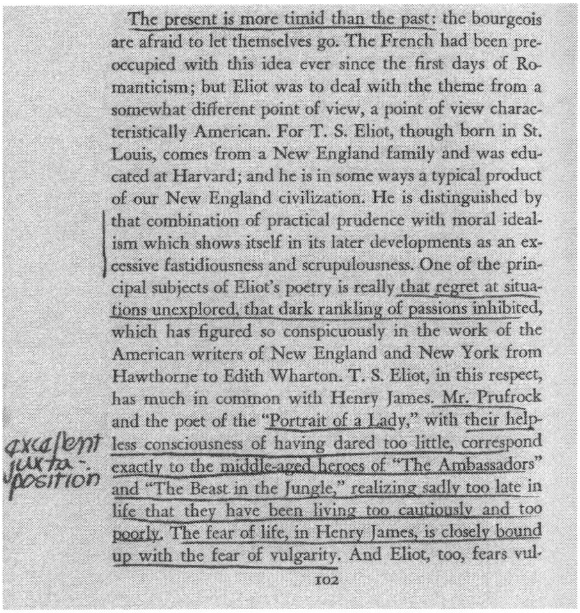

excellent juxta-position

Figure 1.9 Plath's copy of *Axel's Castle*, page 102, Smith.

little, correspond exactly to the middle-aged heroes of "The Ambassadors" and "The Beast in the Jungle," realizing sadly too late in life that they have been living too cautiously and too poorly.

(102; Figure 1.9)

After commenting in the margin that Wilson's comparison of James's and Eliot's characters present an "excellent juxtaposition," Plath adapted it with regard to "The Love Song of J. Alfred Prufrock":

Speaker: helplessness consciousness of having[136] dared too little: realizing sadly
too late in life that they have been living too cautiously and
too poorly. Fear of life. Hesitation: fatal: suspension of decision.

cf. Prufrock & John Marcher, Middle-aged hero of Henry James' [sic] "Beast in [the] Jungle"
Love song: avoid love: too dangerous: heroic "beast" never jumps:
fate to be men without experience: who never force moment to crisis:
men to whom "nothing happens" except the inevitable growing bald,
with all the aridity, sterility of old age this implies.

. . . impulses "to murder & create" conclude neither in suicide nor in release of chosen action, but in the <u>death-in-life of abdication of will</u>. (*TN*)

Plath combined Wilson's observation with Drew's point in *T. S. Eliot: The Design of His Poetry* that "The Love Song of J. Alfred Prufrock" ends "in the <u>death-in-life of the abdication of the will</u>," which Plath had underlined and indicated with a line in the margin (34).

After introducing James's representation of death-in-life in "The Beast in the Jungle," Plath taught four of Lawrence's stories, and introduced four additional stories for the students' essay assignments. Annotating "The Horse Dealer's Daughter" (1922), from the latter category, Plath placed a star and wrote, "life in death," beside Lawrence's explanation, which she also underlined, that the story's daughter "<u>lived in the memory of her mother</u>" (Figure 1.10).[137] When reading Lawrence, Plath was becoming accustomed to the terminology that she would employ to teach *Dubliners*. Her application here of the term "life-in-death" in light of the daughter's lack of engagement with her own desires is closer to the OED's definition of living dead as "not using one's life abundantly."[138] Plath later combined a comparable sense of living death and paralysis in her poem, "Paralytic" (1963). The poem's subject, immobilized in a state of life-in-death, "[a]sks nothing of life" (*Collected Poems*, 267; line 40).[139] The landscape of Dublin that Plath addresses in Joyce's stories is similarly grim and stagnant.

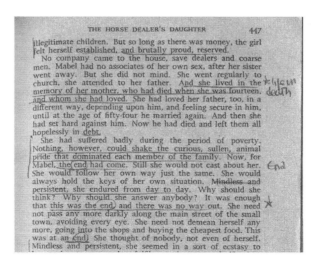

Figure 1.10 Plath's copy of "The Horse Dealer's Daughter" in D. H. Lawrence's *Complete Short Stories*, page 447, Smith.

In her first day of *Dubliners* teaching notes, Plath introduced Joyce's well-known desire to depict Dublin's paralysis, following Kenner's having done so.[140] She then incorporated responses from his *Dublin's Joyce* and Levin's *James Joyce* defining paralysis in relation to death-in-life. Plath followed these notes with quotations from Eliot's *The Waste Land* and "The Hollow Men."[141] Her notes include the following:

Joyce said in letter to publisher:	"I want to write a chapter in the moral history of my country. I chose Dublin for the scene because that city seemed to me the center of PARALYSIS."[142]

CITY: for modern writers no longer has old meaning of COMMUNITY.

T.S. ELIOT: saw the modern city as a WASTELAND [sic]: wrote in poem of that name about <u>london</u>:

"Unreal City,
Under the brown fog of a winter dawn,
A crowd flowed over London Bridge, so many,
I had not thought death had undone so many."

DEATH IN LIFE: PARALYSIS: (utter powerlessness, incapacity of action: state of being crippled, helpless, impotent)[143]

paralysis: key word to stories in DUBLINERS:
FIRST STORY: "The Sisters": Priest paralyzed. . . .

In the midst of PARALYZED CITY, characters move like ghosts, like Eliot's
HOLLOW MEN: . . . "Paralysed force, gesture without motion."
Characters frustrated, ALONE, prisoned in self. ISOLATION
DEATH is one of the few things that happens: first & last
stories. (*TN*)[144]

On her typed page, stressing central words and phrases with capital letters and annotating her notes with red pencil, Plath synthesized the criticism she had read.[145] Levin had observed, for instance, that "[d]eath is one of the few things that happen in *Dubliners*; it is the subject of the first and last stories in the volume" (*JJ*, 35). Drawing on Levin and other scholars, Plath demonstrated that Joyce's Dublin and Eliot's London are sites of solitude and lifelessness.

In her teaching notes for the second class session devoted to *Dubliners*, Plath reminded students that they had been

speaking about the modern city seen by 20th cen.[tury] writers as a wasteland.[146] We mentioned that for writers like Joyce & TSEliot the city has lost its old meaning of community. There is no longer a vital living communion between its citizens. Instead, there is sterility, bar-renness; each man lives alone, prisoned in himself, in his routine job, in his dull, conventional existence.

(*TN*)

Plath elaborated that paralysis is "literally a death-in-life. Not just physical, but emotional, mental. Impotence, crippling. This kind of paralysis in-volves FRUSTRATION: inability to act effectively. Attempts to act decisively are vain, futile" (*TN*).[147] While present throughout *Dubliners*, paralysis takes human form in Joyce's story "The Sisters."

The word "paralysis" haunts and curiously attracts the young narrator of "The Sisters," for whom "it sounded . . . like the name of some maleficent and sinful being. It filled me with fear, and yet I longed to be nearer to it and to look upon its deadly work" (*PJJ*, 19). While the narrator "imagined that I saw again the heavy gray face of the paralytic" (21), Plath too dwelled on this word as she prepared to ask her students: "What effect did we see this word have"? She filled in the response, "FASCINATION, of HOR-ROR, EVIL" (*TN*). This horror extends to those of past and present in *The Waste Land*.[148]

Preparing to teach Eliot's "Unreal City," Plath returned to Drew's *T. S. Eliot: The Design of His Poetry*. As Drew put it,

> The city was a maternal symbol to the ancients, but it is now utterly bar-ren. It is "unreal" because it is cut off from both natural and spiritual sources of life, and because it no longer has anything of its old sense of "community." Each individual exists in drab loneliness, and the mass, "flowing" over the bridge has no more human identity than the river flowing under it. It is "unreal" too because it is indeterminate in its mantle of brown fog, and finally, because, like Baudelaire's Paris, it has taken on the character of a scene in a nightmare, where the spectre in broad daylight stops the passer by.
>
> (*T. S. Eliot*, 72–3)

The "brown fog of a winter dawn" occludes and is polluted by the city. The workers move without ceasing, reduced to a perfunctory, emotionless pres-ence. In her copy of *T. S. Eliot: The Design of His Poetry*, Plath underlined and stressed with a second line the extremity in Drew's explanation that

> In *The Waste Land* . . . one of the elements is the blindness and numb-ness of external contemporary consciousness; its sterility, impotence, emptiness and aridity; its general loss of any vital relationship with the language of symbols, and in general with the human heritage of tradition.
>
> (63)

Plath provided a clearer version for her students on her first page of Eliot notes: "<u>Theme</u>: blindness & numbness of external contemporary consciousness – sterility, emptiness, impotence, aridity – loss of vital relationship with language of symbols & with human heritage of tradition" (*TN*). As she worked with this book, Plath's own copy of the poem provided a space in which she sketched out where Eliot demonstrated the concepts that Drew had articulated (Figure 1.11).

Following Drew's lead, Plath inscribed "death-in-life" beneath Eliot's question in "A Game of Chess," "Are you alive, or not? Is there nothing in your head?" (*Complete Poems and Plays*, 41; line 126; Figure 1.12). The line suggests both a "hollow man" and one who is not responsive. It follows a series of questions: "Do / You know nothing? Do you see nothing? Do you remember / Nothing?" (lines 121–3). The idea of death-in-life, here, as elsewhere, suggests existence without cognizance. In identifying this passage, Plath echoes Brooks's response to it; he had argued that the first speaker mentioned earlier "(is one of the Hollow Men— 'Headpiece filled

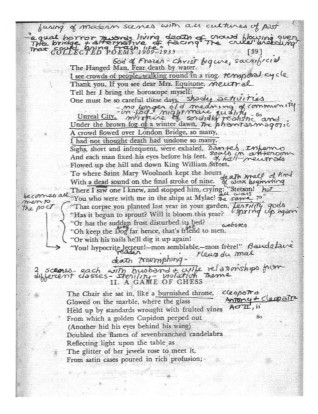

Figure 1.11 Plath's copy of "The Waste Land" in T. S. Eliot's *Complete Poems and Plays*, page 39, Smith.

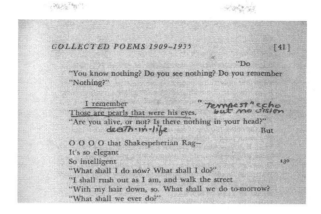

Figure 1.12 Plath's copy of "The Waste Land" in Eliot's *Complete Poems and Plays*, page 41, Smith.

with straw.') These people, as people living in the waste land, know nothing, see nothing, do not even live" ("Modern Poetry," 149). While the speaker's tone may be flippant, or sarcastic in its extremity, it allows us to see Plath's familiarity with death-in-life as a vacuous state in which one's engagement with life is in question, and that this existence is not limited to Eliot's work, but is also present in that of his contemporaries, particularly in Joyce's *Dubliners*.[149]

Plath's emphasis on paralysis, in part, grew out of the criticism that she read. The case may have differed with regard to the more recent poems that Plath taught, as less critical apparatus was available for them.[150] Rachel Sagner Buurma and Laura Heffernan have argued that the classroom provided a site in which Eliot's ideas were deployed. They remind us that "[d]isciplinary historians like [John] Guillory have suggested that Eliot's new canon gave birth to a specifically academic style of literary reading particularly associated with the classroom—a style of reading that attends exclusively to literary technique and form" ("The Classroom in the Canon," 276; citing *Cultural Capital,* 167–9).[151] But in the instances we have seen from Plath's teaching materials, the mediating role of criticism in interpreting modernist texts is often visible. Near the close of the term, Plath also personalized the materials that she introduced, complementing the criticism she had read with further research.

The Waste Land

Plath introduced *The Waste Land* as her professor had, with Eliot's "mythic method." As a student, Plath recorded in notes from a twentieth-century literature lecture Drew gave that the poem presents a "'parallel between contemporaneity & antiquity' (T. S. Eliot's review of Ulysses in 'Dial') <u>Mythical Method</u> to give order & form to modern world. Old religions were moral—social codes now being ignored."[152] Drew pointed out Eliot's "method of implicit contrast—Joyce set frustrated life in modern city against Odessey [sic]: coherent, rich, final home coming." In his image of modernity, Drew added, "Eliot set spiritual drought against grail legend & older fertility cults of rebirth from water of spring rains."[153] Faithful to Drew's example, Plath recorded in her teaching notes that Eliot's "mythical method" is "[p]articularly observable in The Wasteland [sic] where quotes from Shakespeare, Dante, in sordid present situation bring out contrast of old beauty & moral order & present ugliness & moral chaos, or indifference" (*TN*). In this explanation and throughout her teaching notes, Plath is making accessible Eliot's difficult, fragmentary poem, introducing her students to its antecedents.

While Plath's readings of Eliot in her teaching notes often recall those that Drew had introduced in her book, Plath also did her homework and built upon her own interests as she planned her classes. Preparing to introduce the Fisher King and the Holy Grail, she underlined a paperback copy of Jessie Weston's *From Ritual to Romance* that she had recently acquired, its cover displaying a Grail illustration by her colleague Leonard Baskin.[154] When she read the chapter devoted to the symbols of the Grail legend, Plath underlined the beginning and end of Weston's explanation that

> the four treasures of the Tuatha de Danann correspond generally with the group of symbols found in the Grail romances; this correspondence becomes the more interesting in view of the fact that these mysterious Beings are now recognized as Demons of Fertility and Lords of Life.
>
> (77)

Weston elaborated that "we have further evidence that these four objects do, in fact, form a special group entirely independent of any appearance in Folk-lore or Romance. They exist today as the four suits of the Tarot" (77; underlining Plath). Near the bottom of the same page, Plath added a bracket beside Weston's list of the Tarot suits and underlined her description of the "pack of cards, seventy-eight in number, of which twenty-two are designated as the 'Keys'" (77). In her teaching notes, Plath summarized Weston's list, noting the "four suits: Cup, Lance, Sword, Dish & (22 Keys)" (*TN*).[155] In addition, Plath added a note reminding herself to display the "Hanged Man," perhaps from her own Tarot deck (*TN*). By doing so, she would be introducing an artifact that held new significance for her since she was a student and reflects the poetic interest that she shared with Hughes in the occult and mysticism.[156]

As Eliot acknowledged in his notes to *The Waste Land*, he abandoned the significance of the Tarot cards to satisfy the needs of his poem. And in her copy, Plath drew an exclamation point at the close of Eliot's explanation to this effect, beside his admission that he links "quite arbitrarily" The Man with Three Staves and the Fisher King (*Complete Poems and Plays*,

51; underlining Plath). Plath's fidelity to these contexts may appear to date her reading of the poem, but her reference to the Tarot in her teaching notes updates Drew's approach to the poem, and reflects Eliot's association in the popular imagination with the Tarot cards at midcentury.[157] In Plath's copy of *The Painted Caravan: A Penetration into the Secrets of the Tarot Cards* (1954), the author Basil Ivan Rákóczi pointed out on the page opposite the table of contents,

> [a]t the end of the book you find on the left the Hanged man of Gypsy Initiation Rites and on the right, the Drowned Phoenician Sailor, a card under the sign of wands, described by T.S. Eliot in "The Wasteland" [sic].[158]

In *T. S. Eliot: The Design of His Poetry*, Drew elaborated that

> Madame Sosostris . . . is a modern, vulgarized version of the Egyptian diviners and practicers of magic, who professed to control the Nile through the Tarot cards. But she is no longer concerned with the ancient magic which sought to control the sources of life. What originated in a technique of mastery has become a masquerade.
>
> (71)

In her copy of Drew's book, Plath added a line in the margin beside Drew's account of the Tarot cards' significance, and Plath introduced a version of it in her teaching notes: "Traditionally said to be brought from Egypt, to foretell rising & falling of the Nile & forecast & control fertility. Now, modern, vulgarized in gypsy fortune tellings. Ancient magic become masquerade" (*TN*). Joining phrases quickly, Plath winnows down Drew's explanation. Interestingly, in doing so, Plath omits "technique of mastery," as if siding with "masquerade," adopting a more impersonal response that downplays or conceals her own personal interest in the Tarot cards.

Toward the end of her year teaching, Plath contemplated what it would mean to shift away from reading to prepare her courses and focus on reading for her creative work. Reconciling her desires as a reader with the task of preparing texts for an audience of students, Plath complained in the spring of 1958: "I don't like talking <u>about</u> D. H. Lawrence and about critics [sic] views of him. I like reading him selfishly, for an influence on my own life & my own writing" (*LV2*, 189). Plath's sentiment echoes her earlier decision not to pursue the limited focus of doctoral study.[159] She found studying literature to be too removed from everyday life, while "[p]sychology, I imagine, supplies more reality-situations: the people you deal with are bothered with a variety of things, people and ideas, not just the symbolism of James Joyce" (*UJ*, 450). Distinguishing symbolic patterns is the role of a critic and necessitates a certain distance from life. The contrast Plath draws here echoes the distinction she drew on her final day of teaching between living in the world and writing about it.

After she left Smith to devote a year to writing in Boston, Plath faced, as she put it, a "paralyzing fear, that gets in my way and stops me" (*UJ*, 441).[160] Using the language she had once applied to Joyce's Dublin, she takes its sentiments out of academia and places them in the world she now inhabits as a writer.[161] When visiting New York as a college student, Plath similarly described the city by referring to the modernist texts that she had studied. Following their year in Boston, Plath and Hughes returned to England in December 1959, where Plath wrote *The Bell Jar*, finishing it in 1961 (*UJ*, 696).[162] In the novel, Plath brings form to impressions that largely took hold in the summer of 1953 when she spent a month in New York as a Guest Editor for *Mademoiselle* magazine. During and after this experience, Plath's critique of the lifeless city identifies an insufficient presence of conscience and conscientiousness, qualities she sought to awaken in her students.

Life in the margins

Perhaps it is only in the aftermath of World War II that critics could employ the terminology of living death, life-in-death, and death-in-life in their considerations of modernist texts. Robert Jay Lifton proposed in *Death in Life: Survivors of Hiroshima* (1967), "our perceptions of Hiroshima are the beginnings of new dimensions of thought about death and life."[163] Recent history had altered not only the use of the term "death in life," as Lifton's title demonstrates, but also the reading of modernism. Levin asks in *The Portable James Joyce*,

> [h]ow many of those who read John Hersey's *Hiroshima* recognize its literary obligation to *Ulysses*? . . . Is it any wonder, when we live in such an explosive epoch, that even the arts have made themselves felt through a series of shocks.[164]

(1)

While Plath may have encountered this passage when she taught using her copy of *The Portable James Joyce* in 1958, years earlier she eagerly drew upon her reading of modernist texts as she described her surroundings in New York. By doing so, Plath interpreted the midcentury city through a modernist lens, adjusting it to accommodate what she observed.

Plath arrived in Manhattan on the evening of 31 May 1953.[165] In the month to follow, the trial of Julius and Ethel Rosenberg would complicate society's sense of life and living.[166] The media coverage included a terse radio broadcast, reporting that the execution was to occur.[167] Despite the weight of such a decision, those whom Plath encountered on the day that the execution was to take place appeared indifferent:

> the headlines blare the two of them are going to be killed at eleven o'clock tonight. So I am sick at the stomach. I remember the journalists [sic]

report, sickeningly factual, of the electrocution of a condemned man, of the unconcealed fascination on the faces of the onlookers, of the details, the shocking physical facts about the death, the scream, the smoke, the bare honest unemotional reporting that gripped the guts because of the things it didn't say. . . .

The phones are ringing as usual, and the people planning to leave for the country over the long weekend, and everybody is lackadaisical [sic] and rather glad and nobody very much thinks about how big a human life is, with all the nerves and sinews and reactions and responses that it took centuries and centuries to evolve.[168]

(*UJ*, 541)

The members of the workforce exist in a state of living death, lacking the "unconcealed fascination" of onlookers.[169] The "shock" such viewers experience, however, is in response to the physicality, rather than the humanity of the victims.[170] Plath absorbs the strain, experiencing the visceral reaction that others lack.

Processing this information, the style of Plath's reaction also echoes that of an account of the Holocaust's destruction in *A Partisan Guide to the Jewish Problem*. While it is unknown whether Plath encountered them, Milton Steinberg provided recent statistics that reflect what information was available to college students at the time:

Here are the naked, elemental facts, so far as they can be determined in the first months of 1945. At the outbreak of the Second World War there were approximately 16,000,000 Jews on earth . . . Of these, the most reliable estimates have it, 5,000,000 have perished.[171]

(19)

Steinberg's starkness returns as Plath recalls a journalist's account: "the shocking physical facts about the death, the scream, the smoke, the bare honest unemotional reporting" (*UJ*, 541). Both descriptions are unclothed and unguarded, with numbers in the former and smoke in the latter.[172]

In New York, Plath recoiled at "the dry, humid, breathless wasteland of the cliffdwellers, where the people are, as D.H. Lawrence wrote of his society, 'dead brilliant galls on the tree of life'" (*LV1*, 643). In doing so, she reversed Rupert Birkin's observation in Lawrence's *Women in Love* that "mankind is a dead tree, covered with fine brilliant galls of people."[173] Building from Eliot's response to Lawrence in *After Strange Gods* (1934), in her book, *The Novel: A Modern Guide to Fifteen English Masterpieces* (1963), Drew observed that "Lawrence stands for life as against the living death of modern materialism, but it is for quite the wrong sort of life."[174] Plath's misquoting of Lawrence, in which the people are "dead brilliant galls," presents a more disparaging image of lost potential than Birkin's observation that humanity is a "dead tree" on which the people are the "fine brilliant galls." But if the tree is dead, the galls can no longer flourish. Plath also articulated a moral and material contempt for Manhattan, filled with denizens that she caricatured as "slick ad-men," "hucksters," and "wealthy beasts" (*LV1*, 643). The subjects of her 1950s jargon update Eliot's economic response to Lawrence and represent midcentury incarnations of *The Waste Land*'s "Bradford millionaire" and workers traveling over London Bridge.

Following her month in Manhattan, Plath labeled passages with June, July, and August 1953 in the margins of her copies of *Axel's Castle*, Lawrence's *Sons and Lovers* and *The Man Who Died*, and Friedrich Nietzsche's *Thus Spake Zarathustra*.[175] The passage below from *Axel's Castle* that Plath identified as resembling June 1953 recalls her description of New York's ambivalence as the Rosenberg execution drew nearer:

> The <u>terrible dreariness of the great modern cities is</u> the atmosphere in which "The Waste Land" takes place—amidst this dreariness, brief, vivid images emerge, brief pure moments of feelings are distilled; but <u>all about us we are aware of nameless millions performing barren office routines, wearing down their souls in interminable labors of which the products never bring them profit—people whose pleasures are so sordid and so feeble that</u> they seem almost sadder than their pains. And this Waste Land has another aspect: it is the place not merely of desolation, but of <u>anarchy and doubt</u>.[176]
>
> 1953 – yes!
> June – NYC
>
> (Wilson, 106; Figure 1.13)

Even as Wilson's reading of *The Waste Land* was published in the early 1930s, it becomes a lens through which, over 20 years later, Plath interpreted

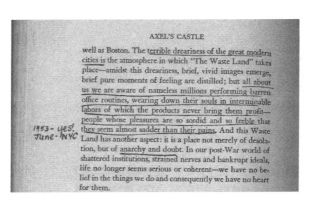

Figure 1.13 Plath's copy of *Axel's Castle*, page 106, Smith.

the recent past.[177] The sentiments in this passage likely became more familiar as Plath prepared her teaching notes, dwelling on the bleakness of Eliot's and Joyce's respective London and Dublin (*TN*).

In her copy of *Sons and Lovers*, Plath similarly inscribed, "cf. July 1953," the month after she would have returned home from New York, beside Lawrence's description of Paul Morel's bewilderment:

> Everything seemed to have gone smash for the young man. He could not paint. The picture he finished on the day of his mother's death— one that satisfied him—was the last thing he did. At work there was no Clara. When he came home he could not take up his brushes again. There was nothing left. . . .
>
> **cf. July 1953**
>
> Everything seemed so different, so unreal. There seemed[178] no reason why people should go along the street, and houses pile up in the daylight. There seemed no reason why these things should occupy the space, instead of leaving it empty. His friends talked to him: he heard the sounds, he answered. But why there should be the noise of speech he could not understand.[179]

Paul's state of death-in-life followed the death of his mother, with whom he was particularly close. While Plath had told her students not to be "nothing," for Paul "there was nothing left" (*TN*). His "unreal" surroundings anticipate the desolation of Eliot's "Unreal City" of *The Waste Land*, which Plath comes to depict in the suburbs to which Esther returns in *The Bell Jar*.

Plath marked moments in two different texts as representing "August 1953," the month in which she had attempted suicide. Robin Peel noticed that in Plath's copy of Nietzsche's *Thus Spake Zarathustra*, she had added

> one of her carefully drawn little stars next to the following paragraph which appears under the heading "Voluntary Death:" "And whoever wanteth to have fame, must take leave of honour betimes and practice the difficult art of—going at the right time."[180]

Peel also points out that "next to this she has written in neat, black ink 'August 1953'."[181] If this passage speaks to the impulse to end one's life, a second in Lawrence's *The Man Who Died* captures the aftermath of doing so. In her copy, Plath commented, "cf. August 1953," beside Lawrence's description of his character's state of paralysis: "He did not open his eyes. Yet he knew that he was awake and numb, and cold, and rigid, and full of hurt[.] . . . Who would want to come back from the dead?" (Figure 1.14).[182] The first part of this response resembles Esther's feelings upon waking from her suicide attempt in *The Bell Jar*. Similarly, the question of Lawrence's

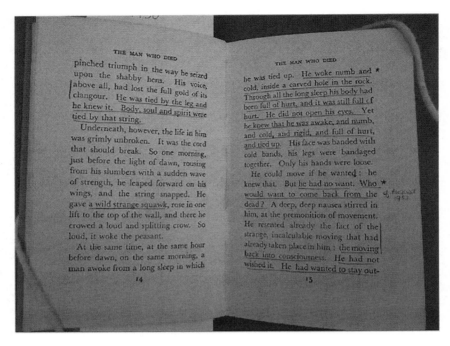

Figure 1.14 Plath's copy of Lawrence's *The Man Who Died*, pages 14–15, Emory.

protagonist anticipates Lady Lazarus's desire "[t]o last it out and not come back at all" (*Collected Poems*, 248; line 38). In these examples, Plath charts a path through the margins of her modernist texts, identifying facets of the world she may have sought to depict.

The focus shifts in the next segment from Plath's interpretation of the midcentury cultural climate using a modernist template to her representation of the post-World War II milieu in *The Bell Jar*.[183] Her critique transforms the New York she encountered as a college student and the modernist landscapes of her interim reading.

The Bell Jar

Plath's depiction of Esther Greenwood's paradoxically enlightening psychological decline in *The Bell Jar* places death-in-life in the paralysis of midcentury Manhattan. Esther's existence resembles that of life-in-death, she is living life without engaging with it. New York's residents occupy a state of living death, emotionally paralyzed as they move in daily routines. Chronicling Esther's breakdown and rehabilitation in *The Bell Jar*, the form of the novel enabled an extensive treatment and redefinition of death-in-life and paralysis at midcentury.[184]

In the novel's familiar opening passage, Esther is keenly attentive to her surroundings, aware that New York is not what it seems:

> It was a queer, sultry summer, the summer they electrocuted the Rosenbergs, and I didn't know what I was doing in New York. I'm stupid about executions. The idea of being electrocuted makes me sick, and that's all there was to read about in the papers—goggle-eyed headlines staring up at me on every street corner and at the fusty, peanut-smelling mouth of every subway. It had nothing to do with me, but I couldn't help wondering what it would be like, being burned alive all along your nerves.
>
> I thought it must be the worst thing in the world.
>
> New York was bad enough. By nine in the morning the fake, country-wet freshness that somehow seeped in overnight evaporated like the tail end of a sweet dream. Mirage gray at the bottom of their granite canyons, the hot streets wavered in the sun, the car tops sizzled and glittered, and the dry, cindery dust blew into my eyes and down my throat.
>
> (*B*, 1)

Midcentury New York is a stalled, dusty world; inhabitants cannot see, their values are impaired, and death is imminent. Forty years after Pound's "In a Station of the Metro" (1913), Plath replaces "faces in the crowd" with "goggle-eyed headlines staring."[185] Words act in the place of petals at rest. Rather than seeing "fear in a handful of dust" (*Complete Poems and Plays*, 38; line 30), dust hinders vision, stifles voice.[186] The city is hostile, and the landscape "unreal."[187]

As she navigates the city and after she returns to the suburbs, Esther encounters versions of the urbanity of *The Waste Land* and the gravity of death-in-life in "The Hollow Men." Early in the novel, Esther encounters the "tomblike morning gloom of the conference room" (*B*, 150).[188] Over time, Esther takes on characteristics of a zombie, a colloquial definition of living dead. She endures a "long, dead walk from the frosted glass doors of the Amazon to the strawberry-marble slab of our entry on Madison Avenue" (*B*, 99). The "strawberry marble" stands out as feminine, yet is childlike and nuanced in its description of the surface. After leaving New York, Esther heard herself speak into a telephone, and her "voice sounded strange and hollow" (*B*, 118). She is unable to recognize this "zombie voice" (*B*, 119). When she can no longer continue speaking during a later call, Esther feels as if "the zombie rose up in my throat and choked me off" (*B*, 126). Esther's experience is gendered, which becomes more apparent as a sense of violence prevents her from speaking. This instance presents a version of Eliot's Philomel in *The Waste Land*. A key difference is in Esther's centrality to Plath's novel, as her character registers the impact of the surrounding world.

The Bell Jar also adds a more visceral dimension to moments in Joyce's story, "The Sisters," from *Dubliners*, and Eliot's poem, "The Love Song of J. Alfred Prufrock," shifting from the impressions of men to the lingering impact that visiting a hospital has on a female college student. While in "The Sisters" the young protagonist encounters a priest's literal paralysis, a form of life-in-death, in *The Bell Jar*, Esther associates the Rosenbergs' imminent death with her memory of what followed after seeing a dead body: "For weeks afterward the cadaver's head—or what there was left of it—floated up behind my eggs and bacon at breakfast" (*B*, 1–2). Unlike Eliot's "patient etherised upon a table" (*Complete Poems and Plays*, 3; line 3), to which Plath referred in her teaching notes as the "living death of [a] patient on [an] operating table," the cadaver Esther viewed was not alive, yet it was on display (*TN*). It realized what Eliot had imagined.

After she had finished writing *The Bell Jar*, Plath received funding from the Eugene F. Saxton Memorial Trust to support the project and composed a series of progress reports concerning the novel's contents. In one dating from 1 May 1962, Plath reflects that Esther finds herself unable to end her life in the sea and "retreats, shamed, defeated by her own cowardly paralysis."[189] Esther's inhibition provides a counterpoint to what will become Lady Lazarus's triumph. Shifting from the novel to the lyric, in "Lady Lazarus" Plath creates a heroine who refuses to suffer any longer.

"Lady Lazarus"

Following her prose assessment of the cultural climate in *The Bell Jar*, the strategies that Plath demonstrates in such late poems as "Lady Lazarus" re-invent in poetic form the modernist discourse with which writers during the first half of the twentieth-century engaged the magnitude of death-in-life. Writing to her mother on the day that she began "Lady Lazarus" in October 1962, Plath's depiction of her Devon workroom is reminiscent of her Lawrence House room, many of her student books possibly remaining on her shelves:[190] "My study is the warmest, brightest room in the house. . . . in the evening, I . . . work again, surrounded by books, photos, cartoons & poems pinned to the wall" (*LV2*, 883).[191] Plath's account returns us to her working materials, the pages from which Lady Lazarus will emerge (*Collected Poems*, 244; lines 6–7).[192] On the clean versos of pink Smith memorandum paper, newly turned over from Plath's revisions of scenes in which Esther braces herself to face life anew, Lady Lazarus confronts a world that has tested the boundaries of humanity.[193]

After finishing "Daddy" and before beginning "Lady Lazarus," Plath insists in another letter to her mother that "what the person out of Belsen—physical or psychological—wants is . . . full knowledge that somebody else has been there & knows <u>the worst</u>" (*LV2*, 874–5; emphasis in the original).[194] Plath's reference recalls "the Jewish Question," but she is also describing the apprehension of unimaginable trauma. In *The Bell Jar*, Esther imagines that electrocution would be "the worst thing in the world."[195] During her teaching year, as we have seen, Plath reflected that "[n]ot writing this year has been the worst of it" (*LV2*, 210). In her final day of teaching notes, Plath referred to death-in-life as the "most moving and troubling" and "most terrible state" (*TN*). While we cannot know the dramatic effect or further explication Plath could have brought to these statements in her classes, her consistency intersects with her reading of modernism and extends to her consideration of the contemporary moment.

To return to "Lady Lazarus," the speaker's request and rhetorical question, "[p]eel off the napkin / O my enemy. / Do I terrify?—" (*Collected Poems*, 244; lines 10–2), recalls Plath's description of "death-in-life" in her teaching notes as one of the "most terrible states of existence." The dust of *The Waste Land* has become the ash of "Lady Lazarus." Vestiges of atrocity and humanity remain: "A cake of soap, / A wedding ring, / A gold filling" (*Collected Poems*, 246; lines 73–8). A central distinction between this world and those that Eliot and Joyce depicted, however, is that Lady Lazarus becomes emboldened: "Out of the ash / I rise with my red hair / And I eat men like air" (*Collected Poems*, 247; lines 82–4). The speaker's threat here has been interpreted in terms of the patriarchy, and implicates figures like Eliot and Joyce. Hammer argued that when Plath rid herself of the earthenware head she was attempting to part with her former student self and its position beside "the canonical texts she read in school" ("Plath's Lives," 71). "Lady Lazarus" radically updates this effort. As a result, in addition to countering the impersonality of modernism with an autobiographical protagonist, "Lady Lazarus" redefines and feminizes the version of death-in-life in Plath's teaching notes. Moreover, the malleability of the lyric form enabled Plath's negotiation in "Lady Lazarus" of issues at stake in her reading of modernism.[196]

In late letters, Plath repurposes the language with which she had addressed the extremity of modernist texts, redefining "the worst," as she had noted in the margin as she prepared to teach "The Beast in the Jungle" (517). In a letter to her therapist Ruth Barnhouse Beuscher after Hughes's infidelity in 1962, Plath confides that until this point, she "really did believe it was the Worst Thing that could happen Ted being Unfaithful; or next worst to his dying" (*LV2*, 798). Ten days later, she raised the bar, proposing that "what would to me have been the real worst, was for Ted to come & say: I want this girl to be my wife & to bear my children" (*LV2*, 805). In a final letter on 4 February 1963, Plath realizes: "What appalls me is the return of my madness, my paralysis, my fear and vision of the worst – cowardly withdrawal, a mental hospital, lobotomies" (*LV2*, 967). In this letter, Plath reconfigures her references to Esther's "cowardly paralysis" in the progress report on *The Bell Jar* and the "paralysis" of Joyce's *Dubliners* in her teaching notes.[197] Continuing to use the language with which she had once taught, Plath documents the extent to which the texts and criticism she read provided her with a means of interpreting the world.

***

The next chapter turns to John Berryman's reading, editing, and teaching of modernist texts. Following the role of Plath's student reading in her later prose and poetry, Berryman's autobiographical persona in *The Dream Songs* (1969) addresses his literary predecessors and contemporaries, including Plath. The allusions Berryman incorporated in *The Dream Songs* followed his first book, which he called a "learned poem" based on the life of Ann Bradstreet.[198] Plath inscribed Berryman's *Homage to Mistress Bradstreet and Other Poems* (1953) with the date of her thirtieth birthday. While she did not underline or annotate her copy, Plath added the date and placed a star on either side of it.[199] According to Edmund Wilson on the dust jacket of Plath's Faber and Faber edition, Berryman had composed "the most distinguished long poem by an American since *The Waste Land*." While *The Waste Land* presented a touchstone for Plath and Berryman, as teachers both poets differed. While Plath demonstrated a certain impersonality as a teacher, after editing Pound's *Selected Poems*, Berryman developed a pedagogy that was more expansive, taking after *The Cantos*.

Notes

1 Karen V. Kukil brought Plath's teaching notes to my attention and learned of them from Susan Van Dyne. Plath's classmate, the late Enid Epstein Mark, generously allowed me to read the notes in her copy of *Ulysses* and brought to my attention her course notebooks in the Smith College Archives.

2 I presented early versions and portions of this chapter as the keynote of "Without Margins" Middle Georgia State College Undergraduate Conference in Macon, Georgia (2015), as "Teaching Modernist Texts: Sylvia Plath Annotating Modernism" at Emory University's Fox Center for Humanistic Inquiry (2010), as well as at the American Conference for Irish Studies, Southern Region in Decatur, Georgia (2013), The Sylvia Plath Seventy-Fifth Year Literary Symposium at Oxford University (2007), the New England Poetry Conference at the University of Massachusetts-Lowell (2007), the Modern Language Association Convention in Philadelphia, Pennsylvania (2006), the Modernist Studies Association Conference in Tulsa, Oklahoma (2006), and the T. S. Eliot Society Annual Meeting in St. Louis, Missouri (2005).

3 Sylvia Plath, "Cambridge, Newnham college; Teaching year at Smith," box 13, f. 10, Sylvia Plath mss. II, The Lilly Library. Indiana University, Bloomington, IN; the Lilly Library will hereafter be cited in the text as "Lilly," and Plath teaching notes will hereafter be cited in the text as "*TN*."

4 *The Bell Jar* was first published under the pseudonym Victoria Lucas in 1963 and republished in England under Plath's name in 1966 and in the United States in 1971. Jo Gill, *The Cambridge Introduction to Sylvia Plath* (New York: Cambridge University Press, 2008), 74; hereafter cited in the text as "*Cambridge Introduction*." Sylvia Plath, *The Bell Jar* (1971; New York: HarperCollins, 1999); hereafter cited in the text as "*B*." With regard to critics' responses to Plath's reading, Robin Peel, for instance, begins "The

Political Education of Sylvia Plath" by stating that "[t]he influence on Plath's writing of her prolonged literary education has been carefully traced by a number of critics." Robin Peel, "The Political Education of Sylvia Plath," in *The Unraveling Archive: Essays on Sylvia Plath*, ed. Anita Helle (Ann Arbor: University of Michigan Press, 2007), 39; hereafter cited in the text as *"Political Education."* Al Strangeways, in *Sylvia Plath: The Shaping of Shadows* (Madison, NJ: Fairleigh Dickinson University Press, 1998), observes that "what is central and often most controversial in her [Plath's] work is clarified through examination of the influences of her literary and academic history" (13), noting that she will address Plath's "often heavily marked collection of books" (13). Concerning Plath's student success, see also A. Alvarez, *The Savage God: A Study of Suicide* (1971; New York: Norton, 1990), 22–3 and Bethany Hicok, *Degrees of Freedom: American Women Poets and the Women's College 1905–1955* (Lewisburg: Bucknell University Press, 2008), 27.

5 In the United States, Harper & Row published *The Bell Jar* under Plath's name and included "Sylvia Plath: A Biographical Note" by Lois Ames. Sylvia Plath, *The Bell Jar* (New York: Harper & Row, 1971). See also Linda W. Wagner-Martin, *Sylvia Plath: A Biography* (New York: St. Martin's Griffin, 1987) and Paul Alexander, *Rough Magic: A Biography of Sylvia Plath* (1991; New York: Viking Penguin, 1999).

6 Plath's annotated books are primarily housed in three archives. The Lilly Library owns approximately 150 books, along with her teaching notes and student notebooks, that she left with her mother before departing for England in December 1959. Approximately 150 more books that Plath had in her possession in England, at least until leaving the home she shared in Devon with Hughes in 1962, are housed at Smith. Emory also owns a selection of Plath's books that are part of Hughes's library. Peter K. Steinberg has catalogued Plath's library and noted the locations of her books on LibraryThing. https://www.librarything.com/profile/SylviaPlathLibrary, accessed 21 February 2020.

7 See also Stephen Gould Axelrod, *Sylvia Plath: The Wound and the Cure of Words* (Baltimore: Johns Hopkins University Press, 1990), 4 and 33–6; hereafter cited in the text as *"The Wound and the Cure of Words."*

8 One can see some of the material that anticipated Plath's own preparation of her course in Drew's lecture notes ("Lecture Notes," box 770.1, Elizabeth A. Drew Papers, Smith College Archives, CA-MS-00056, Smith College Special Collections, Northampton, MA; hereafter cited in the text as "Drew Papers"), and Plath's "Modern Poetry Notebook," box 12, folder 1, mss. II, Lilly.

9 Regarding the ways that archives expand, Anita Helle has observed in her introduction to *The Unraveling Archive* that "archives are, in part, social constructions. They swell, even as we write about them." Anita Helle, "Introduction: Archival Matters," in *The Unraveling Archive*, ed. Anita Helle (Ann Arbor: University of Michigan Press, 2007), 11.

10 Susan R. Van Dyne, *Revising Life: Sylvia Plath's Ariel Poems* (Chapel Hill: University of North Carolina Press, 1991). Tracy Brain has argued that the books in Plath's personal library enable a more expansive consideration of her poetry and prose in *The Other Sylvia Plath* (New York: Longman, 2001); hereafter cited in the text as *"The Other Sylvia Plath."* See also Helle, ed., *The Unraveling Archive* and Lynda K. Bundtzen, *The Other Ariel* (Amherst: University of Massachusetts Press, 2001); hereafter cited in the text as *"The Other Ariel."* Plath's mother also wrote letters to her on stationary from Boston University, where she taught.

11 Sylvia Plath, *The Letters of Sylvia Plath: Volume 2: 1956–1963*, ed. Peter K. Steinberg and Karen V. Kukil (London: Faber and Faber, 2018), 184; hereafter cited in the text as *"LV2."*

12 Adam T. Jernigan notes that "Sylvia Plath typed the early drafts of the pink
    office paper that she had used to prepare lesson plans and quizzes during her
    appointment as a freshman English instructor at Smith College." There is no
    evidence in Plath's teaching notes at the Lilly that she gave quizzes. She used
    the same type of paper in both contexts, but not the same pages, as she left her
    teaching notes behind before departing for England, where she wrote *The Bell
    Jar*. She also did not compose all of her teaching notes on the pink memoran-
    dum paper. Adam T. Jernigan, "Paraliterary Labors in Sylvia Plath's *The Bell
    Jar*: Typists, Teachers, and The Pink-Collar Subtext," *Modern Fiction Studies*
    60, no. 1 (Spring 2014): 1.

13 Henry James, *Portrait of a Lady* (New York: Modern Library, [1951]), for-
    mer owner Plath, Smith. Plath annotated *The Waste Land* in Eliot, *Complete
    Poems and Plays*, Smith. James Joyce, *Ulysses* (New York: Modern Library,
    [1946]), former owner Plath, Smith; hereafter cited in the text as "*U*."

14 Kathleen Connors noted Plath's preference for black ink in her *Eye Rhymes*
    gallery tour. Indiana University Museum of Art, October 2002.

15 Plath also underlined *The Duchess of Malfi* in her copy of John Webster and
    Cyril Tourneur, *Four Plays*, ed. Eric Bentley (New York: Hill and Wang, Inc.,
    1956) in black ink and red pencil (Smith). Plath underlined her teaching notes
    and her books with red pencil in addition to prior underlining. Enid Epstein
    Mark, Plath's classmate, also used red pencil in her student notebooks to un-
    derline. Enid Epstein Mark, "Notebooks," Classes of 1951–1960 records,
    Smith College Archives, CA-MS-01024, Smith College Special Collections,
    Northampton, MA. A character in Plath's classmate Nora Johnson's novel
    A Step Beyond Innocence similarly underlined in red pencil while studying.
    Nora Johnson, *A Step Beyond Innocence* (1961; New York: Dell, 1962), 33.

16 See Jane Baltzell Kopp, "'Gone, Very Gone Youth': Sylvia Plath at Cambridge:
    1955–1957," in *Sylvia Plath: The Woman and the Work*, ed. Edward Butscher
    (1977; New York: Dodd, Mead & Company, 1985), 71–2. See also Lucas
    Myers, *Crow Steered, Bergs Appeared: A Memoir of Ted Hughes and Sylvia
    Plath* (Sewanee, TN: Proctor's Hall Press, 2001), 78.

17 In *A Closer Look at Ariel: A Memory of Sylvia Plath* (New York: Harper &
    Row, 1973), Nancy Hunter Steiner recalls a similar incident regarding Plath's
    disturbance when the contents of her drawers are rearranged, suggesting her
    possessiveness over her property and its organization (54–5).

18 Ellen Bartlett Nodelman, interview with the author, 4 September 2006.

19 James Joyce, *Dubliners* (1914; New York: Modern Library, n.d.), 241, former
    owner Plath, Smith. Plath purchased her copy of *Dubliners* on 17 March 1953.
    Sylvia Plath, *The Letters of Sylvia Plath: Volume 1: 1940–1956*, ed. Peter K.
    Steinberg and Karen V. Kukil (New York: Harper Collins, 2017), 587; hereaf-
    ter cited in the text as "*LV1*."

20 Plath's copy of D. H. Lawrence's *Studies in Classic American Literature*
    (1923; Garden City, NY: Doubleday, 1951) is at Smith.

21 The heroine of Jean Webster's novel *Daddy-Long-Legs* sees her books the
    same way, reluctant to sell them as other students did. Jean Webster, *Daddy-
    Long-Legs* (1912; New York: Random House, 2011).

22 Plath, "Smith Scrapbook," oversize 8, LMC 1862, folder 36, pictures filed in
    folder 36, Plath mss. II, Lilly.

23 Plath owned Cleanth Brooks, *The Well Wrought Urn: Studies in the Structure
    of Poetry* (New York: Harcourt Brace, 1947), Smith, and Ezra Pound, *The
    Pisan Cantos* (New York: New Directions, 1948), former owner Plath, Lilly.

24 Plath's orange/brown clothbound copy of *Ulysses* at Smith lacks a dust jacket
    in the photograph of Plath in front of books in Cambridge that Olwyn Hughes

took in Cambridge in 1956. The next books (with archives where they are housed in parentheses) possibly include Joyce's *Chamber Music* ([New York: Columbia University Press, 1954], former owner Plath, Smith), *Dubliners* (Smith), and *A Portrait of the Artist as a Young Man* ([1916; New York: New American Library, 1948], former owner Ted Hughes, Emory; hereafter cited in the text as "*Portrait*."). After these, she has shelved Woolf's *Orlando: A Biography* ([1928; New York: Penguin Books, 1946], Special Collections, Ekstrom Library, University of Louisville, Louisville, KY) and *To the Lighthouse* ([New York: Harcourt, Brace, & Co., 1927], former owner Plath, former owner Ted Hughes, Emory), followed by Lawrence's *Sons and Lovers* ([1913; New York: Modern Library, 1922], Smith) and Joseph Conrad's *Lord Jim* (Auction, https://www.librarything.com/catalog/SylviaPlathLibrary&collection=-1&deepsearch=lord+jim, accessed 26 June 2019). Plath probably studied *Lord Jim* in English 211 with Drew (Drew Papers). Remaining on the third shelf is Thomas Mann's *The Magic Mountain*, and near the floor on the bottom shelf, miscellaneous prose: Sir James George Frazer's *The Golden Bough: A Study in Magic and Religion* ([New York: The Macmillan Company, 1952], Smith), David Riesman's *The Lonely Crowd: A Study of the Changing American Character.* ([Garden City, NY: Doubleday & Company, Inc., 1953], Smith), possibly Cleanth Brooks and Robert Penn Warren's *Understanding Poetry: An Anthology for College Students* ([1938; New York: H. Holt and Company, 1946], Smith), and Jacques Barzun's *Darwin, Marx, Wagner: Critique of a Heritage* ([Boston: Little Brown, 1947], Lilly).

25 Regarding Plath and Woolf, see, for instance, Sandra M. Gilbert, "In Yeats's House: The Death and Resurrection of Sylvia Plath," in *No Man's Land: The Place of the Woman Writer in the Twentieth Century: Volume 3 Letters from the Front*, ed. Sandra M. Gilbert and Susan Gubar (New Haven: Yale University Press, 1994), 272; *The Other Sylvia Plath*; *The Wound and the Cure of Words*; and Kathleen Connors's contribution to the collection she edited with Sally Bayley, *Eye Rhymes: Sylvia Plath's Arts of the Visual* (Oxford: Oxford University Press, 2007).

26 Behind the typewriter is Plath's slim black hardcover copy of e.e. cummings's *i: six non lectures* ([Cambridge, MA: Harvard University Press, 1954], Smith), which she recently received as a gift. On the desk is her copy of John Dos Passos's *U. S. A.* ([New York: Modern Library, c. 1937], Lilly), which she read in Alfred Kazin's twentieth-century American literature course that spring Beside the lamp is Plath's copy of *The Collected Poems of Wallace Stevens* ([New York: A. A. Knopf, 1955], Smith).

27 See Hammer regarding the composition of this sculpture ("Plath's Lives," 70).

28 As Hammer puts it, "[w]riting endures" ("Plath's Lives," 69). He makes this observation after considering Jaqueline Rose's reading of "The Lady and the Earthenware Head" in *The Haunting of Sylvia Plath* ("Plath's Lives," 69).

29 Hammer observes that "The Lady and the Earthenware Head" is Plath's

> struggle to get rid of an image of herself that . . . is the model head of a model pupil. . . Plath's projected book, *The Earthenware Head*, has displaced the head on her shelf next to the canonical texts she read in school, beside which it hadn't looked right. Plath had rejected one image as being "unlike" her . . . and thus became an author.
>
> (71)

30 Regarding religious and national identity in Joyce see M. Keith Booker, *Ulysses, Capitalism, and Colonialism: Reading Joyce After the Cold War* (Westport, CT: Greenwood Press, 2000), Vincent J. Cheng, *Joyce, Race, and Empire*

(New York: Cambridge University Press, 1995), Laura Doyle, *Bordering on the Body: The Racial Matrix of Modern Fiction and Culture* (New York: Oxford University Press, 1994), and Derek Attridge and Marjorie Howes, eds. *Semicolonial Joyce* (New York: Cambridge University Press, 2000).

31 See James Gourley, "The same anew: James Joyce's Modernism and its influence on Sylvia Plath's *Bell Jar*," in *College Literature* 45, no. 4 (Fall 2018): 695–723.

32 Irving Howe, "The Plath Celebration: A Partial Dissent," *Modern Critical Views: Sylvia Plath*, ed. Harold Bloom (New York: Chelsea House, 1989), 225–35; hereafter cited in the text as "Howe."

33 Howe argues, "[t]here is something monstrous, utterly disproportionate, when tangled emotions about one's father are . . . compared with the historical fate of the European Jews; something sad" (12).

34 Regarding Plath learning about the Holocaust as a student, see also Strangeways.

35 Drew's course was described in the course catalogue as including "Joyce, Yeats, and Eliot." According to her 1953 calendar ("Calendar, Jan–Aug. 1953," box 7, folder 5, Plath mss. II, Lilly), Plath was auditing a course in February and the first week of March with Drew that met at 10 in the morning on Mondays, Tuesdays, and Wednesdays, the time listed in the *Smith College Bulletin* for Drew's English 44a 20th Century British Literature course described as "Joyce, Yeats, Eliot." *Smith College Bulletin: The Catalogue Number 1952–1953* (Northampton, MA), Smith College Archives. Plath also began the first page of her Joyce notebook, "20th Century British Literature—Miss Drew," matching the title in the catalogue. Sylvia Plath, "James Joyce notebook," box 10, folder 10, Plath mss. II, Lilly; hereafter cited in the text as "*JJN*."

36 Nora Johnson, *Coast to Coast: A Family Romance* (New York: Simon and Schuster, 2004), 157. Later in her memoir, Johnson refers to having taken a "Joyce, Yeats, Eliot" course (191).

37 Plath used a slightly darker ink, which may indicate a later addition. The first occurrence of Gilbert's attributes appears on page 71 of Plath's copy of *Ulysses*. Stuart Gilbert, *James Joyce's Ulysses: A Study* (1952; New York: Vintage Books, 1955), 30, former owner Plath, University of Virginia Library, Charlottesville, VA; hereafter cited in the text as "Gilbert." Plath also referred to Gilbert's book as a source regarding the novel's structure (*JJN*), as Drew also noted in her lecture notes. Drew, "Lecture Notes: Joyce," box 770.1, folder 2, Drew Papers.

38 The extra in-text quotation mark at the close of this excerpt is in the original.

39 The resemblance of this comment to one Plath's professor Elizabeth Drew recorded in the notes she prepared for her *Ulysses* lectures suggests that this note is one that Plath transcribed as she audited. Drew, "Lecture Notes: Joyce," box 770.1, folder 2, Drew Papers. Drew uses some abbreviations in her notes. She explains that "St.[ephen] bitterly sees . . . '[symbol for "the"] cracked look. [ing] glass [symbol for 'of'] a servant' as [symbol for 'the'] symbol [symbol for 'of'] Irish art. A servant to Eng[land]: & giving no true reflection [symbol for 'of'] Ireland or [symbol for 'of the'] world in general." Enid Mark, who attended the course, also made a similar comment in her copy of *Ulysses*. James Joyce, *Ulysses* (1922; New York: Random House), 8. Enid Mark's Personal Copy. Owned by Eugene Mark.

40 Drew, "Lecture Notes: Joyce," page 2, box 770.1, folder 3, Drew Papers.

41 Regarding the Aliens Bill, see Harry Defries, *Conservative Party Attitudes to Jews: 1900–1950* (Portland, OR: Frank Cass Publishers, 2001), 18, 16. Attitudes toward Jews in general would also have been affected by the Dreyfus Affair in 1898, which brought into relief the alterity of Jewish people, and, as Amanda Anderson has argued, threatened the cohesiveness of

nineteenth-century conceptions of national identity. Amanda Anderson, *The Powers of Distance: Cosmopolitanism and the Cultivation of Detachment* (Princeton: Princeton University Press, 2001), 125, 126–7, and 139. See also Neil R. Davison, *James Joyce,* Ulysses, *and the Construction of Jewish Identity* (1996; New York: Oxford University Press, 1998) and Richard Sennett, *The Fall of Public Man* (1974; New York: Norton, 1992), 242. Davison points out that

> [t]he term "Jewish question" had a specific and general use throughout the century. After Jewish emancipation, the term became an abbreviation for questions such as "Can the Jews assimilate into Christian society? What should be done with a people who are both religiously and 'racially' different from ourselves?"
>
> (fn. 16, 244–5)

42 Richard J. Bernstein, *Hannah Arendt and The Jewish Question* (Cambridge, MA: MIT Press, 1996), xi.
43 Bernstein, xi.
44 Milton Steinberg, *A Partisan Guide to the Problem.* B'nai B'rith Hillel Foundations in American Universities (Cornwall, NY: The Cornwall Press, Inc., 1945); hereafter cited in the text as "Steinberg." Plath, "Transcript," box 20, folder 25, Plath Collection.
45 Sylvia Plath, "Religion 14 Notebook," box 11, folder 8, mss. II, Lilly. Her notebook reflects a thorough introduction to Jewish religion, holidays, culture, traditions, and contemporary movements such as Zionism.
46 Plath may have been drawing on Stuart Gilbert's observations. When she acquired a copy of his *James Joyce's Ulysses* in or after 1955, she underlined Gilbert's reference to this moment his discussion of the "Cyclops" episode:

> The talk veers round to the Jewish problem whereon Mr Deasy gave wise counsel to Stephen earlier in the day. "Those are nice things," says the Citizen, a Nestor come to judgment, "coming over here to Ireland filling the country with bugs."

This assumption suggests the immigration fears that kept Jews out of England. Plath may also have encountered Gilbert's observation that Deasy "tenders, too, sage counsel on the virtues of economy and airs his views on Anglo-Irish history and the Jewish influence in English affairs" (94). A dash reflects the end of the line in Plath's copy of the novel (Gilbert, 265). Based on the date of Plath's copy of *James Joyce's Ulysses* (1955), she may have annotated it while preparing for her exams during her final term at Smith in 1955, when she also noted in her calendar that she was reviewing *Ulysses*. Plath, "Calendar, July 1954–June 1955," box 7, folder 6, Plath mss. II, Lilly.
47 Writing in her journal, Plath grappled with a similar issue at least two years earlier: "Why do we electrocute men for murdering an individual and then pin a purple heart on them for mass slaughter of someone arbitrarily labeled 'enemy?'" (*UJ*, 46). The line she notes in Joyce echoes the issues at the heart of these sentiments.
48 Christopher Grobe, *The Art of Confession: The Performance of Self from Robert Lowell to Reality TV* (New York: New York University Press, 2017), 42; hereafter cited in the text as "Grobe." Grobe cites Hilene Flanzbaum's point that confessional poets "claim for themselves a 'metaphorical Jewishness'" (Grobe 41). Hilene Flanzbaum, "The Imaginary Jew and the American Poet," in *The Americanization of the Holocaust*, ed. Hilene Flanzbaum (Baltimore: Johns Hopkins University Press, 1999): 29.

49 Ann Keniston, "The Holocaust Again: Sylvia Plath, Belatedness, and Limits of the Lyric Figure," in *The Unraveling Archive: Essays on Sylvia Plath*, ed. Anita Helle (Ann Arbor: University of Michigan Press, 2007), 147, emphasis Keniston; hereafter cited in the text as "Keniston."

50 Keniston is not alone in separating Plath from the world she creates in "Daddy." Tim Kendall dra rs attention to Jacqueline Rose's view that "Daddy" "self-consciously addresses 'the production of fantasy,'" but he finds that she "fails to take adequate account of Plath's developing interest in, and integration into the self of, the Holocaust throughout the last year of her life." Tim Kendall, *Sylvia Plath: A Critical Study* (New York: Faber & Faber, 2001), 121. Kendall's reservation reminds us of the complex poetic identity Plath came to develop. In light of Plath's reading of *Ulysses*, however, her later efforts in "Daddy" also speak to dimensions of Rose's "fantasy" as she creates a character in the poem. A generation after Bloom, the identity of Plath's speaker is less clear. Walter Kalaidjian finds that Plath's

> Holocaust verse . . . goes to the heart of the "Jewish question" as it touches on German identity. . . . In "Daddy" Plath occupies both German and Jewish subject positions so as to confuse, reverse, and ultimately collapse the binary logic that would identify the former through its difference from the latter.

Walter Kalaidjian, *The Edge of Modernism: American Poetry and the Traumatic Past* (Baltimore: Johns Hopkins University Press, 2006), 6.

51 This instance resembles a strategy Keniston sees in Plath's poetry, particularly in "Daddy": "The association of self with Jew leads to a shift into a more purely metonymic mode, one in which a series of objects possessed by and synecdochically associated not with Jews" (147).

52 Plath, "Religion 14 Notebook," Lilly. The underlining is Plath's.

53 Don Gifford, *Ulysses Annotated* (1974; Berkeley: University of California Press, 1988), 478. Gifford cites *Ulysses*, line 1625, page 486. Following the initial list of letters from the Hebrew alphabet, the eclectic list of references includes holidays, practices, and Plath's selections do not appear to follow a pattern, except that some of her choices may have been well-known: "Kosher Yom Kippur Hanukah Hanukah Roschaschana Beni Brith Bar Mitzcah Mazzoth Askenazim [sic] Meshuggah Talith" (*U*, 477). She may have underlined the references based on their appearance, to learn what they mean, or because they may appear later in the novel. She similarly underlined "kol nidre" earlier in the "Circe" chapter (*U*, 470).

54 http://www.theologyweb.com/campus/archive/index.php/t-60184.html, accessed 25 July 2009. http://www.religionfacts.com/judaism/things/tallit.htm, accessed 25 July 2009. In the Gospel of Luke, it is "a certain rich man, and he was clothed in purple and fine linen . . . and a certain beggar named Lazarus was laid at his gate" (Luke 16: 19–20, page 155). In the Gospel of John, "they took the body of Jesus, and wound it in linen clothes with the spices, as the manner of the Jews is to bury" (John 19:40, page 224). *King James Version of A.D. 1611 and The Revised Version of A.D. 1881, The New Testament* (New York: American Book Exchange, 1881). Kathleen Raine traces the imagery and significance of Yeats's phrase in "Byzantium" back to Blake's *Vala*: "That ambiguous advice warns the dreamer to prepare himself for the grave; but equally it tells of rebirth, of 'death-in-life and life-in-death', for as the dead are vested in a shroud." Kathleen Raine, *Death-in-life and Life-in-Death: "Cuchulain Comforted" and "News for the Delphic Oracle"* (The Dolmen Press, 1974), 33; hereafter cited in the text as "Raine."

55 While Plath's annotation in *Ulysses* referring to "English national problem of the Jewish question" accompanies a passage about immigration, "The Perfect Setup," a story Plath published in *Seventeen* in 1952, addresses anti-Semitism. The protagonist sees her job as

> a perfect setup, all right, just so long as people knew what side of the fence they belonged on. I hadn't been sure where *I* belonged, though, even when I had stood in front of Mrs. Bradley saying, "Why yes, of course, I understand." I hadn't understood at all.
>
> (103)

The narrator, objecting to her employer's treatment of a Jewish family, points out "[s]omewhere a mistake had been made. Somehow a little unspoken code had gotten mislaid" (103). I thank Peter K. Steinberg for bringing this story to my attention. Sylvia Plath, "The Perfect Setup." *Seventeen* (October 1952): 76, 101–4. See also Luke Ferretter's response to this story in *Sylvia Plath's Fiction: A Critical Introduction* (Edinburgh: Edinburgh University Press, 2010).

56 In her lecture on "P(l)athography," Heather Clark called Joyce's *Portrait of the Artist* a "template" for Plath's *Bell Jar*. Heather Clark, "P(l)athography: Sylvia Plath and Her Biographers." 19 March 2018. The Center for the Humanities. The Graduate Center, City University of New York, New York, NY.

57 See Kathleen Connors and Sally Bayley, eds., *Sylvia Plath's Art of the Visual* (Oxford: Oxford University Press, 2007).

58 During her sophomore year in the spring of 1952, Plath studied twentieth-century literature with Drew. According to Drew's lectures notes, she taught *A Portrait of the Artist as a Young Man* in this course, and Plath likely read it in during the spring of her sophomore year as well. Drew, "Lecture Notes: The Novel II," box 770.1, folder 19–21, Drew Papers.

59 *Portrait*, 131.

60 *Portrait*, 133.

61 *Portrait*, 172.

62 *Portrait*, 167. The original line reads: "The lyrical form is in fact the simplest verbal vesture of an instant of emotion" (167).

63 Plath is itemizing here what Joyce explains in the novel: "The personality of the artist, at first a cry or a cadence or a mood and then a fluid and lambent narrative, finally refines itself out of existence, impersonalizes itself, so to speak" (*Portrait*, 167).

64 (*Portrait*, 169). The words of this quotation are blurred at the bottom of the notebook cover.

65 Ibid.

66 Harry Levin, *James Joyce: A Critical Introduction* (New Directions: Norfolk, CT, 1941); hereafter cited in the text as "*JJ*."

67 See also Diane Middlebrook's interview on the *A&E Biography* of Sylvia Plath interpreting Plath and Hughes's roles as writers as "vocations." Ilana Trachtman, prod. and dir., *Biography: Sylvia Plath* (Working Dog Productions, A&E *Biography* Series, December 27, 2004).

68 See Wagner-Martin, *Sylvia Plath: A Biography*, 148.

69 During class, Plath had read aloud her student Ellen Bartlett's exam essay on *Portrait of the Artist* as an example. Plath left a note in her teaching notes reminding herself to return Bartlett's paper (*TN*). Nodelman, interview with the author, 4 September 2006. See also Ellen Bartlett Nodelman and Amanda Golden, "Recollections of Mrs. Hughes's Student," *Plath Profiles* 5, Supplement (Fall 2012): 125–39, http://scholarworks.iu.edu/journals/index.php/plath/article/view/4353/3978, accessed 17 February 2020; hereafter cited in

the text as "Recollections." See also Appendix A regarding Plath's preparation and teaching of Joyce.

70 Drew, "Lecture Notes: The Novel II," box 770.1, folder 19–21, Drew Papers.

71 Drew began her lecture notes with a discussion of Joyce's selection of *A Portrait of the Artist as a Young Man* as a title instead of *Stephen Hero*. She noted a progression "[f]rom <u>Stephen Hero</u>, which focusses [sic] attention on the <u>individuality</u> of the <u>man</u>: to 'Portrait of the <u>Artist</u> as a Young Man,' where the accent falls on the A<u>rtist</u>." Drew, "Lecture Notes: The Novel II," lecture materials on *Portrait of the Artist*, page 2, box 770.1, folder 19, Drew Papers.

72 See also Harry Levin's introduction to. *The Portable James Joyce*, ed. Harry Levin (1947; New York: The Viking Press, 1955), former owner Plath, Lilly; hereafter cited in the text as "*PJJ*." Mark A. Wollaeger also observed that "*Portrait*'s historical dimension, greatly underplayed for most of its critical history, has long been as important to Irish writers as its elaborate symbolism was to American New Critics." Mark A. Wollaeger, introduction to *Portrait of the Artist as a Young Man: A Casebook*, 6. See also Sennett, *The Fall of Public Man*, 213, 238, 239.

73 Plath followed Drew, in pointing out the novel's structure as a series of flights and pointed out Joyce's depictions of "clusters" of related symbols. Drew, "Lecture Notes: The Novel II," box 770.1, folders 19–21, Drew Papers.

74 Dena Williams, Public Services, Lilly Library, email to the author, 23 April 2008. Plath also emphasized the first "nets" in red ink and placed a star in black ink and a line in red pencil beside the quotation. Plath may have been working from Levin's introduction to *Portable James Joyce* in her emphasis on this passage. She had underlined, "<u>Language, religion, and nationality</u>," and placed a line in the left margin beside the remainder of Levin's clarification that Stephen imagined them as "a series of nets" (*PJJ*, 3).

75 In her teaching copy of *Portrait*, Plath placed in parentheses in black and underlined the second line of her quotation in her copy in red and blue, and "Welcome, O life! I go to encounter for the millionth time the reality of experience and to forge in the smithy of my soul the uncreated conscience of my race" (*PJJ*, 525).

76 Plath's notes suggest that she worked from the entry for "Fenians," particularly that their efforts communicated that "force and repression were no remedies for Irish discontent." *Encyclopedia Americana*, Volume 11 (1919), page 116. Plath stresses "no remedies for," underlining it in her notes. To some extent, Plath's attention to historical context expands the sense that "[t]he New Critics followed the historians in thinking of literary history as at best a body of preliminary information that, however indispensable, could be set aside once the would-be explicator had done a minimal amount of homework." Gerald Graff, *Professing Literature: An Institutional History* (1987; Chicago: University of Chicago Press, 1989), 183.

77 In her "Modern Poetry Notebook," Plath listed under "Background books," references to critical texts including Richard Ellmann's *Yeats: The Man and the Masks* (New York: Macmillan, 1948); Louis MacNeice, *Poetry of W. B. Yeats* (New York: Oxford University Press, 1941); and Thomas Rice Henn, *The Lonely Tower: Studies in the Poetry of W. B. Yeats* (London: Methuen, 1950). Plath also mentioned in her notebook that Yeats's *Collected Poems* were required for the course. In her copy, Plath also underlined Yeats's "Upon a House Shaken by Land Agitation," and included notes in the margin from MacNeice's *Poetry of W. B. Yeats*. Drew also included the above books in her "Modern Poetry Short Bibliography," Box 770, Drew Papers.

78 W. B. Yeats, *The Collected Poems of W. B. Yeats* (New York: Macmillan, 1952), 204, former owner Plath, Smith; hereafter cited in the text as "Yeats." Plath noted that her report on "1919" was due on March 2 in her 1953 Calendar (Lilly). When Plath annotated her Untermeyer anthology to teach, she included the points from Henn's book that she had inscribed in her copy of Yeats's *Collected Poems* (487, 488).

79 Thomas Rice Henn explains, "This incident, a murder by a burst of machine-gun fire from a passing lorry of Black and Tans near Kiltartan, affected Yeats profoundly." Thomas Rice Henn, *The Lonely Tower: Studies in the Poetry of W. B. Yeats* (1950; New York: Pelligrini & Cudahy, 1952), 216.

80 The tragedy, Sarah Cole explains, involved a pregnant woman who was accidentally shot and killed while she held her child. Interestingly, while Plath underlined Yeats's reference to the mother, her marginalia leaves out the woman and her child, making the instance appear less distinctive among other violent occurrences at the time. Sarah Cole, *The Violet Hour: Modernism and Violence in England and Ireland* (2012; New York: Oxford University Press, 2014), 171; hereafter cited in the text as "Cole."

81 Lewis Carroll, "The Walrus and the Carpenter" from *Through the Looking-Glass and What Alice Found There* (1872; New York: Random House, 1946).

82 Ellmann, *James Joyce*, 12.

83 Peel notes "the separation of politics from 'culture' in the dominant New Critical aesthetic theory of the time," and emphasizing her religion and history classes at Smith, concludes that "the broad American college curriculum that led to acquiring of that knowledge constituted an important, hitherto unacknowledged, ideological apprenticeship" ("Political Education" 41).

84 Richard Larschan also offered useful comments regarding Plath's interview with Orr. New England Poetry Conference, Lowell, MA, 26 April 2007.

85 See Hammer regarding Plath and the New Criticism and Alan Golding, *From Outlaw to Classic: Canons in American Poetry* (Madison: University of Wisconsin Press, 1995), regarding *Understanding Poetry* and the shaping of the modernist canon. Upon graduation from junior high school, Plath received *Understanding Poetry*. See also Alexander, 50.

86 Drew had also noted *Axel's Castle* in her bibliography for the Modern Poetry course Plath completed in the spring of 1953 (Drew Papers). Enid Mark also listed *Axel's Castle* in her Modern Poetry notebook (Smith College Archives), and Plath listed it in her Modern Poetry notebook (Lilly). While she is discussing Plath's time at Cambridge, for treatment of Plath's enthusiasm as a reader in the context of her experience as a Fulbright Scholar, see Merve Emre's *Paraliterary: The Making of Bad Readers in Postwar America* (Chicago: University of Chicago Press, 2017).

87 Plath also noted *Axel's Castle* in her 1955 calendar as a book she wanted to review while preparing for her comprehensive examinations (Lilly).

88 As Strangeways has also observed, Plath's underlining and annotations often reflect her attention to the text's argument.

89 Plath had also recorded Eliot's sense of "poetry [as] an escape from personality" in her notes from Drew's modern poetry course in the fall of 1953. Plath, "Modern Poetry Notebook," Lilly.

90 Plath noted Richards's visit in a letter to Philip McCurdy on 3 March 1954 (*LV1*, 701). Following Richards's talk, Smith's college newspaper *The Sophian* addressed his displays and mentioned his references to Eliot:

Dr. Richards diagrammed the process of communication, with the *source* on one side and the *destination* on the other. . . . The encoding embodies the poem with form and the decoding allows the greatest opportunity for individual derivation.

In talking about inspiration, Dr. Richards quoted from T. S. Eliot, who said that a poet's work has been "the utterance of his secret feelings and the exaltation and despair of a generation." This definition can apply to Eliot's own work, the speaker added.

"Richards Diagrams Estimate of Poetry," *Sophian* (Northampton, MA), 4 March 1954, page 1.

91 I. A. Richards, *Practical Criticism: A Study of Literary Judgment* (London: Routledge and Kegan Paul, 1954), former owner Plath, Lilly.

92 Peter Orr, "Sylvia Plath," in *The Poet Speaks: Interviews with Contemporary Poets Conducted by Hilary Morrish, Peter Orr, John Press, and Ian Scott-Kilvert* (New York: Barnes and Noble, 1966), 169; hereafter cited in the text as Orr.

93 Hugh Kenner quotes Joyce's statement regarding *Dubliners*: "My intention was to write a chapter in the moral history of my country, and I chose Dublin for the scene because that city seemed to me the centre of paralysis." Hugh Kenner, *Dublin's Joyce* (1956; New York: Columbia University Press, 1987), 48; hereafter cited in the text as *Dublin's Joyce*.

94 In preparation to teach, Plath also read Gilbert Highet, *The Art of Teaching* (New York: Vintage Books, 1954), former owner Plath, Lilly. See also Amanda Golden, "Sylvia Plath's Teaching and the Shaping of Her Work," in *Sylvia Plath in Context*, ed. Tracy Brain (Cambridge: Cambridge University Press, 2019).

95 The date of Plath's first Wednesday class was September 25 (*LV2*, 174). The *Smith College Bulletin* described the course as "Practice in expository and critical writing in connection with the study of selected literary forms." *Smith College Bulletin: The Catalogue Number: 1957–1958* (Northampton, MA), page 76, Smith College Archives.

96 Walking distance calculated using Google Maps. 15 September 2018.

97 Plath noted 70 students in one instance and later 65 (*LV2*, 181).

98 See also Appendix A.

99 "Mary Ellen Chase – 'With Feeling' on English 11," *Sophian* (Northampton, MA), vol. II, no. 27, 21 January 1954, page 1, Smith College Archives.

100 Plath asked Robert Gorham Davis on 17 December 1956, "if you think there would be a possibility of my applying to teach on the English 11 staff next year" (*LV2*, 39). She later wrote home from Cambridge on 17 June 1957:

Ijust got my first term syllabus for my English 11 course this morning: fascinating. . . . I am ashamed I haven't read half the novels on the list myself, but I'll get the ones we don't have & take them to the Cape this summer so I'll have read them all, & naturally pick the ones I am best in: a marvellous [sic] choice is given us.

(*LV2*, 149)

101 Robert Lowell, "Foreword," *Ariel* (1966; New York: HarperCollins, 1999), xvi.

102 William James, *The Varieties of Religious Experience: A Study in Human Nature* (1902; New York: The Modern Library, [1929]), former owner Plath, Smith. A paper clip mark remains from approximately pages 3 to 20 in the volume, perhaps indicating the pages she taught.

103 Plath reported to her mother: "The classes are not lectures, but discussions, so I can only prepare the main points to cover & perhaps a little background

material & must learn what I can draw from them" (*LV2*, 172). Plath left a typed list of the books she taught in the course on a half of a page of pink Smith College memorandum paper that follows her notes on the *Duchess of Malfi* in her file of teaching notes at the Lilly. Mary Ellen Chase noted in a letter to Alfred Kazin that the freshman English teachers each selected and taught two novels. Letter, Mary Ellen Chase to Alfred Kazin, n.d. [Fall 1954], Alfred Kazin Collection of Papers, Berg.

104 See *LV2*, 214. According to David Daiches, the "study of Greek tragedy is compulsory in Part II of the Cambridge English Tripos." David Daiches, *English Literature* (Englewood Cliffs, NJ: Prentice-Hall, 1964), 124.

105 The page numbers Plath provided in her teaching notes correspond with Untermeyer.

106 Alexander, 209–10, 213, and 215.

107 See also *UJ*, 358.

108 Sylvia Plath, "20th Century, Miss Drew: Holograph. Notes for English 211 at Smith College," box 20, folder 17, Plath Collection.

109 Plath had demonstrated a similar practice as a student. She mentioned to Philip McCurdy on 1 March 1954, "[I] have several critical books to assimilate" (*LV1*, 698).

110 This topic was of concern to Helen Vendler, who focused in her Mellon Lectures on the ways that in their late work Plath and other writers "wrestled with what Yeats called 'death-in-life and life-in-death': writing about life facing impending death, and writing about death while still immersed in the world." Lecture, National Gallery of Art, Washington, D.C. Rachel Donadio, "The Closest Reader," *The New York Times* (New York, NY), 10 December 2006, page 12.

111 Plath added the words "emerges" and "worse" by hand and changed "IS" to "AS." Toni Saldívar reads this passage in light of her sense that Plath's course was influenced by Romanticism. Toni Saldívar, *Sylvia Plath: Confessing the Fictive Self* (New York: Peter Lang Publishing, 1992).

112 See also Lyndall Gordon, *T. S. Eliot: An Imperfect Life* (1998; New York: Norton, 2000), 181–2 and 206.

113 Another former student from Plath's English 11 class characterized the course texts as "depressing, heavy stuff" and that "the most cheerful thing that we read was some poetry of John Crowe Ransom." Lynda K. Bundtzen and Karen V. Kukil. Radio interview on *The Connection*, 15 December 2000, http://theconnection.wbur.org/2000/12/15/sylvia-plath, accessed 2 February 2015.

114 Plath circled the words "poetry" and "religion."

115 In another context, regarding Plath's poem "Stillborn" (1961), Gill points out: "The interesting aspect of the much-quoted opening line of this poem (which declares that these lines 'do not live') is that it nuances the concept of living, or blurs the boundaries between life and death. As the text goes on to show, it is not that the poems are dead, exactly, it is that they lack life. The distinction is important. The poems, we are told, have all their faculties . . . but somehow they are missing that spark or vital force that other poems . . . had managed to grasp" (*Cambridge Introduction*, 48).

116 The pamphlet I have accessed is in the files of Katherine Gee Hornbeak, instructor of first year English, with whom Plath shared an office during her teaching year at Smith. "Lecture Notes for English 11-Notes, etc." c. 1954, box 6, folder 2, Katherine Gee Hornbeak papers, Smith College Archives, CA-MS-00154, Smith College Special Collections, Northampton, MA. There is no specific copyright information. The bottom of the first page reads, "From MAJOR BRITISH WRITERS ed. G. B. Harrison, copyright, 1954, by

Harcourt, Brace and Company, Inc." Plath's copy of *Poetic Patterns: A Note on Versification* (Northampton, MA: Kraushar Press, 1956) is in the Lilly.

117 Drew, *Poetic Patterns*, 14, former owner Hornbeak.

118 Judith Kroll, *Chapters in a Mythology: The Poetry of Sylvia Plath* (New York: Harper & Row, 1976); hereafter cited in the text as "Kroll."

119 Regarding Yeats's "Byzantium," see Helen Vendler, *Our Secret Discipline: Yeats and Lyric Form* (Cambridge: Harvard University Press, 2007), 42. Kathleen Raine traces the imagery and significance of Yeats's phrase in "Byzantium" back to Blake's *Vala*: "That ambiguous advice warns the dreamer to prepare himself for the grave; but equally it tells of rebirth, of 'death-in-life and life-in-death', for as the dead are vested in a shroud, so are the newborn 'woven' into mortal garments" (33). For Hughes's response to Coleridge, see John Beer, "Coleridge, Ted Hughes, and Sylvia Plath," in *The Monstrous Debt: Modalities of Romantic Influence in Twentieth-Century Literature*, ed. Damian Walford Davies and Richard Marggraf Turley (Detroit: Wayne State University Press, 2006), 123–41. Hughes, as Kroll and other scholars have observed, knew *The White Goddess* well. See *LTH*, 273. Plath and Hughes shared his copy of *The White Goddess* (London: Faber and Faber, 1948), which is at Emory. Regarding *The White Goddess*, see Feinstein, *Ted Hughes: The Life of a Poet* (New York: Norton, 2001), Diane Middlebrook, *Her Husband: Ted Hughes and Sylvia Plath—A Marriage* (New York: Viking, 2003); hereafter cited in the text as "Her Husband," and Karen V. Kukil and Stephen C. Enniss, *"No Other Appetite": Sylvia Plath, Ted Hughes, and the Blood Jet of Poetry* (New York: The Grolier Club, 2005). Regarding Hughes, see Myers, *Crow Steered*, 7.

120 *OED*, s.v. "death," *n.* 2.

121 *OED*, s.v. "life-in-death."

122 *OED*, s.v. "paralysis," *n.* 2.

123 See Jackson's "Editing and Auditing Marginalia" regarding the ways that marginalia introduce readers to a response to a passage, like "eavesdropping" on a conversation.

124 This essay became Brooks's chapter in *Modern Poetry and the Tradition*. As Brooks acknowledged, Matthiessen "puts his finger on the basic theme, death-in-life, but I do not think that he has given it all the salience which it deserves." Cleanth Brooks, *"The Waste Land: An Analysis,"* in T. S. Eliot, *The Waste Land*, ed. Michael North (New York: Norton, 2001), 185; hereafter cited in the text as "Brooks." Originally published in *Southern Review* 3 (Summer 1937): 106–36.

125 F. O. Matthiessen, *The Achievement of T. S. Eliot: An Essay on the Nature of Poetry* (1935; New York Oxford University Press, 1959), 21–22.

126 Cleanth Brooks, *Modern Poetry and the Tradition* (Chapel Hill: University of North Carolina Press, 1939); hereafter cited in the text as "*Modern Poetry*."

127 As Brooks had observed "'Byzantium,' . . . concerns itself directly with . . . the relation of the living to the living dead" ("*Modern Poetry*," 192–3). Plath inscribed in her copy, "condition of fire — relation of living to living dead." Kukil, email to the author, 14 June 2007. Enid Mark noted in her Modern Poetry notebook that students in the class gave presentations (Smith College Archives).

128 Rainey notes that "Brooks . . . in 1939 published an essay that profoundly shaped the course of criticism on the poem for the next forty years" ("*The Annotated* Waste Land," 37).

129 Drew, *T. S. Eliot: The Design of His Poetry*. In Plath's notebook from Drew's modern poetry course, Plath noted the collected volume of Eliot's poetry was a course text. Plath, "Modern Poetry Notebook," Lilly. Brooks's *Modern Poetry and the Tradition*, Wilson's *Axel's Castle*, and her own book on Eliot's poetry. Elizabeth Drew, "Modern Poetry Short Bibliography," Box 770, Drew Papers.

130 In *James Joyce* Levin compared the condition of Joyce's Dublin to that which Eliot depicted in *The Waste Land*:

> "the special odour of corruption," in which he took pride, was by no means peculiar to Dublin. . . . It was perceived by an expatriate American poet, T. S. Eliot, as he watched the lost souls crowding over London Bridge. (*JJ*, 32)

Kenner compared the particularity of Joyce's Dublin to Eliot's London:

> Dublin is not, that is, an agglomeration of residents, but a city. In its present paralysis, it remains a ghost, not a heap of bones: the ghost of the great conception of the City[.] . . . Mr. Eliot saw London as "a heap of broken images"; Joyce's Dublin had none of the random qualities characterized by "heap". It was a shell of grandeur populated by wraiths.
>
> (48)

Kenner's reading of the phantom or immaterial remnants that overshadow Joyce's image of early twentieth-century Dublin is close to the OED's definition of life-in-death.

131 Brooks had also observed in *Modern Poetry and the Tradition* that *The Waste Land* resembles "the death-in-life of Dante's Limbo. Life in the full sense has been lost" (159). Plath may have learned of Kenner's work from Drew, who noted his essay, "The Portrait in Perspective," on what provides a title page for Joyce in her *Portrait of the Artist* lecture notes. Drew, "Lecture Notes: The Novel II," box 770.1, folder 19, Drew Papers.

132 Sylvia Plath, "Notebook from Newton Arvin's Course," and Library, Sylvia Plath Papers, Plath mss. II, 1932–1977, Lilly Library, Indiana University, Bloomington; hereafter cited in the text as "*JN*." Henry James, *The American* (New York: Rinehart and Co., 1949), former owner Plath, Lilly, and *The Ambassadors* (New York: Harper and Brothers, [1948]), former owner Plath, Smith. Regarding Plath's annotating of *The American*, see *The Other Sylvia Plath*. The Henry James Society's panel on the legacy of Adeline Tintner at the MLA Convention in 2006, organized by Pierre Walker, enhanced my understanding of Plath, James, and Tintner's work.

133 Plath also worked as Arvin's grader for his American literature course during the spring of 1958. See Plath's *Unabridged Journals* regarding her reading of James at this time.

134 Henry James, *Selected Fiction*, ed. Leon Edel (New York: E. P. Dutton & Co, Inc., [c. 1953]), 516, former owner Plath, University of Virginia Library, Charlottesville, VA; hereafter cited in the text as "*Selected Fiction*."

135 Henry James, *Selected Short Stories*, ed. Quentin Anderson (New York: Rinehart & Co., Inc., [c. 1950]), 220, former owner Plath, Smith.

136 The transcription does not include two brackets Plath added in the left margin.

137 D. H. Lawrence, "The Horse Dealer's Daughter," *Complete Short Stories* (London: Heinemann, 1955), 447, former owner Plath, Smith.

138 *OED*, s.v. "living."

139 Richard M. Matovich, "Life." *A Concordance to the Collected Poems of Sylvia Plath* (New York: Garland Publishing, Inc., 1986), 283.

140 With regard to "The Hollow Men," Kenner later notes the paralysis "[i]n death's dream kingdom . . . [where] nothing happens." Hugh Kenner, *The Invisible Poet: T. S. Eliot* (New York: McDowell, Obolensky, 1959), 189.

141 Regarding the political implications of paralysis in Joyce, see Luke Gibbons, "'Have You No Homes to Go To?': James Joyce and the Politics of Paralysis," in *Semicolonial Joyce*, ed. Derek Attridge and Marjorie Howes (New York: Cambridge University Press, 2000), 150–71.

142 Kenner quotes this passage in *Dublin's Joyce*, noting that it was from a letter Joyce "wrote to a prospective publisher" (48). Levin also reproduces this statement from Joyce in *James Joyce*, introducing it as his "intention, [as] he told his publisher" (30).

143 The margins and line breaks have shifted from Plath's *TN*. Plath placed parentheses around two lines in red pencil. "PARALYZED" and "paralysed" are spelled as demonstrated.

144 Plath added "ISOLATION" by hand.

145 William York Tindall defines "paralysis" and "living death" as synonyms. William York Tindall, *A Reader's Guide to James Joyce* (1959: Syracuse: Syracuse University Press, 1995), 3.

146 Plath added, "seen by 20th cen. Writers," above this line in her teaching notes.

147 Plath added, "& TS," "for Joyce and Eliot," and "literally" by hand.

148 Reflecting on her teaching year, Plath explained to her Cambridge mentor, Dorothea Krook, that "[g]radually, I became accustomed to preparing in rough question and answer outline the lecture I would have enjoyed giving, and getting the class to give me the half I left out, in a kind of cog-and-wheel cooperation" (*LV2*, 278). Plath employed this strategy as she prepared to question her students on "The Sisters."

149 See also Langdon Hammer's reading of nothingness in *The Waste Land* in Yale Online Classroom, Modern Poetry Lectures, 2007.

150 Regarding Plath's teaching of poetry, see Golden, "Sylvia Plath's Teaching."

151 John Guillory, *Cultural Capital: The Problem of Literary Canon Formation* (1993: Chicago, IL: University of Chicago Press, 1994).

152 Plath, "20th Century" Notes, Plath Collection. Drawing on the English Department files in the Smith College Archives, Anthony Cuda found that these notes are probably from 1955, when Plath attended Drew's lecture as part of the Honors Review Unit. Plath also mentioned having read *The Waste Land* in her application to Smith College (Alexander, 58).

153 Plath, "20th Century" Notes.

154 Plath noted pages 23 and 35 from Weston in her teaching notes (*TN*). Plath inscribed her copy of *From Ritual to Romance*, "Sylvia Plath 1958."

155 Plath left parentheses in pencil around "22 Keys" and added "22" above "Keys" in her teaching notes (*TN*).

156 See *UJ*, Linda Wagner-Martin, *Sylvia Plath: A Literary Life* (New York: St. Martin's Press, 1999), *Her Husband*, and Feinstein, 72.

157 Regarding Plath and Eliot, see also Timothy Materer, *Modernist Alchemy: Poetry and the Occult* (Ithaca, NY: Cornell University Press, 1995), 128. See http://www.wopc.co.uk/tarot/ for Rider-Waite Tarot cards, first printed in England in 1909. Dr. Terry Kidner brought these cards to my attention. This site also attributes the origins of the Tarot to Italy where it originally began as a game. For an image of "The Hanged Man" see http://www.paranormality.com/tarot_meanings.shtml, sites accessed 8 April 2017.

158 Basil Ivan Rákóczi opposite the Table of Contents. Basil Ivan Rákóczi, *The Painted Caravan: A Penetration into the Secrets of The Tarot Cards* (Hague: L.J.C. Boucher, 1954), former owner Plath, Smith. Plath inscribed her copy, "Sylvia Plath London—1956."

159 Plath wrote to Olive Higgins Prouty from Cambridge:

> I also realize that I never will want to become a Phd scholar and know more and more about some minute details of knowledge: I want to read <u>widely</u> in art, philosophy and psychology, my special interests, and to live richly.
>
> (*LV1*, 1047–8)

160 In her presentation during the *Sylvia Plath Seventieth Year Literary Symposium* (2002), Lynda K. Bundtzen discussed Plath's sense of unproductivity during her Boston year. See also Stephen Gould Axelrod, "The Poetry of Sylvia Plath," *The Cambridge Companion to Sylvia Plath*, ed. Jo Gill (New York: Cambridge University Press, 2006), 84.

161 For Plath's later response to paralysis in her poetry, see also Brain's reading of "Paralytic" and her consideration of the environmental contexts surrounding the poem's subject (*The Other Sylvia Plath*, 120–1).

162 See Robin Peel's *Writing Back* regarding the influence of Plath's time in London on the novel. Robin Peel, *Writing Back: Sylvia Plath and Cold War Culture* (Madison: Fairleigh Dickinson University Press, 2002); hereafter cited in the text as "*Writing Back*."

163 Robert Jay Lifton, *Death in Life: Survivors of Hiroshima* (New York: Random House, 1967), 14.

164 Cathy Schlund-Vials brought this text to my attention.

165 Plath, "Calendar, Jan.-Aug.1953," Lilly.

166 See also Linda Wagner-Martin, *The Bell Jar: A Novel of the Fifties* (New York: Twayne Publishers, 1992) and Marie Ashe, "*The Bell Jar* and the Ghost of Ethel Rosenberg," in *Secret Agents: The Rosenberg Case, McCarthyism, and Fifties America*, ed. Marjorie Garber and Rebecca L. Walkowitz (New York: Routledge, 1995), 215–31.

167 See the 19 June 1953 news broadcast available here: "Execution of Julius and Ethel Rosenberg." *History*, A&E Television Networks, 2020, https://www.history.com/speeches/execution-of-julius-and-ethel-rosenberg, accessed 29 March, 2020. and the *New York Times* coverage of the trial, including, "Letter by Mrs. Rosenberg to the President," *The New York Times*, 20 June 1953, page 7; "Kaufman Rejects 11th-Hour Appeal," *The New York Times*, 20 June 1953, page 6; and William R. Conklin, "Pair Silent to the End." Special to the *New York Times*, 20 June 1953, page 1.

168 19 June 1953. See also *Writing Back*, *The Other Sylvia Plath*, and Gill regarding this passage.

169 Plath's response to the Rosenberg execution in her journal also echoes her earlier journal entry contemplating the victims of Hiroshima (*UJ*, 46).

170 See also Sally Bayley, "'I Have Your Head on My Wall': Sylvia Plath and the Rhetoric of Cold War America," *European Journal of American Culture* 25, no. 3 (2006): 155–171.

171 The figure is now six million. United States Holocaust Museum, http://www.ushmm.org/learn, accessed 15 August 2019.

172 Defining the Jewish question as one of national identity, Kalaidjian has argued that Plath's identification with her German background informs her "repetition of issues at [the] heart of the modern 'Jewish question'" (5). See also 6.

173 Letter, Sylvia Plath to Warren Plath, 21 June 1953 (*LV1*, 643) The quotation to which Plath refers is from Chapter 11 of *Women in Love*. Birkin tells Ursula: "mankind is a dead tree, covered with fine brilliant galls of people." The previous spring, Plath noted in her calendar that she began reading *Women in Love* on 25 March 1952 and finished it the following day. Plath, "Calendar, 1952," box 7, folder 5, Plath mss. II, Lilly. Plath inscribed her copy of *Women in Love*, "Hughes 1957," having acquired it after encountering the book as an undergraduate (Smith).

174 Eliot does not use living dead in *After Strange Gods*. http://openlibrary.org/details/afterstrangegods00eliouoft, accessed 28 March 2018. Drew explains in her chapter devoted to Lawrence's *Women in Love* in *The*

Novel: A Modern Guide to Fifteen English Masterpieces (New York: Norton, 1963),

> Eliot's opinion of Lawrence in *After Strange Gods* is unequivocal. He sees him as the perfect example of the diabolic principle in modern tendencies, an instrument of demonic powers. He owns that Lawrence stands for life as against the living death of modern materialism, but it is for quite the wrong sort of life. He quotes Scripture against him: "Woe unto the foolish prophets, that follow their own spirit and have seen nothing."
>
> (209)

While this book was published after Drew had Plath in class, Drew's chapters on Joyce's *Portrait of the Artist* and Woolf's *To the Lighthouse* resemble her lecture notes for each text (Drew Papers).

175 *Axel's Castle* is in Plath's library at Smith with her copies of *Sons and Lovers* and Friedrich Nietzsche, *Thus Spake Zarathustra* (New York: Modern Library, [n.d.]). Plath's copy of D. H. Lawrence, *The Man Who Died* (1931; London: Heinemann, 1950), is in Hughes's library at Emory. Plath noted returning to her Lawrence texts in her journal during the spring of her teaching year, and one of her students recalled that Plath may have read from *Women in Love* while she taught Lawrence's stories in the fall of 1957. Nodelman, interview with the author. See also Appendix A.
     Plath noted in her journal on 22 August 1961 that she had written *The Bell Jar* (*UJ*, 696).

176 My transcription replicates Plath's inscription in her copy.

177 Peel brought to my attention to this passage in his reading of Plath's copy of *Thus Spake Zarathustra* (*Writing Back*, 35). While Plath did not acquire her copy of *Axel's Castle* until December 1953, Drew included it on her "Modern Poetry Short Bibliography," Box 770, Drew Papers.

178 Plath added a line in the right margin beside the next six lines.

179 Lawrence, *Sons and Lovers*, 479. Karen V. Kukil brought this passage to my attention in her exhibition, "A Story of Their Own: Sylvia Plath, Virginia Woolf, and Gloria Steinem" for the *Thirteenth International Conference on Virginia Woolf* held at Smith College in June 2003. In her exhibition caption, Kukil explained that Paul experienced depression following his mother's death. An image of the page Plath annotated is here: http://www.smith.edu/libraries/libs/rarebook/exhibitions/conway/readingnotes.htm, accessed 7 August 2019.

180 *Writing Back*, 35.

181 *Writing Back*, 35. Plath probably acquired the text for her European Intellectual History class in the spring of 1954. Peel mentions notes in it that refer to Plath's Dostoevsky thesis in the fall of 1954, but she was also taking Russian literature in the spring of 1954. On 6 February 1955, (Calendar, Lilly) she also composed a typescript of the poem, "Notes on Zarathustra's Prologue," box 11, folder 177, Plath Collection.

182 Lawrence, *The Man Who Died*, 15. Lynda K. Bundtzen brought Plath's reading of *The Man Who Died* at Cambridge to my attention. See *LV2*, 144. Plath inscribed her copy of *The Man Who Died*, "Sylvia Plath Cambridge 1956," and underlined numerous volumes opposite the title page, possibly indicating that she had read them, including *Sons and Lovers*, *Women in Love*, and *Lady Chatterley's Lover*.

183 See *Writing Back*, regarding Plath's rendering of New York in the fifties in response to the political complexity of London in the sixties.

184 Regarding Esther's detachment, Gill notes that "Elizabeth Wurtzel commends [*The Bell Jar*'s] . . . 'remarkable achievement' and describes it 'as . . . smartly detached'" (*Cambridge Introduction*, 73). Gill also points out that "Plath's own fig tree metaphor . . . represents Esther's paralysis when faced with a multitude of unreachable and indistinguishable opportunities" (*Cambridge Introduction*, 76). She concludes that "Esther's struggle throughout the novel is . . . to feel or be anything at all" (*Cambridge Introduction*, 83).

185 Ezra Pound, *Personae: The Shorter Poems* (1926; New York: New Directions, 1990), 111.

186 See also Brain's reading of pollution in Plath's poetry and prose in *The Other Sylvia Plath*.

187 The simplicity in Plath's phrasing and exaggeration in tone are present throughout Esther's responses to death in the novel. As Vendler has illustrated Plath's encounter at the age of eight with her father's passing informed her subsequent understanding of death. Helen Vendler, "The Contest of Melodrama and Restraint: Sylvia Plath's *Ariel*," "Mellon III" Lecture, 1, 3. Vendler, email to the author, 14 June 2007. Published in *Last Looks, Last Books* (Princeton, NJ: Princeton University Press, 2010).

188 In contrast to Plath's image, Elizabeth Winder notes that neither the *Mademoiselle* offices nor the Guest Editors' rooms at the Barbizon Hotel had working air conditioning. Elizabeth Winder, *Pain, Parties, Work: Sylvia Plath in New York, Summer 1953* (New York: Harper Collins, 2013).

189 Sylvia Plath, "Progress reports: typescripts," 1 May 1962, box 5, folder 47, Plath Collection.

190 The volumes housed at Smith and some at Emory. Before departing for England in 1959.

191 Letter of 23 October 1962. Plath composed "Lady Lazarus" from 23 to 29 October 1962 (*Collected Poems*, 247).

192 Hammer sees Plath's aims in writing on Smith College memorandum paper as

ambiguous. Placing the paper on the desk when she wrote, Plath claimed the school's authority for her own—perhaps in parody (as she parodies, or overturns, Hughes's pages when she writes on the back of them). But the same gesture marked her writing as Smith's, insuring that the institution would be "underlying" her words, backing them up, even as she worked outside of it.

(82)

193 The holograph drafts of "Lady Lazarus" at Smith are on the versos of typescript drafts of *The Bell Jar*. The pages of the novel proceed in reverse with the first typescript draft of the poem on the other side of the scene in which Esther, in the bathtub, "felt pure and sweet as a new baby" (*B*, 20). The typescript draft of the chapter page is numbered 8. Sylvia Plath, Holograph of "Lady Lazarus" and Incomplete Typescript of "Lady Lazarus," 23 October 1962, box 10, folder 129, Plath Collection.

194 21 October 1962. For "Daddy," see *Collected Poems*, 222–4, Plath made more changes to "Lady Lazarus" until December, as the drafts at Smith reflect.

195 Shifting to the personal, however, Plath and other poets of her generation, as Peter Balakian has put it, turned from "Western cultural myths, symbols, and history" of Eliot's "mythic method," as

experience derived from personally inherited history—blood history—became central to the postmodern poet's idea of the past. The impact of World War II, the nightmare of the Holocaust, and the terror created by the atomic and now nuclear age, seem to have discredited for poets much of the meaning and viability accorded to Western Civilization.

Peter Balakian, *Theodore Roethke's Far Fields* (Baton Rouge: Louisiana State University Press, 1989), 2–3. Regarding Plath's responses to the British political climate, see *Writing Back*.

196 Keniston concludes, that in their treatment of the Holocaust, "Plath's poems . . . reveal lyric to be flexible enough to survive such violence" (153).

197 Sylvia Plath, "Progress reports: typescripts," 1 May 1962, box 5, folder 47, Plath Collection. See also Janet Malcolm's discussion of a passage in Plath's journal in which she compares herself to James's character Maggie Verver in *The Wings of the Dove*. Janet Malcolm, *The Silent Woman: Sylvia Plath and Ted Hughes* (New York: Norton, 1993), 152, 155.

198 Peter Stitt, "The Art of Poetry: An Interview with John Berryman," in *Berryman's Understanding: Reflections on the Poetry of John Berryman*, ed. Harry Thomas (Boston: Northeastern University Press, 1988), 23. Reprinted from *The Paris Review* 53 (Winter 1972): 177–207.

199 John Berryman, *Homage to Mistress Bradstreet and Other Poems* (London: Faber and Faber, 1959), former owner Plath, Smith. Plath also placed stars on either side of the date in her journal when she first had a poem accepted by *The New Yorker*. It was "[a] starred day, probably the first in this whole book" (*UJ*, 397).

2 John Berryman annotating modernism

The previous chapter analyzed the ways that Sylvia Plath's engagement with modernist critical discourse as a student and teacher informed her depiction of the postwar scene in *The Bell Jar* and "Lady Lazarus." As a student at Columbia University and Clare College, Cambridge University in the thirties and as a teacher until the early seventies, John Berryman preceded and followed Plath chronologically; his annotated books and teaching notes often present a different image of modernism, in a range of institutions, lectures, and courses. The depth of Berryman's reading enables a different narrative that complements and extends what Plath demonstrates in her marginalia and teaching materials. This chapter illustrates that reading and teaching Yeats, Pound, and other modernist writers informed Berryman's treatment of the midcentury academic and literary landscape in his life poem, *The Dream Songs* (1969).

As teacher and student, Berryman's and Plath's academic careers intersected during the summer of 1954 at Harvard University. Berryman was teaching Shakespeare and creative writing.[1] Plath was studying nineteenth-century literature with Frank O'Connor.[2] As she chronicles in *The Bell Jar*, Plath had not been accepted to O'Connor's fiction writing course in the summer of 1953. Perusing the *Harvard Summer School Catalogue* in 1954, however, Plath may have scanned Berryman's course listing en route to O'Connor's offering.[3] She would have been overqualified for Berryman's course, which was "designed primarily for those who are still experimenting with techniques of fiction."[4] During the summer they lived in Cambridge, Massachusetts, the apartments Berryman and Plath had rented were less than a mile apart. As Plath lived northwest and Berryman lived southeast of Harvard Yard, however, they probably did not cross paths on the way to class.[5]

The simultaneity Berryman and Plath shared, however, is not surprising in light of the academic circles in which they traveled. The fact that there is not a record of their collision is also emblematic of the different paths they did take through a similar field.[6] When he came to write Dream Song 153, Berryman called Plath's death, "a first rate haul" (*DS*, 172; line 4). As if referring to Plath's accomplishments on a resume or transcript, Berryman added in Dream Song 187, "she her credentials / has handed in" (206; lines 9–10).[7] Reading, as we have seen, rested behind Plath's success and this chapter will turn to the role of Berryman's reading in the development of his own career.

While he was teaching at Princeton University in 1947, Berryman began drafting a short story that depicts a professor preparing to teach John Milton's *Lycidas*. In the published version, titled, "Wash Far Away" (1957), Berryman introduces his protagonist as "a systematic man. He opened his Milton and read the poem thoughtfully, twice, before he laid out side by side two other Miltons . . . and began to work his way through the editors' notes" (*FP*, 371).[8] The professor's close reading in "Wash Far Away" subsequently entails annotating his text: "Both times he was gently moved by the exquisite melancholy of a semi-couplet . . . He wrote 'exquisite melancholy' in the margin the second time" (372). For many readers and teachers, this scene is familiar. Inscribing his copy of *Lycidas*, the professor's observation will remain there to return to in class or when writing.[9]

While comparing editions of *Lycidas*, Berryman's professor considers the sources informing Milton's poem and the ways the poem includes and differs from its predecessors in creating something new:

> As Milton's imitations and telescopings multiplied, he commenced to feel restless, distant, smaller. What one editor neglected, another observed, and he began to have a sense of the great mind like a whirring, sleepless refinery . . . through which poured and was transformed the whole elegiac poetry of Greece and Italy and England, receiving an impress new and absolute.[10]
>
> (372)

In this short story of annotating, Berryman makes a claim to which he will refer throughout his career. He argued, for instance, in the essay he prepared as an introduction to Ezra Pound's *Selected Poems* (1948),

> [a]ll the ambitious poetry of the last six hundred years is much less "original" than any but a few of its readers ever realize. . . . A few hours, or days, with several annotated editions of *Lycidas* will transform the reader's view of this matter, especially if he will bear in mind the likelihood that the serious modern poet's strategy resembles Milton's.
>
> (258)

While Berryman is referring here to the annotations in which editors have glossed texts and identified sources, he takes on a similar role as an annotator of the books that he read and taught, including those of

Pound and Milton. In the process, the materiality of his reading informs his sense of literary history and his engagement with modernist discourse.[11]

Berryman's reading and scholarship combined the focus of a student with the lifelong commitment of a professor. Robert Lowell, for instance, recalled that Berryman was "very bookish and also very idiosyncratic." [12] As such, he had "the almost intimate mumble of a don. For life, he was to be a student, scholar and teacher. I think he was almost *the* student-friend I've had, the one who was the student in essence."[13] Berryman's combination of intensity and particularity also meant that his poetry came to reflect, in Stephanie Burt's words, an "unpredictable blend of erudition and comedy" and a "sometimes flaunted learnedness."[14] As a poet and a reader, Berryman was unpredictable and learned, and the modernist books he read were a precedent for the display of knowledge that Burt describes.

Berryman's library contains over 3,000 volumes, housed at Columbia and the University of Minnesota, books that he annotated as a student, teacher, scholar, and independent reader.[15] While critics have investigated Berryman's literary influences, archival material, and personal library, they have yet to consider his annotated books alongside his teaching notes.[16]

Placing these resources side-by-side reveals new connections. For if Berryman developed a humanities pedagogy that was Poundian in its comprehensiveness, annotating his copies of Pound's *Cantos* and writing an introduction for Pound's *Selected Poems* informed Berryman's teaching of modernism in humanities courses and emulation of modernist techniques in *The Dream Songs*.[17] In doing so, he adapted the lyric in order to address both modernism and the midcentury literary and cultural climate. As a textual scholar and teacher of the humanities, Berryman responded to modernist literary and critical discourses throughout his career, and that engagement reflects the significance of the poet's role in shaping the postwar reception of modernism in universities.

Scholarship

After his graduation from Columbia in 1936, Berryman traveled to Cambridge where he studied as an Oldham Shakespeare Scholar from 1936 to 1938.[18] In England, Berryman purchased not only books related to his Shakespeare research but also rare and recent volumes by Pound, W. B. Yeats, and other modernist writers. He later trained himself in methods of textual scholarship while working to complete his edition of *King Lear*. In the process, Berryman encountered different types of libraries than the other midcentury poets in *Annotating Modernism* did.[19]

In Cambridge, Berryman began acquiring rare editions that deepened his interest in the appearance and content of primary sources. Writing to his Columbia classmate, E. M. Halliday, Berryman admits having

> become a pedantic fiend for being able to read things as they were written or first printed, and the more so since the period I am buried in at present is the seventeenth century; marvelously complicated and emphatic page they turned out, infinitely subtle punctuation and capitalization and italicization. . . . Books *and* books. . . . [I] have got together a wonderfully useful set of books, none of which I intend ever to sell.[20]
>
> (Halliday, 126)

Berryman also collected first editions and fine press modern poetry volumes, and by the spring of his second year in Cambridge, a gift of *The Shadowy Waters* (1906) had increased his total of "Yeats firsts to a large fifteen" (150).[21] In 1936, Berryman purchased an autographed, limited edition of Yeats's *A Vision* from 1925, the year it was published (*WD*, 52). Berryman's copy of *A Vision* and his other rare editions were objects of study. Despite the fact that Yeats briefly handled this copy, Berryman still noted inside the back cover, in pencil, the page numbers of Yeats's reference to *The Waste Land*.[22]

After leaving Cambridge, Berryman's relation to his library altered as he relocated for teaching appointments. When teaching at what was then Wayne University in Detroit (1940),[23] he reports to his mother that "my books are here, and my papers are available as I cannot easily make them available elsewhere" (*WD*, 151).[24] New purchases also facilitated further study of textual and bibliographic methods. As an instructor of English at Harvard (1940–3), for instance, he recounts acquiring

> [Ronald Brunless] McKerrow's *Introduction to Bibliography*, which . . . fascinates me; an Oxford book, never issued in this country, and very expensive: even in my 1936–7 debauches in Cambridge I refrained; but Phillips has had a copy since last spring for 3.50 & I snatched it & made off.[25]
>
> (*WD*, 157)

In the archives near Princeton University, Berryman put into practice the methods he had encountered in his reading. After teaching English from 1943 to 1944, Berryman stressed that remaining at Princeton "means . . . access to my materials here in the library while seeing *Lear* through the press [and] access to [Stephen] Crane stuff in Newark" (*WD*, 222).[26] While completing his book *Stephen Crane* (1950), Berryman had positions as an Associate in Creative Writing from 1946 to 1947 and a Resident Fellow in Creative Writing at Princeton from 1948 to 1949. His student William Arrowsmith observed that it was Berryman's "greatest ambition . . . not to write poetry, but to produce the greatest textual edition of Lear, and also the finest commentary."[27] Berryman's research with sixteenth-century manuscripts led to new questions. In 1945, he recounted

> studying Elizabethan handwriting and shorthand methods[,] . . . all I can think of is whether it is plausible that the elaborate entry of *King Lear* in the *Stationers' Register* on 26 November 1608 was really intended to differentiate it from the old play *Leir* to which another publisher had copyright.
>
> (*WD*, 221)

Berryman's awareness that this form of Renaissance shorthand may be an antecedent of the Gregg method provides a connection to a symbolic economy of his own time, when midcentury office workers, often women, used shorthand to transcribe dictation.[28]

As he pursued his research, Berryman not only annotated Shakespeare, but also developed an interest in Shakespeare's reading. Arrowsmith remembers the "endless editions of <u>King Lear</u>" that filled Berryman's Princeton apartment.[29] These volumes leant themselves well to Berryman's marginalia. As Theodore Leinwand observes,

> [t]he broad and inviting margins in his 1927 edition of *The Tragedie of King Lear* are replete with page after page of his conjectures and his punctilious transcriptions of entire Quarto pages. At times, these notes are so meticulous that they call to mind the textual apparatus familiar to any reader of Arden editions of the plays.
>
> (389)

Berryman also investigated the sources that Shakespeare encountered.[30] Writing to the Guggenheim Foundation in 1953, Berryman reported that

> the most important result of my direct, planned work is a manuscript volume called *Shakespeare's Reading*, well advanced, which will presently incorporate, but in chronological order and critically, the whole substance of [H. R. D.] Anders's *Shakespeare's Books*, now 50 years old, and everything learnt since and everything I have learnt myself—I have been gradually reading every book Shakespeare read.[31]
>
> (*JBS*, 281)

In his lecture on "Shakespeare's Early Comedy," Berryman mentioned becoming aware of the possibility that Shakespeare's own annotations had been located:

> A frailer line of enquiry has opened up even more recently. An imperfect copy of Edward Hall's chronicle has come to light containing some

four hundred marginalia (3,600 words) which are claimed as Shake-
speare's; this is the edition of 1550, which he is known to have used.
They occur mostly over the reigns of Richard II, Henry IV, Henry V. It
wants critical examination, paleographic and linguistic.[32]

(*JBS*, 8)

If these notes are authentic, they would provide a vast resource. Berryman's
comment is indicative of his sense of marginalia's scholarly value and may
reflect his approach to his own library.

Berryman's annotating and editing of Pound combined his talents as a
textual scholar with his investment in modern poetry. Berryman was at-
tentive to the sources of Pound's allusions, and his reception as a modernist
poet who was still publishing.[33]

Annotating Pound

Berryman's reading of Pound is emblematic of the role of annotation in
readers' engagement with modernist texts.[34] As Berryman advised in the
essay he prepared as an introduction to Pound's *Selected Poems*: "Occa-
sionally you have to look things up . . . and to be familiar with Pound's
prose, when you read the *Cantos*; the labor is similar to that necessary
for a serious understanding of *Ulysses*, and meditation is the core of it"
(*FP*, 268). In light of his own annotations, Berryman's description of the
research that Pound's poetry calls for is an understatement, but the im-
mersion that Berryman advocated also characterized his own approach.
In a later prose piece, written in 1965 to commemorate Pound's eightieth
birthday, Berryman echoes Pound's breadth of sources:

> the considering reader will have to go through it all, or all that he can
> get hold of: as a *student* of literature and life, as a *reader* of Pound's
> poetry, and as a *do-it-yourself man*: no other criticism, not even Eliot's
> (which is indebted to Pound's), was ever so programmatic. Go and do
> otherwise, go and do thus—these are the burdens; and feel, and think.[35]

Following Eliot, Berryman's annotations record the ways that he put
Pound's strategies into practice.[36]

The appearance of Pound's volumes of poetry and prose shaped Berry-
man's engagement with their contents: his identification of Pound's refer-
ences to his modernist contemporaries reflects a form of midcentury gloss
and anticipates his allusions in *The Dream Songs*.[37] Opening his copy of
Pound's *Pisan Cantos* to Canto LXXIV, Berryman scanned the stressed
syllables in the opening line. A few lines later, Berryman penciled in "TSE"
beside Pound's version of Eliot's lines in "The Hollow Men" in which Pound
refers to Eliot by his nickname: "yet say this to the Possum: a bang, not a
whimper, / with a bang not with a whimper" (see Figure 2.1).

Figure 2.1 Beginning of John Berryman's copy of Ezra Pound's *Pisan Cantos*, Canto LXXIV, page 3, Upper Midwest Literary Archives, University of Minnesota Libraries, Minneapolis, MN.

Berryman's annotations reflect his attention to what critics have referred to as "networks of modernism." He was invested in Pound's role in shaping other modernist texts, and as Berryman argued in his introduction to Pound's *Selected Poems*:

> It is necessary to see Pound under two aspects: as he worked upon poetry and as he worked upon the public. The notion of him as publicist for Joyce, Eliot, Frost . . . his relations with W. B. Yeats, with Imagism, and with *The Waste Land*—with the major poet, that is, the major movement, and the major poem, of the century so far.
>
> (*FP*, 254)

Berryman also filled the insides of the back covers and flyleaves of his Pound volumes with lists of page numbers and references. These indices track Pound's allusions and his midcentury reception.[38] On the back flyleaf of *A Draft of XXX Cantos* (1920), for instance, Berryman records "EP's note in *H&H* [*Hound and Horn*] 'I have no desire either for needless mystery or for writing equally needless explanations.'"[39] Pound's gloss paradoxically sheds light on his method. Berryman mined Pound's *Cantos* for allusions, listing, for instance, in the back of *Cantos LII-LXXI*, Pound's references to the "literati 21, 24," and to himself, "EP 99, 106."[40]

In addition to his annotations, Berryman left small pages of notes in his copies of *A Draft of XXX Cantos* and *The Pisan Cantos* that record his attempt to apprehend the structure of Pound's poem (see Figures 2.2 and 2.3). This technique is reminiscent of what Jackson refers to as "interleaving," the process by which, a century earlier, books could be bound with blank pages between pages of text for commentary; like marginalia, interleaving has an academic history, as students would include pages in course texts (33–4). Schooling himself and creating a guide, in his descriptions of the first 30 Cantos, Berryman worked from his Princeton mentor R. P. Blackmur's "Masks of Ezra Pound" (1933). Berryman's doing so recalls Pound's use of Ernest Fenollosa's translations.[41] The small size of Berryman's notes also resembles Pound's edition of Divus's *Odyssey*, "a serviceable crib, easily slipped into a pocket."[42]

On his page of *Cantos* notes, Berryman itemized the content of each Canto, through the beginning of the *Pisan Cantos* (see Figure 2.2). For

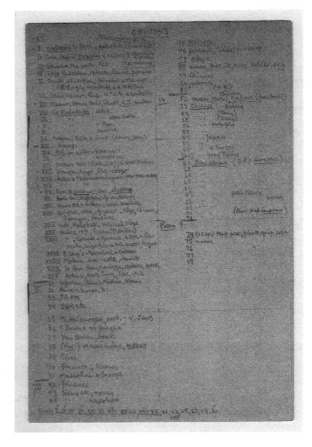

Figure 2.2 Berryman's notes in Pound's *XXX Cantos*, Minnesota.

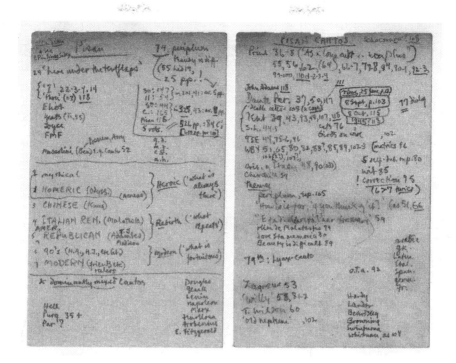

Figure 2.3 Berryman's notes in Pound's *Pisan Cantos*, Minnesota.

instance, he listed the scope of the references in Canto VII: "Eleanor, Homer, Ovid, Dante, H.J., [Henry James] modern."[43] Blackmur's essay preceded the publication of *The Pisan Cantos* (1948), and Berryman left most of the section devoted to this volume open, following the title with a question mark.[44] While near the end of his *Cantos* outline he noted the "tent," "friends, grief, [and] polit[ics]" of Canto 74 (see Figure 2.2), Berryman also devoted two other pages of notes to *The Pisan Cantos* that cover such aspects as its languages, historical periods, and allusions (see Figure 2.3). Consistent with his marginalia and the lists in the backs of his books, Berryman's *Pisan Cantos* notes compile not only the writers to whom Pound refers but also his references to their nicknames.

Berryman's two small pages of notes on *The Pisan Cantos* appear to resume where his prior outline ceased (Figure 2.3).[45] On the page to the left, Berryman listed first the page numbers on which Pound referred to himself. Beneath this cluster Berryman has included literary figures and contemporaries to whom Pound alluded, such as "TSE" and "WBY." At the bottom of the page, Berryman collected more colloquial references, including "Willy," for Yeats, and to the right listed Pound's predecessors, Browning, Swinburne, and Whitman.

Berryman's notes record his investment in Pound's range as a poet and translator.[46] Writing on the verso of his page of *Cantos* notes, Berryman considers Pound's rendering of time and space and his relation to it as poet—"page 3. At top Odys. xi to Hell"—and distinguished "Pound's physical x intellectual travel."[47] He subsequently noted Pound's attention to language and translation. Berryman observed the ways that Pound adapted older forms of languages: "Latin in old heroic Engl Saga – Style / as modified by modern (Pound)." These sketches take shape in Berryman's explanation of the contents of Pound's "Three Cantos" in his introduction to Pound's *Selected Poems*. The first encompasses

> [t]he Poet's, the Hero's, physical and mental travel: what can "I" expect? Persona, Odysseus-in-exile . . . descent to Hell[.] . . . Form: a depth-introduction, heroic Greek (Odyssey, xi) through Renaissance Latin (Divus) in old-heroic-English style as modified by modern style. So the first canto, about sacrifice to the enemy, acknowledgment of indebtedness, and outset.
>
> (FP, 266–7)

Berryman builds from Blackmur's essay in order to interpret Pound's use of others' translations. While Berryman may have desired distance from the New Criticism, he was engaged in and contributed to existing critical conversations.

Editing Pound

While he was at Princeton in 1945, Berryman accepted an offer from James Laughlin to edit Pound's *Selected Poems* for New Directions.[48] The introduction was to familiarize students and casual readers with his poetry (Barnhisel, 130). The inherent paradox was in the request to make Pound appear simple.[49] Berryman's understanding of Pound, as we have seen, was embedded in his larger consideration of Pound's sources and such critics as Blackmur's readings of *The Cantos*. In the introduction that Berryman prepared, he took up the issue of the relationship between texts and their predecessors in a way that responded to what he disagreed with in other critics' separation of form and content, validating Pound's synthesis in the *Cantos*.

Beginning in 1946, Pound's exchanges with Berryman were a combination of mentorship and desire for contact with the larger poetic world.[50] Pound filled pages with his erratic prose, objecting at the opening of one letter, "no! Write me all & often—I live only vicariously."[51] Eileen Simpson, Berryman's first wife, recalled that

> Pound began to bombard him [Berryman] with post cards, firing off sometimes two a day, full of recommendations, orders, miscellaneous bits of esoterica, jokes, epigraphs—the words so abbreviated, so

dressed up or down with capitals, exclamation points and parentheses
that it was a puzzle to make them out.[52]

(165)

Spending time with Pound enabled Berryman to gain more of a sense of
Pound's writing and reading practices. Berryman went with Lowell to visit
Pound at St. Elizabeths Hospital for the first time in 1948, and Berryman
returned for a second visit on his own.[53] In his later account of visiting
Pound, Berryman was attentive to the intellectual constraints that Pound
faced during his imprisonment in Pisa:

> The worst thing in the cage . . . was having no work to do: he was used
> to thinking from two to four at night, then writing it out when he got
> up in the morning; and instead there was the sun on him and he was
> trying to read Mencius in it.

("A Visit," 617)

Visiting Pound also presented the opportunity to discuss his poetry in re-
lation to modernism. Berryman recalled, "[t]o my saying I used to think
Personae the beginning of modern poetry, but now *Ripostes*: [Pound re-
sponded] 'Yes . . . yes'" ("A Visit," 619).

After Berryman published his first volume of poetry, *The Dispossessed*
(1948), he gave a copy to Pound that remains in his library at the Ransom
Center. Berryman inscribed the copy to "Dorothy & Ezra Pound / with ad-
miration & love."[54] To the left of Berryman's note, Pound added in pencil,
"On long loan. Do not return til," followed by a note that remains inexpli-
cable. While Pound may have parted with Berryman's volume in order to
promote it, he also marked his books with instructions.[55] Pound wrote in
and on his copies of his own books, indicating on the cover of his copy of
the *ABC of Reading* (1934), for instance, "Desk Copy please return to Ezra
Pound."[56] While, as we will see, Berryman preferred a particular type of
lead pencil, he and Pound both used pencil to annotate. Both poets would
also compile page numbers at the backs of their books, listing references to
which they could return.[57]

In his introduction to Pound's *Selected Poems*, Berryman argued that
"Pound has no matter *of his own*. Pound—who is even in the most surpris-
ing quarters conceded to be a 'great' translator—is best as a translator"
(*FP*, 258).[58] For Berryman, Pound and poets like him reshape materials
like a refinery does. The difference, however, is that a poem's layers are
visible. Berryman resolves that "[p]oetry is a palimpsest" (258).[59] His lay-
ered image also suggests the appearance of an annotated page. Near the
close of his introduction, Berryman gestured toward his own marginalia:
"Such, according to the notes I once made in my margin, is the beginning
of this famous 'formless' work, which is, according to one critic of distinc-
tion, 'not about anything'" (267).[60] Notes, too, bring form to formlessness.

Berryman's protagonist in "Wash Far Away" also taught with his anno-
tated book, "ransacking like a bookshop the formless minds" (368). As
Berryman's introduction was for new readers and students of Pound's po-
etry, his reference to his notes also models the practice of annotation.

In the wake of the controversy surrounding whether, following his arrest
for treason, Pound's *Pisan Cantos* should receive the Library of Congress's
Bollingen Prize for the best book of poetry published in 1948, William
Barrett argued in his introduction to the issue of the *Partisan Review*
that published Berryman's Pound essay that in it Berryman may have pre-
sented "the strongest possible case for Pound's having a subject matter as
a poet."[61] Berryman's argument presented a contrast to readings that sep-
arated Pound's form from his content because of its political implications.
As Lowell put it in 1948, reading of *The Pisan Cantos* involved "saying . . .
the content doesn't matter i.e. we enjoy Pound's matterless style."[62] Later,
in his discussion of *The Pisan Cantos*, Barrett similarly referred to "that
necessary aesthetic judgment that separates matter from form in a poem."[63]
In the following issue of the *Partisan Review*, Auden similarly underscored
"the excessive preoccupation of contemporary criticism with Form and its
neglect of Content."[64]

In his review copy of Cleanth Brooks's *The Well Wrought Urn* (1947),
Berryman disagreed with Brooks's consideration of poems "not in terms
of 'content' or 'subject matter' . . . but rather in terms of structure."[65]
For Hayden White, "the content of the form" is paradoxically "that nar-
rative, far from being merely a form of discourse that can be filled with
different contents . . . already possesses a content prior to any given ac-
tualization of it in speech or writing."[66] In White's terms, content or
genre brings its own conventions, and for Berryman these conventions
can include allusions to and incorporations of previous work. In the *Par-
tisan Review*'s "State of American Writing" (1948), Berryman continued
along similar lines:

> The nature of *experiment* in writing wants re-stating, and the return-
> to-form in poetry during the last ten years wants general study. Now
> the inevitable bias, in an academic criticism, against "experiment" and
> in favor of "form," is wretched equipment for this task.[67]

In his introduction to Pound's *Selected Poems*, Berryman cited Pound's crit-
ics in order to argue that poems are the product of influence:[68]

> It clearly troubles Eliot that the two first sections of "Near Perigord"
> resemble Browning, Pound's master, though the poem seems to him (as
> to me) beautiful and profound; this poem is extremely original in sub-
> stantial development. Now, though Blackmur is preferring derivation
> and Eliot is deprecating it, they appear to illustrate an identical disorder
> of procedure, that of a criticism which is content to consider in isolation
> originality of either matter *or* manner, without regard to the other, and

with small regard to degree. I term this a disorder rather than a defect, because with regard to a poetry as singular as Pound's, and with such diverse claims upon our attention, it is all but fatal to criticism.

(259)

The translations, to Berryman, are distinct works of art. Responding to Eliot and Blackmur, Berryman stressed that matter and manner are inseparable because of the way Pound complicates the combination or proportion of both elements.

Because he was writing an introduction, Berryman emphasized the possibility of understanding *The Cantos*, bringing cohesion to Pound's endeavor:

> I believe the critical view is that it is a "rag-bag" of the poet's interests, "a catalogue, his jewels of conversation." It can be read with delight and endless profit thus, if at any rate one understands that it is a work of versification, that is, a poem.
>
> (*FP*, 266)

Blackmur, by contrast, underscores Pound's parataxis and contingency, arguing,

> [t]he Cantos are not complex, they are complicated; they are not arrayed by logic or driven by pursuing emotion, they are connected because they follow one another, are set side by side . . . The Cantos are what Mr. Pound himself called them in a passage now excised from the canon, a rag-bag.[69]
>
> (Blackmur, 92)

The passage to which Blackmur referred appeared early in the first of Pound's "Three Cantos," published in *Poetry* magazine (1917):

> say I take your whole bag of tricks,
> Let in your quirks and tweaks, and say the thing's an art-form,
> Your *Sordello*, and that of the modern world
> Needs such a rag-bag to stuff all its thought in.[70]

Blackmur clarified and expanded his comparison, linking Pound's allusions in *The Cantos* to their contexts:

> we have a rag-bag of what Mr. Pound thinks is intelligent conversation about literature and history. As you pull out one rag, naturally, so well stuffed is the bag, you find it entangled with half the others. Since it is a poetical bag the entanglements are not as fortuitous as they at first seem, the connections may be examined, and some single pieces are large and handsome enough to be displayed alone.
>
> (93)

Blackmur's claim that readers must understand the interconnectedness of Pound's references echoes Berryman's own approach to annotating Pound's poem. As Blackmur elaborated,

> [e]ach person was someone, each letter written, each voice spoken, each deed historical—or each invented, cohesive power of obvious design or continuing emotion, cling together, a quilt in the patch work, a string of rags from the inexhaustible bag.
>
> (98–9)

While Blackmur argued that Pound's words form a design of available pieces, the jumble of rags also takes a shape that would differ if one spilled them from their container.[71]

Perhaps unsurprisingly, Pound characterized Berryman's introduction as too academic.[72] Writing to Berryman in December, Laughlin expressed concern as to "whether it [the essay] is not too difficult and too profound for the purpose. . . . and in some ways so difficult, that it would simply put the students off from reading the poetry."[73] Berryman replied, "[your] letter astonished me. My essay is deliberately SIMPLE-MINDED."[74] While Laughlin was attempting to be diplomatic, Pound reported to Laughlin that Berryman's introduction was "NOT good. it is clumsy. unreadable [sic] And the facts are not accurate . . . NOT stuff to go into a permanent volume as an introduction. which ought to point at essentials for the reader."[75] Strident that "[i]t is simply NOT an introduction at all," Pound stressed that Berryman devoted too much time to critical conversation instead of marketing *The Cantos* to less informed readers: "Berry[man] is criticizing the critics. NOT whetting anyone's appetite for the text" (*EPJL*, 179). Reclaiming his rag bag, Pound resolved that "Berry's [is] . . . a ragbag of EVERYTHING except an introd[uction]" (*EPJL*, 179). Unlike Blackmur, however, Pound does not propose that Berryman's scraps form a quilt. With regard to Berryman's scholarship, Pound volunteered that the essay "makes one or two points . . . The bit on the Cantos . . . [is] rather good" (*EPJL*, 179). He added to Laughlin, "make clear to him [Berryman] that E. did not object to his essay qua essay" (*EPJL*, 186). Pound later sent Berryman a "compliment on yr selection from the earlier stuff" adding, "@ any rate appreciate hard work."[76] Despite the rejection, Berryman published the essay in 1949 in the *Partisan Review* (Mariani, 218).

When Pound composed a forward to his *Selected Cantos* (1966), he reproduced his own lines from the Ur-Cantos, to which he alluded in his response to Berryman's introduction.[77] In simpler terms, what Pound proposes may be "the best introduction to the *Cantos*" is Pound's description of a "rag-bag."[78] As the next segment of this chapter illustrates, writing Pound's introduction informed Berryman's treatment of modern poetry as a lecturer and professor of humanities. Lowell understood Pound as a source from whom Berryman "learned the all-inclusive style, the high spirits, the flitting from subject to subject, irreverence, and humor."[79] Berryman's lectures flout convention at times in a fashion that echoes Pound's tone in his letters. Doing so enables Berryman to distance himself from aspects of modernism that he disliked.

Teaching

The following segment turns to Berryman's modern poetry lectures at the University of Cincinnati (1952) and teaching of a course called Humanities 54 at the University of Minnesota (1955–72). In addition to the materials Berryman prepared as a lecturer and teacher, his former students and colleagues' recollections provide a complementary narrative of the role of literary history in his approach to teaching and mentoring.

Recommending Berryman for a position as a Resident Fellow in Creative Writing (1948), Donald A. Stauffer, Princeton's English department chairman, praised Berryman's "particular ability of engaging the respect and rousing the best talents of the specially chosen students who are allowed to elect creative writing."[80] Bruce Berlind, one of the poets who came to know Berryman at Princeton,[81] similarly remembered that

> [f]riendship with John inevitably meant discipleship. It's not merely that he was older by ten or a dozen years, or that he was brilliant and a marvelous talker, or that he was publishing his poems in the "best" places. It wasn't even that we especially admired the poetry he was publishing then—those gnarled, impenetrable, postured pieces that are the latest in <u>The Dispossessed</u>. In part it was his monumental arrogance, which continuously asserted his superiority even when there was no question of competition. . . . he struck some of us . . . as the walking archetype of the brilliant, erratic, guilt-laden poet. Beneath all the posturing, he was somehow the real thing.[82]

Part of what enabled Berryman's convincing performance was the thoroughness of his reading and the background informing his gestures and statements. The poet William Meredith, also at Princeton in Berryman's time, recalled that "[h]e was formidable in his learning and in his pride of learning."[83]

While waiting for the publication of his first poetry volume, *The Dispossessed*,[84] Berryman articulated in the *Partisan Review* what he saw as the conflict between the materials one prepares for teaching and reading that would better inform his poetry:

> For poets and fiction writers, as for critics, it might be claimed that teaching is valuable because in a seat of learning one keeps on learning. I have no faith in the claim. . . . the writers I know outside universities read more, on the whole, more that counts, than those inside. I have no faith in the claim even for critics; and it is not widely enough understood that literary criticism is an activity which bears no relation whatever to good teaching.[85]

Berryman here was also rejecting the recommendation of his Columbia mentor, Mark Van Doren, who had suggested a potential appointment in a Great Books program in 1938, stressing that its focus "upon the classics, upon the tradition: the best emphasis in my opinion for a living poet, who can thereby become alive. Also, you will constantly be reading the best books: a superb opportunity for a critic of contemporary literature."[86]

In Berryman's ten Cincinnati lectures, he attended to poems of the previous generation and the present moment. On Tuesday and Thursday afternoons at four, Berryman spoke in 127 McMicken Hall, addressing an audience that was likely to have comprised faculty, students, and community members (Ames).[87] The lectures presented an opportunity for Berryman to discuss what he had come to value in the poems that preceded his own, and their contribution to a broader sense of modern poetry.

Modern poetry

The notes that Berryman prepared for his series of lectures as the George Elliston Chair of Poetry at Cincinnati in the spring of 1952 comprised a skeletal outline of the poems that he had selected to read and discuss.[88] Berryman's colleague, Van Meter Ames, however, typed copious notes that he sent to John Haffenden for his inaugural Berryman biography (Ames).[89] These notes, which remain with Haffenden's papers at Columbia University, provide a glimpse of the narrative Berryman brought to his treatment of modern poetry, particularly regarding Yeats, Pound, and Eliot.[90]

The subjects of Berryman's Cincinnati lectures ranged from Walt Whitman to Robert Lowell, enabling Berryman's assessment of contemporary poetry in light of what had preceded it. The university had publicized the lectures as "Commentary with readings." Beginning on Thursday, 21 February, Berryman delivered, "Modern Poetry—an introduction," which he followed on later dates with two lectures on Whitman, a lecture each on Hopkins, Yeats, and Pound, two lectures on Eliot, and one lecture on Auden, concluding with a lecture devoted to Lowell, Thomas, and other recent poets (Ames). With wit, Berryman proposed in his first lecture that

> Whitman is the greatest American poet. In my next lecture it will take five minutes to show that he is great. Read the 60-page <u>Song of Myself</u>. Eliot is the greatest living poet, and it will take two lectures to show his development.
>
> (Ames)

In the first Whitman lecture, Berryman underscored that his opinion was not typical of his time, stressing that

> Whitman is, without rival, the American poet. Yet in all the literary conversations I have had I have never heard anyone recommend or even

mention him. The cultivated, literary, academic audience ignores him. He is not being written about. It is a strange discrepancy between his being our national poet and the fact that 15 or 20 others in our poetry are more read and assented to. There is a curious unease and doubt about him.

(Ames)

Whitman had fallen out of favor among academics, perhaps due to the perception that he lacked difficulty. Berryman pointed out that Whitman "is very difficult in thought and means of expression, as difficult as Eliot" (Ames). Even so, however, Berryman qualified that "Song of Myself, 100 years old now, is not much more accessible now than then" (Ames). At the time, Pound's *Pisan Cantos* would have presented a recent example of difficult verse.

Perhaps in light of Berryman's experience editing Pound, the Bollingen controversy, or the enormity of *The Cantos*, Berryman had not included Pound in his preliminary draft for the Cincinnati lectures. Responding to Berryman's plans, William S. Clark urged "that many persons would wish you to include Pound as one of the poetic figures whom you would interpret in some detail."[91] The lecture notes that Berryman prepared, like his introduction to Pound's *Selected Poems*, feature Pound's translations. In his lecture notes, for instance, Berryman noted "(EP as translator)" beside his reference to "The River Merchant's Wife: A Letter," and lower on the page, listed page numbers to address in "Homage to Sextus Propertius."[92] In a note, Berryman also gestured toward the modern poets whom Pound encouraged: "early career: not only Eliot but Frost [, and] not only Joyce." In addition, after mentioning Eliot, Berryman indicated that Pound's efforts included "cut[ting] <u>Wasteland</u> [sic]."[93] In his lecture, Berryman clarified his approach:

> I shall talk about Pound only as a poet, not as a critic. There are several ways of approaching him as a poet: as dictator of the means of expression, comparable to Ben Jonson at the beginning of the 17th century; or as a profound energizer of poetry and criticism . . . or as an immense virtuoso, comparable to Stravinsky or Picasso, one of the few in the 20th century to have remade his art.
>
> (Ames)

The analogues that Berryman suggested recall his investment in poetic inheritances. Ames's notes also bring to light the rarity of Berryman's comparison of Pound to Jonson. As Berryman specified his focus in the lecture, he also referred his audience to the piece he had prepared as an introduction to Pound's *Selected Poems*: "I shall present him here as a poet and versifier (see my essay on him in the Partisan Review, April 1949)" (Ames).

As he delivered his lecture, Berryman refined the sense of Pound as a poet that he introduced. "Near Perigord," Berryman found, may be regarded "generally and, I think, correctly as Pound's best poem" (Ames). Before concluding his discussion of Pound's "Hugh Selwyn Mauberley," Berryman acknowledged that "we can't explain all the allusions and that would spoil the poem. So not to worry about them" (Ames). Berryman's handling of Pound's references suggests the range of readers who may have been in the audience. While Berryman devoted time in his Eliot lectures to his references, Berryman similarly cautioned that *The Waste Land* includes "[e]ndless allusions. Don't worry about them. Everything fundamental is made plain. The anthropological hocus pocus is unimportant, as compared with the human, personal, spiritual substance" (Ames).

Pound's role in Eliot's career anchored Berryman's first Eliot lecture. Berryman indicated at the top of the first page of his notes for the lecture that Eliot was "[y]ounger than WBY & EP, & appeared later, but first & 'original.'"[94] At the middle of the page, he enumerated Pound's contributions to Eliot's career, including that Pound "got him printed" and "cut [*The Waste Land*] W.L."[95] By contrast, Ames's more fulsome account brings to life the anecdotes that Berryman told, impressing upon his audience the measures to which Pound went to ensure the publication of Eliot's poems: "Pound got <u>Prufrock</u> printed in the Chicago <u>Poetry</u> magazine in 1915 by threatening to resign from the editorial staff if they didn't print it. And he was responsible for getting Eliot's other early work published." Berryman informed his audience that "Eliot says that after a nervous breakdown in Switzerland he wrote a sprawling poem from which Pound cut <u>The Waste Land</u>. This makes Pound directly the critic behind the most impressive poem in English of the century" (Ames). Even as Pound had a powerful influence on Eliot's career, however, Berryman clarified that "a poet of Eliot's size is fundamentally responsible for his own work, which remains extremely original" (Ames). In his own notes, Berryman had placed "original" in scare quotes. His doing so also questions the concept of originality, suggesting that what makes Eliot's work distinctive is in part due to the work of others.

Writing Pound's introduction and lecturing on modern poetry informed Berryman's subsequent development of a pedagogy that was Poundian in its extensiveness. As we will see, Berryman's Humanities courses at Minnesota enabled his interdisciplinary consideration of materials of larger historical and generic scope.[96]

Humanities

From the mid-fifties to the mid-sixties, Berryman taught twentieth-century literature, history, and culture in his Humanities 54 courses at Minnesota.[97] These courses demonstrated a form of modernist pedagogy in their range of texts and discourses.[98] However, unlike his prior readings of Pound, which focused on his poetics without attending to his politics, Berryman's Humanities 54 course materials addressed the literary, historical, and ethical complexity of modernism from a midcentury perspective.[99]

In a proposal that Berryman drafted for a Humanities 54 textbook (1958), he argued that the course's method of combining contents is indicative of the contribution of interdisciplinary studies as a field itself.[100] Because his colleagues in other departments at Minnesota did not feel that it could "represent a discipline," Berryman made demonstrating that this was the case "[t]he first purpose of this book."[101] Shifting from his previous investment in the "matter" of poetry to the "subject matter" of courses, Berryman continued,

> [i]t has also been contended . . . that interdisciplinary studies have no subject matter; indeed the term "subject-matter departments" is now regularly used . . . for all departments except mine. The second purpose of this book is to show that Humanities has a subject matter, and that the sort of things here studied is it.[102]

Berryman stressed that his textbook was innovative in "the <u>arrangement</u> of the materials and the points made about them."[103] For students' assignments, however, Berryman made his expectations clear: "Originality will not be expected. If I were reporting on my course in . . . psychoanalysis and literature, <u>of course</u> originality would be expected."[104]

Berryman's Humanities 54 syllabi reflect the course's cohesive and thematic design that accommodated chronological breadth.[105] The first unit addressed what Berryman on his 1966 syllabus called "Political and Social Confidence, Political and Moral Despair" (Figure 2.4), referring to fiction and primary sources concerning the Russian Revolution published within ten years of World War II. The texts included Edmund Wilson's *To the Finland Station: A Study in the Writing and Acting of History* (1940), Vladimir Lenin's *State and Revolution* (1917), Arthur Koestler's *Darkness at Noon* (1941), and George Orwell's *Nineteen Eighty-Four* (1949).

In 1965 and 1966 syllabi, Berryman placed Eliot and Joyce beneath the category, "Degradation, Nostalgia, affirmation, [sic] Religious Despair" (Figure 2.4). His language recalls that of the midcentury Joyce and Eliot criticism we encountered in Chapter 1. For instance, Berryman noted at the bottom of one page of notes on *The Waste Land*, "<u>Death-in-life</u>." He indicated "varieties of death" beside the opening of Eliot's first segment, "Burial of the Dead." Plath had similarly inscribed "varieties of death" at the beginning of her copy of poem (*Complete Poems and Plays*, 37). Berryman also noted beside "TSE" on a list of Humanities 54 themes, "paralysis of will despair" and "paralysis".[106] Such references allow us to see some of the ways that Berryman's teaching and understanding of modernism intersected with Plath's, even as the courses they taught differed.

After teaching Eliot's "The Love Song of J. Alfred Prufrock" and *The Waste Land*, Berryman devoted two class sessions to a selection of chapters from Joyce's *Ulysses*. In Berryman's copy of the novel, he compiled page numbers inside the back cover and indicated in the margins passages that

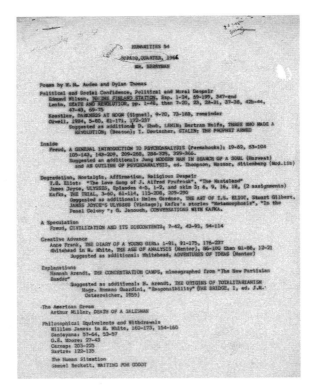

Figure 2.4 Berryman's Humanities 54 Syllabus, fall 1966, Teaching notes, box 1, folder titled, "Humanities 54," John Berryman Papers (Mss043), Minnesota.

suggested aspects of *The Waste Land*. In the "Circe" chapter, for instance, he noted a passage of dialogue reminiscent of Lil's abortion in "A Game of Chess."[107] In the *Ulysses* chapters that he assigned, Berryman had his students encounter Leopold Bloom before Stephen Dedalus. Berryman listed in his 1966 syllabus that students should read "Episodes 4–5, 1–2, and skim 3; 6, 9, 16, 18" (Figure 2.4).[108] Rearranging the readings emphasized the introduction of Joyce's Jewish protagonist. The remaining episodes Berryman selected had students navigate Bloom and Stephen's collective wanderings, concluding with "Eumaeus," in which Bloom brings Stephen home, and Molly Bloom's "Penelope" monologue.[109]

Anne Frank's *Diary of a Young Girl* (1947) was a text that Berryman sought to teach. In his proposal for a Humanities 54 textbook, Berryman notes that Frank's *Diary*

> constitutes in several ways the climax of the course, and from which the course fans out: [including] . . . explanations by Hannah Arendt . . .

into what used to be called logical positivism and French atheistic existentialism . . . into some consideration of justice, and into some prognostic suggestions about the question of survival.[110]

In what appear to be a series of midquarter exam questions from the fall of 1958, Berryman asked students to "[c]ontrast Anne Frank & Molly Bloom in temperament, interests, & character."[111] In a similar instance, Berryman noted a page number inside the back cover of his copy of D. H. Lawrence's *Lady Chatterley's Lover* (1928) that was "almost Exactly the end of Anne Frank's diary!" In the novel, Berryman added a line to mark the gamekeeper Mellors's exasperation as he desires to be with Constance Chatterley: "'If only there weren't so many other people in the world,'—he said lugubriously."[112] At the end of Anne Frank's *Diary*, Berryman drew two lines in the margin at the end of the final diary entry, which concludes: "what I could be, if . . . there weren't any other people living in the world."[113] Each example suggests an attempt to address characters' existence apart from the circumstances of modernity, before and during World War II.

Berryman's Humanities 54 courses invited students to consider the psychological dimensions of the atrocities of World War II alongside their reading of *The Waste Land*. His teaching materials include an outline of the evolution and current state of psychological treatment. Drawing on his own experience, he cautioned his students, "some of <u>you</u> will spend time in a mental hospital."[114] In response to Freud's *Civilization and Its Discontents*, Berryman requested that his students "[s]ummarize the nature of the instinctual renunciations demanded by culture, in Freud's view; and compare the dramatization of the consequences in <u>The Waste Land</u>."[115] For a final examination in winter of 1958, Berryman asked that students "[d]iscuss Hannah Arendt's picture of the concentration camps as an illustration of Freud's notion of aggression."[116] Berryman also proposed a more expansive question in an undated final exam:

> If Freud's description of our society as ill, in something like the way an individual mental patient is ill, producing symptoms, etc., draw on at least three other works read in the course (including Hannah Arendt's account of the purpose of the concentration camps) to illustrate the nature of and some of the results of this illness.[117]

The type of inquiry that Berryman's Humanities 54 courses pursued represents a midcentury version of what critics might now characterize as a cultural studies approach. In his interview with *The Paris Review* (1972), Berryman explained the way that his scholarship informed his teaching of humanities courses:

> I give courses in the history of civilization, and when I first began teaching here I nearly went crazy. . . . I worked it out once, and it took me nine hours to prepare a fifty-minute lecture. I have learned much

more from giving these lecture courses than I ever learned at Columbia or Cambridge. It has forced me into areas where I wouldn't otherwise have been, and since I am a scholar, these things are connected. I make myself acquainted with the scholarship.[118]

Berryman added that the reading for the humanities courses proved more compatible with his interests as a writer: "I wouldn't recommend [teaching creative writing] . . . to a poet. It is better to teach history or classics or philosophy or the kind of work I do here in the humanities."[119] As we will see in the next segment, the form of the long poem in *The Dream Songs* enabled Berryman's combination of innovation and allusion within the stanza form he had developed. In Lowell's words, Berryman's "bookishness . . . lets him draw on whatever models will serve him."[120] Emulating certain modernist techniques, Berryman's decisions privileged his poem's aesthetic.

The Dream Songs

Before removing Berryman's books from the Minneapolis house where he had lived since 1964,[121] Richard J. Kelly made a map so that scholars could see the order of Berryman's surroundings.[122] Berryman stored his Shakespeare collection in his study with a selection of the books he taught frequently. In the dining room, Berryman displayed, in the following order, a substantial portion of his Yeats collection, his copies of Pound's *Cantos LII-LXXI*, *The Pisan Cantos*, *A Draft of XXX Cantos*, *Homage to Sextus Propertius*, *Polite Essays*, and *The Letters of Ezra Pound*, and volumes of poetry of which Berryman was the author.[123] Berryman's placement of his own poems after those of Yeats and Pound symbolizes Berryman's continuation and reinvention of their contributions to modernism.[124]

The form, style, and content of *The Dream Songs* reflect Berryman's selectivity in engaging with his modernist predecessors.[125] Allen Tate called *Homage to Mistress Bradstreet* (1953) "a fourth to the three first-rate long poems by Americans in this century—the others being by Pound (*Cantos*), Eliot, (*Wasteland* [sic]), and (Hart) Crane (*The Bridge*)" (qtd. in *WD*, 298).[126] Perhaps in response to Tate, Berryman explained in his acceptance speech for the National Book Award (1969), "I set up the Bradstreet poem as an attack on *The Waste Land* . . . no anthropology, no Tarot pack, no Wagner" (qtd. in Haffenden, 352).[127] Tate had considered *Homage to Mistress Bradstreet* to be a part of a tradition that Berryman had distanced himself from. Brendan Cooper sees Berryman's statement that *Homage to Mistress Bradstreet* would be "spectacularly NOT *The Waste Land*" as "a generative hostility, a postwar anxiety of influence in which opposition and antagonism exist as catalysts for dialogue and interaction."[128] Following Pound's example, Berryman addresses Eliot by his nickname in *The Dream Songs*. Ultimately, the poem benefits from Berryman's reading and teaching of modernism, engaging and transforming modernism's midcentury presence.[129]

Berryman had argued in his introduction to Pound's *Selected Poems* that the issue at stake in addressing Pound's poetry was not to "consider in isolation originality of either matter *or* manner, without regard to the other, and with small regard to degree" (*FP*, 259).[130] Berryman also looked to Pound with regard to the form and structure of *The Dream Songs*. Publishing the first installment of *77 Dream Songs*, Berryman expressed his concern to Lowell: "I can't help feeling that it's *irresponsible* to publish—not 16 and 30 cantos as Pound did—but a large number of sections" (Qtd. in Haffenden, 327). In *The Dream Songs*, Berryman also shared Pound's use of song units. As a student in 1937, Berryman had admired "the hard vigor of Pound's versification, and tightening his stanza forms by comparison with good speech" (*WD*, 91).[131] When Berryman annotated his copy of *Cantos LII-LXXI*, he also expressed his excitement over Pound's stressed syllables, writing, "spondees!" to the right of Canto LII.[132]

While Pound's incorporation of writers and artistic figures' names blended with his enigmatic combination of phrases, terms, places, and objects, Berryman's use of writers' names in *The Dream Songs* speaks both to the content of his reading and to the contexts suggested by his poetry. These references provide a form of Pound's luminous details, "a sudden insight into circumjacent conditions."[133] As Pound clarified, "[t]he artist seeks out the luminous detail and presents it. He does not comment."[134] The detail's vibrancy also recalls Berryman's account of close reading in "Wash Far Away": "seizing one brightness, another, another, [and] locking them in place" (*FP*, 372). While writing *The Dream Songs*, Berryman adapted this metaphor with regard to his poems: "I've written out 14 new songs in the last week, and moreover have made a breakthrough: I'm now doing lower-keyed, *narrative & necessary* architecture, as well as flashing units as usual" (*WD*, 350).[135]

In Berryman's well-known explanation, his persona in *The Dream Songs* is

> an imaginary character (not the poet, not me) named Henry, a white American in early middle age sometimes in blackface, who has suffered an irreversible loss and talks about himself, sometimes in the first person, sometimes in the third, sometimes in the second; he has a friend, never named, who addresses him as Mr Bones [sic] and variants, thereof.[136]

In the Eliotic, epigrammatic lines that form his predominately three stanza *Dream Songs*, Berryman's approach enabled his manipulation of his contents and construction of dialogue.[137] The conventions of Vaudeville stage comedy informed one of the more prominent forms of exchange among Berryman's speakers in *The Dream Songs*. As Helen Vendler has illustrated, the protagonist, Henry, and his "friend, never named," represent end men who would joke between acts of a performance. The straight man contributed to the principal actor's completion of jokes. It was also common in

Vaudeville and minstrel performances, Vendler notes, for end men to refer to each other during their routines using nicknames.[138] Berryman resituates Pound's allusive strategy in *The Dream Songs*, particularly when he refers to Eliot as Possum.[139]

Following Pound's placement of lines and allusions in unfamiliar contexts in *The Cantos*, in the second stanza of Dream Song 53 Berryman gives Eliot speech regarding popular culture in the voice of Henry's interlocutor:

> —I seldom *go* to *films*. They are too exciting, / said the Honourable Possum. / —It takes me so long to read the 'paper, / said to me one day a novelist hot as a firecracker, / because I have to identify myself with everyone in it, / including the corpses, pal'.[140]
>
> (*DS*, 60; lines 7–10)

As an interlocutor in Berryman's scheme, Eliot here contradicts himself; as an end man he speaks against the form of entertaining to which he contributes, not unlike his end notes to *The Waste Land* undermine the quality of his poem. While critics have since attended in greater detail to the ways that Eliot's poetry combined high and low culture, including film, Berryman had acknowledged in his Cincinnati lecture that "A Game of Chess" "divides into the wrought scene of the society woman and the pub scene of life horribly futile at bottom" (Ames).[141] The context in which Berryman places Eliot in the poem also extends the simplicity of Pound's nickname.[142] The behavior of a possum and the light verse of *Old Possum's Book of Practical Cats* (1939) offset the gravity that Eliot's stature commands. Berryman also recalled that during a visit to St. Elizabeths, Pound "showed me his new way of writing . . . 'Pos O. M.'"[143] Berryman's British spelling of the title he bestows upon Eliot in Dream Song 53 ("Honourable Possum") suggests his citizenship while distinguishing his persona from the rhetoric of film and newspapers. As a student in Cambridge, Berryman had found

> [t]he temptation is very great to identify one's self with the rich valid history of English literature—Eliot could not resist it, and Pound has gone further in taking European culture for his personal tradition. But you never get there, I think: what you write is pastiche in . . . [Eliot's *Murder in the Cathedral*] and the *Cantos*.[144]
>
> (*WD*, 62)

In a fashion that gestures to Pound's range of allusions, in the final stanza of Dream Song 53, Berryman presents an interdisciplinary critique of intellectual and mass culture. The philosophers and poets that the narrator names present a contrast to Eliot's contributions in *The Waste Land* notes:

> Kierkegaard wanted a society, to refuse to read 'papers, / . . . / Tiny Hardy, toward the end, refused to say *anything*, / a programme adopted

early on by long Housman, / and Gottfried Benn / said:–We are using
our own skins for wallpaper and we cannot win.

(Lines 13–18)

Suggesting here the existence of an intellectual discourse that exists apart
from the media also gestures toward Pound's statement that poetry is "news
that stays news" and poets are "antennae of the race."[145]

Later in Dream Song 224, Berryman shifted from dialogue to narrative,
meditating on Pound's august stature on the occasion of Eliot's funeral.[146]
Berryman's poem gestures toward a potential state of poetry after *The
Cantos* are complete and without Pound as a powerful influence. In doing
so, Berryman also underscores his own contribution to the perpetuation
and reinvention of modernist poetics.

Berryman's Dream Song 224, titled "Eighty," depicts Pound as an aged,
silent prophet whose reign is near completion. Pound's physical and liter-
ary presence is dwindling. In the first stanza, he is alone, pale, and infirm:
"Lonely in his great age, Henry's old friend / leaned on his burning cane . . .
Pound white as snow / bowed to them with his thoughts—it's hard to know
them though / for the old man sang no word" (*DS*, 243; lines 1–6). Ber-
ryman's phrasing throughout combines the colloquial and simplistic with
the nostalgic: "Gone. Gone them wine-meetings, gone green grasses / of
the picnics of rising youth" (lines 8–9). What Pound does say will be sig-
nificant, not a casual, irritated mechanical movement of the tongue, but
one that merits respect: "Gone all, slowly. Stately, not as the tongue / wor-
ries the loose tooth, wits as strong as young, / only the albino body fail-
ing" (10–12). The rhyme of "tongue" and "young" suggests that despite
his weak body, Pound's voice retains its power. Berryman begins the final
stanza with an obfuscating line gesturing toward the impact of Pound's
aesthetic: "Where the smother clusters pinpoint insights clear" (13). In the
poem's closing lines, Berryman's speaker alludes to Pound's conclusion of
The Cantos, asking, "[t]he last words are here? / What, in the world, will
they be?" (14–15).

Reflecting on his experience meeting Pound, Berryman recounted learn-
ing that Pound "had gone to London to learn from Yeats how to write
poetry . . . Exactly as I did, a quarter-century later [in 1937]" ("A Visit,"
617).[147] In Dream Song 312, Berryman returned to Pound in one of the
poems in his late series of *Dream Songs* set in Dublin (Section VII; Dream
Songs 279–379).[148] For Berryman, Yeats presented a means of returning
to Pound and poetic innovation: "For years then I forgot you, I put you
down, / ingratitude is the necessary curse / of making things new" (*DS*, 243;
lines 7–10).[149] Addressing making "things" new instead of making "it"
new, Berryman suggests the "matter" of Pound's poetry. Closing with an
image of "making things" like a "refinery" indicates material production.
In his introduction to Pound's *Selected Poems*, Berryman similarly called
Pound "the motor" in Yeats's poetic development (*FP*, 254).[150] As the "it"

in Pound's aphorism signifies tradition, the process captures Berryman's ability in *The Dream Songs* to sustain and reinvent modernist discourse.[151]

In his responses to Pound, Berryman reflects his attention to the integral role of history in the study and continuation of modernist discourse. Berryman's assessments of the present context in his teaching notes emulate Pound's strategies in the *Pisan Cantos* and anticipate Berryman's range in *The Dream Songs*. A central difference between both poets, however, lies in Berryman's investment in the ethical complexity of artistic expression at midcentury, which emerged in the humanities courses that he taught. As he returned to Pound's aphorism, Berryman underscored in *The Dream Songs* that modernism too must be made new.

***

In the fall of 1968, Houghton Mifflin requested that Sexton select seven readers for the proofs of her new book, *Love Songs* (1969). From the list they provided, she was to "check off seven names that you think would be most effective. These people will receive proofs with a note . . . Others will be sent books with a special letter."[152] From the numbered list of 16 poets and critics, Sexton initially checked the misspelled, "John Beryman," but in an afterthought, crossed it out.[153] Her decision may signify any number of concerns such as her familiarity with other figures on the list.[154] Hughes had invited Sexton and Berryman to read their work in London at the Poetry International Festival in July 1967.[155] While Berryman had been scheduled to read twice in the festival, as Middlebrook recounts, he did not appear for his first reading, and Sexton read in his place during the same session as Auden and Pablo Neruda (*AS*, 278).[156] Regardless of the fact that they may have met in England, Sexton reconsidered having Berryman read *Love Songs*. More boldly, Sexton's eliminated check mark suggests that she feared his gaze as a reader, particularly of her late lyrics with predominately feminine subjects. Perhaps considering his intimidating stature, she chose that he receive a book, but not critique an advanced proof.[157] With this small mark, Sexton indicated that she changed her mind about having Berryman evaluate her work.

Following Berryman's allusions to his predecessors and contemporaries in *The Dream Songs*, Sexton began her unpublished poem, "March 4th": "The high ones, Berryman said, die, die, die" (*Complete Poems*, 601; lines 1–2). While one might assume that the poem refers to Berryman's suicide, it had not occurred yet.[158] Sexton was responding to Berryman's Dream Song 36, which begins, "The high ones die, die. They die" (*DS*, 40; line 1). In doing so, she defers to him as an influence. Both Sexton and Berryman were also pedagogically innovative. As we will see in the next chapter, Sexton taught a course on her own poetry and shared her own poem drafts with those in the class. Teaching in this way, she introduced students to the creative process and invited their feedback on her work.

Notes

1 Berryman was teaching "English Composition: Practice in Writing Fiction." *Harvard Summer School Final Catalogue* 1954, Official Register of Harvard University, LI, No. 4 (1954), Harvard University Archives. John Berryman, *We Dream of Honour: John Berryman's Letters to His Mother*, ed. Richard J. Kelly (New York: Norton, 1988), 259, 283; hereafter cited in the text as *"WD."* See also John Berryman, *Berryman's Shakespeare: Essays, Letters and Other Writings of John Berryman*, ed. John Haffenden (New York: Farrar, Straus and Giroux, 1999); hereafter cited in the text as *"JBS."*

2 Plath had already taken Shakespeare. See also *UJ*, 543–6.

3 Philip Levine has recalled his unfamiliarity with Berryman a year earlier: "in 1953 his reputation was based on *The Dispossessed*, that first book, and it was no larger than it should have been." Levine, "Mine Own John Berryman," 19.

4 *Harvard Summer School Final Catalogue* 1954, page 67.

5 Plath lived in Bay State Apartments 1572 Massachusetts Avenue, apartment 4 (*LV1*, 781–2). Berryman lived at 7 Ware Street. Letter of "[7 July 1954?]" (*WD*, 259; bracket and question mark by editor). According to Google Maps, this is 0.8 miles and a four-minute drive or 0.7 miles and a 14 or 15-minute walk, depending on whether one walks through or around Harvard Yard. Google Maps accessed 8 February 2015.

6 See also John Haffenden, correspondence with William Arrowsmith, 9 March 1976. John Haffenden Collection of John Berryman Papers, 1952–1978, Rare Book & Manuscript Library, Columbia University Libraries, New York, NY; hereafter cited in the text as "Haffenden-Berryman Papers."

7 See also Jeffery Meyers, *Manic Power: Robert Lowell and His Circle* (New York: Arbor House, 1987), 140–1.

8 John Berryman, *The Freedom of the Poet* (1966; New York: Farrar, Straus and Giroux, 1976); hereafter cited in the text as *"FP."* See also E. M. Halliday, *John Berryman and the Thirties: A Memoir* (Amherst: University of Massachusetts Press, 1987); hereafter cited in the text as "Halliday."

9 As Jackson argues in *Marginalia*, "[t]he essential and defining character of the marginal note throughout its history is that it is a responsive kind of writing permanently anchored to preexisting written words" (81). I thank Daniel L. Manheim for introducing me to "Wash Far Away" in his call for papers for the American Literature Association Conference in 2006.

10 See also Lea Baechler, "A 'Deeper—Deepest—Acquaintance' with the Elegy: John Berryman and 'Wash Far Away,'" in *Recovering Berryman: Essays on a Poet*, ed. Richard J. Kelly and Alan K. Lathrop (Ann Arbor: University of Michigan Press, 1993), 129.

11 Combining nineteenth-century poetics and Baudelaire, Marjorie Perloff has characterized Berryman and Lowell as "*Poètes Maudits* of the Genteel Tradition." As such, she explains that Berryman presents an "outsider poet, alienated from his society, who is really an insider, the quintessential fellowship holder and prize winner" (32). As Perloff observes, Lowell and Berryman combined academic prestige and psychological instability (33). Coming after modernism, as Perloff acknowledges, however, Berryman and Lowell differed "from their Modernist predecessors [in] . . . their single-minded *literariness*" (33). Marjorie Perloff, "*Poètes Maudits* of the Genteel Tradition: Lowell and Berryman," *American Poetry Review* 12, no. 3 (May/June 1983).

12 Robert Lowell, "The Poetry of John Berryman" (1964), in *Collected Prose*, ed. Robert Giroux (New York: Farrar, Straus and Giroux, 1987), 108. See also Travisano, 28.

13 Robert Lowell, "For John Berryman, 1914–1972" (1972), in *Collected Prose*, ed. Robert Giroux (New York: Farrar, Straus and Giroux, 1987), 111.

14 Stephen [Stephanie] Burt, "My Name Is Henri: Contemporary Poets Discover John Berryman," in *Reading the Middle Generation Anew: Culture, Community, and Form in Twentieth-Century American Poetry*, ed. Eric Haralson (Iowa City: University of Iowa Press, 2006), 233.

15 Twenty-eight of Berryman's books are housed in the William Meredith Collection of John Berryman Papers and Library, 1952–1972, Rare Book and Manuscript Library, Columbia University, New York, NY. Other books are in the John Berryman Papers (Mss043), Upper Midwest Literary Archives, University of Minnesota Libraries, Minneapolis, Minnesota; hereafter cited in the text as "Minnesota." Richard J. Kelly, *John Berryman's Personal Library: A Catalogue* (New York: Peter Lang, 1999); hereafter cited in the text as "Kelly." Kelly lists 3,257 books, not including 387 periodicals with periodicals, 3,644 (411, 415–33). See also Richard J. Kelly, "Introduction" to *Recovering Berryman: Essays on a Poet*, ed. Richard J. Kelly and Alan K. Lathrop (1993; Ann Arbor: University of Michigan Press, 1996), 5, 6.

16 See Harold Bloom, ed., *Modern Critical Views: John Berryman* (New York: Chelsea House, 1989), which includes Edward Mendelson, "How to Read Berryman's *Dream* Songs," 53–70 and Jerome Mazzaro, "The Yeatsian Mask: John Berryman," 111–32. See also Richard J. Kelly, preface to *"After Thirty Falls:" New Essays on John Berryman*, ed. Philip Coleman and Philip McGowan (New York: Rodopi, 2007), xvi. Other critics have addressed Berryman's poems and the form of the elegy, minstrelsy, and impersonality. For instance, see Samuel Fisher Dodson, *Berryman's Henry* (Netherlands: Rodopi, 2006) and Peter Maber, "'So-called *black*': Reassessing John Berryman's Blackface Minstrelsy," *Arizona Quarterly* 64, no. 4 (Winter 2008): 129–49.

17 In 1945, Berryman accepted an offer from James Laughlin to edit and compose an introduction for Pound's *Selected Poems* for New Directions. Letter, Berryman to Laughlin, 30 July [1945], box 30, Minnesota. While Hugh Witemeyer dates this letter as 1946, it is probably 1945, as Berryman also mentions his essay "The Imaginary Jew" (1945). In what is probably a subsequent letter from Berryman to Laughlin, 27 September 1945, Berryman refers to the same amount of money (box 30, Minnesota). Hugh Witemeyer, "The Making of Pound's *Selected Poems* (1949) and Rolfe Humphries' Unpublished Introduction," *Journal of Modern Literature* XV, no. 1 (Summer 1988): 74. Witemeyer cites a copy of this letter in James Laughlin's personal files. See also Gregory Barnhisel, *James Laughlin, New Directions, and the Remaking of Ezra Pound* (Amherst: University of Massachusetts Press, 2005); hereafter cited in the text as "Barnhisel."

18 Dates and titles are from Richard J. Kelly, *John Berryman: A Checklist* (Metuchen, NJ: Scarecrow Press, 1972), xxxiii–xxxiv. Theodore Leinwand emphasizes that Berryman was the Oldham Shakespeare Scholar at Cambridge. Theodore Leinwand, "Berryman's Shakespeare/Shakespeare's Berryman," *The Hopkins Review* 2, no. 3 (Summer 2009), 389; hereafter cited in the text as "Leinwand." This chapter of *Annotating Modernism* investigates the ways in which Berryman's archival materials record the relationship among what his former student, Peter Stitt, linked in the title of his essay, "John Berryman: His Teaching, His Scholarship, His Poetry," in *Recovering Berryman: Essays on a Poet*, ed. Richard J. Kelly and Alan K. Lathrop (1993; Ann Arbor: University of Michigan Press, 1996): 43–56.

19 Berryman referred to these bibliographic techniques in a proposal for a book based on one of his humanities courses: "Shakespearean textual criticism (recension, editorial decision, conjectural emendation)." John Berryman,

"Teaching Notes/Class Files," box 1, folder 10, Minnesota. Haffenden also notes in his introduction to *John Berryman's Shakespeare* that when Berryman entered the field, W. W. Greg had combined bibliographical work and textual criticism. Haffenden explains that

> Peter W. M. Blayney, in the introduction to his majestic *The Texts of "King Lear" and their Origins*, Vol. I (1982), finds it necessary—in order to clear the ground for a fresh analysis of the texts—to take [W. W.] Greg severely to task on two specific points. His first complaint is that Greg muddles his definitions of the areas of study that constitute "bibliography." There are in fact three related areas of study: (i) "pure" bibliography (dealing with books as material objects), (ii) textual criticism, which is strictly non-bibliographical, and (iii) the 'metacritical' form of textual criticism, which includes the science or art of conjectural emendation. Greg's misleading, and indeed damaging, answer to the problem was to collapse the first two of those three distinct disciplines when, in "Bibliography—An Apologia" (1932), he coined the term "critical bibliography" to cover the whole case and subsequently to argue, in his influential lecture, "The Function of Bibliography in Literary Criticism Illustrated in a Study of the Text of *King Lear*'"(1933), that in any case bibliography and textual criticism are "the same."
>
> (*JBS*, xxxi)

20 Letter of 31 January 1937. See also *WD*, 2, 44.
21 Letter of 15 March 1938. Berryman purchased in London, for instance, W. B. Yeats's *Celtic Twilight: Men and Women, Dhouls and Faeries* (London: Lawrence and Bullen, 1893), former owner Berryman, Minnesota. Berryman inscribed his copy, "12 April 1937."
22 Berryman noted that this reference appears on pages, 211–2. W. B. Yeats, *A Vision* (London: T. Werner Laurie Ltd., 1925), former owner Berryman, Minnesota. He inscribed the volume, "London / 30 September 1936." Berryman's second copy of *A Vision* contains "A Packet for Ezra Pound," which Berryman also marked. He inscribed this copy, "John Berryman 1937." W. B. Yeats, *A Vision* (London: MacMillan & Co., Ltd., 1937), former owner Berryman, Minnesota. Berryman also noted Pound's listed references to "Yeats 11, 14," "H. J.," and "Eliot 20" in his fine edition of *Hugh Selwyn Mauberley* (The Ovid Press, 1920), former owner Berryman, Minnesota.
23 Kelly, *John Berryman: A Checklist*.
24 Kelly recounts that in Cambridge, Berryman "began in earnest the book buying which, over the years, would form his remarkable collection of elegant editions of most of the important English and American poets" (*WD*, 44). Eileen Simpson adds that Berryman "owed money to every bookseller in Boston. He owed Clare College so much that they had impounded the splendid library he had acquired in London and Cambridge" (75). Eileen Simpson, *Poets in Their Youth* (1982; New York: Farrar, Straus, and Giroux, 1990); hereafter cited in the text as "*Poets in Their Youth*. After moving to Minneapolis (1955), Berryman exclaimed, "my books have arrived from Iowa!!!!!! So that I have the core of my own Sh'n [Shakespearean] collection to work with" (*WD*, 290). Writing from Minneapolis in 1958, however, he "still cherish[ed] hopes of soon getting my library out of storage in Princeton: I need it" (316).
25 Letter of 27 October 1941. See also Simpson and Kelly, *John Berryman: A Checklist*.
26 Letter of 16 May 1946.
27 Letter, Arrowsmith to Haffenden, 9 March 1976, page 3. The third page of the letter is dated 9 March, and the second page of the letter is dated 8 March, Haffenden-Berryman Papers. John Berryman, Faculty and Professional Staff

files, Subgroup 4: E, AC107.04, Princeton University Archives, Department of Special Collections, Princeton University Library, Princeton, NJ; hereafter cited in the text as "Princeton." In Haffenden's biography, he notes that William Arrowsmith was Berryman's student (164).

28 Berryman added,

> [i]t was very difficult to get the Librarian at the Gregg Institute to understand that I do not share her generalized interest in shorthand – that my attention to it stops in the year 1608—but when I succeeded she told me that Mr [John Robert] Gregg has a copy of [Timothy] Bright's 1588 treatise *[Characterie: An arte of Shorte, Swifte and Secret Writing by Character]*, of which I have only seen facsimiles heretofore, and will bring it into New York . . . On Peter Bales and John Willis, who invented the more likely system, she had nothing – like everyone else. It is the devil: the Quarto text, wretched from any other point of view; is unutterably good from the early-stenographic point of view.
>
> (*WD*, 211)

Letter of 3 October [1944]. *Berryman's Shakespeare* contains the note: "It is not certain that we possess even all the systems *published* by 1607; of three registered in 1621, none has survived" (*JBS*, 206). See also 249.

29 Letter, Arrowsmith to Haffenden, 9 March 1976, Haffenden-Berryman Papers.

30 See Leinwand, 386–7.

31 H. R. D. Anders, *Shakespeare's Books: A Dissertation on Shakespeare's Reading and the Immediate Sources of His Works* (Berlin: Publisher & Printer Georg Reimer, 1904), 7. Anders begins with section on Shakespeare's "school-books." He explains in the preface, "[t]he present work was intended to serve as an introduction to a new edition of Collier-Hazlitt's 'Shakespeare's Library'" (XIV).

32 This lecture dates from 1969 to 1970 (*JBS*, 28). Berryman's footnote, reproduced in *JBS*, cites scholarship dating from 1938, 1949, 1950, 1951 (*JBS*, n. 24, 368–9), so his evidence could have been collected earlier.

33 Leinwand argues that Berryman's *Dream Songs* "drew heavily on the habits of textual scholarship rooted in Berryman's 'Shakespearian study'" (397).

34 See also Poirier, 104–5.

35 John Berryman, "A Tribute [To Ezra Pound on his Eightieth Birthday]," *Michigan Quarterly Review* 45, no. 4 (Fall 2006), 624. Originally published in *Agenda* 4, no. 2 (October/November 1965).

36 See also Meyers, 140, 148.

37 Among these were the following: Pound, *Cantos LII-LXXI* (Norfolk, CT: New Directions, 1940); Pound, *The Classic Anthology Defined by Confucius* (Cambridge, MA: Harvard University Press, 1954); Pound, *Culture* (Norfolk, CT: New Directions, 1938), printed in England and published in London under the title *Guide to Kulchur*; Pound, *A Draft of XXX Cantos* (New York: Farrar & Rinehart, 1935); Pound, *Eleven New Cantos: XXXI-XLI* (New York: Farrar & Rinehart, 1934); Pound, *The Fifth Decad of Cantos* (Norfolk, CT: New Directions, 1937); Pound, *Homage to Sextus Propertius* (London: Faber and Faber, 1934); Pound, *Make It New: Essays by Ezra Pound* (New Haven, CT: Yale University Press, 1935); Pound, *Polite Essays* (London: Faber and Faber, 1937); Pound, *The Pisan Cantos* (New York: New Directions, 1948); Pound, *Selected Poems*, ed. T. S. Eliot (London: Faber and Faber, 1934); Pound, *Patria Mia: A Discussion of the Arts and Their Use and Future in America* (Chicago, IL: Ralph Fletcher Seymour, 1950); Pound, *Personae* (New York: Boni and Liveright, 1926); Pound, *The Letters of Ezra Pound: 1907–1941* (New York: Harcourt Brace, 1950); *Certain Noble Plays*

of Japan: From The Manuscripts of Ernest Fenollosa, Chosen and Finished by Ezra Pound, trans. Ernest Fenollosa (Churchtown, Dundrum: The Cuala Press, 1916); Pound, *Hugh Selwyn Mauberley*; and F. R. Leavis, *How to Teach Reading: A Primer for Ezra Pound* (Cambridge: Gordon Frazer, The Minority Press, 1932), former owner Berryman, Minnesota. See also Kelly, *John Berryman's Personal Library*, 213, 278–0. Regarding Pound's allusions to his contemporaries in *The Pisan Cantos*, see Ira B. Nadel, "Introduction: Understanding Pound," in *The Cambridge Companion to Ezra Pound*, ed. Ira B. Nadel (New York: Cambridge University Press, 1999), 7. Archivists at Minnesota were unable to locate Berryman's copy of T. S. Eliot's *Collected Poems*, which Kelly lists in *John Berryman's Personal Library*.

38 Among the techniques that Jackson identifies in *Marginalia*, the tendency of readers to create their own indexes is one that both Berryman and Pound shared (*Marginalia*, 37).

39 Berryman's annotations on the back flyleaf of Pound's *A Draft of XXX Cantos*, former owner Berryman, Minnesota.

40 Berryman's notes in the back of *Ezra Pound's Cantos LII-LXXI*, former owner Berryman, Minnesota.

41 R. P. Blackmur, "The Masks of Ezra Pound," 1933, in *Form and Value in Modern Poetry* (1946; rpt. New York: Doubleday, 1957), 93–5; hereafter cited in the text as "Blackmur." Regarding Berryman and Blackmur, see also James D. Bloom, *The Stock of Available Reality: R. P. Blackmur and John Berryman* (Lewisburg: Bucknell University Press, 1984).

42 Hugh Kenner, *The Pound Era* (1971; rpt. Berkeley: University of California Press, 1973), 350.

43 Berryman's notes inside Pound's *A Draft of XXX Cantos*, Minnesota.

44 Ibid.

45 In addition to the pencil marks with which we have observed Berryman filled his library, (and his professor in "Wash Far Away," close reading, "pencil in hand" [*FP*, 373]), the dark print of Berryman's *Pisan Cantos* notes suggests his "soft lead pencils . . . Eberhard Faber, 6325, Ebony, Jet black, extra smooth" (*WD*, 315). Letter of 1958. In an interview with the author, Kate Donahue remembered that Berryman preferred pencils of a dark lead. While he annotated in pencil, he did inscribe the inside covers of his books, perhaps after purchasing them, more often with blue or black ink, often with a long slash beneath his last name or his initials. The protagonist of "Wash Far Away" also prepared "a dozen notes made compactly on a small yellow pad," not unlike the appearance of pages in some of Berryman's books at Columbia (*FP*, 374). Henry in Dream Song 261 uses "A stub point . . . / . . . of more dignity than my typewriter, / than my marvellous [sic] pencils darker" (*DS*, 280, lines 13–15). See also Haffenden, 153. For the type of pencil, see http://www.pencilthings.com/servlet/the-752/Design-Ebony-Sketching-Pencil/Detail, accessed 14 December 2008.

46 Regarding Berryman and Pound, see also Stitt, "John Berryman: His Teaching, His Scholarship, His Poetry," 54.

47 Berryman's notes inside *A Draft of XXX Cantos*, Minnesota.

48 Letter, Berryman to Laughlin, 27 September 1945, Minnesota. See also Barnhisel.

49 See also *WD*, 230–1 and Richard Taylor, "The texts of *The Cantos*," in *The Cambridge Companion to Ezra Pound*, ed. Ira B. Nadel (New York: Cambridge University Press, 1999), 172. Berryman mailed the introduction on 30 November 1948 (*WD*, 230).

50 See Letter, Pound to Berryman, "12 or 13 Oct," box 29, Minnesota.

51 Letter, Pound to Berryman, 17 February, box 29, Minnesota.

52 See also *Poets in Their Youth*, 165, 197; *WD*, 233.

53 Lowell, "For John Berryman, 1914–1972" (1972), 113. See Lowell's letter to J. F. Powers, Feb. 5 [1948], in *The Letters of Robert Lowell*, ed. Saskia Hamilton (New York: Farrar, Straus and Giroux, 2005), 83.

54 John Berryman, *The Dispossessed* (New York: William Slone Associates, Inc. Publishers, 1948), former owner Pound, Ransom Center.

55 Ezra Pound, *Selected Letters 1907–1941*, ed. D. D. Paige (1950; New York: New Directions, 1971), 193. See also Noel Stock, *The Life of Ezra Pound: An Expanded Edition* (1970; San Francisco, CA: North Point Press, 1982).

56 Ezra Pound, *ABC of Reading* (London: George Routledge and Sons, 1934), former owner Pound, Ransom Center. See also from Pound's library in the Ransom Center, Ezra Pound, *Make it New: essays by Ezra Pound* (London: Faber and Faber, 1934) and *Instigations*. See also Noel Stock, *Poet in Exile: Ezra Pound*, 209.

57 See Adams, *History of the United States of America*, former owner Pound, Ransom Center.

58 Berryman's introduction to Pound's *Selected Poems* was published as the essay, "The Poetry of Ezra Pound" in *FP*.

59 By addressing form, content, and poetic originality, Berryman was also responding to Eliot's response to the topic in his introduction to Faber and Faber's collection of Pound's *Selected Poems* (1928):

> People may think they like the form because they like the content, or think they like the content because they like the form. In the perfect poet they fit and are the same thing; and in another sense they *always* are the same thing. So it is always true to say form and content are the same thing, and always true to say that they are different things.
>
> (363)

Eliot had also discussed the concept of poetic inheritance that Berryman engaged:

> True originality is merely development; and if it is right development it may appear in the end so *inevitable* that we almost come to the point of view of denying all "original" virtue to the poet. He simply did the next thing.
>
> (363)

T. S. Eliot, "Introduction: 1928" (1929/1948), *New Selected Poems and Translations* by Ezra Pound, ed. Richard Sieburth (1926; Norfolk, CT: New Directions, 2010). Berryman owned Ezra Pound, *Selected Poems*, ed. T. S. Eliot (London: Faber and Faber, 1934), Minnesota (Kelly, 280).

60 Berryman is referring to Allen Tate. The phrase Berryman repeats is quoted in Dudley Fitts, "Pound and the 'Cantos,'" *Saturday Review of Literature*, 8 (26 December 1931), 416. Quoted in *Ezra Pound: The Contemporary Reviews*, ed. Betsy Erkkila (New York: Cambridge University Press, 2011), xxxv.

61 William Barrett, "A Prize for Ezra Pound," in *A Casebook on Ezra Pound*, ed. William Van O'Connor and Edward Stone (New York: Thomas Y. Crowell Company, 1959), 50. From the *Partisan Review*, April 1949. Berryman's essay was also reprinted in Ezra Pound, *New Selected Poems and Translations*, ed. Richard Sieburth (1926; Norfolk, CT: New Directions, 2010): 373–8.

62 Letter, Robert Lowell to Leonie Adams "[n.d. late November 1948]," *Letters of Robert Lowell*, 118. Lowell later observed in an 18 March 1962 letter to Alfred Kazin, "I feel about Pound that his content is very important, and that it is a content we are scared to define" (403).

63 Barrett, "A Prize for Ezra Pound," 52.

64 W. H. Auden et al., "The Question of the Pound Award," in *A Casebook on Ezra Pound*, ed. William Van O'Connor and Edward Stone (New York: Thomas Y. Crowell Company, 1959), 54. From the *Partisan Review*, May 1949.

65 Cleanth Brooks, *The Well Wrought Urn: Studies in the Structure of Poetry* (New York: Reynal & Hitchcock, 1947), 177, former owner Berryman, Minnesota. Citation from Kelly, 47. The passage follows Berryman's comment in the margin. Haffenden also notes Berryman's response to *The Well Wrought Urn*.

66 Hayden White, *The Content of the Form: Narrative Discourse and Historical Representation* (Baltimore, MD: Johns Hopkins University Press, 1987), xi.

67 Berryman et al., "State of American Writing," *Partisan Review*, 859.

68 See also Bloom, 40.

69 Blackmur quotes Canto XI.

70 Ezra Pound, "Three Cantos I," *Poetry* X, no. 3 (June 1917): 113.

71 See also Brown, "The Secret Life of Things." Blackmur concluded that

> here the Cantos differ from such works as Joyce's *Ulysses* . . . in that it is neither the structural framework and some of the ornament, nor the key to the meaning that is hidden in symbolism, complex allusion, and difficult thought, but the substance of the poem itself. The movement of the reader's mind is thus either from the poem as a unit to the verse as such, or from the poem to the material alluded to. Thus the poem is either lost in the original or becomes an attachment to it: it is scholia not poetry.
>
> (106)

72 Berryman mailed his arrangement of Pound's poems, cut from the copies of *The Cantos* that Laughlin had sent, with his introduction for Pound's *Selected Poems* to Laughlin in late November 1948. Berryman had requested "copies of <u>Personae</u> & the Cantos volumes because I don't want to tear up my own." Berryman to Laughlin, 30 July [1945?], Minnesota. From Berryman to Laughlin 18 April, "Many thanks for Pound's translation" (Barnhisel, 131). Barnhisel brought Berryman's correspondence with Laughlin to my attention.

73 Letter, Laughlin to Berryman, 3 December 1948, box 30, Minnesota.

74 Letter, Berryman to Laughlin, 9 December 1948, box 30, Minnesota.

75 Ezra Pound and James Laughlin, *Ezra Pound and James Laughlin Selected Letters*, ed. David M. Gordon (New York: Norton, 1994), 178; hereafter cited in the text as "*EPJL*."

76 Letter, Pound to Berryman, 20 March, box 29, Minnesota. See also *WD*, 232.

77 Ezra Pound, "Foreword," *Selected Cantos* (1934; New York: New Directions, 1970), 1. James McDougall brought this passage to my attention in his paper "Pound's Sea as Pedagogy and Paideuma" on the Ezra Pound Society panel, "Language, Literature, Learning: Ezra Pound as Teacher, Teaching Ezra Pound" at the 2012 Modern Language Convention in Seattle. Lise Jaillant's paper, "Woolf in the Modern Library Series: Bridging the Gap between Academics and Common Readers," on the International Virginia Woolf Society panel, "Institutional Woolf" also shaped my response to Pound's introduction.

78 See also Daniel Albright, "Early Cantos I–XLI," in *Cambridge Companion to Ezra Pound*, ed. Ira Nadel (New York: Cambridge University Press, 1999), 59–91.

79 Lowell, "The Poetry of John Berryman," 109.

80 Donald A. Stauffer, Chairman of Department to the President, "John Berryman appointment of Resident Fellow in Creative Writing. Department of English," 5 May 1948, Berryman, Faculty and Professional Staff files, Princeton.

81 Letter, Bruce Berlind to Haffenden, 22 October 1972, Haffenden-Berryman Papers.
82 Letter, Berlind to Haffenden, 22 October 1972, Haffenden-Berryman Papers.
83 William Meredith, "In Loving Memory of the Late Author of The Dream Songs," foreword to Kelly, *John Berryman: A Checklist*, xii. He also explained,

> The appointment as R. P. Blackmur's assistant in the creative writing courses at the university was an annual one; that is, one person couldn't hold it for more than one year consecutively, and for several years Berryman and I held it alternately.
>
> (xi)

84 Berryman's biography in the issue.
85 Berryman et al., "State of American Writing," *Partisan Review*, 858–9. See also Haffenden, 204.
86 Letter, Mark Van Doren to Berryman, 25 March 1938, box 3, Minnesota.
87 Regarding the building, see Spencer Tuckerman, "The Rise and Fall of McMicken Hall," *Oh Varsity!*, 4 June 2018, https://www.ohvarsity.com/blogs/2018/5/25/the-rise-and-fall-of-the-original-mcmicken-hall, accessed 29 June 2019.
88 In an article in Berryman's file at Minnesota Winter 1951, page 7. "John Berryman Critic-Poet-Lecturer To occupy the George Elliston Chair of Poetry 1952." The article may refer to the title of the publication, "the PROFILE."
89 See also *DS*, 244 and *WD*, 240.
90 Haffenden-Berryman Papers, http://www.columbia.edu/cu/lweb/archival/collections/ldpd_4078432/, accessed 31 July 2019.
91 Letter, William S. Clark to Berryman, 21 December 1951, Teaching Materials, box 1, Cincinnati File, Minnesota.
92 Berryman, "Teaching Materials/Class Files," box 1, Cincinnati File, Minnesota.
93 Ibid.
94 Berryman, "Teaching Materials/Class Files," box 1, Minnesota.
95 Ibid.
96 Saul Bellow, "John Berryman," in *Berryman's Understanding: Reflections on the Poetry of John Berryman*, ed. Harry Thomas (Boston, MA: Northeastern University Press, 1988), 77.
97 Haffenden explains that "[t]he Humanities Program was an old one . . . It was run by Ralph Ross . . . who had formerly headed the Humanities Program (a part of Adult Education) at New York University" (249).
98 Berryman had some experience in a humanities program. As a Hodder Fellow (1950–1) at Princeton, a press release announced that Beryman "will present several lectures next year to undergraduates enrolled in Princeton's Special Program in the Humanities." "Release: Monday, March 20, 1950," Berryman, Faculty and Professional Staff files, Princeton.
99 See also Berryman, "Humanities 54," "FOREWORD," page 2, "Teaching Notes/Class Files," box 1, folder 10, Minnesota.
100 Berryman was an "Associate Professor of Interdisciplinary Studies" (*WD*, 306). He served as Regents' Professor of Humanities until 1972. Dates and Berryman's position and fellowship titles from Kelly, *John Berryman: A Checklist*, xxxiii-xxxiv.
101 Berryman, "Humanities 54," "FOREWORD," page 1, box 1, folder 10, Minnesota. The foreword is dated "24 May 58."
102 Berryman, "Humanities 54," "FOREWORD," page 1, box 1, folder 10, Minnesota
103 Berryman "Humanities 54 (Book)," "Teaching Notes/Class Files," box 1, folder 10, Minnesota.

104 Berryman, "Humanities 54 (Book)," box 1, folder 10, Minnesota.

105 See Haffenden, 250. See also Haffenden's listing of the course's contents.

106 In an earlier contribution to the *Partisan Review* (1948), Berryman also articulated that in midcentury culture "[t]here is a political, perhaps a moral, paralysis." John Berryman et al., "The State of American Writing, 1948: A Symposium," *Partisan Review* 15, no. 8 (August, 1948): 857.

107 Berryman had read *Ulysses* with Blackmur at Princeton (*Poets in Their Youth*, 85). Berryman may have owned a previous copy. Donohue, interview with the author. James Joyce, *Ulysses* (New York: Random House, 1934), former owner Berryman, Minnesota.

108 While this chapter does not list, "Circe," other final exams in his file include it, as he probably altered which chapters he covered in different iterations of the course.

109 From Berryman's *Ulysses* chart. He included a question with choice of "Molly Bloom's soliloquy <u>or</u> the Circe episode."

110 Published in 1947 in Holland in 1952 in the United States. Berryman owned two copies of Anne Frank, *Diary of a Young Girl*. Second copy, Anne Frank, *Diary of A Young Girl*. Trans. B. M. Mooyaart-Doubleday (1947; New York: Pocket Books, 1953), 237, former owner, Berryman. Berryman, "Humanities 54," "I. THE READING," page I-2, "Teaching Notes/Class Files," box 1, Minnesota.

111 John Berryman, "<u>Hum.</u> 54 – Spr. '61, mid.- qu," handwritten notes, "Teaching Notes/Class Files," box 1, Minnesota.

112 D. H. Lawrence, *Lady Chatterley's Lover* (1928; New York: Grove Press, 1959), 139, former owner Berryman, Minnesota.

113 Frank, *Diary*, 237, ellipses in the original; former owner Berryman, Minnesota.

114 "Psychiatry," he clarified, at midcentury also used "shock / surgery / drugs." Handwritten page of notes dated "<u>Fall '60</u>," "Teaching Notes/Class Files," box 1, folder 8 or 9, Minnesota.

115 Berryman, "Hum. 4 Final Examination. Winter 1958," Handwritten, "Teaching Notes/Class Files," box 1, folder 14, Minnesota.

116 Ibid.

117 Berryman, "Teaching Notes/Class Files," box 1, folder 14, Minnesota.

118 Peter Stitt, "The Art of Poetry," 18.

119 In his interview with the *Harvard Advocate* (1969), Berryman responded to the question, "How do you see your role as a teacher in relation to your poetry?" "There is no connection." Plotz, "An Interview with John Berryman," *Berryman's Understanding*, 15.

120 Robert Lowell, "John Berryman," in *Collected Prose*, ed. Robert Giroux (New York: Farrar, Straus and Giroux, 1987), 108. Lowell, "The Poetry of John Berryman" (1964). See also Travisano, 28.

121 Haffenden, x. See also 335.

122 In Kelly, *John Berryman's Personal Library*. It was at this time that Berryman had "his library removed from store in Princeton (after 11 years) and transported to his new home, where Berryman had for the first time in his life designated one room as his study" (Haffenden, 335).

123 For Berryman's ordering of his Yeats books, see Kelly, *John Berryman's Personal Library*, 406–9 and 401. According to the numbers that Kelly gave each of the books, Berryman's order of his books included *Cantos LII-LXXI* 246, *The Pisan Cantos* 247, *A Draft of XXX Cantos* 248, *Homage to Sextus Propertius* 255, *Polite Essays* 251, and *The Letters of Ezra Pound* 252. Also in the dining room were some of his Auden volumes (Kelly, 16, 17), and many books by Freud. Other Pound volumes were in the attic and marked "other," if not

located with the other books at the time of the inventory (Kelly, 278–80). Berryman's own books begin at number 278. See Kelly 30–4.

124 James D. Bloom addresses Blackmur and Berryman's responses to Pound in *The Stock of Available Reality: R.P. Blackmur and John Berryman* (Lewisburg, PA: Bucknell University Press, 1984); see, for instance, 95–106.

125 As Jane Coil Cole and other scholars have argued, as a long poem, *T⸍e Dream Songs* followed Whitman's *Leaves of Grass* and Pound's *Cantos*. "'To Terrify & Comfort': John Berryman's *Dream Songs* and the Quest of the Poetic Imagination" (PhD diss., Drew University, 1982), 3, 6–7. See also Gareth Reeves, "Songs of the Self: Berryman's Whitman," *Romanticism* 14, no. 1 (2008): 47–56. Cole also addresses Berryman's use of the long poem (42–4).

126 "The parenthetical insertions are JB's own" (*WD*, 298). See also Mariani, 305.

127 See also John Plotz, et al., "An Interview with John Berryman," in *Berryman's Understanding: Reflections on the Poetry of John Berryman*, ed, Harry Thomas (Boston, MA: Northeastern University Press, 1988), 5. Reprinted from John Plotz, et al., "An interview with John Berryman," *Harvard Advocate* 103, no. 1 (Spring 1969): 4–9.

128 Brendan Cooper, "'We Want Anti-Models': John Berryman's Eliotic Inheritance," *Journal of American Studies* 1 (2008): 3; hereafter cited in the text as "Cooper." Cooper quotes Berryman's statement while discussing *Homage to Mistress Bradstreet*: "Narrative! Let's have narrative, at least one dominant personality, and no fragmentation! In short, let's have something spectacularly NOT *The Waste Land*." John Berryman, "One Answer to a Question: Changes," in *The Freedom of the Poet* (New York: Farrar, Straus and Giroux, 1976), 327.

129 Regarding Eliotic aspects of *The Dream Songs*, see Cooper, 11–8.

130 Marjorie Perloff has also observed that "*The Dream Songs . . .* has been called 'Poundian' in its range and allusiveness, its shifting from humor to pathos, from high style to black slang." Marjorie Perloff, "The Contemporary of Our Grandchildren: Pound's Influence," in *Ezra Pound Among the Poets*, ed. George Bornstein (Chicago, IL: University of Chicago Press, 1985), 212. She cites Joel Conarroe's *John Berryman: An Introduction to the Poetry*. John Bayley also compares *The Dream Songs* to *The Cantos* in "A Question of Imperial Sway," 1973, *Berryman's Understanding: Reflections on the Poetry of John Berryman*, ed. Harry Thomas (Boston, MA: Northeastern University Press, 1988), 169.

131 Pound, *Cantos LII-LXXI*, 7, former owner Berryman, Minnesota. Berryman dated his copy 1941.

132 Ezra Pound, "I Gather the Limbs of Osiris," 1911–1912, in *Selected Prose 1909–1965*, ed. William Cookson (1950; New York: New Directions, 1973), 22.

133 Pound, "I Gather the Limbs of Osiris," 23.

134 Letter, "25 November [1962]."

135 Qtd. in Helen Vendler, *The Given and the Made: Strategies of Poetic Redefinition* (Cambridge, MA: Harvard University Press, 1995), 35.

136 See also Peter Denman, "Form and Discontent: The Prosody of *The Dream Songs*," in *After Thirty Falls: New Essays on John Berryman*, ed. Philip Coleman and Philip McGowan (New York: Rodopi, 2007), 87–100.

137 See also Vendler, *The Given and the Made*, 35–6.

138 Maber sees Berryman's incorporation of minstrelsy as "ambivalent in relation to high modernism, [it] has no unqualified investment in the freeing power of dialect" (134).

139 There is a closed single quotation mark in the poem, but not an opening one.

140 Regarding Eliot and popular culture, see David E. Chinitz, *T. S. Eliot and the Cultural Divide* (Chicago, IL: University of Chicago Press, 2003) and David Trotter, "T. S. Eliot and Cinema," *Modernism/modernity* 13, no. 2 (2006): 237–365.

141 Pound recounted during one of Berryman's visits that "Fordie [Ford Madox Ford] saw through the Possum right away . . . you know that academization, intellectualism" ("A Visit," 619).

142 John Berryman, "A Tribute [To Ezra Pound on his Eightieth Birthday]," *Michigan Quarterly Review* 45, no. 4 (Fall 2006): 623–4, 570. Originally published in *Agenda* 4:2 (Oct/Nov 1965).

143 Letter of 27 October 1936 from Cambridge. The editor of *We Dream of Honour* inserted the phrases in brackets.

144 "Literature is news that STAYS news." Ezra Pound, *ABC of Reading* (1934; New York: New Directions, 1960), 29.

145 See also Bloom, *Stock of Available Reality*, 224 and 139–40 and Dodson, 113.

146 See also *WD*, 55 and "A Visit," 619. During his visit, Pound also displayed "British illustrated papers about the removal of Yeats's body to Ireland."

147 See also Mariani, 420, 426, 428, Joseph Mancini, Jr., *The Berryman Gestalt: Therapeutic Strategies in the Poetry of John Berryman* (New York: Garland Publishing, 1987), Haffenden, 341, *WD*, 72, Philip Coleman's Introduction to *After Thirty Falls* (2007), 1–2, and Philip Coleman, "'What Am I Myself Here Doing?': Revisiting Henry in Dublin," *Thumbscrew* 15, http://www.bristol.ac.uk/thumbscrew/thum_rev.html#coleman, accessed 5 June 2007.

148 Dodson reads this passage: "At the heart of the Songs is the freedom implied in Pound's dictum to make it new" (35). He continues to address Berryman's revision of the sonnet form (35). See also Dodson's treatment of the elegy.

149 See also Smith, 433, 434, 435, and 431.

150 See Dodson. David Wojahn also addresses the writers to whom Berryman alludes in *The Dream Songs* in "'In All Them Time Henry Could Not Make Good': Reintroducing John Berryman," *Blackbird* 4, no. 2 (Fall 2005). 12 December 2008, http://www.blackbird.vcu.edu/v4n2/nonfiction/wojahn_d/berryman.htm, accessed 5 April 2018. Peter Maber's article brought this essay to my attention.

151 Letter, Anne Rowland, Assistant to Miss Anne Ford, of Houghton Mifflin Company, to Anne Sexton, 16 October 1968, box 21, folder 2, Sexton Papers.

152 The list follows the letter on a separate page. Sexton Papers.

153 Sexton selected Lowell, George Starbuck, beside whose name there also remains a crossed-out check mark, followed by a new check mark, Dan Wakefield, May Swenson, Babette Deutsch, Marianne Moore, and Louis Untermeyer. The remaining names without checks were Robert Bly, James Dickey, Eugene McCarthy, Allen Tate, Archibald MacLeish, Robert Graves, and Alfred Kazin.

154 "Programs and information sheets," box 182, folder 47, Hughes Papers. The location of the Purcell Room is from a letter addressed "To All News Editors" regarding a press conference for the festival. The letter is dated 16 June 1967. Hughes's schedule, titled, "POETRY INTERNATIONAL SIXTY SEVEN," listed Hugh MacDiarmid, Patrick Kavanagh, Berryman, Sexton, and Bella Akmadulina. Hughes had initially scheduled Berryman and then Sexton to read their poems at 8:15 in the evening on 14 July 1967 in London's Purcell Room in South Bank at the Poetry International Festival. Berryman also requested to be placed early in the program. Telegram, Berryman to Hughes, 7 June 1967, box 182, folder 25, Hughes Papers. I thank Gillian Groszewski

for bringing this document to my attention. See Mariani regarding Berryman's Guggenheim fellowship.

155 Berryman ostensibly did eventually arrive to read his poems on Friday. Middlebrook also notes that Sexton was eager to see him (279). According to Hughes's plans for the festival, Berryman and Sexton were also to stay at the same hotel in Chelsea. "Programs and information sheets," box 182, folder 47, Hughes Papers. List of "Participating Poets" and "Where to Contact Them." Berryman and Sexton stayed at the 69 Hotel at 69 Cadogan Gardens.

156 See also Jo Gill, "*The Colossus* and *Crossing the Water*," in *The Cambridge Companion to Sylvia Plath*, ed. Jo Gill (New York: Cambridge University Press, 2006), 91.

157 Berryman ended his life on 7 January 1972. Charles Thornbury, "Chronology," *Collected Poems 1937–1971*, ed. Charles Thornbury (New York: Farrar, Straus and Giroux, 1989), lxvii.

3   Annotating herself
Anne Sexton's teaching notes

Following John Berryman's reading and teaching of Ezra Pound, W. B. Yeats, and other modernist writers, Anne Sexton's library and the teaching notes for her "Anne on Anne" course on her own poetry at Colgate University in 1972 provide the subject of this chapter. While she lacked Plath and Berryman's academic training, Sexton may resemble a larger segment of the mid-to-late twentieth-century poetry reading population. In preparing and teaching a course with her own poems as the subject, Sexton combined close reading strategies she had acquired with revisions of content she had composed for public lectures, poetry readings, and interviews. Sexton had a certain degree of flexibility, crafting a teaching presence that shared with her public persona the illusion of ease, despite her effort and preparation.

Sexton's library of over 750 volumes reflects the breadth of texts she collected and received from peers and publishers.[1] The annotations that Sexton inscribed in her books lie behind the development of her poetry and poetic career.[2] While previous treatments of Sexton's teaching notes have emphasized her confessional techniques and assessed her pedagogical strategies, this chapter turns to Sexton's engagement with materiality and literary history in order to examine the contexts informing her reading practices.[3] The artifacts in this chapter include the books Sexton owned, her copies of her own poetry volumes, her poem drafts, notes she prepared for lectures, her correspondence, and the small pieces of paper she collected, which included quotations that she hung above her desk, kept on her person, and reproduced in letters. These materials are housed with Sexton's teaching notes in the Ransom Center.

***

There was probably snow on the ground when Anne Sexton returned to Colgate University. In the spring of 1972, Sexton flew each week from Boston to the vaguely familiar, icy campus near where she and her husband lived following their marriage in 1948 (*AS*, 23). At least 40 minutes from Syracuse and Utica, rural farming communities surround the village of Hamilton, New York that houses the Colgate campus.[4] Looking ahead at the students and beyond to the hills and farms visible in the distance,[5] Sexton taught her "Anne on Anne" course on Wednesdays in the esteemed Shakespeare professor Jonathan Kistler's classroom, 320 Lawrence Hall, at the top of the hill on which the academic buildings sit.[6] Even as the college had started admitting women the previous year, Sexton feared isolation upon her return.[7] In a poem she composed around this time, "O Ye Tongues" (1971–2), the speaker "prays that she will not cringe at the loneliness of the exile in Hamilton" (*Complete Poems*, 399; line 48).[8]

Inviting Sexton to serve as the Crawshaw Professor of Literature in the spring of 1972, Colgate's English Department Chairman, Bruce Berlind, proposed "two courses: one would be a poetry-writing workshop in which we would collaborate. . . . For the other course you could do anything you wanted, whatever's on your mind."[9] Despite trepidation, Sexton developed her course, inquiring with Berlind as to the parameters and materials[10]:

> The book order for Anne on Anne course is going to cost those students a hell of a lot, because it will be all the books. Everything is in paperback except for TRANSFORMATIONS. . . . I am working slowly, trying to structure the Anne on Anne course. It's harder than I thought it would be. I hope for that course I can have a chair and a table, not a lecturn. I could never stand up for two and a half hours. Do you think it is too sophomorish to structure the course around narrative poems and then again lyric poems and then again persona poems and then again confessional and so forth? Maybe I'll do one just with worksheets. . . . I need to talk with you for at least five hours. My husband has promised . . . that we can make a trip to Colgate this fall. . . . I'd like to get the lay of the land so perhaps I wouldn't be quite so apprehensive. Hold the Anne on Anne course to 30.[11]

Sexton followed through with several of her early suggestions, including teaching her "worksheets," the drafts of her poems that she mentioned to Berlind. In class, her manner was casual. Rather than standing at a lectern, one of her students remembers Sexton, at the beginning of class, sitting on the "desk, crossing her legs, leaning forward, taking a drag on the omnipresent cigarette and launching into her 'lectures.'"[12]

After she received a formal offer from Colgate's Provost and Dean of the Faculty, Sexton reminded the administration that she had been to Hamilton before: "It is a great pleasure to return to Colgate in another guise. My husband is a Colgate man and we lived off campus there one year."[13] The brief autobiographical sketch that Sexton sent *What's New at Colgate* may have differed from other responses that the college would have received from visiting faculty:

> I don't know how to write a little homely faculty sketch for you. I will just tell you in telegram style a little about my life. In 1948 I married

Alfred M. Sexton II and that year we returned to Colgate and lived off campus at Reg Scott Dairy Farm which was right on the road to Syracuse. We lived with Reg and I did the laundry and kept house. . . . It will be something really fine to return to Colgate as a teacher instead of washing the sour milk overalls out on the road to Syracuse.[14]

The distinctiveness of Sexton's response was part of her persona, one of sarcasm and understatement. Perhaps unknowingly, her blend of formality ("Alfred M. Sexton II") and farm life also speaks to Colgate's combination of prestige and rural surroundings.

Writing on her "[b]right yellow-orange 'lucky paper'" (*AS*, 385),[15] Sexton composed teaching notes for "Anne on Anne" that contain close readings of her poems, questions and answers regarding the meaning of her lines, and creative exercises for her students.[16] In her teaching notes, Sexton not only reinvents and revisits her creative process but also revises her responses from former interviews and annotates the poems she had published. She articulated an expansive, yet traditional, understanding of poetry that reflects her independent reading, her experiences in workshops, and 20 years as a poet. Sexton's teaching notes extend beyond the scope of her poems and interviews to augment the content of her oeuvre.

Teaching "Anne on Anne" allowed Sexton to accomplish what she had envisioned over a decade earlier when she received a fellowship from the Radcliffe Institute for Advanced Study in May 1961. Based on her experience as a poet and in workshops, she responded to her therapist Dr. Martin Orne that she could teach poetry writing and even literature with preparation: "If I took a course in twentieth-century poetry, I could teach it the next year."[17] Without additional training, she felt that "I could teach, tomorrow I could teach creative writing poetry . . . But I could teach it and I could teach it well." She resolved, "I want to show them what I know."[18] Sexton's connection between writing and teaching combines familiar phrases from midcentury fiction writing workshops, "write what you know" and "show don't tell."[19] Sexton, however, meant writing about her life, and her "Anne on Anne" course addressed these aims, including class sessions devoted to her "worksheets," in which students analyzed her poem drafts.

Despite others' skepticism, Sexton's preparation for her "Anne on Anne" course permitted a sense of distance while teaching her own poetry. The poet Richard Murphy, who taught at Colgate the year before Sexton arrived, explained to Ted Hughes that she would be teaching a course "on her own poetry. It seems a bit narcissistic, but I suppose she won't need to do any preparation, except her customary call on her analyst."[20] By contrast, C. K. Williams, who visited an "Anne on Anne" class while he was at Colgate to give a poetry reading, recalls

being sort of amazed that Anne would dare do a class on her own work, and, though I don't remember many details, I was struck as she did by how calmly and with such illumination she could speak about it, and herself, really as though she was separate from it all.[21]

Berlind remembers Sexton demonstrating a similar distance when he observed her class: "she ran through her poems and was honest about them except for being explicit about the ones that are about affairs: she would occasionally plead that the poems were fictional."[22]

When student reporter Brian Rooney visited Sexton's "Anne on Anne" class, he was surprised that she could "be unpretentiously ignorant of her own life in front of a large audience. It borders on naivete. She can, at times, approach treating herself as material rather than a person."[23] Rooney's response suggests a familiarity with modernist impersonality that recalls Joyce's artist "within or behind or beyond or above his handiwork . . . paring his fingernails" (157).[24] Sexton's course synthesizes the "self" who created the material with the "self" who teaches it, incorporating her memories of the composition process to do so.

A student in public

Sexton adopted the practices of a student to craft her image as a poet without an education. Reluctantly, Sexton admitted to a reporter that "my little introductory notes, are, I hate to tell you, not in the least spontaneous with the exception of one or two sentences . . . I hate to admit I am so studied, but there it is" (*AS*, 319–20).[25] The texts that Sexton wrote and revised contribute to what Diane Middlebrook has called Sexton's "life narrative she was evolving for public consumption" (*AS*, 151).[26] Turning to her reading, we see the material contours that lie behind what Jo Gill has identified as "the profound self-consciousness with which Sexton approaches the [poetry] field" (*Anne Sexton's Confessional Poetics*, 192).

As she often recounted, Sexton happened to catch I. A. Richards demonstrating how to write a sonnet on television in 1956 (*SP*, 29).[27] She remarked during an interview with *The Hudson Review* (1965/6) that she found his explanation clear enough to follow:

> I thought, "Well, so that's a sonnet." Although I had learned it in high school, I hadn't ever done anything about it. And so I thought, "I'll try that, too. I think maybe I could." So I sat down and wrote in the form of the sonnet.[28]

After seeing Richards on television and later meeting him at a party that Lowell hosted in 1960 (*Lost Puritan*, 283), Sexton skillfully offered Richards's name in her response to the interviewer.[29] Richards had spent over two decades at Harvard and Sexton was also gesturing toward a familiarity with its academic and literary landscape.[30]

Sexton's lack of the formal academic training that shaped her contemporaries' poetry was a perpetual source of insecurity.[31] In February 1957, she contemplated attending Boston University or Newton Junior College (*AS*, 46, 418n). In September 1958, Lowell granted Sexton permission to attend his Boston University workshop that fall (which Plath would join in the spring of 1959):

> Of course your poems qualify. They move with ease and are filled with experience[.] . . . I am not very familiar with them yet, but have been reading them with a good deal of admiration and envy this morning after combing through pages of fragments of my own unfinished stuff.[32]

Sexton responded humbly,

> I am more than a little shy of the great factories of humanity, like B.U. . . . I am not sweetened with a background of knowledge . . . ("I don't know anything.")—but if you can squeeze me in, I will be there.[33]

Lowell remembered that in his class "Anne was more herself, and knew less [than Plath]."[34] As we will see, Sexton's approach to literary study was more expansive, and idiosyncratic, than she or Lowell admitted.

Literary scraps

As a reader, Sexton was a blend of what Virginia Woolf called a "common reader" and a sort of literary *voyeur*. In her essay, "The Common Reader" (1925), introducing her collection of the same name, Woolf draws on Dr. Samuel Johnson's description in his "Life of Gray" of places "full of books, where the pursuit of reading is carried on by private people" (*CR*, 1). Sexton initially appears to fit the profile of the common reader who "differs from the critic and the scholar. He is worse educated, and nature has not gifted him so generously. He reads for his own pleasure rather than to impart knowledge or correct the opinions of others," and critics may assume that this continues to be the case (1). Sexton, however, was acquiring books because of her aspirations as a poet.

Johnson's common reader, "snatching now this poem . . . without caring where he finds it or of what nature it may be so long as it serves his purpose and rounds out his structure," resembles Sexton as she collects fragments (qtd. in *CR*, 1). Sexton saved quotations, hanging them above her desk, as her daughter remembers, at "eye level."[35] Returning to these passages, Sexton brought new meaning to them. She found inspiration and literature in found artifacts that took the shape of scraps and gifts. Sexton's accounts of coming upon these pieces in interviews, her teaching notes, and correspondence suggest an unmethodical nonchalance that complicates her role as a common reader.[36] Tillie Olsen, whom Sexton met at Radcliffe,

> recognized from reading *Bedlam* what a reader Anne was, what a hunger for ideas she had. Yet she would say to me over and over, "It's Maxine [Kumin] who's the real intellectual! I'm a poet, but I don't have real brains."[37]
>
> ("Circle of Women Artists," 18)

Sexton's modest gesture enables her to make a distinction between poet and intellectual. She also learned that Olsen had

> copied out treasured passages from library books, which she would annotate with her own thoughts. She brought with her to Radcliffe an enormous collection of them, bundles of loose pages accumulated over the years, all shapes and sizes. With Anne she shared translations from Rilke and pages of copy-outs from the letters of Emily Dickinson, and from James's and Kafka's notebooks.
>
> ("Circle of Women Artists," 20)

Subsequently, Middlebrook recounts, "Sexton borrowed Olsen's notes; she and her secretary spent many hours typing the 'copy-outs' to keep in her own files: sixty-three pages of them" ("Circle of Women Artists," 21). As if attempting to harness Olsen's own sources of inspiration, Sexton's secretary helped her to create an archive. In her files and on her walls, these notes became sources of education and inspiration.

In December 1964, the Sextons moved from 40 Clearwater Road in Newton Lower Falls to 14 Black Oak Road in Weston, Massachusetts (*AS*, 230), where, Gray Sexton remembers, her mother's study was a darker room that also served as the family's den. Sexton enjoyed working in this room less and instead wrote in the kitchen (*SP*, 329).[38] Late in her career, Sexton was probably focusing on her study in this house in her short piece called, "Some things around my desk" (1971):

> there are some anonymous quotations Scotch-taped up. *Poets and pigs are not appreciated until they are dead.* And: *The more I write, the more the silence seems to be eating away at me.* And here is Pushkin, not quite anonymous: *And reading my own life with loathing, I tremble and curse.* And: *Unhappiness is more beautiful when seen through a window than from within.*[39]
>
> (*NES*, 24)

Cataloging these contents, Sexton describes her manner of collecting and displaying passages that may later take on new meaning in her poetry.

Sexton often narrated the routes that her fragments traveled, underscoring her distance from conventional literary study. During her interview with Harry Moore (1968), for instance, Sexton recounted the origins of the passage that inspired the title and graces the front cover of *All My Pretty Ones*:

> The title was given to me by a friend who stole it from Shakespeare in the first place. . . . She said in her letter. "Oh no, Anne, your mother in March and your father in June. All of your pretty ones at once?" And then she added, "Anne this quote is from *Macbeth*, in case you don't know." (I have little formal education and little informal education.). So I read to the end of *Macbeth*—almost the end—looking for it, and I found it. . . . "I cannot but remember such things were / That were most precious to me." Then I knew what my title was. "All My Pretty Ones" was the name for my dead.[40]
>
> (*NES*, 43)

Unlike Johnson's reader, "snatching" a poem "without caring where he finds it," Sexton knew the source of her title for *All My Pretty Ones*, and where a more traditional reader, like her friend, would have found it. But, like Johnson's reader, the passage was "precious" to her because she was able to use it for her own poetry.

In her accounts of the evolution of her work, Sexton recounted her fragments' significance in her poems and in relation to her writing. For instance, Saul Bellow sent Sexton a note on a page of his manuscript for *Herzog* (1964) that provided her epigraph to *Live or Die* (1966).[41] She explained during her interview with *The Paris Review* that

> in circling that and in sending it to me, Saul Bellow had given me a message about my whole life. . . . So I stuck that message up over my desk and it was a kind of hidden message. You don't know what these messages mean to you, yet you stick them up over your desk or remember them or write them down and put them in your wallet. One day I was rereading a quote from Rimbaud that said "Anne, Anne, flee on your donkey," and I typed it out because it had my name in it and because I wanted to flee. I put it in my wallet, went to see my doctor, and . . . In the hospital, I started to write the poem, "Flee on Your Donkey," as though the message had come to me at just the right moment.
>
> (*NES*, 96–7)

Such accounts act to legitimate Sexton's work and record the particularity of her literary encounters. Carrying the Rimbaud fragment on her person underscores the physicality of Sexton's relationship to language and inspiration.[42]

Textuality, for Sexton, included the surfaces of objects. She wore a necklace that was a gift from her friend Lois Ames in 1969, inscribed, "Don't let the Bastards Win."[43] Sexton continued this practice, reporting to an interviewer in 1974:

> I have these little medals I give to people: "Don't let the bastards get you." I ought to give one as a present to every single student who graduates from my class. I try to tell them. 'You think you're going to get a teaching job? . . . You've got a hard climb, particularly in poetry.
>
> (*NES*, 205)

Sexton's transition in this reply from her own sources of strength to the advice she gives her students reflects her practices in her teaching notes, in which she tells stories of the fragments that inspired her poems.

Sexton acquired materials in the form of comments, feedback, passages she encountered, courses she attended, and books she annotated. She affixed above her desk, for instance, Ted Hughes's advice that others' reviews stand in the way of the remove writers need to maintain, separating themselves from the interpretation of their work.[44] While Sexton's means of encountering literary sources of inspiration were unorthodox, her library took a more conventional shape.

Sexton's library

Arriving at her therapy session in October 1961, Sexton proudly handed Dr. Orne a copy of *Newsweek* and asked him to turn to the Education section.[45] In their "Women of Talent" piece, the magazine featured the Radcliffe Fellows, and introduced Sexton:

> In her book-lined study in Newton Lower Falls, Mass., Mrs. Anne Sexton, a 32-year-old poet, turned from typewriter to greet her two children on their return from school. It was a welcome interruption, but of interruptions per se Mrs. Sexton observed: "When some people call me and I say I've been reading a book, they just keep chattering away. But if I say I'm baking a cake, they apologize and hang up. Unfortunately, some educated women reach a point where a fallen angel-food cake is almost more important than a lost idea."[46]

Sexton differentiates herself from the woman with whom she has been compared, those who are more educated, but have become consumed with baking over books. *Newsweek*'s photographer Vytas Valaitis photographed Sexton at her desk in the workroom she added to her home following her Radcliffe acceptance the previous May.[47] The magazine borrowed Sexton's response for a caption: "Poet Anne Sexton at Radcliffe: Research for lost ideas" (97).

How Sexton searched for "a lost idea" takes on new meaning when paired with an image of Sexton at her desk. Gillian White observes that three years earlier,

Sexton expressed concern . . . about the frequently heard admonition that she needed still to "find her voice." To Nolan Miller (editor at *Antioch Review*) she wrote in November 1958, "People keep telling me that I haven't found my 'voice' yet and I have spent considerable time fishing around in my desk drawers and under old ms. and have found no new notable sound." . . . Sexton figures poetic "voice" as a thing she will find not in her self but in her desk.[48]

Even as Sexton's response to Miller may have been partly in jest, *Newsweek*'s selection of her line as a caption reflects the fact that her environment became a subject for her work.

For Sexton, building a study meant altering her home.[49] A screened-in porch became her workroom, with long glass windows filling the room with light.[50] There were books above Sexton's desk and two walls were lined with bookshelves.[51] When Sexton built this study, she had not yet read *A Room of One's Own* (1929), but after reading Woolf's essay at Radcliffe in 1963 she referred to it as "health."[52] Creating a space for her professional life, Sexton, like those of the early twentieth-century writers whom Victoria Rosner addresses in *Modernism and the Architecture of Private Life*, "signal[s] an unwillingness to carry on with things as usual" (5). Sexton and her predecessors enact "rebellions located in that most sacred and custom-bound site, the home" (5). For Sexton, this meant changing domestic structures to make room for poetic ones. Books were necessary to this process.

Linda Gray Sexton's impression is that while her mother might not have seen herself as acquiring a library as such, she purchased books that she wanted to keep and revisit, stocking her bookshelves with them.[53] In the "Second Psalm" of Sexton's "O Ye Tongues," the speaker "pray[s] that the wooden room I live in will faithfully hold more books as the years pass" (*Complete Poems*, 399; line 40). Sexton's first work space not only became a location for her writing but also for her arrangement of her manuscripts and her library:

> I used to write in the dining room, books, papers . . . all over the place. . . .
> The rest of my room is book shelves. I hoard books. . . . I think it is too
> bad that monks are not allowed to keep books . . . I mean lots of them.[54]
>
> (*SP*, 142–3)

As Sexton stressed in a therapy session, she wanted to impress upon her husband the significance of this accomplishment and the space that it provided:

> when I got the Radcliffe grant with *my money* this is what I want to
> shout at him, with the thing that I've done, we built a room, the room
> is built with the thing I've done. A room is built so everything is out of
> the way.[55]

Visiting a female therapist whose waiting room displayed a vast library, Sexton felt that the books conveyed a sense of the doctor's intellectual prowess:

> there are all sorts of books. In other words this woman is intelligent. She's thinking. There are quarterlies for instance that I print in. She has books of poetry, although not just poetry, all sorts of things. . . . See I am sizing her up.[56]
>
> (Qtd. in Skorczewski, 115)

One could infer that by acquiring a library, Sexton wanted others to see her as a woman who thinks as well. Working in her study and glancing upward at her collection would also produce a feeling of gratification for Sexton, who could imagine others' responses to her library and herself as the poet whom it reflects.[57] These impressions extended to the image that Sexton crafted for others to accompany her books of poetry.[58]

When she selected a photograph for the back cover of her first volume, *To Bedlam and Part Way Back* (1960), Sexton wanted readers to see a plain woman: "I was very careful about the picture on my book: [I] didn't want it to look suburban, wanted just to be a face, a person whose life you couldn't define" (*AS*, 65). The studio portrait on the back jacket cover displayed a head shot against a matte backdrop.[59] For her second volume of poetry, *All My Pretty Ones* (1962), Sexton's author photograph in front of her library suggests intellectual, academic conventions that critics were reluctant to associate with her work. A series of Rollie McKenna photographs displaying Sexton at her desk depict a writer surrounded by the tools of her craft.[60] The back cover of *All My Pretty Ones* displays McKenna's headshot of Sexton in front of a bookshelf. This image contributes to the volume's combination of literary history and femininity. The front cover includes a lavender daffodil against a black background.[61] To the left is a thin column of lavender italicized lines from William Shakespeare's *Macbeth*.[62] Sexton's choice of this excerpt also reflects the eclectic, yet often canonical, contents of her own reading.

While describing her poetry writing process, Middlebrook has called Sexton "virtually an autodidact," and the characterization also applies to her reading.[63] The material in Sexton's lecture notes, therapy sessions, and annotated books illustrates that her sense of writing in books is linked to her experience as a student.[64] The contents of her library and teaching notes reflect that Sexton demonstrated more of a concern with literary history and the traditions that inform her work than critics may have previously assumed.[65]

As we have seen throughout *Annotating Modernism*, the material condition of texts shapes readers' encounters with them. In her poem, "Eighteen Days Without You" (1969), Sexton's speaker reports that there was "[n]o rain last night, but an icestorm. / Jewels! Today each twig is important, / each ring" (*Complete Poems*, 212; lines 125–7). After the storm, one sees what remains differently. Sexton's speaker notes the particularity of each item, not unlike that of each artifact in an archive. Such remains become the jewels of *"A Life of Things"* (1971): "When I die, who will put it all away? Who will index the letters, the books, the names, the expendable jewels of a life" (*NES*, 30).[66] While such remnants are "expendable," and could be discarded, a cataloger will attempt to understand their meaning for their owner. Books in a personal library provide a similar challenge, and like Sexton's jewels, when taken together these artifacts may complement each other in unexpected ways, shedding new light on their reader.

Sexton owned not only poetry books and novels but also collections of essays accompanying many writers that academics of the time were reading. These critical volumes are visible in the upper right hand corner of photographs of Sexton at her desk in her Weston study.[67] Sexton's library contains a broader range of texts than critics may have previously assumed she had encountered, from *Aristotle on the Art of Poetry* to Joyce's *A Portrait of the Artist as a Young Man*.[68] In the spring of 1961, Sexton suggested to her therapist that after "a course in twentieth century poetry, I could teach it the next year."[69] Sexton's accumulation of books may reflect a similar impulse, becoming immersed in the field, and even prepared to teach a course if the opportunity arose. While the degree to which Sexton read her books is difficult to determine, their presence in her library indicates her familiarity with the writers, texts, and appearance of the volumes.

Resting on shelves above and around her desk, Sexton's books presented the comfort and irritation of what she called, "people who do not leave" (*SP*, 142–3). The books that she and others wrote reinforced her accomplishments as a poet and suggested all that there remained to read. In a different instance, Plath described a similar sense of frustration: "all reading mocks me (others wrote it, I didn't.)" (*UJ*, 284). In several uncollected poems, Sexton gave voice to texts with which she had surrounded herself. As she did not include these poems in her books of poetry, she may have considered them to be of a lesser quality or a form of procrastination. The protagonist in "The Thought Disease," for instance, complains, "[o]verhead the books are noisy. / I try to write" (qtd. in *Anne Sexton's Confessional Poetics*, 193). In "Some Things Around My Desk" (1971) the speaker advises, "[i]f you put your ear closer to a book, you can hear it talking" (*NES*, 24).[70] Imagining conversations among her library's residents, the persona of Sexton's poem "February 20th" (1971) blends gossip with poets' autobiographies and idiosyncrasies: "I concentrate. / My books hypnotize each other. / Jarrell tells Bishop to stare / at the spot. Tate / tells Plath she's going under. / Eliot remembers his long lost mother" (*Complete Poems*, 599, lines 1–6). In the process, Sexton not only recorded her knowledge of anecdotal details but also gestured toward associations that books' covers and spines suggest to viewers.

As we will see in the following segment, attending literature courses informed Sexton's annotation of the books she added to her library. She not only underlined texts by the writers whom she encountered in the courses she audited, but she also recounted her excitement for an audience. As a result, Sexton incorporated her emulation of student practices in her public repertoire alongside understatements regarding her academic background.

Inscribing texts

Describing an incident that took place in 1951, Alice Munro's story "The Love of a Good Woman" includes a book inscribed with

> all the names of previous owners, some of whom were middle-aged housewives or merchants around the town. You could not imagine them learning these things, or underlining "Edict of Nantes" with red ink and writing "N.B." in the margin.[71]

Unlike Plath, who wrote N.B. in the margin of Woolf's *A Writer's Diary*, Sexton was not trained to mark her text with a student's attention.[72] Even so, Sexton came to acquire habits and books, leaving behind a material record of her engagement with language.

Sexton treated books with a certain functionality; it was vital to acquire them, and in some cases, reading led to underlining or marking them. Linda Gray Sexton remembers her mother annotating her books and, while they may not have discussed it directly, she grew up with an impression that writing in books was an acceptable part of the reading process. Books were "tool[s] to be used," and Sexton "wrote in them endlessly."[73] While they also visited the library, Gray Sexton recalls that her mother felt "owning a book . . . was important," it meant you "could underline it, [and] could write marginalia."[74] Sexton's daughter remembers her mother using pencil to annotate her books, but also sometimes resting drinks on them.[75] Such texts were functional for different reasons at different moments, both the subject of care and attention, and objects in and of themselves.

In the summer of 1960, Sexton attended Philip Rahv's and Irving Howe's literature courses at Brandeis University. Rahv introduced Sexton to many of the writers whom she read and annotated.[76] Robert Lowell may also have suggested Rahv to Sexton,[77] and after the course, she told Lowell that she found Rahv to be "a fascinating man . . . a great teacher."[78] As Middlebrook has argued, Lowell's workshop had motivated Sexton to pursue what she felt was lacking in her education (126):

> Sexton took what she wanted from her summer at Brandeis: a feeling for such writers as Kafka, Dostoevsky, and Rilke, whose names she had learned from her mentors. She complained to Dr. Orne that she seemed

incapable of following her professors' lectures on the books, but reading them stimulated her creativity and fed her hunger for knowledge. "After two hours a day of Rahv on Dostoevsky or Kafka etc. I swallowed fire with the excitement . . . and returned home to . . . let a sonata bear away the heat, the intensity," she later recalled. "Anne kept on being a wide-eyed, gaga student right up until the end," [George] Starbuck commented.

(*AS*, 128)

The quotation that Middlebrook includes is from a eulogy that Sexton composed for Rahv in 1973.[79] By this time, she had been returning to Dostoevsky and Kafka as touchstones in her accounts of her reading and the development of her work for over a decade. While Starbuck depicts a clichéd image of femininity, his observation speaks to her peers' surprise regarding her exuberance and motivation.[80]

Following Rahv's course, Sexton continued to read and annotate the texts and writers he had taught. At the beginning of October she reported to Rahv, "I am still reading . . . [Thomas] Mann's essays at this point" (*SP*, 113).[81] She was impressed, for instance, with

[h]ow beautiful and sick and morbid . . . [Dostoevsky's *Crime and Punishment*] was. By God, if this is what great books are all about—maybe I could just write anyhow and stop worrying that it would be too "sick and morbid" a view of life.[82]

(*AS*, 127)

Sexton's introduction to nineteenth- and twentieth-century literature becomes a subject of conversation in her letters and she emphasizes her former distance from literary study. In October 1960, Sexton's letter complimenting W. D. Snodgrass combines her excitement and the informality of an initiate: "I liked your article on Dosty—most especially because I had just finished reading *Crime and Punishment*. I had never read any Russian stuff and just love it. It is right down my alley!" (*SP*, 115).[83] The following month, Sexton sent Nolan Miller a laundry list of the nineteenth- and early twentieth-*century* writers whom she was reading:

Kafka, Mann, Dostoyevsky, Rilke, Faulkner, Gide—etc. A mixed bunch, picking and delighting. I wasn't kidding when I told you once that I had never read anything. I hadn't. So I'm forming, eating books, words, thinking and now and then worrying about all this intake and no output.[84]

(*SP*, 116–7)

While for Sexton these texts presented an eclectic collection, she listed predominately canonical modernist writers.

Rainer Maria Rilke became integral to Sexton's accounts of her reading, particularly his *Letters to a Young Poet* (1929). She told Brother Dennis Farrell, "I am very fond of that book and read it often, going to it when I am thirsty or lonely" (*SP*, 138).[85] Sexton's interest recalls Rilke's sentiments as he wrote to his correspondent:

> Of all my books, just a few are indispensable to me, and two even are always among my things, wherever I am. They are about me here too: the Bible, and the books of the great Danish writer Jens Peter Jacobsen.[86]

Sexton later insisted to Jonathan Korso that *Letters to a Young Poet* is a book to "read and reread. Read it like a Bible. I wish for myself that I could care [carve?] it into my eyes, word by word" (*SP*, 268).[87] Sexton's image metaphorically suggests the possibility of one's reading through Rilke's lines, permanently. While her word choice may be due to her correspondent's profession, her paraphrasing of Deuteronomy 6:8, "let them be a symbol before your eyes," speaks to Orthodox Jewish ritual.[88] The verse alludes to the act of tying a religious text, enclosed in a box, to the forehead in prayer.[89]

In her response to Rilke, Sexton may have also recalled sentiments she underlined in pencil in her copy of H. F. Peters's *Rainer Maria Rilke: Masks and the Man* (1960): "Things: that is what he wanted to make now, realities. . . . He would work like a sculptor, carve his words, deliberately, patiently, and with the utmost regard for detail" (98).[90] On the following page, Sexton wrote "precise!" and "Control," one above the other, adding a line to the right of the following passage:

> Meticulous care with the use of language is as much a prerequisite for the expression of precise emotion as it is for the expression of precise thought. . . . Words, he now realized . . . are tools that demand careful and precise handling. . . . Now he wanted to control them.
>
> (99)

Writing in texts becomes an act of mastery not unlike the process to which Rilke aspired.

For Sexton, carving and carpentry become metaphors as she describes writing and its purpose. In her late piece, "The Freak Show" (1973), Sexton clarified, "[p]oetry is for us poets the handwriting on the tablet of the soul" (*NES*, 35). It is sacred, essential, and inscribed in the essence of one's being, like having words in one's eyes. Shaping and honing impressions become "like carving on a statue, trying to get down to the bone" (127). While overseeing the production of her play, *Mercy Street*, Sexton compared herself to "a carpenter who maybe was building a cathedral and had little to do with it. I don't even feel like the architect, just the carpenter"

(129). Gray Sexton's recollection of her mother's use of books as "tools" also allows us to shed new light on Sexton's adoption of the metaphor in her well-known poem for Plath, "Wanting to Die" (1966): "suicides have a special language. / Like carpenters they want to know *which tools*. / They never ask *why build*" (*Complete Poems*, 142; lines 7–9). As a form of carving, annotating becomes part of the process of building. It is the vestige of research, isolating what one has found, but it is also a physical act, denting, shaping, and irrevocably changing a text. Linking the carving in texts with the carving of texts, Sexton engages the intersection of form and content as she excavates language and literary history.

After seeing the continuity between Sexton's navigation of texts and her descriptions of the writing process, we will turn to her annotating of books. For Sexton, annotations become extensions of emotion and voice, like poems themselves.

Annotating in public

During one of Sexton's therapy sessions, she exclaimed to her doctor, "[m]y copy of this damn book *Henderson* is all underlined: that is the way *I* feel, that is it!" (*AS*, 162). Underlining suggests a form of emphasis that Sexton cannot put into words. Not long after Saul Bellow's *Henderson the Rain King* (1959) was published, Sexton dramatically observed in a 1960 letter, "I would rather read it than breathe" (*SP*, 102).[91]

In another instance, Rahv's introduction to Franz Kafka's *Selected Stories* (1952) elicited a similarly powerful reaction from Sexton. Perhaps during Rahv's course, Sexton opened her hardcover copy of Kafka's stories and underlined the following phrases in black ink (Figure 3.1):

> In *The Metamorphosis*, I would say, Kafka for the first time fully realized his own innermost conception of writing—<u>a conception of inexpressible urgency</u> <u>and inwardness</u>. Long before the composition of the story, he attempted to explain what writing meant to him when he said in a letter to his friend Oskar Pollak that "<u>the books we need are of the kind that act upon</u> us <u>like a misfortune, that make us suffer like the death of someone we love more than ourselves.</u>"[92]

Sexton's response as she read can itself be described as one of "inexpressible urgency." Beneath this passage, Sexton added in blue ink, "Yes! Yes!"[93] The two ink colors suggest that she may have returned to this passage more than once. Sexton continued using blue ink, drawing a bracket in the left margin around the conclusion of this passage at the top of the next page ("feel as though we were on the verge of suicide, or lost in a forest remote from all human habitation—a book should serve as the ax for the frozen sea within us."), and noted a final "Yes" (Figure 3.2).[94]

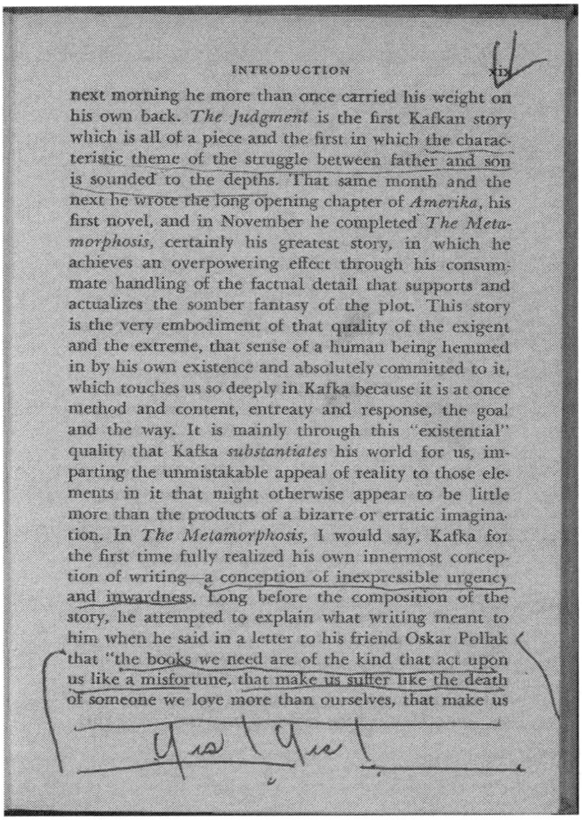

Figure 3.1 Anne Sexton's annotations in Philip Rahv's introduction to Franz Kafka's *Selected Stories*, page xix, Harry Ransom Center, The University of Texas at Austin.

Sexton recounted annotating Kafka's observation in a series of undated presentation notes. Seeking to entertain and provide a glimpse of her inspiration, she confided in her listeners:

> One of my secret instructions to myself as a poet is . . . "whatever you do, don't be boring." However, I don't attempt to entertain an audience, but to get them caught up in the story I am trying to tell. Most of my poems tell stories, Therefore it was quite natural for me to choose the words of a prose writer when I was looking for something that would explain the kind of writing I try to do. When I read the following quote in the introduction to Kafka's short stories I wrote YES YES in the margin . . . this is what I want, YES YES. . . . Kafka said . . . "The books we need are of the kind that act upon us like a misfortune, that

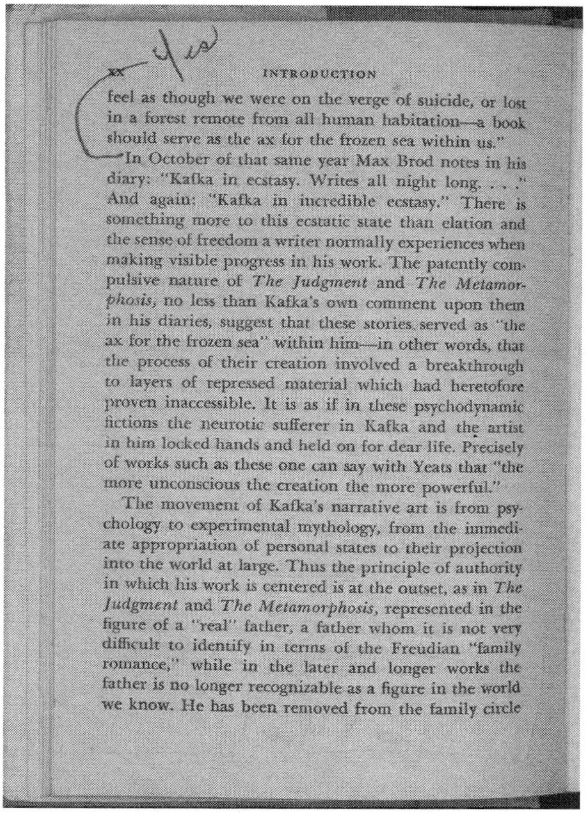

xx INTRODUCTION

feel as though we were on the verge of suicide, or lost in a forest remote from all human habitation—a book should serve as the ax for the frozen sea within us."

In October of that same year Max Brod notes in his diary: "Kafka in ecstasy. Writes all night long. . . ." And again: "Kafka in incredible ecstasy." There is something more to this ecstatic state than elation and the sense of freedom a writer normally experiences when making visible progress in his work. The patently compulsive nature of *The Judgment* and *The Metamorphosis*, no less than Kafka's own comment upon them in his diaries, suggest that these stories served as "the ax for the frozen sea" within him—in other words, that the process of their creation involved a breakthrough to layers of repressed material which had heretofore proven inaccessible. It is as if in these psychodynamic fictions the neurotic sufferer in Kafka and the artist in him locked hands and held on for dear life. Precisely of works such as these one can say with Yeats that "the more unconscious the creation the more powerful."

The movement of Kafka's narrative art is from psychology to experimental mythology, from the immediate appropriation of personal states to their projection into the world at large. Thus the principle of authority in which his work is centered is at the outset, as in *The Judgment* and *The Metamorphosis*, represented in the figure of a "real" father, a father whom it is not very difficult to identify in terms of the Freudian "family romance," while in the later and longer works the father is no longer recognizable as a figure in the world we know. He has been removed from the family circle

Figure 3.2 Sexton's annotations in Rahv's introduction to Kafka, page xx, Ransom Center.

> make us suffer like the death of someone we love more than ourselves, that make us feel as though we were on the verge of suicide, or[95] lost in a forest remote from all human habitation—a book should serve as the ax for the frozen sea within us". . . . and that is what I want from a poem . . . a poem should serve as the ax for the frozen sea within us.[96]

Sexton adopted "a book should serve as the ax for the frozen sea within us" as the epigraph for *All My Pretty Ones* (1962) and discussing the quotation became part of her interview repertoire. In *The Hudson Review* (1966), Patricia Marx asked Sexton whether her epigraph to *All My Pretty Ones* captures "the purpose you want your poetry to serve?" Sexton responded, "Absolutely. . . . it should be a shock to the sense[s]. It should almost hurt" (*NES*, 71–2).[97] The epigraph alone lacks the remaining portion of the passage, particularly the extremity of the portions that Sexton noted. When she adds, "I put it in the book to show the reader what I felt" (72), Sexton's phrasing also recalls her response to Bellow, "that is the way *I* feel."[98] In both cases, an underlined or annotated book prompts a sensation that Sexton cannot find words to describe. The sentiments she notes are those to which she connects in essence, and on which she can build.

Weaving writers and passages into her public performances, Sexton gestured toward her reading. She did so with a degree of ambiguity and extremity that contributed to her construction of a public persona that is at a distance from academia. As she prepared to teach her "Anne on Anne" class at Colgate, she drafted questions and answers that would guide students through close readings of her poems. In doing so, Sexton demonstrated an awareness of academic conventions and combined them with details and methods she had acquired along the way. In the process, she introduced her students to her poems and the circumstances informing their composition.

Annotating herself

Sexton was at Colgate, but not of it. When Ted Hughes visited in 1971, he encountered a quintessential Central New York winter: "There is about 15 inches of snow everywhere, except for the roads. Beside the roads the snow is banked up as high as myself."[99] Despite the cold weather, one of her students remembers Sexton's clothes as "diaphanous."[100] In a photograph from the evening reading she gave after her first "Anne on Anne" class session in February 1972, Sexton is dressed formally in a black and white sheath tied with a bow. Poised, mid-gesture, her hand is clenched (Figure 3.3).[101] One of her students remembers Sexton's ease as she taught,[102] she "didn't lecture. She thought out loud. . . . She planned the class very carefully and then inspiration took over. . . . Someone can't be . . . musing for ten minutes and reading notes."[103] But the marginalia and passages that two of Sexton's students noted in their books from the course indicate that she addressed the lecture material, questions, and answers she had prepared.[104] Even so, she demonstrated a certain candor; after observing her class, Rooney concluded that Sexton "has a wonderful casualness with her own work. While she is proud of herself she does not feign genius and will admit she is ignorant of something in her own poem."[105]

In her "Anne on Anne" class, Sexton introduced her students to the creativity, close reading, and public role that comprised her experience as a poet.[106] While Sexton was teaching a course on her own poetry and not a poetry workshop, she asked the students to complete creative exercises in which they might "write a character sketch using a persona" (*CL*, Preface; 2). As she put it in her preface to the lectures, the students "will know a lot more about writing and the way a writer thinks" (2). In the process, Sexton's students became acquainted with the gravity that her poems demonstrate.[107] She added, offsetting her anxiety with a typical self-deprecating

Anne Sexton, author of five volumes of poetry, gave a reading of her own work last Wednesday night in the Jerome Room. Miss Sexton, who won a Pulitzer prize in 1961 for her *Live o r Die* included mainly selections from that book, as well as *To Bedlam and Part Way Back*. The Crawshaw professor of English will offer two courses this semester, one in her own poetry, and one in poetry writing.

(photo by Madison)

Figure 3.3 The Colgate News, 11 February 1972, page 8.

remark, "[y]ou don't need to worry about spelling or punctuation because I am terrible at both. You need to worry more about a certain sense of style" (3). In doing so, Sexton underscored the significance of craft for her students, some of whom were probably aspiring writers.

The primary assignment for students in the course was a 30- to 50-page interview with Sexton—asking new questions and fabricating answers—or a publishable essay on her work (*CL*). At the close of teaching notes for the introductory session, Sexton advised students to read her interviews in *The Paris Review* and *The Hudson Review* and also noted that she would read the second interview aloud during the same class period (Preface, 3). Unlike responding to an interviewer's questions, which involves a certain degree of spontaneity, writing her teaching notes provided Sexton with an opportunity to prepare and revise.[108]

Sexton's ten "Anne on Anne" classes began with what she called "mini-lectures" introducing the theme and poems for the session (*CL*, Preface; 2). Sexton also prepared questions (with answers in parentheses) to lead her students through explications of her poems. While many of these answers may result from Sexton's prior discussions of her poems in workshops and interviews, the range of determinate and indeterminate answers she provides—sometimes one word, sometimes three, sometimes she does not know—creates a text of her reading of her own work.

The structure of Sexton's "Anne on Anne" classes revised Lowell's division of his workshop into two segments:

> During the first hour Lowell would discuss a poem or two from the assigned anthology; he could spend a long time talking about the effects of just one or two lines by master poets. Then he would turn to the students' poems.
>
> (*AS*, 91)

In Sexton's course, her work provided the subject of both segments, with students' creative exercises filling an additional role. She departed from aspects of Lowell's "burly sorcery" that she found less engaging (*Complete Poems*, 32; line 13).[109] As she recalled in "Classroom at Boston University" (1961), "[u]nused to classes of any kind, it seemed slow and uninspired to me. But I had come in through a back door and was no real judge" (*NES*, 3). She later complained to *The Paris Review*,

> At first I felt an impatient desire to interrupt his slow, line-by-line readings. He would read the first line, stop, and then discuss it at length. I wanted to go through the whole poem quickly and then go back. I couldn't see any merit in dragging through it until you almost hated the damned thing, even your own poems, especially your own. At that point, I wrote to Snodgrass about my impatience and his reply went this way, "Frankly, I used to nod my head at his every statement, and he taught me more than a whole gang of scholars could." So I kept my mouth shut, and Snodgrass was right.[110]
>
> (91)

In her own classes, Sexton offered backstories for her poems. Her thoroughness is perhaps a desire to overcompensate and fill ten lectures with discussions of her own work.

Sexton's "Anne on Anne" teaching notes—composed predominately on her confidence-inspiring yellow paper—remain piled in her file folder, itself stained with coffee rings inside the back cover. On the back of the folder, using "her traditional thick black felt-tip pen," Sexton indicated for posterity, "Lectures (Colgate University) Chair – Crawshaw Professor DO NOT Publish except for an occasional excerpt if deemed proper by literary executor or heirs. Anne Sexton 1973" (Gray Sexton, 4; *CL*).[111] The personal contents present an ostensible reason for restricting publication. Her hesitancy to publish the entirety of her teaching notes may also reflect an insecurity regarding the accuracy of the historical and literary information she introduced.

Sexton opened her third lecture on narrative poems with an overview of the genre:

> Poetry was initially an oral art before it was written down. It was cast in rhyme because rhyme was easier for troubadours to remember. A roving troubadour travelled from village to village singing his ballads and narrative tales. The tradition is less strong now because today story telling takes place largely in prose. We have the short story and we have the novel, but in my poetry I have revived along with quite a few of my contemporaries the art of telling a story in a poem. It's something I like very much to see when I read a poem. I like poems that tell stories. Many of my persona poems tell stories as you have seen, but they will present a voice with the eye outside myself. Lyric poems very seldom tell stories. The lyric poem more generally seizes a moment, a situation, an instant in time and kind of encapsulates it[.] . . . The earliest narrative poems, of course, were epic. They told tales of grandure [sic] and heroism in the manner of Beowolf [sic][.] . . .
>
> We'd have to follow all the great novels down through history to understand this technique, but today we're interested in the use of this technique in poetry where it still lives and thrives.
>
> (CL, 3; 1–2)

While misspelling *Beowulf*, Sexton's overview of the lyric poem frames her introduction of her own poems that "tell stories," and pays homage, of which she may not have been aware, to predecessors that she notes not having read. Her note, for instance, that "the lyric poem . . . seizes a moment . . . an instant in time," alludes to Pound's definition of an image as "that which presents an intellectual and emotional complex in an instant of time."[112] It is possible that Sexton was repeating a version of what she had heard it in a workshop.[113]

In a portion she crossed out, Sexton introduced the epistolary novel in order to frame her own incorporation of correspondence in her poems. In an offhand manner riddled with spelling errors, Sexton recounted that

> the first novel in English history was a lovely little thing called PAMELA by Richardson. [She then adds] Tom Jones by Fielding [above the following line, which is crossed out]. As some of you probably know it was an epistolitory [sic] novel. It was written in letter form. Poor little Pamela was a serving girl who was forced to do her master's wishing very much against her own will. But it was very much a tongue-in-cheek novel, because of course it was a great romantic tale. I forget exactly who her letters were addressed to, but I think they were to her family and they all were in the tone of help, help, I am being held prisoner. Techniques are a little more sophisticated now, but it's still a good story.
>
> (CL, 3; 2–3)

Sexton's inability to reproduce central details is not as interesting as the fact that she, at least initially, prepared to discuss the origins of the English novel in a course on her own poetry. As she began to plan this session, Sexton was not projecting as uninformed a persona as that which she often presented to interviewers. Even while being glib, Sexton prepared a history that she may have felt obligated to gesture toward in a college course.

The arc of Sexton's course, however, introduced the genres and central concerns that her poems engage. In her seventh lecture on prosody, for instance, after noting her "great respect" for poetic form, she added,

> When I was in high school and dabbling in poetry, I was very aware of metrics, the stress, iambic pentameter and so forth. I've since forgotten every definition. I can barely remember what iambic means. My secretary had to tell me what pentameter was.
>
> (*CL*, 7; 2)

Sexton's anecdotes depict her casual handling of facts. While perhaps telling the story for dramatic effect, she contradicts her earlier account of writing sonnets following Richards's demonstration, during which she may have practiced iambic pentameter prior to hiring a secretary. Sexton's response to prosody in her youth also suggests a position comparable to the members of her audience, for whom fewer years had passed since high school.

Perhaps assuming that her Colgate students would be familiar with her nineteenth- and early twentieth-century predecessors, Sexton added, "I had never read Williams or Elliott [sic] or Pound or Whitman or Dickenson [sic]. Don't ask me what kind of school I was attending. It was mostly boy-crazy school anyway" (*CL*, 7; 3). While belittling her performance as a student, she demonstrates her awareness, in the misspelled shape it takes, of five canonical poets. In the final stanza of Sexton's poem "Three Green Windows" (1962), her persona concludes, "I have misplaced the Van Allen belt, / . . . / I have forgotten the names of the literary critics. / I know what I know" (*Complete Poems*, 106; lines 31–5). Recording what may have been Sexton's comment during class, one of her students wrote in her book beside the first three lines beginning with the "Van Allen belt" reference, "may have misplaced them, but still can name them."[114] Sexton's final line also recalls her comment to her therapist (a year before completing this poem), regarding her desire to teach, "I want to show them what I know."[115] As she taught, Sexton was able to do so. While in her poem and her teaching notes Sexton drew a contrast between academic knowledge and life experience, the casualness with which she listed names (and references to writers elsewhere) reminds us that she knows more than she lets on.

As Gill has argued, Sexton engaged critics' assessments of her confessional techniques and her construction of personae in her "Anne on Anne" notes. In her penultimate lecture, Sexton quoted from A. R. Jones's "Necessity and Freedom: the poetry of Robert Lowell, Sylvia Plath and Anne

Sexton."[116] Near the close of her course, she may have felt it was obligatory not only to bring in preeminent considerations of her use of personal material, but also to quote Jones's assessment of her response to Eliot's "Tradition and the Individual Talent," underlining the phrases indicated below:

> for . . . [Sexton], poetry is a way of handling and coming to terms with painful and intensely personal experience. T. S. Eliot's assertion that, "the more perfect the artist, the more completely separate in him will be the man who suffers and the mind which creates" indicates the dualism that is operating in these poems[.] . . . "[T]he artist creates the poem within which the suffering is contained and given meaning".
>
> (*CL*, 9; 5)

The passage from Eliot, which Gill and other critics have invoked to assess Sexton's response to his theories of poetic impersonality, signals the detachment that a persona enables.[117]

Introducing Eliot's separation of the artist from his work, however, also raises larger questions regarding the strength and content of Sexton's poetry. Her references to *Beowulf* and *Pamela* suggest a broader desire to justify her work as the subject of a literature course. Sexton also interrogates the literary throughout her lectures. Introducing the poem "It is a Spring Afternoon" in the sixth lecture, she recounts that

> Some years ago Cosmopolitan Magazine sent me a picture of a woman lying on a tree limb over a river and offered me $300 if I'd write a poem to go with it. She looked a little lewd, but that was because of her marcel permanent, something left over from the nineteen thirties. But the more I thought about it, the more I felt that she deserved to lie there if it were spring, so I wrote this poem. I didn't sell it to Cosmopolitan. They turned it down as too literary. The New Yorker published it.
>
> (*CL*, 6; 8)

While her poem transcended the suggestions of *Cosmopolitan*'s photograph, Sexton's anecdote underscores her ability to achieve literary recognition. Plath had praised *All My Pretty Ones* for being "so blessedly unliterary" (*LV2*, 811). While earlier in Sexton's career the term "literary" may have appeared synonymous with masculine, formal, or conservative, in this instance it legitimizes her work without silencing its irreverence.

Annotating "Her Kind"

In December 1959, Sexton began a reading of her own poetry at Harvard University with her poem "Her Kind." It was still a new poem then, one she had composed a year earlier. Sitting in the front row was the wife of the English Department Chairman, Harry Levin.[118] After Sexton read "Her

Kind," Mrs. Levin removed herself from the auditorium. When Sexton gave a reading of her poetry at Colgate in 1965, she told this story, and even as it may have prompted a few glances toward the door, perhaps laughter followed that would have put those in attendance at ease.[119] Sexton may not have shared their calm, admitting, "It's kind of scary for me to be back here, but you'll have to take me the way I am."[120] *The Colgate Maroon* printed a dimly lit photograph of Sexton leaning back with arms crossed, her high heels visible. Her pose is not inviting.[121] But it also speaks to the seriousness with which she took her work, impressing upon her audience, "[a]ll poetry is poetry of rebellion."[122] "Her Kind" is a poem born out of this sentiment, and in her teaching notes Sexton demonstrates how this is the case.

Preparing her "Anne on Anne" teaching notes, Sexton worked from strategies that had brought her success in her poetry readings. She recounted in her fifth lecture, which addressed lyric poetry:

> The first poem I'd like to consider is my standard introductory poem. I have never given a reading without reading "Her Kind" first off. I always say "I'll read you this poem, and then you'll know just what kind of poet I am, just what kind of woman I am. And then if anyone wishes to leave, they may do so." The first time I made this statement and read the poem—and this was at Harvard—the wife of the head of the English Department rose solemnly from her front row seat and walked out.
> (*CL*, 5; 1–2)

While Sexton opened her poetry readings with "Her Kind," she hesitated to teach the poem until halfway through the semester. This seems counterproductive, since it was a poem that brought her such confidence, but since she had given a reading of her poetry at Colgate on the night of their first class meeting, the students may also have already heard the story.[123] Sexton's decision also suggests her consideration of the poem's role in different contexts. She did not choose "Her Kind" as the opening poem in the book in which it was first published, *To Bedlam in Part Way Back*, and it would not have necessarily fit as a beginning to the progression that Sexton charts in her course.

Composing her teaching notes gave Sexton a certain degree of control. For a short time, she was able to be a teacher, student, critic, and poet. The questions Sexton drafted for "Her Kind" begin with her persona's eccentricities:

> In each of the three stanzas I portray myself as a witch. In the first stanza what kind of witch (mad, lonely, disfigured). In the second stanza what kind of witch (domestic, obsessional, mother-like, a lover of possessions, a whiner). In the third stanza what kind of witch (the adulteress, the Salem witch, the sexual witch). Why in the first stanza do I say "a woman like that is not a woman quite"? (too crazy, too

possessed) Why in the second stanza do I say 'a woman like that is misunderstood' (is not always loved because she is so obsessional, is not always understood because she is so female. The implication is that <u>men</u> don't understand her.) Why do I say in the third stanza "a woman like that is not ashamed to die"? (her death is a consumation [sic] of their wicked love—ashamed is the key word, to die is what witches do).

(*CL* 5; 2)

Sexton's terse explanation of what constitutes "not a woman, quite" emphasizes normality and possession, suggesting that the protagonist's will is not her own (*Complete Poems*, 15; line 6). When she composed her teaching notes, Sexton left out the comma that separates "quite" from the rest of the line and leads to a pause accentuating the word's suggestion of propriety.[124] Sexton's answer suggests, in part, that a more socially acceptable woman is sane, self-motivated, and not driven by inappropriate concerns, or those that come from less socially acceptable sources. Her definition not only speaks to both sanity and femininity as socially defined categories, but also is unexpectedly simple considering all that "not a woman, quite" could suggest. The word "quite," in particular, suggests a sense of formality, class, and decorum that the persona's behavior questions and subverts.

As Sexton became more comfortable preparing close readings of her poems, her answers to her questions became more expansive. Initially, as we will see in the following segment, it appears that she felt more obligated to provide clear, concise answers for the meaning of her lines and significance of her images. As her teaching notes progress, she acknowledged greater ambiguity in her verse, leaving room for students' contributions. In the process, she also documented an awareness of the types of questions to which readers or literary critics might have answers that she could not, or declined to, supply.

Parenthetical annotations

The questions and answers that Sexton prepared in her teaching notes emphasized how poems work. One of her students recalled that the class "read the poems aloud. We'd analyze the poems line by line. She allowed for a lot of student input."[125] In some instances, Sexton did not provide answers to the questions to which students might contribute most. At the close of her questions on "Unknown Girl in the Maternity Ward," for example, she asked, "[w]ould anyone like to comment on the form of this poem?" (*CL*, 1; B).

Sexton's questions resemble those she may have encountered in poetry workshops and the associative discourse of psychiatric sessions. As Starbuck recalled a 1961 meeting in Sexton's home,

> [n]one of us in this group was the psychiatrist kind of workshop teacher, poem teacher; we didn't try to do the kind of thing Anne later learned

to do as a teacher—insistently but noncoercively asking simple little questions about where does this come from, how did you dream this up, how old were you when this first happened to you.

(AS, 98)

In her teaching notes, Sexton posed these questions to her students about her work, providing background information to which they would not otherwise have access.

Sexton's responses to her own questions reflect a degree of indeterminacy, yet also annotate her poems with answers so that she would not be caught off guard before the class. In some instances, Sexton's teaching notes may record her first attempt to answer questions regarding the significance of her lines, and in others, she may be recording her understanding of poems that she had discussed for several years. As a result, Sexton records her close reading of her own poems and an awareness of the conventions of literary analysis.

In an interview after teaching her "Anne on Anne" class, Sexton described her hesitation to read her work as a critic might: "something might block me and say, 'Hey, wait a minute, I'm not sure I want to know that' (the superego or ego or whatever). I'm not saying I don't read them and couldn't explicate them. . . . Sometimes I do" (*NES*, 185). Sexton's use of the term explicate suggests her knowledge of Brooks and Warren's terminology in *Understanding Poetry*. Out of an interest in her own preparation or an assumption that in the classroom she, or her students, should be able to answer questions as to the significance in her poems, some of the questions and answers Sexton prepared did, in fact, assume and produce a single response. In other instances, however, she replied to her own queries with question marks or multiple answers that suggest indecision or acknowledgment of a range of interpretations. Sexton's reservation speaks to her later response during an interview that in explicating "[y]ou might be fooling yourself or lying to yourself. The critic might be way off, too. If you look into enough criticism, that can be well established. . . . the poem should be what it means to its *readers*" (186).[126]

Sexton's questions and answers for the poems she introduced in her lectures served as review and close reading. Writing her first lecture, Sexton prepared precise answers to her questions for the poem "Portrait of an Old Woman on a College Tavern Wall" from her first book:[127]

Who is singing "Did you hear what it said"? (the poet) Why are the poets lying? (they think they are immortal) What is the best line in the poem? (poets are sitting in my kitchen) How does the old lady feel as she speaks to them? (jealous because they are alive, prophetic because they will die.) She wants to stop them with a chill finger. How does she do it? (in the last line).

(CL, 1; A)

One of Sexton's students in the class recorded notes in the margins of her copy of this poem suggesting that Sexton asked the questions and supplied the answers she had prepared.[128] Beside "Poets are sitting in my kitchen" (*Complete Poems*, 19; line 29), the student added, "favorite line."[129] In doing so, she interpreted what may have been Sexton's indication of quality or effectiveness as a reflection of Sexton's own interest.[130]

As the course progressed, Sexton included a more extensive range of answers in parentheses. During her fifth lecture, for instance, Sexton introduced "Noon Walk on Asylum Lawn," also from her first book:

> Next we have a very early poem. It is about madness and although you may not be specialists in madness I would ask you to read it and describe what kind of person this is. . . .
> What kind of person? (suspicious, distrustful, skeptical, doubting, unsafe, paranoid) How is this seen? (through nature) Can you tell me what the psalm does for the poem (it brings in an old familiar litany turned sour but what else). How would you characterize this lyric (it is an anti-lyric, a dark song).
>
> (*CL*, 5; 3)

In her first parenthetical annotation, Sexton provided six adjectives describing the persona, several of which are interchangeable. She subsequently turned to perspective, asking, "How is this seen? (through nature)." The poem captures the persona's sense that a "suspicious tree" "sucks the air" (*Complete Poems*, 27, 28; lines 2, 4). Sexton communicates the persona's impressions using pathetic fallacy and synesthesia as "[t]he grass speaks," and the speaker "hear[s] green chanting all day" (*Complete Poems*, 28; lines 6, 7). As the persona concludes that "[t]here is no safe place" (line 15), the poem becomes what Sexton calls "an anti-lyric, a dark song."

Sexton's directness as she addressed her relationship with her parents in her teaching notes recalls C. K. Williams's impression of "how calmly and with such illumination she could speak about it, and herself, really as though she was separate from it all."[131] Discussing "All My Pretty Ones," she asked:

> What is mean [sic] by "this year's jinx? From the list of things he left, what can you tell about my father? Do you think I did the right thing to throw the pictures out? In what way did I keep the pictures and yet throw them out? What is meant by the mother saying in her diary, "you overslept"? After I had written this, my psychiatrist said, of course you have forgiven your father. It says so in the poem. What did I have to forgive him for? What do I leave out of the poem that you could surmise?[132]
>
> (*CL*, 3; 5)

Sexton reviewed more obscure aspects of the poem and asked questions attending to remaining elements:

> What do I mean by "this year's jinx rides us apart"? What is the jinx? (the fates, the additional death). What do I mean by "a second shock boiling its stone to your heart"? (It is the way a child would see a shock, and poetry should be written by the child in you.) In the second stanza who is the small boy? (my father) In the second stanza the commodore in the mailman's suit reminds me of Van Gogh's painting of his postman. Why do I throw out the book? (Because I don't know the people.).
>
> (*CL*, 3; n.p.)

A jinx spurs an unfortunate outcome, and Sexton's choice becomes clearer when she notes "the fates, the additional death."[133] In response to her lines, "I'll ever know what these faces are all about / I lock them into their book and throw them out" (*Complete Poems*, 50; lines 19–20), Sexton asked why her persona discards the book. Her answer, "[b]ecause I don't know these people," echoes her lines in the poem: "boxes of pictures of people I do not know. / I touch their cardboard faces" (lines 9–10). In her copy of *All My Pretty Ones*, Sexton's student recorded the explanation Sexton had prepared and added to it: "[d]idn't know these people & didn't know father."[134]

One of the questions that Sexton proposed in her teaching notes for "All My Pretty Ones" was "[w]hat do I leave out of the poem that you could surmise? (*CL*, 3; 5). While students may not have been aware at the time, later in the course they would be able to answer such a question without guessing. As we will see in the following segment, Sexton's teaching of her own draft pages introduces students to the materials she removed from poems. Distributing copies of her poem drafts enabled students' encounters with the development of the poems they had analyzed. In doing so, Sexton adapts academic conventions to suit her materials.

Teaching raw material

In a course on reading and understanding Sexton's poems, her worksheets brought students closer to her writing process. Over 30 years later, a former "Anne on Anne" student recalled "[t]he excitement of stuff in her hand." This student not only found seeing Sexton's drafts remarkable but was also impressed with her openness to the undergraduates' feedback.[135] During the seventh and eighth class sessions, Sexton distributed copies of her drafts of two long poems, "Flee on Your Donkey" (1966) and "Eighteen Days Without You" (1969). A course on Sexton's work may have been considered plausible because her published volumes had received a degree of acceptance, including a Pulitzer Prize in 1967.[136] Introducing students to the particular character of her manuscripts, Sexton also demonstrated the significance of texts and versions of them that remained outside of anthologies and the canon to which they may have been accustomed.[137]

As Sexton recounted during her interview with *The Hudson Review*, her process of composition was integral to her understanding of her poems:

> Often I keep my worksheets, so that once in a while when I get depressed and think that I'll never write again, I can go back and see how that poem came into being. You watch the work and you watch the miracle. You have to look back at all those bad words, bad metaphors, everything started wrong, and then see how it came into being, the slow progress of it, because you're always fighting to find out what it is that you want to say.
>
> (*NES*, 73)[138]

Sexton's practice of revisiting her drafts contributes to her understanding of poetic language and her own voice. For Sexton, manuscripts preserve early starts that are "never really lost, they're on a worksheet" (127).[139] In doing so, Sexton engaged in a process like that which Kumin described as she recalled their writing practices: "We hammered stuck pieces into form rather than abandon them. We preserved the raw works that refused to cohere."[140] Sexton's worksheets were "raw works" that, in facsimile, became texts for her students.

Sexton introduced her drafts of "Flee on Your Donkey" in the seventh lecture:

> Now we're going to play detective. We're going to see how a poem is made and remade and remade. I have made copies of two sets of worksheets, both strangely enough not poems in form. . . . Houghton Mifflin sent me a copy of Rimbaud's poetry and as I glanced through it one day in June I saw my name. It said "Anne, Anne", and then in French it said flee on your donkey. Because it was written to me, or my namesake, I wrote it down on a slip of paper and put it in my wallet. . . . The reason I tell you these details is that you will see them on the worksheets. No one else in the world knows them. . . . So when I got to the hospital, I took out my little Rimbaud quote "Anne, Anne, flee on your donkey" and flee I should and would, seeing my sickness as the old dress that I would put on. That night and the next morning I wrote my first draft of the poem, a poem that would take me from June 1962 to June 1966 to complete.
>
> (*CL*, 7; 7–8)

The fact that Sexton had an anecdote prepared regarding her composition of this poem may have inspired her teaching of its drafts. Earlier in this chapter, we encountered her account of carrying the Rimbaud lines in her wallet. This story was in her interview with *The Paris Review*, which some of her more diligent students may have read. Preparing to speak to English students, however, Sexton noted the book of avant garde poetry she had received. Casually leafing through the unnamed book (which may have been the copy of *A Season in Hell* in her library), Sexton recognizes her own name as a child might.[141] At the same time, dropping his name acts as a form of parenthetical citation, noting to readers that she has become aware of such poets and knows that they are significant.

While revising "Flee on Your Donkey," Sexton eliminated references to her academic accomplishments and the breadth of her reading.[142] Students would have seen their presence and learned of their deletion. As such, these pages also record the development of Sexton's career and the ways that she revised her accounts of it. The second stanza that Sexton removed from the second page (C2), alluded to Sexton's Radcliffe grant: "I sold cosmetics from door to door. / Since then I sold some poems / and got a grant."[143] In another instance, however, Sexton makes fun of her ambitious interests: "Sometimes I read / Freud and Marx at teatime / and tried hard to be / a bogus intellectual."[144] These lines provide a contrast to Sexton's admission in her notes for her first lecture that she was once "a reader of psychoanalytic journals and not for any particular reason except that I was in therapy and wanted to know more, more, more" (*CL*, 1; 3).[145]

Unlike the sprawl of "Flee on Your Donkey," the orderly segments of Sexton's later poem, "Eighteen Days Without You," provided the subject of her eighth "Anne on Anne" class session. As we observed regarding "Flee on Your Donkey," Sexton also discussed her composition of "Eighteen Days Without You" with *The Paris Review*:

> my husband said to me, "I can't stand it any longer, you haven't been with me for days." That poem originally was "Twenty-One Days Without You" and it became "Eighteen Days" because he had cut out the inspiration; he demanded my presence back again, into his life.
>
> (*NES*, 101)

Before teaching at Colgate, Sexton had selected to read portions of "Eighteen Days," as she referred to it (*CL*, 8; 1), when she was invited to speak at Harvard's Phi Beta Kappa ceremony in 1968 (*AS*, 302). In her draft material for the presentation, she observed that the poem addresses "the little things we all live by daily." [146] Introducing "Eighteen Days" in her fourth Colgate lecture, Sexton expanded upon this idea, explaining that the poem

> is a cycle of love poems written to a lover while he is gone . . . The diary device helps you catch all the little daily domestic mundane things; the

little whims of nature, in this case the snow and ice storms, the birds that visit, and the dreams. This poem also tells a story. There is exposition as well as a series of little lyrics.

(*CL*, 4; 4)

Drawing out the facets of daily life to which the poem speaks, she also introduces how it works, and what makes this long poem an effective one.

The questions Sexton composed regarding "Eighteen Days" point to its specificity, from its obscure references to whether it invites comparison to the poet's life. She asks,

What do I mean by Christ's lights. [sic] What do I mean by cat green ice? What do I mean by the hemlocks are the only young thing left? In December 2nd, how do the nuthatches jailed to the spine of the feeder symbolize my emotion on that day?

(*CL*, 4; 4)

Sexton asked questions for which she did not have an answer: "December 10th. What is a beaver moon? (I don't know.)" (*CL*, 4; 6). Other questions elide the persona with the poet, yet interrogate the poem on its own terms: "December 11th. Describe the lover as you see him? I think this is the only description of him" (*CL*, 4; 6). She presses further on the poem's veracity: "December 16th. This poem gives a little of their history. Do you think it is my history? Do you think it is his history? Does he exist? Is there a cabin[?]" (*CL*, 4; 7). In addition to testing whether the poem invites comparisons to her own life, Sexton is demonstrating the ways that each of the poem's days contribute to its overall scheme, and more broadly, the way that words and images form a poem.

Beginning her eighth lecture, Sexton introduced her "Eighteen Days" drafts with an account of how she came to finish the poem:

When you sit down to write a poem, you often have no idea what you want to say. I started eighteen days without you in November, I think with a poem entitled "The Call". . . . Then on the last day of November my psychiatrist left with his family for Europe for three weeks, and it occurred to me that I could use my manic energy writing a poem for every day he was gone. Of such dependencies the creative act evolves. So I put a piece of paper in the typewriter on December 1st and wrote at the top "Twenty-one days without you". . . . I had never done it before, a poem a day, a stiff requirement. . . .

I purposely have not reread these. What they will show you of my personal life I have no idea. It is a very vulnerable position to show your worksheets, but I felt it would greatly enhance your knowledge of me as well as showing you how badly a poem can begin and then how it can be rescued. We will play detective together. We will look at the beginnings, the early fumblings and jottings and find clues. I want you to look as hard as I will look.

The reason I showed you "The Call" to begin with was that about half-way through the poem I said to this fellow who I was teaching with "how the hell will I ever end it?" And he said, "Why don't you end it with "The Call". . . . You will notice that at one point the pages will say "Eighteen Days Without You". I think I was about on December 15th or 16th when my husband said, "I never see you any more." . . . And thus the poem became eighteen days not twenty-one[.] . . . Still, one never knows what one could have written had they had the solitude and time to pursue it.[147]

(*CL*, 8; 1–3)

Near the close of the term, Sexton's composition of "Eighteen Days" also introduced the difficulty of finishing poems.[148] Recounting her decision to end the poem earlier than she had anticipated and to use another poem as the conclusion presented both an anecdote and textual evidence to which she could direct students.[149]

After sharing her own drafts with her students, at the end of her last lecture, Sexton recalled receiving a page of Bellow's *Herzog* manuscript:

Now we come to the last poem ["Live"]. Saul Bellow marked his man-uscript for me and he said "With one long breath, caught and held in his chest, he fought his sadness over his solitary life. Don't cry, you idiot! Live or die, but don't poison everything . . ." And I used part of that quote for my last poem "Live". What would you say the quo-tation meant? (don't foul up the world.) . . . There are a lot of obscure references in this poem, but perhaps you understand every one of them knowing me as you do. Why don't you ask me the questions.

(*CL*, 10; 14–5)

In her final statement, Sexton distances herself from the texts that she has presented, asking the students to do the work of critics.

The peculiarity of Sexton's "Anne on Anne" course enabled her redefi-nition of the roles of poet, teacher, critic, and student. In earlier chapters, we observed midcentury critics defining interpretive practices in relation to modernist texts. In her teaching notes, Sexton responds to and reshapes these practices. Following Berryman's interdisciplinary experiments, how-ever, the idea of Sexton's course suggests an even greater degree of flexibility with regard to content and method. While she had provided students with the option of composing either a new interview with her or a publishable es-say, Rooney observed that Sexton "seems to enjoy being the subject of forty people's intensive attentions. 'I can't wait to read these papers,' she said."[150]

After "Anne on Anne," Middlebrook observed that Sexton's poems

in 1972 . . . show her trying to fit her own experiences into frame-works of cultural critiques she absorbed from her reading and from circulating in academic environments. Never a critic herself, Sexton knew her strengths lay in the indirect ways in which new ideas filtered into her consciousness.

(*AS*, 362)

Sexton's negotiation of academic contexts was inseparable from her poetic strategies. Her library and teaching notes illustrate the extent to which she contributed to her self-presentation as a writer who preferred the types of association that Middlebrook suggests. From her acquisition of literary and critical texts to her grading practices, Sexton demonstrated a greater degree of conscientiousness than critics may have assumed informed her public, poetic, and teaching personae.

***

Like Sexton, as a poet Ted Hughes maintained a peripheral relation to academic institutions. Following Plath's death, Hughes's correspondence with Sexton provided poetic advice from outside of academia.[151] When Sexton taught her own poetry, the sort of detachment that Hughes advocated as a writer and a teacher enabled her to maintain a sense of distance while teaching poems dealing with personal subject matter.

When Hughes read at Colgate during what he called "a pleasant scramble around the colleges,"[152] one of the student newspapers compared *Crow* to *The Waste Land*.[153] But despite the high praise anticipating his reading, Hughes may not have had fond memories of it. His host, Richard Murphy, remembers:

> Ted gave a solo reading on Friday in a large overcrowded room, he got angry with a cameraman who kept moving his camera after Ted had told him to stand still. I sensed hostility to Ted in the audience, and only discovered the cause after he had gone. An associate professor had told his students that an English poet called Ted Hughes would be reading on the campus and they should bear in mind that he had married an American called Sylvia Plath, who was a far better poet, and that many people thought he was responsible for her suicide.[154]

Murphy adds that Hughes's reading was made more awkward by efforts to record it. In the photograph that *The Colgate News* printed following the event, Hughes is in shadow at the podium, leaning forward slightly.[155] His sharply folded collar is visible beneath his jacket and his hand, as his book rests on his forefinger in his grasp, catches the eye. He is stiff and serious, yet also poised, blending delicacy and strain as he holds the book. According to the newspaper's caption, the reading was "packed with students, faculty[,] and many visitors," and "Hughes' poetry, laden with visceral and sexual imagery, enraptured the audience and skirted the border between provocative and shocking." After the visit, Murphy wrote to Hughes, proposing that he come teach at Colgate, as Sexton would be doing so the following year.[156] Murphy added that the chair, Berlind, had

> offered Auden $20, 000 for a term, but Auden turned this down. I have nothing to do with the appointment, but Bruce did say that he would love you to come, but he was afraid you mightn't want to stay here for four months. How about it?[157]

And while nothing came of this, the exchange sheds light on the circumstances preceding Sexton's arrival at Colgate, and the extent to which she differed from the male contemporaries whom the department had entertained as possible visiting faculty.

In 1970, Sexton had sent Hughes a letter admiring his poems in *Crow*, stating that they "are brilliant. They go further than anything you've done. They go into that unknown land where spirits live—crow spirits."[158] Sexton's comment echoes a quotation on the back jacket flap of her hardcover copy that "in *Crow* he [Hughes] reaches deep into the primeval consciousness, penetrating to the very source of the life force itself."[159] Sexton went on to contribute the first endorsement on the back cover of the Harper and Row paperback of *Crow* (1971): "Let all the poets of the world bow down their heads in admiration and awe. Ted Hughes' [sic] *Crow* has done it and it will last for generations."[160]

In *Anne Sexton's Confessional Poetics*, Gill argues that Sexton's teaching notes for her first Colgate lecture address her construction of a confessional persona. *Crow* anchored this effort. Early in her lecture Sexton clarified, "[t]hat is what a persona is, the taking on of a voice, an ancient tradition, a clown show" (*CL*, 1; 1).[161] Such an attempt to perform, embody, and apprehend a perspective is reminiscent of Hughes's accomplishment in *Crow* of inhabiting "the unknown land where spirits live." At the close of her notes for the lecture, Sexton drafted an assignment that she may not have used that included examples of persona poems, adding, "to get a little more contemporary and perhaps more interesting Ted Hughes' [sic] book CROW is all persona" (*CL*, 1; 12).

Annotating for Hughes presented a type of persona, a form that enabled his preparation for teaching in a fashion that adapted contemporary academic practices. As we will see in the Coda: "Ted Hughes and the Midcentury American Academy," teaching provided experience with the life of universities, which Hughes would later encounter as executor of Plath's estate.

Notes

1 A list of the volumes in Sexton's library can be generated from the Ransom Center's Online Catalog: http://catalog.lib.utexas.edu/search/x, accessed 6 May 2019. I thank Richard Oram for bringing this resource to my attention. Richard B. Watson, Head of Reference and Research Services at the Ransom Center checked this figure. Email, Richard B. Watson to the author, 7 February 2020.

2 Recent Sexton scholarship has approached the relationship of her poetry to lyric form, popular culture, the Cold War, juridical discourse, suburban culture of the Fifties, formalism, trauma and incest, and earlier criticism addressed Sexton's poetry in confessional, feminist, and psychological contexts. Regarding the form of the lyric, see Mutlu Konuk Blasing, *Lyric Poetry: The Pain and the Pleasure of Words* (Princeton: Princeton University Press, 2007). For popular culture see, Karen Alkalay-Gut, "The Dream Life of Ms. Dog: Anne Sexton's Revolutionary Use of Popular Culture," *College Literature* 32, no. 4 (2005): 50–73. For juridical discourse, see Deborah Nelson, *Pursuing Privacy in Cold War America* (New York: Columbia University Press, 2002). Concerning the suburbs, see *Anne Sexton's Confessional Poetics* and Clare Pollard, "Her Kind: Anne Sexton, the Cold War and the Idea of the Housewife," *Critical Quarterly* 48, no. 3 (Autumn 2006): 1–24. For formalism, see Philip McGowan in *Anne Sexton and Middle Generation Poetry: The Geography of Grief* (Westport, CT: Praeger Publishers, 2004). Considering Sexton and trauma, see Kalaidjian, *The Edge of Modernism*. For confession, see M. L. Rosenthal, *The New Poets: American and British Poetry since World War II* (New York: Oxford University Press, 1967); Nelson also gives a helpful genealogy in *Pursuing Privacy in Cold War America*. And pertaining to feminist and psychological contexts, see Diana Hume George, *Oedipus Anne: The Poetry of Anne Sexton* (Urbana: University of Illinois Press, 1987), Suzanne Juhasz, *Naked and Fiery Forms: Modern American Poetry by Women, A New Tradition* (New York: Farrar, Straus & Giroux, 1976), 117–43.

3 Diane Wood Middlebrook argues that Sexton's teaching notes for "Anne on Anne" are a valuable resource regarding Sexton's response to her contemporaries Diane Wood Middlebrook, *Anne Sexton: A Biography* (1991; New York: Random House, 1992), 358; hereafter cited in the text as "*AS.*" Gill argues in *Anne Sexton's Confessional Poetics* that these teaching notes "offer an insight into Sexton's understanding of the confessional mode and of her place in it" (26). In *Anne Sexton: Teacher of Weird Abundance*, Salvio assesses Sexton's pedagogical strategies in relation to the field of educational studies.

4 One of Sexton's students explained, "Colgate looked so much different in those days—more like an outpost." Steven Peiffer, email to the author, 17 September 2007.

5 Sexton's arrival coincided with changes at Colgate that reflected the social and political climate of the time. Professor Anthony Aveni remembers student protests in the late sixties and the year before Sexton arrived, Irish activist Bernadette Devlin had visited the campus. Near the close of the term that Sexton spent at Colgate, sophomore Gloria Borger became the first woman to join the editorial board of *The Colgate Maroon*, before becoming a world-renowned journalist. Anthony Aveni, *Class Not Dismissed: Reflections on Undergraduate Education and Teaching the Liberal Arts* (University Press of Colorado, 2014), Kindle Location 1177. Chris Minarich, "Leftist Bernadette Devlin to Give Lecture Tonight," *The Colgate Maroon* (Hamilton, NY), 11 February 1971, page 1. "Maroon Names Three Associate Editors," *The Colgate Maroon*, 18 April 1972, page 12.

6 Paula M. Salvio, *Anne Sexton: Teacher of Weird Abundance* (Albany, NY: State University of New York Press, 2007).

7 Bruce Berlind mentioned, "Colgate's co-ed, which it wasn't when you were here." Letter, Bruce Berlind to Anne Sexton, 13 August 1972, box 18, folder 1, Sexton Papers. While this letter is dated 1972, it is more likely from 1971. One of Sexton former students had a similar impression of the "lonely experience" someone in Sexton's position at Colgate could have. Lydia Woodward, interview with the author, 10 November 2005.

8 Sexton began writing this poem in December 1971, before her first class at Colgate in February 1972 (*AS*, 349). She completed the poem around March 1972, with about a month remaining in the semester. Middlebrook observes that Sexton "was working on the Crawshaw lectures during the months she was writing the celebratory poems of 'O Ye Tongues,' and it seems likely that these two activities encouraged each o 'her" (359). Sexton finished the poem "near Easter 1972" (355). As Middlebrook's endnotes record, Sexton did so before 29 March (456, n355). In 1972, Easter was 2 April, http://www.wheniseastersunday.com/year/1972/, accessed 31 July 2019.

9 Letter, Berlind to Sexton, 13 August 1972, Sexton Papers. Sexton had met Berlind years earlier when she was giving a poetry reading at the University of Rochester, where he was teaching for a term. Berlind, interview with the author. In a therapy session, Sexton notes a Rochester reading in 1961. Diane Middlebrook binder, 1987–1988 (disbound), box 1, folders 2–7, audiotapes and papers of Anne Sexton, 1956–1988, Schlesinger Library, Radcliffe Institute, Harvard University, Cambridge, MA; hereafter cited in the text as "*APAS*."

10 Linda Gray Sexton, conversation with the author, 17 June 2013. Sexton's daughter pointed out that the "Anne on Anne" course was different from other workshops that her mother had taught.

11 Letter, Sexton to Berlind, 27 October 1971, box 18, folder 1, Sexton Papers. Carbon, Ransom Center; Original, Colgate University Special Collections and Archives, Hamilton, NY. See also *AS*, 23. It is likely that Sexton and her husband carried out their suggested visit, as she sent a card notifying Berlind that their flight was due in on 11 December, and she expressed interest in seeing where she would be teaching. Letter, Sexton to Berlind, 1 December 1971, Colgate University Special Collections and Archives.

12 Richard D. Enemark, email to the author, 28 September 2005.

13 Letter, Franklin W. Wallin to Sexton, 5 October 1971, box 18, folder 7, Sexton Papers. Letter, Sexton to Wallin, 20 October 1971, box 18, folder 7, Sexton Papers. Sexton and Kayo may have lived in Hamilton for three months. Kayo knew during Thanksgiving that he wanted to leave college (*AS*, 23), and the editors of Sexton's letters agree with this statement. Anne Sexton, *Anne Sexton: A Self-Portrait in Letters*, ed. Linda Gray Sexton and Lois Ames (1977; Boston, MA: Houghton Mifflin, 1991), 21; hereafter cited in the text as *SP*.

14 Letter, Sexton to Marion L. Blanchard, 17 November 1971, box 18, folder 7. Sexton Papers. After Sexton had brought to the administration's attention her husband's attendance at Colgate, the associate editor of *What's New at Colgate* wrote to Sexton:

> you may well have wondered why we did not include the information that you are the wife of a Colgate alumnus who will be returning to the campus in a very different role 20 years after you first came to the University as a student wife. I regret that we did not have this information.

Letter, Blanchard to Sexton, 8 November 1971, box 18, folder 7, Sexton Papers. See also Jo Gill, *Anne Sexton's Confessional Poetics* (Gainesville: University Press of Florida, 2007), 86 and 87; hereafter cited in the text as "*Anne Sexton's Confessional Poetics*."

15 Sexton also referred to it as "yellow working paper" (*SP*, 325).

16 Anne Sexton, "Colgate University lecture notes," [1972], box 16, folder 5, Sexton Papers; hereafter cited in the text as *CL*. See also Middlebrook, "Anne Sexton: The Making of 'The Awful Rowing toward God,'" in *Rossetti to Sexton: Six Women Poets at Texas*, ed. Dave Oliphant (Austin, TX: Harry Ransom Humanities Research Center, 1992), 223.

17 CD-3, reel 23, 30 May 1961, *APAS*. Sexton later taught a poetry writing course as a fellow (*AS*, 169).

18 CD-3, reel 23, 30 May 1961, *APAS*.

19 McGurl, *The Program Era*, 81. Regarding "show don't tell," see 235.

20 Letter, Richard Murphy to Ted Hughes, 27 September 1971, box 5, folder 7, Hughes Papers.

21 C. K. Williams, email to the author, 10 March 2008. Bruce Berlind brought Williams's attendance of Sexton's class to my attention. Berlind, email to the author, 15 July 2006.

22 Bruce Berlind, email to the author, 22 October 2006. During my interview with Richard D. Enemark, he mentioned that Berlind observed the class.

23 Brian Rooney, "Anne Sexton: Once a Charming Hostess," *The Colgate Maroon* (Hamilton, NY), 7 March 1972, page 11. The author of this article is the son of journalist Andy Rooney.

24 See McGurl for further consideration of the role of impersonality in academia at midcentury.

25 Middlebrook cites "A. S. to John Mood, 21 July 1970, HRHRC" (*AS* 452, n 319). Regarding Sexton's anecdotes, see also Linda Gray Sexton, *Searching for Mercy Street: My Journey Back to My Mother, Anne Sexton* (Boston, MA: Little, Brown and Company, 1994) and Salvio. Following Sexton's reading at Colgate in 1965, Gary Hummel recalled that "Before beginning, Mrs. Sexton put the audience at ease and perhaps surprised it." Gary Hummel, "Anne Sexton, Acclaimed Poet, Reads Work," *The Colgate Maroon* (Hamilton, NY), 10 November 1965, page 1.

26 Middlebrook distinguishes the origins of this narrative in Sexton's interviews in "Becoming Anne Sexton," in *Anne Sexton: Telling the Tale*, ed. Steven E. Colburn (Ann Arbor: University of Michigan Press, 1988), 7–8. In her biography, Middlebrook elaborates that

> [t]he interviews Sexton gave these researchers [at Radcliffe in 1961] provide an index to the life narrative she was evolving for public consumption, which included not mere information but consciousness about the significance of her transformation from housewife into poet.
>
> (*AS*, 151)

27 See Skorczewski, xvi.

28 Anne Sexton, *No Evil Star: Selected Essays, Interviews, and Prose*, ed. Steven E. Colburn (1985; Ann Arbor: University of Michigan Press, 1997), 70; hereafter cited in the text as *NES*. The editors of Sexton's *Self-Portrait in Letters* explain, "In December 1956, Anne had seen the program, 'How to Write a Sonnet' on Educational Television" (*SP*, 29). Middlebrook adds that Sexton "found some ingenious ways to apply the doctor's advice; for instance, she bought a new antenna for her television set so she could watch cultural programs on educational television" (*AS*, 42). Richards was at Harvard at the time, as Middlebrook and Russo note. See also John Paul Russo's *I. A. Richards: His Life and Work* (Baltimore, MD: Johns Hopkins University Press, 1989) regarding Richards's programs teaching English. The station may have been WGBH-TV Channel 2 in Boston. See also http://www.wgbhalumni.org/people/wheatley-parker.html, accessed 16 September 2016.

29 This anecdote and what Gill has called Sexton's "preexisting script[s]" presented a source of confidence and enabled an illusion of candor (*Anne Sexton's Confessional Poetics*, 171). Sexton's anecdote stresses her distance and mediation; she encountered Richards by chance, and on television, which in her interview with *The Paris Review* (1968) she attributed to her psychologist's recommendation (*NES*, 84–5). See also *Anne Sexton's Confessional Poetics*, 1 and *AS*, 179.

30 I. A. Richards taught at Harvard from 1939 to 1963. "I. A. Richards," *Poetry at Harvard*, https://poetry.harvard.edu/i-richards, accessed 14 August 2019.

31 Middlebrook explains in "Poet of Weird Abundance [Excerpts]," in *Critical Essays on Anne Sexton*, ed. Linda Wagner-Martin (Boston, MA: G.K. Hall & Co., 1989), that Sexton

> was not an intellectual. Sexton had only a high school education; she got her training as a poet in workshops. Though she had a quick mind and read widely, her thinking was intuitive rather than systematic. She did not identify herself with a literary tradition, she did not measure herself in terms of precursors, she did not acquire a critical language by which to classify and discriminate.
>
> (78)

"Reprinted . . . from *Parnassus* . . . 1985." Kathleen Spivack also notes Sexton's "lack of formal education and . . . her own insecurity." Kathleen Spivack, *With Robert Lowell and His Circle: Sylvia Plath, Anne Sexton, Elizabeth Bishop, Stanley Kunitz, & Others* (Boston, MA: Northeastern University Press, 2012), 37.

32 Letter, Robert Lowell to Sexton, 11 September 1958, box 22, folder 3, Sexton Papers. Regarding Lowell's workshop see *AS* and Peter Davison, *The Fading Smile: Poets in Boston: From Robert Lowell to Sylvia Plath* (1994; New York: Norton, 1996).

33 Letter, Lowell to Sexton, 15 September 1958, box 22, folder 3, Sexton Papers.

34 Ian Hamilton, "A Conversation with Robert Lowell," 1971, *Robert Lowell: Interviews and Memoirs*, ed. Jeffrey Meyers (1988; Ann Arbor: University of Michigan Press, 1991), 170.

35 Linda Gray Sexton, conversation with the author, 17 June 2013.

36 Regarding Dickinson's fragments, see Marta Werner, *Emily Dickinson's Open Folios: Scenes of Reading, Surfaces of Writing* (Ann Arbor: University of Michigan Press, 1995).

37 Diane Middlebrook, "Circle of Women Artists: Tillie Olsen and Anne Sexton at the Radcliffe Institute," in *Listening to Silences: New Essays in Feminist Criticism*, ed. Elaine Hedges and Shelley Fisher Fishkin (New York: Oxford University Press, 1994), 17; hereafter cited in the text as "Circle of Women Artists." Kumin received her B.A. and M.A. from Radcliffe and Harvard.

38 Gray Sexton, conversation with the author, 17 June 2013.

39 The chance also exists that Sexton composed this piece earlier and completed it later or is depicting her first study.

40 Middlebrook notes that "James Wright had suggested the title" (*AS*, 165).

41 Images of Bellow's letter are included on pages 7 and 8 of *This Business of Words: Reassessing Anne Sexton*, ed. Amanda Golden (Gainesville: University Press of Florida, 2016).

42 At the time of her death, Sexton's wallet still held James Dickey's "ax-job" *New York Times* review of *All My Pretty Ones* (Gray Sexton, 102).

43 Letter, Sexton to Lois Ames, 17 February 1969, box 17, folder 3, Sexton Papers.

44 Writing to Kathleen Spivack, Sexton mentioned "a section of a letter Ted Hughes wrote to me that I have pasted over my desk, and I find it one of the wisest and to me most helpful words about reviews that I have come upon." Letter, Sexton to Kathleen Spivack, 19 June 1974, box 26, folder 5, Sexton Papers. Letter, Ted Hughes to Sexton, 9 August 1967, box 20, folder 7, Sexton Papers.

45 CD-3, reel 50, 17 October 1961, *APAS*.

46 No author, "Women of Talent." *Newsweek*, vol. LVIII, no. 17, 23 October 1961, page 94; hereafter cited in the text as "Women of Talent." This photograph is on the cover of *This Business of Words*. A month before she arrived with *Newsweek* issue, Sexton remarked in a therapy session that during the

summer she had added a study to her home. CD-3, reel 47, 3 October 1961, *APAS*. See also Middlebrook, who brought the full citation of the *Newsweek* article to my attention (*AS*, page 150 and note 150, page 430).

47 Sexton discusses receiving the Radcliffe Grant in CD-3, reel 23, 30 May 1961, *APAS*.

48 White is quoting *SP*, 44–5. Gillian White, *Lyric Shame: The "Lyric" Subject of Contemporary American Poetry* (Cambridge, MA: Harvard University Press, 2014), 107; hereafter cited in the text as "White."

49 Regarding the home in Sexton's poetry, see Jo Gill, "'This house / of herself': Reading Place and Space in the Poetry of Anne Sexton," in *This Business of Words: Reassessing Anne Sexton*, ed. Amanda Golden, 17–37 (Gainesville: University Press of Florida, 2016).

50 Gray Sexton, conversation with the author, 17 June 2013.

51 Ibid.

52 Middlebrook, "Circle of Woman Artists," 19. Middlebrook explains, "Sexton read it [*A Room of One's Own*] too: sandwiched between books on psychiatry and witchcraft, in contrast to which '*A Room of One's Own* was health'" ("Circle of Woman Artists," 19). Middlebrook cites Sexton's 21 March 1963 therapy session ("Circle of Woman Artists," note 10, page 22). Olsen became a Radcliffe Fellow in 1963 ("Circle of Woman Artists," 19). A copy of *A Room of One's Own* does not remain in Sexton's library in the Ransom Center.

53 Gray Sexton, conversation with the author, 17 June 2013.

54 From Sexton's letter of 16 July 1962 to Brother Dennis Farrell, a monk with whom she corresponded. Middlebrook recounted that in 1959, "Anne took her mother's writing desk and a large collection of books" (*AS*, 137). See also *SP*, 395–6. Gray Sexton also noted, "I was at my happiest amid stacks of books, as was she [Sexton]" (114).

55 Dawn M. Skorczewski, *An Accident of Hope: The Therapy Tapes of Anne Sexton* (New York: Routledge, 2012), 92; hereafter cited in the text as "Skorczewski."

56 Sexton had casual working habits, as he tells her doctor: "I spend a lot of time *thinking* or reading. And I like to put my feet up. I like to lean back" (qtd. in Skorczewski, 114). See also 116.

57 As Skorczewski recounts, during the earlier session with Dr. Orne, Sexton dwelled on her response and her desire to add her own poetry books to this doctor's library (116).

58 See Anita Helle, "Anne Sexton's Photographic Self-Fashioning," in *This Business of Words: Reassessing Anne Sexton*, ed. Amanda Golden (Gainesville: University Press of Florida, 2016), 38–72.

59 Photograph by T. Polumbaum (Boston, MA: Houghton Mifflin, 1960).

60 This image may depict Sexton at her desk in the dining room before moving to her wood paneled study. I am indebted to conversations with Anita Helle regarding the conventions of author photographs and Salvio's discussion of the photograph of Sexton reading *To Bedlam and Part Way Back* with her family.

61 Initially, there were more options, including the publisher's proposal of a "sea motif for a jacket theme . . . since your poems have the strength and depth this almost too subtly implies." Letter, Anita Bleecker of Houghton Mifflin to Sexton, 23 February 1962, box 21, folder 1, Sexton Papers.

62 Subsequent book jacket photographs depict Sexton in front of her library. A 1966 film of Sexton in her home depicts her at her desk and the pages she hung up are visible. National Education Television Video. See also *Anne Sexton's Confessional Poetics* regarding this documentary.

63 Middlebrook, "Anne Sexton: The Making of 'The Awful Rowing Toward God,'" 223.

64 Sexton's library includes her daughter's copy of Dante's *Inferno* that she appears to have annotated as a student. Dante Aligheri, *The Inferno: A Verse Rendering for the Modern Reader,* trans. John Ciardi (New York: New American Library, 1954), former owner Gray Sexton, former owner Sexton, Ransom Center. Sexton also refers to Dante's *Inferno* in a letter of 12 February 1964, "I like making sections of poems that interrelate. Maybe I'll call it (the section) 'The Wood of Suicides' (from Dante's *Inferno*)" (*SP*, 232).

65 As a result of her time in therapy, Middlebrook observed that Sexton not only became interested in psychology, but she started to acquire books and demonstrated intellectual curiosity (*AS*, 53).

66 The date of the segment is "Dec. 2, 1971."

67 See http://media.web.britannica.com/eb-media/96/19296-004-E5A41693.jpg, accessed 30 March 2018.

68 Aristotle, *Aristotle on the Art of Poetry: With a Supplement, on Aristotle on Music,* ed. Milton C. Nahm and trans. S. H. Butcher (New York: Liberal Arts Press, 1956), former owner Sexton, Ransom Center.

69 CD-3, reel 23, 30 May 1961, *APAS*.

70 This excerpt is from "All God's Children Need Radios," which was titled, "A Small Journal" in *Ms.* Magazine (1973).

71 Alice Munro, *The Love of a Good Woman: Stories* (New York: Random House, 1998), 48. "The Love of a Good Woman" (1996). Munro's housewives and the type of reader to whom she refers suggest a midcentury reading population.

72 Plath wrote "N.B." in Virginia Woolf's *A Writer's Diary* (1953; London: Hogarth Press, 1954), 139; former owner Plath, former owner Hughes, Emory.

73 Gray Sexton, conversation with the author, 17 June 2013.

74 Ibid.

75 Ibid. Sexton used pencil to underline and annotate an uncorrected proof of Plath's *Ariel* (London: Faber and Faber, 1965), former owner Sexton, Emory. In her memoir, Gray Sexton recalls Sexton's "copy of Betty Friedan's *The Feminine Mystique*, complete with her scribbled notes across the pages— notes that showed her identification with the problems Friedan described" (Gray Sexton, 98).

76 As the editors of Sexton's *Self-Portrait in Letters* put it, "she was finally able to do much of the reading she had missed earlier in her life" (111).Following John Holmes's workshop in 1958, she also acquired his book, *Writing Poetry* (Boston, MA: The Writer Inc., 1960), in which the second section includes essays by poets and critics including W. H. Auden, Robert Frost, Wallace Stevens, William Carlos Williams, Marianne Moore, and Richard Wilbur (Ransom Center).

77 It is also possible that Sexton had encountered Rahv in Lowell's *Life Studies* (1959) poem "Man and Wife." The poem's speaker "outdrank the Rahvs in the heat" (87, line 17). Robert Lowell, *Life Studies and For the Union Dead* (1956; New York: Farrar, Straus and Giroux, 1997), 87, line 17.

78 Letter, Sexton to Lowell, 18 November 1961, Item 1012, Robert Lowell Papers, Houghton Library, Harvard University.

79 Anne Sexton, "Eulogy for Philip Rahv," 1973, box 9, folder six, Sexton Papers.

80 See also Maxine Kumin, "Introduction," *Complete Poems* xxvii–xxviii.

81 The ellipses are Sexton's. Letter of 8 October 1960. Elspeth Healey of the Ransom Center checked this letter, email to the author, 5 August 2009.

82 For instance, Sexton annotated her copy of Dostoevsky's *The Possessed*. Fyodor Dostoevsky, *The Possessed*, trans. Constance Garnett (1872; New York: The Modern Library, c. 1930), former owner Sexton, Ransom Center;

hereafter cited in the text as "Sexton Library." The forward by Avrahm Yarmolinsky, which Sexton underlined, is dated 1935.

83 Letter, Sexton to W. D. Snodgrass, 11 October 1960.

84 Letter, Sexton to Nolan Miller, 14 November 1960.

85 Letter of 12 February 1962.

86 Rainer Maria Rilke, "Viareggio, near Pisa (Italy)," April 5th, 1903, *Letters to a Young Poet*, trans. M. D. Herder Norton (1934; New York: Norton, 2004), 20. See also *AS*, 365.

87 12 August 1965. The bracket with "[carve?]" is in the published letter. Middlebrook suggests that this letter is to an aspiring poet and Korso is a pseudonym (*AS*, 241, 442n).

88 "Deuteronomy 6 verse 8: Bind (7194) them for a sign (226) on your hand and shall be frontlets (2903) between your eyes." See http://www.karaitejudaism. org/talks/Deuteronomy6v4-9_figurative.html. Also, in versions of the Jewish prayer the *Shema*, "Let them be a symbol before your eyes."

89 The line in Deuteronomy also repeats in the central Jewish prayer, the *Shema*, which alludes to the ritual practice.

90 H. F. Peters, *Rainer Maria Rilke: Masks and the Man* (Seattle: University of Washington Press, 1960), 98, former owner Sexton, Ransom Center; hereafter cited in the text as "Peters."

91 Letter, Sexton to Hollis Summers, 16 March 1960.

92 Philip Rahv, Introduction to Franz Kafka, *Selected Stories*, trans. Willa and Edwin Muir (1936; New York: Modern Library, 1952), xix, former owner Sexton, Ransom Center.

93 I thank Richard Oram for checking the color of Sexton's ink.

94 Sexton's copy of Kafka, xx. See also Blasing, 189 and Gill, *Anne Sexton's Confessional Poetics*, 12–13.

95 "It looks as though Sexton originally typed 'of,' but then typed an 'r' over the 'f' to correct the quotation." Andrew Gansky, Public Services Intern, Ransom Center, email to the author, 9 August 2013.

96 Anne Sexton, "Presentations 1968–1974 nd," box 16, folder 4, Sexton Papers.

97 While the date of the interview in the collection *No Evil Star* is 1965/66, *The Hudson Review* dates it as Winter 1966. See http://hudsonreview.com/ 1966/01/interview-with-anne-sexton/#.UmAzNRYdO5c, accessed 17 October 2013.

98 Following Marx's lead, when Barbara Kevles of *The Paris Review* asked Sexton to define "the purpose of poetry," Sexton responded, "As Kafka said about prose, 'A book should serve as the axe for the frozen sea within us.' And that's what I want from a poem" (*NES*, 83).

99 Letter, Ted Hughes to Frieda Hughes, ca. 1970s, box 1, folder 1, MSS 1014, Letters to Frieda Hughes, Emory.

100 Enemark, interview with the author, 19 March 2008. One student, writing in *The Colgate Maroon*, was critical of the brief amount of time Sexton would be spending on campus. No author, "*Dollars. . . . and Sense*," *The Colgate Maroon* (Hamilton, NY), 16 November 1971, page 4. Berlind responded in a subsequent issue that Sexton would be at Colgate for two days each week, and he refers to "Anne on Anne" as English 336: "The Poetry of Anne Sexton." Bruce Berlind, "Poetic Justice," *The Colgate Maroon* (Hamilton, NY), 7 December 1971, page 5. Sexton stayed two nights a week in Merrill House, on the periphery of the campus, and the college installed a phone line in her room so that she could call her friend Maxine Kumin. Berlind interview. Hamilton, NY. Berlind notes that Sexton's room was Merrill House B-4. Letter, Berlind to Sexton, 14 January 1972, box 18, folder 1, Sexton Papers.

101 See *The Colgate News*, Vol. 4, No. 12, 11 February 1972, page 8.
102 Woodward, interview with the author, 10 November 2005.
103 Enemark, interview with the author, 19 March 2008.
104 Craig Carlson and Nancy Flanagan Kinsella, annotations in books from "Anne on Anne" class. Carlson and Kinsella sent photocopies to the author. Sexton had some experience teaching literature. Sexton taught Ralph Ellison's novel, *The Invisible Man* (1933), at Wayland High School in 1967. While Salvio observes that Sexton did not keep notes for her teaching of the novel, perhaps her lack of preparation anticipates her copious teaching notes for the "Anne on Anne" class. Salvio also mentions that Sexton annotated her copy of the novel and recorded "in her journal, 'The discussion of *Invisible Man* has put me off my stride because it is beyond me, and I am incapable of discussing it intelligently'" (107).
105 Rooney, 11.
106 See also *AS*, 358.
107 Sexton also used creative exercises in her Boston University workshop. See Polly C. Williams, "Sexton in the Classroom," in *Anne Sexton: The Artist and Her Critics*, ed. J. D. McClatchy (Bloomington: Indiana University Press, 1978), 98.
108 Gill emphasizes that in Sexton's response to A.R. Jones's "Necessity and Freedom" she is responding to his pivotal essay on the confessional persona (*Anne Sexton's Confessional Poetics*, 33). In response to Sexton's final assignment, Salvio

> felt overwhelmed by the excessive accumulation of personae—fabricate a persona from Sexton's poems, formulate a question a week for Sexton, formulate an answer, see how close you come to her response as the term moves on? . . . And why an interview?
>
> (41)

109 Anne Sexton, "Elegy in the Classroom" (1959, 60) (*AS*, 110). Salvio also discusses this poem. See Diane Wood Middlebrook's essay, "'I Tapped My Own Head': The Apprenticeship of Anne Sexton," in *Coming to Light: American Women Poets in the Twentieth Century*, ed. Diane Wood Middlebrook and Marilyn Yalom (Ann Arbor: University of Michigan Press, 1985), 195–213 and *AS*.
110 See also *NES*, 4.
111 Sexton, box 26, folder 1, Sexton Papers. Sexton may have collected these papers the summer before her death when she "put her manuscripts and correspondence in order" (Gray Sexton, 185).
112 Ezra Pound, "A Few Don'ts by an Imagiste," *Poetry* 1, no. 6 (March 1913): 200.
113 Sexton provided a similar explanation in her fifth lecture addressing the lyric poem: "The lyric more or less enshrines a moment, an event, a situation, a single part of time" (*CL*, 5; 1).
114 Kinsella notes, *Live or Die*.
115 CD-3, reel 23, 30 May 1961, *APAS*.
116 The article was published in *Critical Quarterly*. See *Anne Sexton's Confessional Poetics* for further treatment of the significance of Sexton's response to this article and what Gill calls "the confessional mode" (27–8).
117 Sexton owned T. S. Eliot, *Complete Poems and Plays 1909–1950* (New York: Harcourt, Brace and Co., c. 1952), Ransom Center. Sexton marked Eliot's play *The Family Reunion*. She also owned T. S. Eliot, *The Waste Land and Other Poems* (New York: Harcourt, Brace and Co., 1955), Ransom Center.
118 Sexton is probably referring to the Morris Gray reading at Harvard in December 1959 (*AS*, 119). She told Lowell that Harry Levin's wife left "in the middle

of the reading." Letter, Sexton to Lowell, 11 December 1959, Item 1098, Robert Lowell Papers, MS Am 1905, Houghton Library, Harvard University, Cambridge MA. Levin had advised Maxine Kumin's undergraduate thesis at Radcliffe, which may have been how Sexton knew who he was. Heather Treseler, "Making History: An Interview with Maxine Kumin," *Notre Dame Review* 39 (2015): 142.

119 Sexton's reading at Colgate was on 3 November 1965. Bruce M. Buck, "Register Shows Faculty Plans Few Fall Lectures," *The Colgate Maroon* (Hamilton, NY), 3 October 1965, page 6.

120 Hummel, "Anne Sexton, Acclaimed Poet," *The Colgate Maroon*, page 1. Hummel mentions that the chairman's wife left after one poem.

121 Hummel, "Anne Sexton, Acclaimed Poet," *The Colgate Maroon*, page 1.

122 Ibid.

123 See Appendix B. Sexton prepared to tell the students during her first class session, "tonight I'm giving a reading, one that I have prepared exclusively for this class" (*CL*, Preface, 1). Colgate student Stanley Yorsz reviewing Sexton's poetry reading explained, "[w]hile the final applause was hardly tumultuous, the appreciation of her work was readily apparent despite the obvious mixed emotional response of the persons present" (10). He called her, "in a sense, a fusion of the traditional poet and those of the *beat* generation. The poems express raw feelings. She is capable of *letting it all hang out*, yet still retaining respect for the word" (10). Stanley Yorsz, "The Confessions of A Poetess," *The Colgate Maroon* (Hamilton, NY). 15 February 15, 1972, page 10. Regarding the New Criticism and workshops see McGurl.

124 See Blasing for further exploration of Sexton's typos.

125 Enemark, interview with the author, 19 March 2008.

126 The interviewer reminded Sexton, "You said earlier you're not too willing to explicate a poem's meaning" (*NES*, 185).

127 Sexton recounted in her interviews and teaching notes that she wrote this poem while attending a workshop with Snodgrass at Antioch College.

128 In response to Sexton's first question, her student underlined the final line of the first stanza, "Did you hear what it said?" (5), and wrote in the margin, "People (or poet) speaking of portrait." Kinsella copy of Anne Sexton, *To Bedlam and Part Way Back*, 25.

129 Kinsella copy of *To Bedlam and Part Way Back*, 25.

130 While Sexton asks, "How does the old lady feel as she speaks to them" and observes that "She wants to stop them with a chill finger. How does she do it? (in the last line)," Kinsella writes beside the last stanza, "nostalgic for life & she lied when she was young." Kinsella copy of *To Bedlam and Part Way Back*, 26. Kinsella recorded what may have been the poet's preferences among her canon. Beside the poem, "I Remember," she added a star and "Favorite." "You, Doctor Martin," the first poem in *To Bedlam and Part Way Back*, contains the lines, "There are no knives / for cutting your throat" (15–16), and Kinsella wrote, "favorite line" beside "knives." "The Bells" contains the lines, "I, laughing, / lifted to your high shoulder / or small at the rough legs of strangers, / was not afraid / You held my hand and were instant to explain the three rings of danger" (11–17). Kinsella noted, "favorite image—/ shows her smallness" beside "was not afraid. / You held my hand." Regarding the poem "Hutch," Kinsella noted, "[s]ome say this is Sexton's best poem." Kinsella copy of *To Bedlam and Part Way Back*, 3, 10, and 38.

131 C. K. Williams, email to the author, 10 March 2008.

132 Kinsella wrote at the end of her copy of the poem, "does not really forgive him—poem an attempt—didn't forgive him for not loving her—caught up in own life." Kinsella copy of *All My Pretty Ones*, 5.

133 *OED*, s.v. "jinx," *n*. In her copy, Sexton's student added, "same year mother had died." Kinsella wrote in her copy of *All My Pretty Ones* beside the line, "a second shock boiling its stone to your heart" (3), "Child might see shock as stone traveling to the heart."

134 Kinsella, copy of *All My Pretty Ones*, 4.

135 Enemark, interview with the author, 19 March 2008.

136 The term before she arrived, *The Colgate Maroon* (Hamilton, NY) ran the article, "Anne Sexton, Pulitzer Poet to Join Faculty in Spring," 26 October 1971, page 8. *The Colgate News* (Hamilton, NY) also published "Poet will Teach Here Next Spring" on 29 October 1971, which mentioned Sexton's "honorary Doctor of Letters Degree from Tufts University in 1970" (page 10).

137 Sexton may have known the value of her manuscripts. Mary-Elizabeth Murdock, Curator of the Sophia Smith Collection at Smith College, wrote to Sexton during the fall before she began teaching at Colgate, explaining that the collection "contains the personal and professional papers of some of the nation's most accomplished women" and "would be further enhanced by acquiring yours." Murdock also sent Sexton a catalog introducing "the quality of our holdings as well as the types of papers that we hope to acquire." Letter, Mary-Elizabeth Murdock to Sexton, 21 September 1971, box 26, folder 5, Sexton Papers.

138 Sexton discussed the drafts of "All My Pretty Ones," in a telephone interview with Harry Moore. Even while she specified having six pages before her, it is unclear which drafts she used as there are three pages numbered six in her draft (*NES*, 43).

139 As Salvio has noted, Sexton's technique of teaching with her drafts was one she learned from John Holmes (97–8). Salvio explains,

> Sexton drew a good deal on the pedagogical approach taken by John Holmes in her writing workshops, often informing her students on the first day of class that they will learn "how badly a poem can begin," and then, through revision, and a series of what she referred to as her "tricks," how her drafts evolved into a complete poem. . . . as I read through Sexton's discussions with her student, I felt she practically imitated Holmes word for word. In a 1972 workshop she gave at Colgate University, Sexton presents her students with a set of her manuscripts for her poem, "All My Pretty Ones."
>
> (99)

140 Maxine Kumin, *Always Beginning: Essays on a Life in Poetry* (Port Townsend, WA: Copper Canyon Press, 2000), 61–2.

141 Sexton also noted purchasing Rimbaud's *A Season in Hell* in 1964 (*SP*, 232–3). Arthur Rimbaud, *Une Saison en Enfer & Le Bateau Ivre. A Season in Hell & The Drunken Boat*, trans. Louise Varèse (Norfolk, CT: J. Laughlin, 1961), former owner Sexton, Ransom Center.

142 J. D. McClatchy observes that

> "Flee on Your Donkey" struggles with the ambiguous impatience, introducing it first as weariness with "allowing myself the wasted life": "I have come back / but disorder is not what it was. / I have lost the trick of it! / The innocence of it!"

J. D. McClatchy, "Anne Sexton: Somehow to Endure," in *Sexton: Selected Criticism*, ed. Diana Hume George (Chicago, IL: University of Chicago Press, 1988), 56. McClatchy also identifies the title of the poem from which the epigraph comes, "Rimbaud's 'Fêtes de la faim'" (55).

143 Sexton, "Flee on Your Donkey" draft, page 2C, box 9, folder 7, Sexton Papers. It is unclear which pages Sexton distributed from the drafts of "Flee on Your Donkey" and "Eighteen Days Without You." On the first page of Sexton's handwritten worksheet of "Flee on Your Donkey," however, she added in the margin, "Read aloud," and included the names of three students from her "Anne on Anne" class. Elsewhere in her teaching notes, Sexton also included a longer list of students' names, and "Read aloud." Perhaps prior to introducing her worksheets, Sexton added numbers and letters to the pages of her "Flee on Your Donkey" drafts. It is likely that she distributed the sequences marked III C, which differ from the version of the poem published in *Live or Die*. Sexton also numbered the pages of the final set of worksheets, marked IV D, which include textual additions, but read as a cleaner, more fluid version.

144 Sexton, "Flee on Your Donkey" draft, page 2C, Sexton Papers.

145 See also *AS*.

146 Sexton, "Poetry reading at Harvard Phi Beta Kappa," [11 June 1968] "Presentations, 1968–1974, nd," box 16, folder 4, Sexton Papers. See *AS*, 302.

147 See letter, Sexton to Richard B. McAdoo, Houghton Mifflin Company, 31 June 1970, box 21, folders 1–2, Sexton Papers.

148 See also Middlebrook's consideration "Eighteen Days Without You" (*AS* 288, 294–5). Sexton left notes on pages of her "Eighteen Days" worksheets to a potential secretary requesting copies. Sexton, "Eighteen Days Without You," "[1967]," box 6, folder 6, Sexton Papers.

149 At the Ransom Center numerous mimeographed copies of Sexton's poem "The Call" remain together, perhaps left from her class, if she distributed some, or saved for future classes. These copies are not filed with "Eighteen Days," but instead are with her poems not included in published volumes. Sexton, "The Call," box 9, folder 4, Sexton Papers. In Sexton's draft file for "Eighteen Days," she labeled the drafts of each section with a letter, with December 16 having Q, Sexton Papers.

150 Sexton mentioned these options in the introduction to her teaching notes. Rooney, 11.

151 See Amanda Golden, "Ted Hughes and the Midcentury American Academy," *The Ted Hughes Society Journal* 3 (2013): 49; hereafter cited in the text as "Hughes and the Midcentury American Academy."

152 Letter, Hughes to Peter Redgrove, "[late 1970 ALS]," box 1, folder 3, MSS 867, Hughes Letters to Peter Redgrove, Emory. Even though this letter is cataloged as tentatively late 1970, it is probably 1971 as Hughes refers to Richard Murphy. I thank Neil Roberts for bringing Redgrove's later teaching at Colgate to my attention and Stephen Enniss for noting Redgrove's correspondence in "Ted Hughes, archives and alligators: How – and why – writers' papers end up in British and American libraries" *The Times* (27 April 2011). Reprinted from the *Times Literary Supplement*. http://entertainment.timesonline.co.uk/tol/arts_and_entertainment/the_tls/article7174360, accessed 30 April 2011. Hughes's poetry reading at Colgate was on Friday 19 March 1971. Letter, Murphy to Hughes, 17 January 1971, box 5, folder 7, MSS 644, Hughes Papers, Emory; hereafter cited in the text as "Hughes Papers." I thank Jane Pinchin for bringing Hughes's Colgate visit to my attention and Carol Hughes for telling me the year of Hughes's visit with Murphy.

153 "Hughes to Read Poetry," *The Colgate Maroon* (Hamilton, NY), 16 March 1971, page 5.

154 Richard Murphy, *The Kick: A Life Among Writers* (2002; London: Granta, 2003), 296. I thank Christopher Reid for bringing this book to my attention in the *Letters of Ted Hughes*.

155 *The Colgate News* (Hamilton, NY), Friday, 26 March 1971, page 7. http://diglib.colgate.edu/digital/collection/ColgateNP04/id/27538/rec/86, accessed 25 August 2018. The caption notes "photo by Johnston."
156 Letter, Murphy to Hughes, 27 September 1971, box 5, folder 7, Hughes Papers.
157 Ibid.
158 Letter, Sexton to Hughes, 24 November 1970, box 20, folder 7, Sexton Papers. The letter in Sexton's file at the Ransom Center is a copy, and the original letter that she had sent to Hughes is at Emory. This letter was published in *SP*, 369.
159 Ted Hughes *Crow: From the Life and Songs of the Crow* (New York: Harper and Row, 1971), former owner Sexton, Ransom Center. The back jacket flap also contains an endorsement from Alan Brownjohn of the *New Statesman*: "In this set of harshly beautiful, alarming poems, Hughes has found both a structure which gives his vision a new power and coherence, and a persona through which he can explore reality well beyond his previous limits."
160 Ted Hughes, *Crow: From the Life and Songs of the Crow* (New York: Harper and Row, 1971), former owner Sexton, Ransom Center. Sexton owned two copies of *Crow*, a hardcover and a paperback.
161 See Middlebrook's discussion of this quotation in *AS*.

Coda
Ted Hughes and the midcentury American academy

The preceding chapters addressed the ways that Sylvia Plath, John Berryman, and Anne Sexton contributed to midcentury constructions of modernist discourse. Each poet's means of material engagement, in annotations and teaching materials, anchored their consideration of the previous generation. Plath's modernism was intertwined with critical interpretations of it. And while her teaching style may have reflected the impersonality of the modernism she had inherited, she also brought humanity to it, particularly in the wake of World War II and the atrocities that overshadowed the world in which she lived. Berryman's training as a textual scholar brought him closer to the practice of annotation. His sense of modernism became one he blended with the contemporary world, returning in his poems to modernist writers, addressing their legacies in form and content. Sexton's teaching shifted the focus to her students. Inviting their feedback on her poems, Sexton introduced students to her composition strategies.

A final case study, that of Ted Hughes, analyzes the marginalia of one new to the American university. If Plath is the student, Berryman is the scholar, and Sexton is the teacher, then Hughes is the poet. In the materials he created as he taught, Hughes, to a greater extent than the other poets in the previous chapters, sought to maintain his fidelity to creative work. His approach to teaching intersects with his approach to writing, and the materials that he annotated and composed preserve his attention to the ways that texts make meaning.

***

Ted Hughes's personal library is a less frequently used collection for considering midcentury academic practices, but its contents record the material dimensions of his preparation for teaching at the University of Massachusetts, Amherst (UMass) in the spring of 1958. This early immersion in academic life also provides a background for his later responses to critics as Plath's literary executor and Hughes revisits Plath's relationship to academia as he writes *Birthday Letters*.

Hughes taught three courses at UMass Amherst, spending time on a changing university campus.[1] His Great Books course for sophomores met on Tuesdays, Thursdays, and Saturdays at eight and nine in the morning. On Tuesdays and Saturdays at ten in the morning, Hughes also taught "a class of freshmen . . . the elements of various literary forms & authors: this is mainly a course in grammar, lay-out, & so on."[2] Hughes also had a creative writing class of ten students. He commuted 9.5 miles to UMass, which he characterized as "a queer place — like a great sprawling unfinished building site, with great square box-buildings standing about a sort of raw landscape. A main road runs through the middle of it."[3] UMass was initially an agricultural college, and Plath suggests this history in her journal when she refers to Max Goldberg, the professor who had hired Hughes, and his "tales of the steelworkers course in humanities" (*UJ*, 304).[4] While Hughes knew the formality of Cambridge and taught in the Coleridge Secondary Modern School for Boys (Bate, 126), in important ways he was also self-taught, preparing himself to compose the poetry he sought to write.

In letters, Hughes compared his time at UMass to Groucho Marx's university satire *Horse Feathers* (1932).[5] Writing to his friend Glen Fallows, Hughes reported that Plath

> is teaching at Smith College—a high class girl's college—and . . . I am . . . teaching at the University of Mass—the kind of State University you see in Marx brother films. Very amusing, & the work is light. The wages are extraordinarily good.[6]

The University of Massachusetts was growing, as its name had changed from Massachusetts Agricultural College to Massachusetts State in 1931, and in 1947—a little over a decade before Hughes arrived—it became the University of Massachusetts, Amherst.[7] Following World War II, this university, like so many others, increased in size.[8] In the same letter, Hughes also captured the state of demand in the postwar academic marketplace:

> In fact, teaching in America is rapidly becoming the coddled profession i.e. the reverse to England. Apparently what is known as "the bulge" is now about 14 years old, & the colleges are in a panic, mustering men & courses & new buildings to prepare for it, and to encourage teachers wages are being pushed up. The cost of living is very high too, however.[9]

While financial reasons partly motivated Hughes's teaching, he ended up contributing to a particular moment in American academic history.

Part of the reason that Hughes commuted to Amherst, instead of joining Plath in Northampton, was due to Smith's reluctance to grant him a position. The poet Anthony Hecht felt that this was a slight to Plath and Hughes:

> Smith contrived profoundly to offend Ted and Sylvia in a manner that made them decide to leave after a single year. Sylvia was teaching the

same courses as I, and Ted stayed at home, writing, keeping house, but fretful, with too much time on his hands. He wanted to teach too, and Sylvia arranged a meeting for him with the chairman. Ted was told they couldn't hire him because he had no teaching experience, though this had been no barrier to their having appointed Sylvia, who had none either. But of course she was a Smith graduate. The indignation Sylvia felt about this, and which Ted probably felt as well, though he kept his feelings under better control than she, was little short of explosive. They firmly resolved to leave at the end of the year, and they did so, to the utter astonishment of the chairman, who hadn't the slightest clue that he had offended them.[10]

If this was the case, it might have informed Hughes's and Plath's subsequent responses to Smith.[11] Ultimately, it meant a broader range of experiences for Hughes, teaching different texts and a different student population than he would have otherwise encountered.[12]

After the term began, Hughes gathered his impressions of the time he had spent in the classroom, filling his sister in on the success that he had found: "Yes, I am teaching. The State University of Massachusetts is one to which anyone can go who pays quite a small sum, $200 I think a year."[13] He adds that work was scarce, "So when the University approached me, and offered 2200 dollars to teach 14 weeks, I accepted. £50 a week I thought. Now I teach three courses, eleven hours a week in all."[14] The schedule meant less depth, with the class "spending not more than six hours in all on any one author."[15] The fact that Hughes found intellectual satisfaction in teaching may have come as a surprise to him, and the experience was less onerous than he had anticipated: "I am taking the work lightly, and yet I'm doing better than I thought I would. In front of a class my mind is clearer and more free than in say, speaking with one other person."[16]

In what is now a well-known story, Hughes left a concentration in literature to pursue one in Archaeology and Anthropology at Pembroke College, Cambridge. His poem "The Thought-Fox" speaks to Hughes's realization that the critical work of literary study would stifle his ability to create.[17] In the time that had passed since Hughes ceased formally studying literature and began teaching it at UMass, however, he had become a different kind of reader. The years that he had spent attending to the ways that texts work, both those he wrote and those he read, prepared him to do so as he taught. Continuing his letter to Olwyn, Hughes reflects:

> I think I'm probably quite a good teacher. This business of pulling a work to pieces, into its main themes, development, implications etc was something which I had always considered utterly alien to my way of thinking, but my way of thinking must have just been idleness because if I have a gift for anything it is for this dismantling a long work and keeping all its pieces in the air together, and all clear, and to show how inevitable and purposefully they all come ~~together~~ back into place. I get

completely ~~lost~~ absorbed in this, so that teaching time is to me literally no time at all. My classes are interested. I'm very relieved to find that I do it so easily and confidently. I was expecting to find it hard slogging minute by minute labour, but the whole lesson just pours into my head. I wonder where all this was when I was at Cambridge.[18]

Perhaps emulating the style of courses like the one Plath taught at Smith, Hughes's approach recalls the manner of close reading that Brooks and Warren modeled in *Understanding Poetry*.[19] Hughes's account also possesses a sense of the ease and grace that he brought to the process as a poet immersed in the crafting of verse.

Hughes, however, remained wary regarding the negative effect that close reading can have on creative work. He elaborated in his letter to Olwyn:

> This is why teaching is dangerous. It accustoms the habit of mind with which you attend to a piece of writing to drop automatically into the habit of mind with which you teach a piece of writing – into a bringing out the artful effects, the surface meaning, the symbolic meaning of every detail, the purpose and effect of every word, as to a class of curious but slightly misunderstanding people. This secondary expository and almost completely analytical self-conscious state of mind, with a slight cast of deliberate virtuoso putting-over of effects, becomes strong enough to completely resist the unconscious invention-absorbed state in which good writing comes out. This is what inevitably happens to all teachers of literature and why I shall not stay in it beyond May17th (end of half-year) and why I never think about the classes when I'm outside them and have finished the six or so hours of preparation that each week needs.[20]

Hughes annotated his copies of some of the texts he taught. He added marginalia and markings as he made his way through the readings, developing the impressions that he would communicate to his students. The books themselves became guides to which he could return, consulting the thoughts he had collected.

Great Books

Apart from teaching or reviewing books, annotating was not a practice in which Hughes often indulged as a reader.[21] One reason that he may not have done so may stem from his experience as a child reading comic books in his parents' Yorkshire store, and returning them to the shelves when he had finished.[22] Hughes's Great Books course included the poetry of John Milton, William Wordsworth, and John Keats, Fyodor Dostoevsky's *Crime and Punishment*, three Molière plays, the first part of Johann Wolfgang von Goethe's *Faust*, and Henry David Thoreau's *Walden*.[23] When he prepared to teach *Crime and Punishment*, however, Hughes added his annotations to a copy of the novel that Plath had already filled with her own notes and marginalia. Their shared copy of *Crime and Punishment* and the books that Hughes subsequently annotated—Molière's *The School for Wives* and *Walden*—reflect the extent to which Hughes learned from Plath's reading and annotating strategies and brought his own techniques to them.

As Hughes later reflected during his interview with *The Paris Review*:

> Between the age when I began to write seriously and the time I left the university at the age of twenty-four, I read very little in poetry, novels, and drama apart from the great authors—the authors I considered to be great. Within that literature I was a hundred-great-books reader.[24]
>
> (296)

Hughes's own definition of a great book coincides with some of the texts that he taught by the writers whom he revered: "By the time I got to university, at twenty-one, my sacred canon was fixed: Chaucer, Shakespeare, Marlowe, Blake, Wordsworth, Keats, Coleridge, Hopkins, Yeats, Eliot" (*Paris Review*, 274). As Hughes turned to fiction, he included Dostoevsky: "I have a deep hatred of all novels except Singer, Tolstoy, Dostoevsky, and a few odd other volumes" (*LTH*, 484).[25]

When Hughes began teaching in late January, Plath had recently prepared "two weeks of lectures" on *Crime and Punishment* (LV2, 206).[26] This novel was the first she taught in her course and she had planned to devote a class session to each "part" of it (*TN*).[27] While both Plath and Hughes underlined and annotated the whole of *Crime and Punishment*, Plath's written comments appear with the greatest frequency earlier in the novel. Hughes marked the copy throughout, often noting key points and plot development where Plath's notes cease. Her annotations return, however, at central moments, and both she and Hughes note the novel's climactic scenes.

As Plath had already indicated themes and patterns on the pages of *Crime and Punishment*, Hughes was more selective when he annotated the novel. He responded to Plath, but also made points that reflected his own pedagogical style. Hughes added brief comments above the passages that Plath had underlined, writing in the top margins and, infrequently, on the sides of the pages. Hughes's annotations in Dostoevsky's novel—in black ink, pencil, and sometimes in red pencil—serve as a form of shorthand for teaching. In order to be thorough, at times he repeated points Plath had made and, in at least one instance, added his own. Beside a description of Raskolnikov's home, Plath noted, "crowded-" and "isolation." In a darker black ink, Hughes added below them, "effect" (22).[28] He was generalizing as to the impact of the list that Dostoevsky provides of those who filled the house, including the "tailors, locksmiths, cooks, . . . low-grade civil servants, and so on. People entering or leaving the house seemed to be darting to and fro" (22). Hughes's directness as an annotator in this instance, capturing the impression that the passage makes, reflects the influence of his education at Cambridge.

Neil Roberts has argued that despite Hughes's claims otherwise, his brief experience studying literature at Pembroke College was formative in the development of his writing.[29] Further, Roberts points out that critics have deferred to "a caricature view" of Cambridge lecturer F. R. Leavis's teaching style when assessing the impact of Hughes's education on his work ("Hughes and Cambridge," 25). According to Roberts, part of Leavis's style was to provide an overall impression of the text, one that would unfold as he demonstrated it. Roberts elaborates that Leavis's

> typical method was to quote, make an incisive critical judgement, and invite the reader's agreement that this is self-evident; for example, his comment on Milton's line "Th'earth cumber'd, and the wing'd air dark't with plumes": "the crowding of stressed words, the consonantal clusters, and the clogged movement have a function that *needs no analysis*".
> ("Hughes and Cambridge," 27, emphasis, Roberts)

Similarly, Roberts points out that "The Thought-Fox"

> does not *state* that the fox's shadow is distorted by the irregular terrain over which it passes. Rather that sense-impression is completely saturated by the figurative displacement of the fox's natural fear on to its shadow, leaving the fox itself free to represent a bold venturesomeness.[30]
> ("Hughes and Cambridge," 30)

By noting "effect" in *Crime and Punishment*, Hughes is referring to an impression that does not require an explanation. But Hughes's annotations throughout the novel served different purposes. Elsewhere, Hughes's annotations mark what a passage may communicate, making clear for students the kind of interpretations that Leavis left implicit.

Plath summarized the political theories that the characters discuss in *Crime and Punishment*, writing at the top of one page, "[s]elfishness for good of society as a whole." Hughes noted beside it, "Ras's idea" (167).[31] Hughes may have been rereading the novel as he added notes like this one. Lucas Myers recalls that in Hughes's bedroom at his family's Yorkshire home, he had "the complete works of Dostoevsky."[32] Hughes's annotations are both thorough and informal. Because Hughes characterized UMass as somewhat casual, the latter style of his notes is fitting, but the former aspect may also be a reaction to it.[33] His close attention to texts reflected his expertise, prior education, self-study, and teaching at the secondary level. Further, working in close proximity to Plath, he also reacts to her engagement with the text, which began as an undergraduate.

At Smith, Plath studied Russian literature with George Gibian in the spring of 1954, and he advised her senior thesis on *The Double* and *The*

Brothers Karamazov, "The Magic Mirror: A Study of the Double in Two of Dostoevsky's Novels," the following fall (*LV*1, 861). Plath confided in her friend Gordon Lameyer, "I'll never get over the experience of reading 'The Idiot' and 'Brothers Karamazov' and fear that I shall walk around carrying the muchunderlined books in a small satchel and quoting voluminously from them at the slightest provocation!" (*LV*1, 705).[34] The Penguin paperback copy of *Crime and Punishment* that Plath and Hughes annotated to teach was acquired at a later date.[35] But the passages that she once envisioned reading dramatically may have also been those that she had also studied. In this sense, the new book presents an extension of a material process, one informed by engaging the text critically.

The year that Plath graduated, Gibian published the essay, "Traditional Symbolism in *Crime and Punishment*" (1955), addressing "the anti-rationalistic tenor of the novel."[36] Gibian points out that "Dostoevsky held that . . . exclusive reliance on reason ('reason and will' in Raskolnikov's theories and again in his dream of the plague) lead to death-in-life."[37] In other words, Gibian argues that for Dostoevsky, a state of "death-in-life" can result from overdependence on logic. In another passage, Gibian describes Raskolnikov as living dead:

> The crucial final scene . . . They seem to be men of the age of Abraham and his flocks, truly free and living people, not living dead as Raskolnikov had been. Now he can identify himself with these nomads, although he has only one thing in common with them, the most important thing of all—humanity.
>
> (540)

Even if Plath did not encounter this article by the time she taught *Crime and Punishment*, the fact that Gibian refers to "death-in-life" and "living dead" presents a point of intersection between his work and the Eliot criticism that Plath read. Further, the article introduces another application of the concept at roughly the same critical moment.[38]

By turning to their shared copy of *Crime and Punishment*, we can see that the differences in Plath's and Hughes's annotations reflect their backgrounds as readers, and indicate their respective approaches to the courses they were teaching. While both annotators share a certain efficiency, Plath's notes bear the weight of the criticism she read. In response to one passage, Plath added, "SUICIDE – NOT a way out." Hughes then added, "Suicide Projection" (188). Hughes's annotation reflects that he noted what Plath marked, and, as if having considered the passage at a distance, categorized it for further reference. Plath's note also makes sense in the context of her course and the role of death-in-life in it. Other annotations present echoes of Joyce's "The Dead," which Plath had taught earlier in the term. Plath recorded in her teaching notes for the third part of the novel that Raskolnikov is "like one DEAD" (*TN*). She linked this idea to what she called the

"LAZARUS Theme family recalls him to ties of earth – what he has done" (*TN*). Early in the novel, Plath notes its "naturalistic description" (23), indicating an awareness of the conventions that distinguish Dostoevsky's style from that of the modernist texts that would follow.[39] But she also sees the "WORLD [as] DEAD" in *Crime and Punishment*, as she had in Joyce's *Dubliners* (*TN*). The latter is the result of reading criticism, but as she identifies a similar presence in Dostoevsky's novel, her gaze as a reader reflects the order of the texts she taught.

While Hughes may not have shared Plath's priorities as a student, his notes in the remaining spaces of her densely packed first page of *Crime and Punishment* teaching notes record where he placed additional emphasis (*TN*). For instance, on the left side of the page, Plath had listed attributes of Raskolnikov's "ATMOSPHERE," and that the novel describes his "garret: [as the] lair of animal [,] trap – cupboard [,] [a] cloister [, and a] beastly hole" (*TN*).[40] Plath's response lists Dostoevsky's descriptions of Raskolnikov's dwelling, which includes attributes ranging from the monastic to the vile. She wants students to understand the way Dostoevsky's text works. Beneath Plath's note, Hughes had added, Raskolnikov's "state: weak, coma, dreams, imbalanced mind" (*TN*).[41] Hughes addresses Raskolnikov's physical and emotional condition. Plath noted Raskolnikov's "calculation & arithmetic," which recalls her professor's attention to rationality in the novel, and Hughes added beside her comment, "Free!" (*TN*).[42]

In his brevity as an annotator, Hughes rebelled against academic conventions while using a text for teaching that is the result of them. As critics have noted, Plath learned her style of annotating from her mother, and it could be argued that it is emblematic of midcentury practices in academic institutions.[43] While at times Hughes's annotating style resembled Plath's, one can also distinguish his darker, quick inscriptions from her neater comments.[44] In his teaching copy of Molière's plays, Hughes annotated *The School for Wives*, *Tartuffe*, and *The Misanthrope*.[45] Hughes may have started preparing to teach these plays around 10 February, when Plath noted in her journal that Hughes "outlined his Molière" (*UJ*, 329). Annotating the text, Hughes drew lines from passages to his comments at the top of the pages, as he had done when annotating *Crime and Punishment*. While Plath does not appear to have shared this tendency, Hughes adopted other techniques that she used, including noting "c.f." for cross references (Figure 4.1) and drawing short lines in the margin. In his comments, Hughes ponders the significance of characters' actions and their relationship to the play as a whole. In *The Misanthrope*, he noted: "Alceste seeking motive for his indignation" (Figure 4.1). In *The School for Wives*, Hughes reflected at the bottom of page 40: "Purpose of all this: Arnolphe is a countryman & though he wants to be an aristocrat his servants still treat him casually. He is deceived here" (Figures 4.2 and 4.3).

Hughes's annotations in *School for Wives* contain cues to himself—notes regarding irony, motive, and character—to which he could draw students' attention. In one instance, he commented on an early scene's

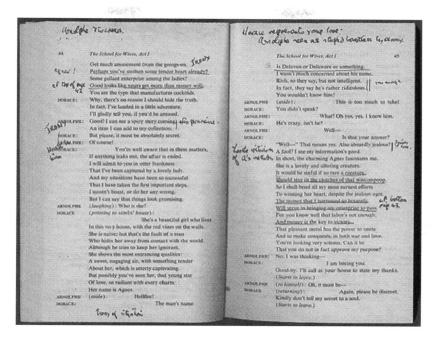

Figure 4.1 Ted Hughes's copy of Molière, *The School for Wives*, pages 44–5, Emory.

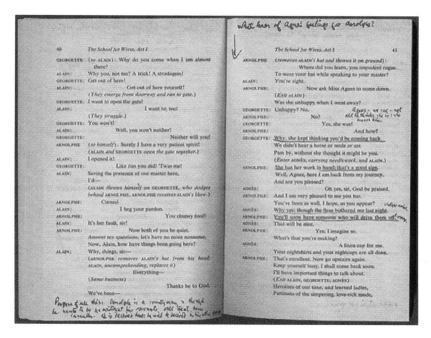

Figure 4.2 Hughes's copy of Molière, *The School for Wives*, pages 40–1, Emory.

ARNOLPHE: Curses!
ALAIN: I beg your pardon.
ARNOLPHE: You clumsy fool!
ALAIN: It's her fault, sir!
ARNOLPHE: Now both of you be quiet.
Answer my questions; let's have no more nonsense.
Now, Alain, how have things been going here?
ALAIN: Why, things, sir—
(ARNOLPHE *removes* ALAIN'S *hat from his head;* ALAIN, *uncomprehending, replaces it*)
Everything—
(*Same business*)
Thanks be to God.
We've been—

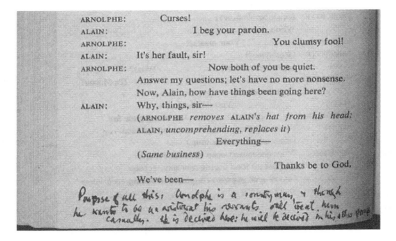

Figure 4.3 Hughes's copy of Molière, *The School for Wives*, page 40, Emory.

42 *The School for Wives, Act I*

I defy you and all your prose and poems,
Your novels and your billets-doux, to equal
This decent, modest, honest ignorance.
(*Enter* HORACE)
In marriage, money's not the important thing.
If honor's there— Who's this? It can't be— Yes!
Or maybe not. It is, though! Yes, it's Horace!
HORACE: My dear Ar—
ARNOLPHE: Horace!
HORACE: Arnolphe!
ARNOLPHE: What a surprise!
How long have you been in town?
HORACE: Just eight days.
ARNOLPHE: Really!
HORACE: I called first at your house, but you weren't there.
ARNOLPHE: I'd gone to the country.
HORACE: Yes; two days before.
ARNOLPHE: Well, how young people grow in a few short years!
It's really amazing to see you as you are.
When I remember you no bigger than that!
HORACE: You see—
ARNOLPHE: Enough of that. Your father Oronte,
My excellent friend, whom I esteem and honor,
What is he up to? He's still gay and hearty?
He knows I'm interested in all his news.
We haven't seen each other for four years;
In fact, we haven't written in all that time.
HORACE: Seigneur Arnolphe, he's gayer than you and I are!
He gave me a letter to present to you.
But now a later message has informed me
He's coming in person; he hasn't told me why.
Do you perhaps know of a local man
Who's coming home soon with a lot of money
He's made in fourteen years in America?

The School for Wives, Act I 43

ARNOLPHE: No; no. You wouldn't know his name?
HORACE: Enrique.
ARNOLPHE: No; no.
HORACE: Well, father speaks of his return
As if I ought to be acquainted with him.
And they expect, he says, to travel together
To treat an important matter; he doesn't say what.
(*He hands letter to* ARNOLPHE.)
ARNOLPHE: I'll certainly be glad to see him again,
And I shall give him a proper welcome here.
(*Reads letter, and pockets it*)
Old friends hardly require such protestations;
He needn't waste his time in mere politeness.
Without a word from him, I would have offered
To let you draw on me, if you need cash.
HORACE: Since you're so cordial, I'll take you at your word.
I do in fact need some pistoles. A hundred.
ARNOLPHE: Why, it's a pleasure to have you act so frankly;
And by a fortunate chance I have them on me.
(*Hands a fat purse to* HORACE, *who starts to empty it*)
Keep the purse, too.
HORACE: But I must give you—
ARNOLPHE: Nonsense!
Tell me, Horace, how do you find our city?
HORACE: Busy; and with some very handsome buildings.
And I suspect that people enjoy themselves.
ARNOLPHE: Everyone seeks for pleasures to his taste.
And those they call the gay Lotharios
Find plenty of opportunity in this town.
Our women know the tricks of coquetry,
And both brunettes and blondes are—very kind.
And husbands are uncommonly indulgent.
Why, it's a happy hunting ground! I often

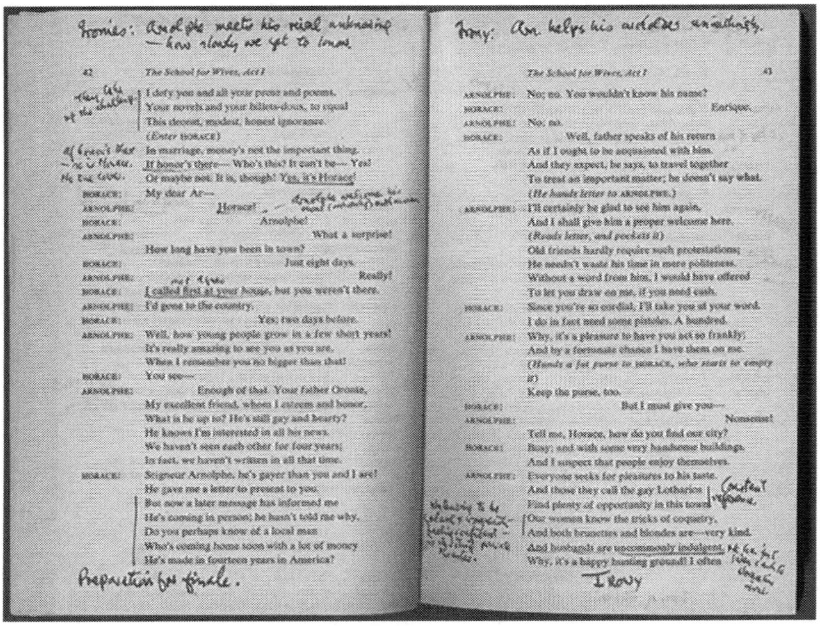

Figure 4.4 Hughes's copy of Molière, *The School for Wives*, pages 42–3, Emory.

"Ironies: Arnolphe meets his rival unknowing –how slowly we get to know" (Figures 4.4 and 4.5). As the play continues, Hughes turned to Arnolphe's character, noting his "Humiliation," "Pain at loss," and "Vanity" (Molière, 68; Figure 4.6). Subsequent annotations suggest an invitation for students to probe further regarding the characters' impulses. Beneath Arnolphe's

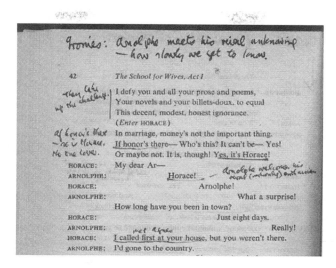

Figure 4.5 Hughes's copy of Molière, *The School for Wives*, page 42, Emory.

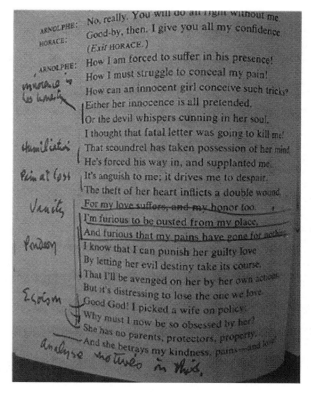

Figure 4.6 Hughes's copy of Molière, *The School for Wives*, page 68, Emory.

complaint that his love interest Inez "betrays my kindness," Hughes added: "Analyse motives in this."

When Hughes read *Walden*, his attention to Thoreau's reflections on art, creativity, and education speaks to Hughes's perspective as a writer and the distance he sought from academia.[46] At the top of page 37, he glossed that "All life to be related to the inner creative life." Later, on page 79, Hughes drew an arrow to Thoreau's statement that "[t]he poet or the artist never yet had so fair and noble a design but some of his posterity at least could accomplish it," which he underlined. Hughes also summarized Thoreau's favoring of exploration in nature over the expertise of academic institutions: "Practical experience the only valuable education. American distrust of education." Hughes added this note above the following passage from Thoreau, which Hughes also indicated with a line in the left margin:

> If I wished a boy to know something about the arts and sciences, for instance, I would not pursue the common course, which is merely to send him into the neighborhood of some professor, where anything is professed and practiced but the art of life;—to survey the world through a telescope or microscope, and never with his natural eye, to study chemistry, and not learn how his bread is made[.] . . . Which would have advanced the most at the end of a month,—the boy who had made his own jackknife from the ore which he had dug and smelted, reading as much as would be necessary for this—or the boy who had attended the lectures on metallurgy at the Institute in the meanwhile.

Crafting his own tools, Hughes came to know the Great Books that he selected to teach and continued to admire.[47] While Hughes separated himself from the academy, his understanding of texts did not exist solely outside of it. Teaching prompted his further meditation regarding the texts he read, how they worked, and the directions in which he would proceed.

While teaching at UMass, Hughes resolved in a letter to his Cambridge friend Lucas Myers that "Teaching in these Universities is the death of the artist in whatever person tries it."[48] But, after some time had passed, Hughes expressed a sense of the impact that his teaching experience had on his work.[49] In 1961, Hughes wrote again to Myers that he and Plath

> were at first dismayed to hear you were going to teach, but then considering our own teaching thought it might be one of the best things you could do. The equivalent that I did of the "representative master pieces" was the most valuable thing I ever did, in the way of study: 1000 times more valuable than my academic experience of Cambridge. I envy you the Greek plays cycle & the Dante.[50]

As we observed in Chapter 2, John Berryman similarly felt that by teaching humanities courses he was able to understand "much more . . . than I ever learned at Columbia or Cambridge. It has forced me into areas where I wouldn't otherwise have been."[51] In the same interview, Berryman also recommended teaching this type of course over creative writing.[52] In his letter to Myers, Hughes added that teaching writing helped to refine his sense of composition: "In my 'advanced writing' I really taught myself how to put together my imaginations to make an effective story, since I didn't have the art by nature." Teaching allowed Hughes to continue his education. Even so, he cautioned Myers that for teaching, "A year, is the maximum, though, I should think."[53]

Birthday Letters

When Hughes served as executor of Plath's estate, his prior experience provided an introduction to the genres he encountered, but he continued to distance himself from academia, both his experience and Plath's. In his essay, "Notes on the Chronological Order of Sylvia Plath's Poems" (1966), Hughes mentioned Plath's "muse of death in life and life in death," reversing the order with which Yeats referred to "Life in Death and Death in Life" in "Byzantium."[54] Hughes's doing so may be due to Plath's familiarity with the term as a teacher, and perhaps suggests her even more frequent use of the term in relation to her own poetry or her reading. Hughes also switched the order of death-in-life and life-in-death when he addressed Plath's teaching in his *Birthday Letters* poem, "Blue Flannel Suit." In it, he depicts Plath's "dummy stiffness," performing a role that she had since she was a student (*BL*, 67, line 11). His choice of a "straitjacket" suit links academic and psychiatric institutions.[55] It recalls the role that her desire for success had on her breakdown as a student and as she adopted the uniform of the academy when she returned to teach.

When he composed a response to Jacqueline Rose's book *The Haunting of Sylvia Plath* (1991), Hughes underscored the blurriness of influence, and that it was not just Graves's book that would have influenced Plath, but also the anthropological and mythological antecedents that informed Graves's sense of poetic myth. In his notes on Rose's manuscript, Hughes went as far as to say that "Graves was not an important influence" for Plath. Rather, "The important influences were in earlier sources (Graves' own sources)."[56] Lived reality differs from the paths that scholars subsequently weave through texts, pointing out threads of which writers and speakers are unaware. But Hughes also stressed that the attempt to pin down Plath's "sense of archetypal figures" is pointless.[57] These are impressions she and other writers absorb from reading, education, and society.

Mythological sources are unclear, and there are untraceable elements of them. Graves's composition of *The White Goddess* demonstrates this process to some extent, as when he researched the book during World War II, his access to the British Library was limited.[58] As we observed in Chapter 1, Plath's encounter with death-in-life was not limited to Graves's mentioning of it in *The White Goddess* (1948). Her use of the term in her teaching notes intersected with its presence in the Eliot and Joyce criticism

she read. The larger bodies of knowledge to which Hughes gestured, how-
ever, would also include source texts that she consulted, such as Weston's
From Ritual to Romance.

Critics have noted Hughes's familiarity with Graves's *White God-
dess* and Hughes revealed in a letter to Nick Gammage in 1995: "it was
the Graves maybe that made the link directly to that lineage in English
poetry—from the Sycorax figure to La Belle Dame and the Nightmare Life
in Death. Made it conscious and obvious" (*LTH*, 681).[59] Hughes discusses
this trajectory in his essay, "The Snake and the Oak."[60] When alluding to
Coleridge in his *Birthday Letters* poem, "Moonwalk," however, Hughes
replaced Life-in-Death with Death-in-Life as he addressed Plath in apostro-
phe: "Your mask / Bleak as cut iron . . . / And angering moon-devil – here
somewhere / The Ancient Mariner's Death-in-Life woman / Straight off the
sea's fevered incandescence."[61] Here, Hughes blends Coleridge's figure with
the image Plath creates in her late poem, "Edge" (*Collected Poems*, 272–3).
In "Moonwalk," the anchor of death-in-life is Coleridge's poem, but after
examining the contents of Plath's library and teaching notes, such a refer-
ence can also be interpreted in relation to them, part of a material history
that is different from, yet simultaneously rests behind, lived experience.[62]

While Hughes's library has been underexplored, its contents open new
directions for understanding not just his navigation of words and pages, but
also his sense of texts over time. Taken independently and in relation to the
writers in previous chapters, we see the role of annotated books and teach-
ing materials in making engagement with language—for teaching, writing,
or independent reading—visible. By annotating, Hughes contributed to a
larger cultural history, and his perspective as an outsider to the American
academy presents a counterpoint to the previous case studies, one that re-
flects certain consistencies in annotating style across texts and genres, from
nineteenth-century Russian fiction to seventeenth-century French drama.
The common denominator, making clear to students how texts work, is one
that Hughes brought to light.

Future digitization of writers' teaching notes, personal libraries, and
other materials will prompt broader, more detailed, global conversations
regarding modernism's relationship to midcentury poetry, academic institu-
tions, and literary history.[63] As we have seen throughout *Annotating Mod-
ernism*, contextualizing writers' annotations enables further consideration
of the teaching, reception, and criticism of modernist texts. The result is a
new sense of the role that readers and teachers continue to play in the for-
mation of modernism as a discourse.

Notes

1 Plath noted in her journal that Hughes had an "interview-lunch" in Amherst
on 8 January (*UJ*, 308). Hughes subsequently wrote to his parents that he was
teaching three courses. Letter, Ted Hughes to parents, [January 1958], box 1,
folder 17, MSS 980, Olwyn Hughes Papers, Emory; hereafter cited in the text

as "Olwyn Hughes Papers." At the request of the Hughes Estate, brackets will not be used in quotations from Hughes's unpublished materials.

2 Qtd. in Golden, "Hughes and the Midcentury American Academy," page 48. Letter, Hughes to parents, [January 1958], box 1, folder 17, Olwyn Hughes Papers.

3 Qtd. in Golden, "Hughes and the Midcentury American Academy," page 48. Letter, Hughes to parents, [January 1958], box 1, folder 17, Olwyn Hughes Papers. Distance from Google Maps, 28 March 2020.

4 See http://www.umass.edu/umhome/about/history.html, accessed 1 February 2010.

5 Hughes reported to his brother Gerald,

> I have led an utterly unreal life for a year, because there is no friendship with these people, only acquaintance. All churning over the same mechanical trash, which passes for modern criticism etc . . . My spell of teaching at the State University near here was amusing, a sort of Marx brothers episode, and a great relief.
>
> (*LTH*, 130)

Letter to Gerald and Joan Hughes and family, late August with additions dated 7 and 8 September 1958.

6 Letter, Hughes to Glen [Fallows], box 53, folder 1, Hughes Papers. This item contains the date [Fall 1957], but Hughes began teaching in the spring of 1958.

7 See http://www.umass.edu/umhome/about/history.html, accessed 1 February 2010.

8 See http://www.umass.edu/umhome/about/history.html, accessed 1 February 2010. The University of Massachusetts's online history lists a student population of 4,000 for 1954.

9 Letter, Hughes to Glen [Fallows], box 53, folder 1, Hughes Papers.

10 Philip Hoy, *Interviews with Anthony Hecht* (London: Between the Lines, 2004), 48–9. See also Hughes comments on *Letters Home* to Aurelia Plath. Hughes Papers.

11 Hughes, for instance, critiques Plath's relationship to Smith in a letter to Lucas Myers:

> The most useful thing about this last year so far is that it has forced Sylvia out of several of her easy delusions. . . . Sylvia would have been an adoring Smith Sophomore all her life but for this job—which has very brutally disenchanted her. Now she sees what an utter kindergarten the whole place is, and she is really a different person.
>
> (*LTH*, 118)

12 Regarding Hughes's time at UMass, see Golden, "Ted Hughes, Isaac Bashevis Singer, and an Interview with Jules Chametzky," *The Ted Hughes Society Journal* 3, no.1 (2013): 59–66.

13 Letter, Ted Hughes to Olwyn Hughes, [February 1958], Add MSS 889 48/1/1, British Library.

14 Ibid.

15 Ibid.

16 Ibid.

17 Ted Hughes, *Collected Poems*, ed. Paul Keegan (London: Faber and Faber, 2005), 21. Regarding Hughes's departure from literary study, see Heather Clark, *The Grief of Influence: Sylvia Plath and Ted Hughes* (New York: Oxford University Press, 2011), Jonathan Bate, *Ted Hughes: The Unauthorised Life* (New York: Harper Collins, 2015), 75; hereafter cited in the text as "Bate," Roberts, *Ted Hughes*, 19–20. Hughes also explains this story in the following clip from *A*

Tribute to Ted Hughes: http://www.youtube.com/watch?v=18DdJO9Lg-s, accessed 28 March 2018.

18 Letter, Ted Hughes to Olwyn Hughes, [February 1958], British Library.

19 See Guillory regarding Brooks and Leavis. Neil Roberts, however, has argued that for Hughes, "the values of Cambridge English were much closer to his poetic practice, as it emerged in the years immediately following his graduation, than his dismissive comments suggest." Neil Roberts, *Ted Hughes: A Literary Life* (New York: Palgrave Macmillan, 2006), 19.

20 Letter, Ted Hughes to Olwyn Hughes, [February 1958], British Library. Brooks and Warren use the terms "surface meaning" and "symbolic meaning" in *Understanding Poetry*, 615.

21 Books at Emory contain Hughes's underlining or lists of page numbers, particularly when he was preparing to write a review.

22 Drue Heinz, "Ted Hughes: The Art of Poetry," in *The Paris Review Interviews, III*, ed. Philip Gourevitch (New York: Picador, 2008), 272; hereafter cited in the text as *"Paris Review."*

23 Henry David Thoreau, *Walden and On the Duty of Civil Disobedience* (1854; New York Rinehart & Company, 1957), former Owner Hughes, Emory. Anita Helle brought Hughes's copy of *Walden* to my attention. Hughes explained in a letter to Lucas Myers ("[Early 1958]"),

> I shall teach 14 weeks—which is ½ an academic year—at the University of Massachusetts. I take two classes three times a week on a "Great book" [sic] course—Milton's shorter poems & Samson Agonistes, Goethe's Faust Pt I, Crime & Punishment, Keats, Wordsworth, Yeats, Thoreau's Walden, 5 plays by Moliere [the book contained five; three are annotated].
>
> (*LTH*, 117)

Hughes and Plath's copy of *Crime and Punishment* contains his cross reference to Goethe's *Faust* and his copy of *School for Wives* includes a cross reference to Milton. Molière, *Eight Plays by Molière*, trans. Morris Bishop (New York: The Modern Library, 1957), 59, former owner Hughes, Emory

24 Robin Peel also notes that Hughes "later reflected on how useful both the creative writing and the 'great works' courses had been for his own development." "From *Dogs* to *Crow*: Ted Hughes and a 'world lost' 1956–1970," *English 55* (Summer 2006), 169.

25 Amy Hildreth Chen brought this passage to my attention.

26 Plath taught *Crime and Punishment* from approximately Wednesday 8 January to Saturday 18 January 1958, after her Smith students had returned from the winter vacation and before their midterm exams. She wrote in her journal on 8 January that she had "[u]nderlined notes in Crime and Punishment" (*UJ*, 308). Around this time, she also noted that she had either received or had to fill a "request for Dostoevsky book from library" (*UJ*, 309). See also Appendix A and *UJ*, 305, 308, and 309.

27 Inside the back cover, Plath listed each of the novel's six sections and its epilogue with each segment's range of pages and total number of pages.

28 See image in Golden, "Hughes and the Midcentury American Academy," 49. In this article, I quoted the word as "effort," but now believe it may be "effect."

29 Neil Roberts, "Ted Hughes and Cambridge," in *Ted Hughes: From Cambridge to Collected*, ed. by Mark Wormald, Neil Roberts, and Terry Gifford (Houndmills, Basingstoke: Palgrave, 2013), 31; hereafter cited in the text as "Hughes and Cambridge."

30 Hughes published this poem before he began teaching.
31 See image in Golden, "Hughes and the Midcentury American Academy," 50.
32 I thank Neil Roberts for bringing this passage to my attention. Lucas Myers, *An Essential Self: Ted Hughes and Sylvia Plath* (Nottingham: Richard Hollis, 2011), 21.

   Hughes also observed in a later interview, "[a]part from the more monumental classics—Tolstoy, Dostoyevsky, and so on—my background reading was utterly different from hers. But our minds soon became two parts of the same operation" (*Paris Review*, 289).
33 Letter, Ted Hughes to Parents, [1958], box 1, folder 17, Olwyn Hughes Papers.
34 Letter of 16 March 1954. Fyodor Dostoevsky, *The Brothers Karamazov*, trans. Constance Garnett (New York: Modern Library, [c. 1950]), former owner Plath, Smith.
35 Fyodor Dostoevsky, *Crime and Punishment*, 1886, trans. David Magarshack (1951; Middlesex: Harmondsworth, 1956), former owner Hughes, Emory.
36 George Gibian, "Traditional Symbolism in *Crime and Punishment*," in Feodor Dostoevsky, *Crime and Punishment*, ed. George Gibian (1964; New York: Norton, 1989), 526. Originally published in *PMLA LXX* (1955), 979–96. Peter Gibian brought his father's edition of *Crime and Punishment* to my attention. When Plath wrote her senior honors thesis, "The Magic Mirror: A Study of the Double in Two of Dostoevsky's Novels" (1955), analyzing *The Double* and *The Brothers Karamazov*, Plath also cites Ruth Mortimer, "The Design of Dreams in *Crime and Punishment*" (unpublished honors essay), Northampton: Smith College, 1953. Mortimer later became Curator of Rare Books at Smith. I consulted the copy of Plath's thesis in the Raymond Danowski Poetry Library, Emory. Sylvia Plath, "The Magic Mirror" (1955; 1989).
37 Gibian, 526.
38 It is possible that the affection for identifying "death-in-life" by critics as they interpreted earlier texts was a reaction to the desire for normality at midcentury. Regarding the interest in normality, see Anna G. Creadick, *Perfectly Average: The Pursuit of Normality in Postwar America* (Amherst: University of Massachusetts Press, 2010).
39 For an image of this page, see figure 1 in Golden, "Hughes and the Midcentury American Academy," 49.
40 Qtd. in Golden, "Hughes and the Midcentury American Academy," 49.
41 Ibid.
42 Ibid.
43 See Axelrod and Alexander.
44 Karen Kukil has also suggested that Plath taught Hughes about prose. See also Clark, *The Grief of Influence*.
45 Molière, *Eight Plays by Molière*, Emory. Hughes also owned an earlier copy of Molière's plays in French. Molière, *Théatre choisi de Molière* (Paris: Garnier Frères: 1937?), former owner Hughes, Emory.
46 Regarding Plath, Hughes, and America, see Clark, *Grief of Influence*, and Gillian Groszewski, "Hughes and America" in *Ted Hughes in Context*, ed. Terry Gifford (Cambridge: Cambridge University Press, 2018): 155–64.
47 See also Tracy Brain, "Hughes and Feminism," in *The Cambridge Companion to Ted Hughes*, ed. Terry Gifford (New York: Cambridge University Press, 2011).
48 Ted Hughes, *The Letters of Ted Hughes*, ed. Christopher Reid (London: Faber and Faber, 2007), 118; hereafter cited in the text as *LTH*.
49 Myers had taught at the English Language Institute in Rome in 1957. This information is on an envelope that enclosed letters from Hughes and Plath.

Letter, Hughes to Myers, 1957, box 1, folder 3, MSS 865, Letters to Lucas Myers, Emory.

50 Clark brought this passage and letter to my attention in *The Grief of Influence*. Letter, Hughes to Lucas Myers, "[Winter / Spring 1961]," box 1, folder 7, MSS 865, Letters to Lucas Myers, Emory.

51 Stitt, "The Art of Poetry," 22–3.

52 In his interview with the *Harvard Advocate* (1969), Berryman responded to the question, "How do you see your role as a teacher in relation to your poetry?" "There is no connection." Plotz, "An Interview with John Berryman," *Berryman's Understanding*, 15.

53 Letter, Hughes to Myers, "[Winter / Spring 1961]," MSS 865, Emory. See also Hugh Dunkerley, "Hughes and Creative Writing," in *Ted Hughes in Context*, ed. Terry Gifford (Cambridge: Cambridge University Press, 2018): 315–24.

54 Ted Hughes, "Sylvia Plath (1966)," in Ekbert Faas, *Ted Hughes: The Unaccommodated Universe* (Santa Barbara, CA: Black Sparrow Press, 1980), 181. The essay was printed as "Notes on the Chronological Order of Sylvia Plath's Poems" in *Tri-Quarterly* no. 7 (Fall 1966): 81–8 (Cited in Faas, 149).

55 For further consideration of both institutions in midcentury poetry, see Kamran Javadizadeh, "Anne Sexton's Institutional Voice," in *This Business of Words: Reassessing Anne Sexton*, ed. Amanda Golden (Gainesville: University of Florida Press, 2016): 73–103.

56 Hughes, "Rose, Jacqueline, *The Haunting of Sylvia Plath* (1991) [1 of 3]," Note "79: P 251 – 1 – 7," box 148, folder 3, Hughes Papers.

57 Hughes, "Rose, Jacqueline, *The Haunting of Sylvia Plath* (1991) [1 of 3]," Note "79 252," box 148, folder 3, Hughes Papers.

58 See Robert Perceval Graves, *Robert Graves and the White Goddess 1940–85* (London: Weidenfeld and Nicolson, 1995), Martin Seymour-Smith, *Robert Graves: His Life and Work* (1982; London: Bloomsbury, 1995), 390–1, and John B. Vickery, *Robert Graves and the White Goddess* (Lincoln: University of Nebraska Press, 1972), 44–5.

59 Regarding Hughes and Graves's *White Goddess*, see Kroll, Myers, *Crow Steered*, 7. As Weissbort underscores, Hughes and his friends took to

> what now might be called his [Graves's] "non-canonical" approach, and especially his writings about the White Goddess, Diana, the spectral female figure seen by Coleridge's Ancient Mariner etc.), by embodying the eternal feminine, the pagan principle of matriarchy, appeared to challenge the Judeo-Christian male culture, that of the establishment which was treated by us as inimical.
>
> (1–2)

Daniel Weissbort, "Sylvia Plath and Translation," *Theme and Vision: Plath and Ronsard*, ed. Anthony Rudolph (London: The Menard Press, 1995), 1–2.

60 Ted Hughes, "The Snake in the Oak," in *Winter Pollen: Occasional Prose*, ed. William Scammell (1994; New York: Picador, 1995), 396, 423, 426, 437, 457.

61 Ted Hughes, "Moonwalk," *Birthday Letters* (New York: Farrar, Straus and Giroux, 1998), 41. In his essay, "The Snake in the Oak," Hughes describes the origins of Coleridge's female figure.

62 I thank Alicia Ostriker for her comments at my talk on Plath and Joyce at New York University.

63 For considerations of poetry across national boundaries, see Jahan Ramazani, *A Transnational Poetics* (Chicago, IL: University of Chicago Press, 2009).

Conclusion

Marginalia and modernism are forward thinking. A difference between the two, however, is that readers add notes in books with the thought of returning to them, even if they know this may not be the case. The resulting artifacts record impulses. Such marks become a part of the artifacts to which they respond. As poets prepare to teach, their notes become points for discussion, concepts to which they may give new life in future work. In the process, midcentury poets' reading and teaching materials can contribute to a broader understanding of modernism. These items form part of an incomplete archive of notes and fragments, memories and impressions.

This prospect becomes apparent when addressing resources housed in different archives. Laura Hughes argues that Derrida's library comprises

> literary artifacts . . . as they cross limits between animate and inanimate matter, between archives and authors, between moments of creation and consultation. What is *vivant* about the artifact is not solely the material content, nor any textual content, but the unexpected connections made possible between artifacts, across collections.[1]

Writers' reading and teaching materials can similarly be held in different locations, and considering such artifacts in relation to each other enables more thorough treatment of them. To take Plath as an example, new insights emerge when examining her student copy of *A Portrait of the Artist as a Young Man* (at Emory), her student copy of *Ulysses* (at Smith), her teaching copy of *The Portable James Joyce* containing *Portrait of the Artist*, and the Joyce notebook she kept as a student (both at the Lilly Library).

Evidence of responses to reading is detectable because it forms material impressions and recollections, captured in conversations. In *Making Literature Now*, Amy Hungerford, critiquing Bruno Latour's "Actor-Network Theory", reminds us of the futility of

> raking the archives not for recollection or record but for the actual trace of a social act as it unfolded, and not just one social act but an

infinite series of them; cramming them, by force of method into the book one writes.[2]

The materials in an archive can never allow one to experience a past event. Instead, the archive becomes the site where scholars read the materials that authors created and knew. Such records are scattered and disconnected, repetitive and textured. Still, Hungerford insists, "the context recoverable by live conversation cannot be archived . . . until context materializes in an artifact" (170). In the case of teaching, the archive provides access to pages that writers prepared and may have consulted as they addressed the class, with the presence of students altering what one might have imagined in advance.

Teaching and reading are performances, and the attempt to reconstitute them will only be that. As Christopher Grobe puts it,

> performance is ephemeral in general and so it fills the archive with ephemera for us to study. Performance theorist José Muñoz has defined ephemera as "anti-evidence"—"traces, glimmers, residues," a "kind of evidence of what has transpired but certainly not the thing itself." Literary scholars are too used to beholding "the thing itself," an authorized text between their hands. Deny yourself that feeling for a while, and whole new horizons will open up to you. Even poems on the page will have more to offer the scholar who treats them as "traces, glimmers, residues" of an embodied event.
>
> (51)

Grobe's point is that working with the illusion brings the real into focus. It is remarkable when poets' student notes, or the notes of their students, surface, or when a phrase in a book is underlined.[3] While neither present definitive answers, both present artifacts. They are remnants of conversations, documents of their aftermath.

The archival materials addressed throughout *Annotating Modernism* teach us about the means by which users navigate texts. As Margaret Konkol observes in a different context, "[m]aterial selection is a deliberate meaning-making act."[4] We have seen the implications of such actions, and the role that modernism played in generating the marginalia that readers brought to it. For the New Modernist Studies, such archival materials are part of an expanding archive that will anchor considerations of twentieth-century literary history.[5]

The introduction of marginalia to modernist studies troubles its marginal role. Paul K. Saint-Amour, introducing *Modernism/modernity*'s special issue on Weak Theory, argues that "[w]eakness comes with a lot of baggage. It sits at the center of a dense array of slurs by which marginal subjects have been kept marginal."[6] Making marginalia a subject of inquiry means attending to its placement on the page. In this way, it has never been central. Further, interpreting midcentury annotations and the critical and cultural landscapes to which they respond certainly does not mean a return to the fifties' methods of scholarly exploration. With regard to modernist studies, Saint-Amour clarifies that

> we have learned to focus on questions other than, "But is such-and-such a work really modernist?" In fact . . . the field's formation qua field appears to have required a weaker theory of modernism than that Harry Levin-era question permits. I value the strong field that resulted from this weakening-in-theory and mostly celebrate that weakening and the chances it affords us.
>
> ("Weak Theory," 451)

The radical transformation that modernist studies has undergone over the past two decades has led to the consideration of new materials, in both print and digital form, and engaging such texts means asking again what modernism was and what it can be.

Digital projects can make writers' reading practices accessible to a broader audience, with searchability and visualization meaning the ability to survey a vast array of details.[7] When the markings that writers have made can be readily seen and called forward, scholars can better understand both trends and specific occurrences, interpreting writers' styles as readers. A digital archive devoted to John Stuart Mill's library catalogs different types of markings, teaching readers about the particularity with which he responded to his reading.[8] More recently, *Derrida's Margins* not only reproduces the contents of his library but also contains an interactive visualization of the books that Derrida cites in *Of Grammatology*. Dots accumulating horizontally across the page indicate when the books that he cites are also in his library, and when clicked, they display the reference.[9] As a result, readers gain a new sense of his book, one keyed to the texts on which it rests.

The capabilities of digital resources have already inspired the creation of new teaching archives, including the *Open Syllabus Project*.[10] Such data can have far-reaching implications for the changing role of the humanities in academic institutions. To this end, in "The Teaching Archive: A New History of Literary Study," Rachel Sagner Buurma and Laura Heffernan assess a large corpus of syllabi. They underscore in *The Chronicle of Higher Education* that the liberal arts have been a part of various institutions since their origins, regardless of their emphasis and socioeconomic status. The longevity of the liberal arts, they argue, is indicative of its enduring value.[11] In addition to a better understanding of the discipline, the ability to search syllabi at the level of the word can also enable new considerations of modernism's formation in academic institutions.

Digital and material modernist scholarship returns us to the spaces that surround texts. We can devote new attention to teaching and the process of creating materials, as well as the ongoing relationships that writers have to the texts they read and teach. Even as marginalia take on new digital forms, such markings will continue to register reactions, providing new data. These observations will take on new life in creative work, poetry and prose awaiting comments. The resulting annotations will form part of a story, one that readers will continue in the margins.

Notes

1 Laura Hughes, "In the Library of Jacques Derrida: Manuscript Materiality after the Archival Turn," *New Literary History* 49, no. 3 (Summer 2018): 403–24.

2 Amy Hungerford, *Making Literature Now* (Palo Alto, CA: Stanford University Press, 2016), 4; hereafter cited in the text as "Hungerford."

3 As Buurma and Heffernan put it with regard to the University of London's materials related to Eliot's teaching, "[t]he survival of so many of these documents is unusual. More often, teaching materials are archived only by accident and are catalogued in less detail than the evidence of published scholarship" ("The Classroom in the Canon," 167).

4 Margaret Konkol, "Prototyping Mina Loy's Alphabet," *Feminist Modernist Studies* 1, no. 3 (October 2018): 300.

5 See Rachel Sagner Buurma and Laura Heffernan, "The Common Reader and the Archival Classroom: Disciplinary History for the Twenty-First Century," *New Literary History* 43, no. 1 (Winter 2012): 113–35. Other volumes addressing marginalia include Dirk Van Hulle and Mark Nixon, ed., *Samuel Beckett's Library* (New York: Cambridge University Press, 2013) and Stephen Collis and Graham Lyons, ed., *Reading Duncan Reading: Robert Duncan and the Politics of Derivation* (Iowa City: University of Iowa Press, 2012).

6 Paul K. Saint-Amour, "Introduction: Weak Theory, Weak Modernism," *Modernism/modernity* 25, no. 3 (September 2018): 438; hereafter cited in the text as "Weak Theory."

7 With regard to the scope of book history, Allen Liu includes "approaches to digital texts rooted in revisionary textual editing, bibliography as the sociology of texts, and the materiality of the digital." Allen Liu, "The Meaning of the Digital Humanities," *PMLA* 128, no. 2 (2013): 410.

8 *Mill Marginalia Online*, University of Alabama Libraries, http://millmarginalia. org/; the spines by volume, http://millmarginalia.org/shelf; marginalia types http://millmarginalia.org/marginalia-examples, all accessed 9 March 2019.

9 *Derrida's Margins*, Visualization, Center for Digital Humanities at Princeton, Princeton University, https://derridas-margins.princeton.edu/references/ histogram/de-la-grammatologie/, accessed 9 March 2019. After conducting a broad survey of readers' markings, Jackson observes in *Marginalia* that she found that while readers often thought that their tendencies were unique, in reality they were not, as readers tended to employ similar approaches.

10 *The Open Syllabus Project*, https://opensyllabusproject.org/, accessed 9 March 2019.

11 Regarding "The Teaching Archive: A New History of Literary Study," see http://rachelsagnerbuurma.org/research/, accessed 23 February 2020; Rachel Sagner Buurma and Laura Heffernan, "Elite Colleges Have No Monopoly on the Liberal Arts," *The Chronicle Review*, 15 July 2018, https://www.chronicle. com/article/Elite-Colleges-Have-No/243915, accessed 18 July 2018; and "The Classroom in the Canon."

Appendix A
Sylvia Plath's teaching syllabus
A chronology

The chronology below draws on Plath's teaching notes, correspondence, and journal entries. In addition to information that Plath recorded, 1957 and 1958 calendars also provided dates and days of the week.[1] Plath's afternoon classes met on Wednesdays, Thursdays, and Fridays and her morning classes met on Thursdays, Fridays, and Saturdays (LV2, 174). Following her first meeting with the Wednesday afternoon class, the three sections progressed at slightly different paces. At points in her teaching notes Plath indicated the amount she had covered in specific class sessions and what to address next. In addition to the readings the students prepared for class meetings, Plath also assigned different texts for the students' essays. When possible, the chronology acknowledges the material she covered by day and course section as well as the texts she assigned students to navigate independently. On an additional page, Plath listed poems she planned to teach through the end of the term. Perhaps as the poetry unit progressed, she crossed out poems and revised the number of class days to devote to individual poets. The chronology indicates the time period Plath devoted to each poet, and both the poems she selected to teach and those she eliminated.

1957

During her second year as a Fulbright Scholar at Newnham College, Robert Gorham Davis offered Plath a teaching position at Smith the following year (LV2, 87). In June, Plath received a book list from Smith (318).[2]

September and October
William James: *Varieties of Religious Experience*, two chapters (LV2, 175).[3]
Plath wrote that she was preparing James on Tues. 10.1 (UJ, 618, 620).

Nathaniel Hawthorne: Plath taught the following stories, "The Birthmark," "Rappaccini's Daughter," "Ethan Brand," "Lady Eleanore's Mantle," and "Goodman Brown" (Thurs.–Sat. 10.10–12) (UJ, 620).[4]

November
Henry James: Stories, "The Pupil" (Thurs. 10.31) and "The Beast in the Jungle" (10.31, Fri. 11.1, Sat. 11.2, Fri. 11.8).[5]

> When considering the days on which she would teach James, she placed a question mark beside Wed. for "The Pupil."

> Plath indicated for "Oct. 30 (31)" a "Library Assignment" in Seelye Hall, the building in which the English department was located. The students defined terms from James's "The Pupil" in the *Oxford English Dictionary*, his French vocabulary in Fowler's *Dictionary of Modern English Usage*, and compiled from the *Dictionary of American Biography* details from James's background relevant to the story (*TN*).

D. H. Lawrence: Stories, "The Rocking-Horse Winner" (11.8), "The Blind Man" (11.8), "The Prussian Officer" (c. Thurs. 11.14), and "The Princess" (Fri. 11.15) (*TN*).[6]

> Plath noted in her Journal Fragment of November 5, that her former poetry professor, Alfred Young Fisher, would be observing her class on her first day teaching Lawrence (Fri. 11.8), (*UJ*, 622).

> On Plath's first page of notes for Lawrence's stories, she noted to go over "The Beast in the Jungle" and address chapters 5 and 6 (*TN*).

> For their essays, the students selected from Lawrence's stories, "The Woman Who Rode Away," "Mother and Daughter," The Man Who Loved Islands," and "The Horse Dealer's Daughter."[7] The thousand-word essays were due Fri. 11.22 and Sat. 11.23 (*TN*).

James Joyce: Stories, "The Sisters," "Grace," "Araby" (Thurs. 11.21), "A Little Cloud" (Thurs. 11.21), "A Painful Case" (Fri. 11.22), "Clay" (Sat. 11.23), and "The Boarding House" (Sat. 11.23). Plath noted that "Ivy Day in the Committee Room" and "The Dead" for "Thurs. and Fri," which may have been 12.5 and 12.6 (*TN*).

> One page of notes on "A Painful Case" indicates points in the story "newspaper / life's feast" for the Wednesday afternoon section and "Average / common" for the morning classes. In addition, a page of notes on "A Painful Case," give the date "Dec. 5" [Thurs.] above a list of stories, "Clay," "The Boarding House," and "Ivy Day in the Committee Room (*TN*)."

1958

January
Fyodor Dostoevsky: *Crime and Punishment* (c. Wed. 1.8–Sat.1.18) (*LV1*, 678). Plath planned to divide the novel into "[a] Part a day" (*TN*).[8]

February
Joyce: *A Portrait of the Artist as a Young Man* (c. Thurs. 2.6 to Fri. 2.14).[9]

Sophocles: *Oedipus* (Fri. 2.21) (*UJ*, 335).[10] *Antigone* (Thurs. 2.27) (*TN*) (*UJ*, 340).

Webster and Tourneur: *The Duchess of Malfi* and Middleton and Tourneur, *The Revenger's Tragedy* (Fri. 2.28) (*UJ*, 339).[11]

March
Henrik Ibsen: *Ghosts, Rosmersholm,* and *The Master Builder* (*TN*). In her journal, Plath noted completing her preparation of Ibsen on Wed. 3.5. She may have taught Ibsen from Thurs–Sat. 3.6–8 (*UJ*, 344).[12]

August Strindberg: *Miss Julie, A Dream Play,* and *Ghost Sonata* (Thurs. 3.13, afternoon) (*UJ*, 348) (*TN*).

April
Gerard Manley Hopkins: In her journal, Plath noted covering three Hopkins poems a class session for a week (*UJ*, 363). She wrote and circled a number six (days) above the Hopkins poems on her list for the unit. Some of the poems she underlined, placed in parentheses, or noted with check marks ("✔") or asterisks, which the symbols below indicate.

> Hopkins poems, "Pied Beauty," "Spring," "Hurrahing in Harvest," "Inversnaid," "*God's Grandeur," "*What I do is Me," "The Caged Skylark," "(Felix Randall)," "(Heaven-Haven)," "*Spring & Fall," "No, Worst, There is None," "✔Thou Art Indeed Just, Lord," "✔The Habit of Perfection," "✔The Windhover," "That Nature is a Heraclitean Fire and of the Comfort of the Resurrection" (Thurs.-Sat. 4.3–5) (*TN*).

W. B. Yeats: In her list of poems for the term, Plath planned to devote four days to Yeats's poems, "(*Nineteen Hundred and Nineteen)," "*The Second Coming," "Leda and the Swan," "* Sailing to Byzantium," "*Among School Children" (Sat. 4.26 (*UJ*, 373), Wed. 4.30), "An Irish Airman Foresees His Death," "Crazy Jane on God," and "A Friend Whose Work Has Come to Nothing" (*TN*).

> Plath noted for Wednesday afternoon class to cover "Nineteen Hundred and Nineteen" with "The Second Coming" on what may have been 4.30 (*TN*).

May

T. S. Eliot: (c. Fri. 5.2–Sat. 5.10) (*UJ*, 377). "The Love Song of J. Alfred Prufrock" and "Journey of the Magi" on Fri. 5.2 (*TN*).

> In her list of poems to teach, Plath crossed out "The Hollow Men." Plath planned to devote five class sessions to Eliot, with four on *The Waste Land* (*TN*).[13]

> For one day teaching *The Waste Land*, Plath noted the following stopping points for the nine a.m., eleven a.m., and three p.m. classes, "Here she said / is your card," "Madame Sosostris," and "Belladonna" (*TN*).

> The following session, she indicated that the nine and eleven a.m. classes covered "to Lil's Husband" and "The Fire Sermon," respectively (*TN*). Plath also noted in her journal that she taught "The Fire Sermon" on Sat. 5.10 (*UJ*, 380).

Dylan Thomas: Plath initially scheduled three days for Thomas's poems, which she later shortened to two. On her list of poems, she placed some of the titles in parentheses or preceded the titles with asterisks, indicated in the symbols below.

> Poems, "*The Hand That Signed the Paper Felled a City," "*The Force through which the Green Fuse Drives the Flower," "*The Hunchback in the Park," "*Twenty-Four Years," "(In Memory of Ann Jones)," "*Fern Hill," and "Do Not Go Gentle into that Good Night," and "Over Sir John's Hill" (*TN*).

> Plath eliminated "The Hand that Signed the Paper Felled a City" and "The Force through which the Green Fuse Drives the Flower" (*TN*).

> Poems for students' papers on one of the following poems due Wed. 4.16 and Thurs. 4.17: Thomas, "A Refusal to Mourn the Death, by Fire, of a Child in London," and "And Death Shall Have No Dominion" and Auden, "Chorus from a Play" and "Lay Your Sleeping Head My Love" (*TN*).

W. H. Auden: For one day on Auden's poems, Plath listed the following poems, indicating some with markings, "*In Memory of W. B. Yeats,"[14] "*Law, Say the Gardeners is the Sun," "*Musee des Beaux Arts," "Look, Stranger," "*As I Walked Out One Evening," and "—Fish in the Unruffled Lakes" (*TN*).

> A later list for Fri. and Sat. of Thomas's and Auden's poems, "The Hunchback in the Park," "Twenty-Four Years," "Fern Hill, "Over Sir

John's Hill," "Do Not Go Gentle into that Good Night," "In Memory of W.B. Yeats" [Fri. afternoon class], "Musee des Beaux Arts," "Law, Say the Gardeners, is the Sun," and "As I Walked Out One Evening" *(TN)*.

John Crowe Ransom: Two days for the following poems, "*Painted Head," "*Winter Remembered," "Parting Without Sequel," "*Captain Carpenter," "Antique Harvesters," "(Bells for John Whiteside's Daughter)," and "*Prelude to an Evening."

Plath gave what she called an "hour exam: open book" on Ransom's "The Equilibrists" on Thurs. 5.1 *(TN)* *(UJ,* 376, 378).

e. e. cummings: For the final day of class, Plath initially selected "Chanson Innocente," Portrait," and "Poem, or Beauty Hurts Mr. Vinal" *(TN)*.

Additional Poems: Beneath the heading "If Possible," Marianne Moore, "Poetry" and "Nevertheless"; Wallace Stevens, "Sense of the Sleight-of-Hand Man"; Elizabeth Bishop, "The Fish"; Richard Wilbur, "Potato" *(TN)*.[15]

Remainder of Poetry Unit: Essays due Fri. 5.16 analyzing two to three of the following poems, Stevens, "The Motive for Metaphor" and "The Idea of Order at Key West"; Moore, "The Mind is an Enchanted Thing" and "Nevertheless"; Ransom, "Bells for John Whiteside's Daughter," "Here Lies a Lady," and "Janet Waking" *(TN)*.

Final day of class (Thurs. 5.22): Plath listed the following poems: Ransom, "Captain Carpenter," "Winter Remembered," and "Parting Without Sequel"; e.e. cummings, "When God Lets My Body Be," "Portrait," and "Chanson Innocente"; Edith Sitwell, "Aubade"; Bishop, "The Fish"; (Wilbur, "Potato") *(TN)* *(UJ,* 388–9).

Notes

1 Even as they draw on available sources, the dates are approximations and draw on the online calendars at the following sites: http://www.hf.rim.or.jp/~kaji/cal/cal.cgi?1957 and http://www.hf.rim.or.jp/~kaji/cal/cal.cgi?1958, accessed 16 August 2008; http://home.comcast.net/~s.astorino/Calendars/1957_Calendar.htm and http://home.comcast.net/~s.astorino/Calendars/1958_Calendar.htm, accessed 7 July 2009.
2 See also Calendar, *Sophian* (Northampton, MA), October 17, 1957, page 3.
3 Daniel Aaron, Director of English 11, noted that the two chapters from James were "The Religion of Healthy-Mindedness and "The Sick Soul." Letter, Aaron to Plath, 11 June 1957, Sylvia Plath Papers, Smith College Archives, CA-MS-00142, Smith College Special Collections, Northampton, MA.

4 Plath may have taught using her copy of *Hawthorne's Short Stories*, ed. Newton Arvin (New York: Vintage Books, 1955), Smith.

5 The page numbers in Plath's teaching notes correspond with James, *Selected Fiction*, Virginia.

6 Plath taught Lawrence's stories using Diana Trilling's edition of *The Portable D.F. Lawrence* (TN).

7 Plath annotated these stories in her copy of Lawrence, *Complete Short Stories*, Smith.

8 See also *UJ* 305, 308–9, and 312.

9 Plath noted the following entries in her journal regarding her preparation of *Portrait of the Artist*. Dates are in brackets: two chapters (Thurs. 2.6) (*UJ*, 324); "finish 3 chapter Joyce outline tomorrow" [for Mon. 2.8] (*UJ*, 327); "outlining this week's first chapter of Joyce – two more to go" (Tue. 2.10) (*UJ*, 329). In her teaching notes, she added, "Thursday & Friday" for Chapter Four (*TN*).

10 See also Plath's journal entries regarding Sophocles (*UJ*, 331), *Oedipus*, and *Antigone* (*UJ*, 333).

11 Plath's copies of Webster and Tourneur, Ibsen, and Strindberg are at Smith. She also owned a copy of Strindberg's plays that is in Hughes's library at Emory.

12 See Bundtzen regarding the role of *Ghosts* in *The Bell Jar*. See also *UJ*, 344.

13 See also *UJ*, 377.

14 See also *UJ*, 358.

15 See also Axelrod.

Appendix B

Poems in Anne Sexton's teaching notes from Colgate University

Sexton listed the following poems and volumes using her own abbreviations (which the citations below replicate) with the page numbers in her books on a page preceding each lecture in her teaching notes. When possible, a title or topic of the lecture is provided. In addition, the list below includes poems Sexton initially included and later eliminated, marked with a strikethrough. Sexton's check marks are represented by a "✔."

The titles of the volumes to which she refers are *To Bedlam and Part Way Back* (1960), *All My Pretty Ones* (1962), *Live or Die* (1966), and *Love Poems* (1969). The class met once a week, and the dates below follow a 1972 calendar.[1] In initial correspondence, Bruce Berlind noted that there was "a twelve-day recess period in April."[2] Sexton also noted that the final assignment would be due "May 3rd, the next to the last class" (*CL*, Preface; 1).

2.9 Preface[3]
2.16. Lecture One
"Laurel Tree" (*Bedlam*, 24), "Portrait of an Old Woman on a College Tavern Wall" (*Bedlam*, 25), "The Moss of His Skin" (*Bedlam*, 37), "Old" (*Pretty*, 37), "Unknown Girl in Maternity Ward" (*Bedlam*, 34), In the Deep Museum" (*Pretty*, 25), "Doors, Doors, Doors" (*Pretty*, 49).

2.23. Lecture Two: "persona [sic] from later books" (*CL*, 2; 1).
"Interrogation of the Man of Many Hearts" (*Love Poems*, 6), "Song for a Lady" (*Love Poems*, 44), "The Legend of the One-Eyed Man" (*Live or Die*, 22), "Two Sons" (*Live*, 33), "Protestant Easter" (*Live*, 41), "In the Deep Museum" (*Pretty*, 25).

3.1. Lecture Three: Narrative Poems (*CL*, 3; 1).
"Some Foreign Letters" (*Bedlam*, 13), "The Operation" (*Pretty Ones*, 12), "All My Pretty Ones" (*Pretty*, 4), "The House" (*Pretty*, 41), "Flight" (*Pretty*, 62), "Letter on L.I. Ferry" (*Pretty*, 55).

3.8. Lecture Four
"Cripples & Other Stories" (*Live*, 80), "The Break" (*Love*, 23), "Eighteen Days Without You" (*Love*, 46).

3.15. Lecture Five: "Lyric poetry" (*CL*, 5; 1).
"Her Kind" (*Bedlam*, 21), "Noon Walk on the Asylum Lawn" (*Bedlam*, 39), "The Bells" (*Bedlam*, 10), "Lullaby" (*Bedlam*, 41), "Hutch" (*Bedlam*, 38), "The Farmer's Wife" (*Bedlam*, 27), "I Remember" (*Pretty*, 11), "Starry Night" (*Pretty*, 9), "Young" (*Pretty*, 6), "Lament" (*Pretty*, 6), "Old" (*Pretty*, 37).

3.22. Lecture Six: "the lyric poem again" (*CL*, 6, 1).
"The Sun" (*Live*, 3), "Three Green Windows" (*Live*, 12), "Consorting With Angels" (*Live*, 20), "Love Song" (Live, 25), "Man and Wife" (*Live*, 27), "Wanting to Die" (*Live*, 58)✔, "Self in 1958" (*Live*, 73)✔, "Suicide Note" (*Live*, 75), "In the Beachhouse" (*Live*, 78), "Live" (*Live*, 87), "Nude Swim" (*Love*, 14), "It is a Spring Afternoon" (*Love*, 26)✔, "Just Once" (*Love* 28), "Us" (*Love*, 41)✔ ✔, "Knee Song" (*Love*, 45)✔.

3.29. Lecture Seven: "prosody" (*CL*, 7; 1).
"Flee on Your Donkey" (*Live*), "Pain for a Daughter" (*Live*).

4.5, 4.12, or 4.19. Lecture Eight: "Eighteen Days Without You" (*CL*, 8; 1).
"Eighteen Days Without You" (*Love Poems*, 46).

4.26 or 5.3. Lecture Nine
"You, Dr. Martin" (*Bedlam*, 3), "Music Swims Back To Me" (*Bedlam*, 8), "Ringing the Bells" (*Bedlam*, 40), "The Double Image" (*Bedlam*, 53), "The Truth the Dead Know" (*Pretty*, 3), "All My Pretty Ones" (*Pretty*, 4), "The Operation" (*Pretty*, 12), "The Abortion" (*Pretty*, 20), "With Mercy for the Greedy" (*Pretty*, 22).

5.10. Lecture Ten
"The Fortress" (*Pretty*, 31), "The House" (*Pretty*, 41),[4] "Letter Written on Long Island Ferry" (*Pretty*, 55), "And One For My Dame" (*Live*, 1),[5] "Somewhere in Africa" (*Live*, 14)✔, "Imitations of Drowning" (*Live*, 16)✔, "Sylvia's Death" (*Live*, 38)✔, "For the Year of the Insane" (*Live*, 44)✔, "Crossing the Atlantic" (*Live*, 47)✔, "Walking in Paris" (*Live*, 49), "Little Girl, My Stringbean, My Lovely Woman" (*Live*, 62)✔, "A Little Uncomplicated Hymn" (*Live*, 66)✔, "Suicide Note" (*Live*, 75)✔, "The Addict" (*Live*, 85), "Live" (*Live*, 87)✔.

Notes

1 http://www.timeanddate.com/calendar/index.html?year=1972&country=1, accessed 7 February 2015.
2 Letter, Berlind to Sexton, 13 October 1972, box 18, folder 1, Sexton Papers. While the letter is dated 1972, it is probably from 1971.
3 Letter, Berlind to Sexton, 13 October 1972, Sexton Papers.
4 Sexton wrote, "done before" beside "The House" and above "Letter Written on Long Island Ferry."
5 Sexton wrote, "done."

Bibliography

Adams, Henry. *History of the United States of America* New York: A&C Boni, 1930. Former Owner Pound, Ransom Center.

Adelman, Gary. *Reclaiming D. H. Lawrence: Contemporary Writers Speak Out.* Lewisburg, PA: Bucknell University Press, 2002.

Albright, Daniel. "Early Cantos I-XLI." In *Cambridge Companion to Ezra Pound*, edited by Ira Nadel, 59–91. New York: Cambridge University Press, 1999.

Alexander, Paul. *Rough Magic: A Biography of Sylvia Plath.* 1991. New York: Viking Penguin, 1999.

Aligheri, Dante. *The Inferno: A Verse Rendering for the Modern Reader.* Translated by John Ciardi. New York: New American Library, 1954. Former Owner Gray Sexton, Former Owner Sexton, Ransom Center.

Alkalay-Gut, Karen. "The Dream Life of Ms. Dog: Anne Sexton's Revolutionary Use of Pop Culture." *College Literature* 32, no. 4 (2005): 50–73.

Altieri, Charles. *The Art of Twentieth-Century American Poetry: Modernism and After.* Malden, MA: Blackwell, 2006.

Alvarez, Al. *The Savage God: A Study of Suicide.* 1971. New York: Norton, 1990.

Anand, Mulk Raj. *Conversations in Bloomsbury.* 1981. Oxford: Oxford University Press, 1995.

———. *Untouchable.* 1935. New York: Penguin, 1940.

Anders, H. R. D. *Shakespeare's Books: A Dissertation on Shakespeare's Reading and The Immediate Sources of His Works.* Berlin: Georg Reimer, 1904.

Anderson, Amanda. *The Powers of Distance: Cosmopolitanism and the Cultivation of Detachment.* Princeton: Princeton University Press, 2001.

Annas, Pamela J. *A Disturbance in the Mirrors: The Poetry of Sylvia Plath.* New York: Greenwood Press, 1988.

"Anne Sexton, Pulitzer Poet to Join Faculty in Spring." *The Colgate Maroon* (Hamilton, NY). October 26, 1971. Page 8.

Arata, Stephen. *Fictions of Loss in the Victorian Fin de Siècle: Identity and Empire.* New York: Cambridge University Press, 1996.

Ardis, Ann. "Review of *The Feminist Avant-Garde: Transatlantic Encounters of Early Twentieth Century.*" *Modernism/modernity* 16, no. 3 (September 2009): 627–628.

Aristotle. *Aristotle on the Art of Poetry: With a Supplement, on Aristotle on Music.* Edited by Milton C. Nahm and Translated by S. H. Butcher. New York: Liberal Arts Press, 1956. Former Owner Sexton, Ransom Center.

Ashe, Marie. "*The Bell Jar* and the Ghost of Ethel Rosenberg." In *Secret Agents: The Rosenberg Case, McCarthyism, and Fifties America*, edited by Marjorie Garber and Rebecca L. Walkowitz, 215–231. New York: Routledge, 1995.

Ashton, Jennifer. *From Modern to Postmodern*. New York: Cambridge University Press, 2005.

Atherton, James S. *The Books at the Wake: A Study of Literary Allusions in James Joyce's* Finnegans Wake. London: Faber and Faber, 1959.

Attridge, Derek, and Marjorie Howes, eds. *Semicolonial Joyce*. New York: Cambridge University Press, 2000.

Aveni, Anthony. *Class Not Dismissed: Reflections on Undergraduate Education and Teaching the Liberal Arts*. University Press of Colorado, 2014.

Axelrod, Stephen Gould. "The Poetry of Sylvia Plath," *The Cambridge Companion to Sylvia Plath*, edited by Jo Gill, 73–89. New York: Cambridge University Press, 2006.

———. *Sylvia Plath: The Wound and the Cure of Words*. Baltimore, MD: Johns Hopkins University Press, 1990.

Baechler, Lea. "A 'Deeper—Deepest—Acquaintance' with the Elegy: John Berryman and 'Wash Far Away.'" In *Recovering Berryman: Essays on a Poet*, edited by Richard J. Kelly and Alan K. Lathrop, 125–140. Ann Arbor: University of Michigan Press, 1993.

Balakian, Peter. *Theodore Roethke's Far Fields: The Evolution of His Poetry*. Baton Rouge: University of Louisiana Press, 1989.

Barnard, Caroline King. *Anne Sexton*. Boston, MA: Twayne Publishers, 1989.

———. *Sylvia Plath*. Boston: Twayne Publishers, 1978.

Barnhisel, Gregory. *James Laughlin, New Directions, and the Remaking of Ezra Pound*. Amherst: University of Massachusetts Press, 2005.

Barzun, Jacques. *Darwin, Marx, Wagner: Critique of a Heritage*. Boston: Little Brown, 1947. Former Owner Plath, Lilly.

Bate, Jonathan. *Ted Hughes: The Unauthorised Life*. New York: Harper Collins, 2015.

Baumel, Judith. "Robert Lowell: The Teacher." In *Robert Lowell: Interviews and Memoirs*, edited by Jeffrey Meyers, 277–280. Ann Arbor: University of Michigan Press, 1988.

Bayley, John. "A Question of Imperial Sway." 1973. In *Berryman's Understanding: Reflections on the Poetry of John Berryman*, edited by Harry Thomas, 192–212. Boston, MA: Northeastern University Press, 1988.

Bayley, Sally. "'I Have Your Head on My Wall': Sylvia Plath and the Rhetoric of Cold War America." *European Journal of American Culture* 25, no. 3 (2006): 155–171.

———. "'I Need a Master': Sylvia Plath Reads D. H. Lawrence." *English* 57, no. 218 (2008): 127–144.

———. and Tracy Brain, eds. *Representing Sylvia Plath*. Cambridge: Cambridge University Press, 2011.

Beck, Charlotte H. "'Solely *The Southern Review*': A Significant Moment in the Poetic Apprenticeship of John Berryman." In *Recovering Berryman: Essays on A Poet*, edited by Richard J. Kelly and Alan K. Lathrop, 113–124. Ann Arbor: University of Michigan Press, 1993.

Becker, Jillian. *Giving Up: The Last Days of Sylvia Plath*. London: Ferrington, Bookseller & Publisher, 2002.

Beer, John. "Coleridge, Ted Hughes, and Sylvia Plath: Mythology and Identity." In *The Monstrous Debt: Modalities of Romantic influence in Twentieth-Century Literature*, edited by Damian Walford Davies and Richard Marggraf Turley, 123–141. Detroit, MI: Wayne State University Press, 2006.

Bellow, Saul. *Henderson the Rain King*. 1958. New York: Penguin, 1996.

———. "John Berryman." In *Berryman's Understanding: Reflections on the Poetry of John Berryman*, edited by Harry Thomas, 74–79. Boston, MA: Northeastern University Press, 1988.

Benjamin, Walter. *The Arcades Project*. Translated by Howard Eiland and Kevin McLaughlin. Cambridge, MA: Harvard University Press, 1999.

Berlind, Bruce. Correspondence with Anne Sexton. Box 18, Folder 1, Sexton Papers.

———. Emails to the Author. 15 July 2006, 22 October 2006, and 24 October 2006.

———. Interview with the Author. Hamilton, NY. March 2007.

———. "Poetic Justice." Letter to the Editor. *The Colgate Maroon* (Hamilton, NY). December 7, 1971. Page 5.

Berman, Jessica. *Modernist Commitments: Ethics, Politics, and Transnational Modernism*. New York: Columbia University Press, 2011.

Bernstein, Richard J. *Hannah Arendt and The Jewish Question*. Cambridge, MA: MIT Press, 1996.

Berryman, John. *Berryman's Shakespeare*. Edited by John Haffenden. New York: Farrar, Straus and Giroux, 1999.

———. *Berryman's Sonnets*. 1952. New York: Farrar, Straus and Giroux, 1969.

———. "The Cage." *Michigan Quarterly Review* 45, no. 4 (Fall 2006): 621–622.

———. *Collected Poems 1937–1971*. Edited by Charles Thornbury. New York: Farrar Straus Giroux, 1989.

———. Correspondence and Teaching Notes. John Berryman Papers (Mss043), Upper Midwest Literary Archives, University of Minnesota Libraries, Minneapolis, Minnesota. Minneapolis, MN.

———. *The Dispossessed*. New York: William Slone Associates, Inc. Publishers, 1948. Former Owner Pound, Ransom Center.

———. *The Dream Songs*. 1969. New York: Farrar, Straus and Giroux, 2001.

———. Faculty and Professional Staff files, Subgroup 4: E, AC107.04, Princeton University Archives, Department of Special Collections, Princeton University Library. Princeton, NJ.

———. *The Freedom of the Poet*. 1966. New York: Farrar, Straus and Giroux, 1976.

———. Library of John Berryman. Upper Midwest Literary Archives, University of Minnesota Libraries, Minneapolis, MN.

———. "1969 National Book Award Acceptance Speech." *Great River Review* 48 (Spring/Summer 2008): 1–2.

———. "One Answer to a Question: Changes," in *The Freedom of the Poet* (New York: Farrar, Straus and Giroux, 1976), 323–31.

———. "The Poetry of Ezra Pound (1949)." In Ezra Pound, *New Selected Poems and Translations*, edited by Richard Sieburth, 373–388. Norfolk, CT: New Directions, 2010.

———. *Stephen Crane*. New York: Sloane, 1950.

———. "A Tribute [To Ezra Pound on His Eightieth Birthday]." *Michigan Quarterly Review* 45, no. 4 (Fall 2006): 623–624, 570.

————. "A Visit to Ezra Pound in St. Elizabeths Hospital." 1948. *Michigan Quarterly Review* 45, no. 4 (Fall 2006): 617–620.

————. *We Dream of Honour: John Berryman's Letters to His Mother.* Edited by Richard J. Kelly. New York: Norton, 1988.

————. and R. P. Blackmur, Robert Gorham Davis, Leslie A. Fiedler, Clement Greenberg, H. L. Mencken, John Crowe Ransom, Wallace Stevens, and Lionel Trilling. "The State of American Writing, 1948: A Symposium." *Partisan Review* 15, no. 8 (August 1948): 855–893.

————. John Haffenden Collection of John Berryman Papers, 1952–1978, Rare Book & Manuscript Library, Columbia University Libraries, New York, NY.

————. William Meredith Collection of John Berryman Papers and Library, 1952–1972, Rare Book and Manuscript Library, Columbia University Libraries, New York, NY.

Birmingham, Kevin. *The Most Dangerous Book: The Battle for James Joyce's Ulysses.* New York: The Penguin Press, 2014.

Bishop, Edward L. "The 'Garbled History' of the First-edition *Ulysses.*" *Joyce Studies Annual* 9 (Summer 1998): 3–36.

————. "Re: Covering *Ulysses.*" *Joyce Studies Annual* 5 (Summer 1994): 22–55.

Bishop, John. *Joyce's Book of the Dark.* Madison: University of Wisconsin Press, 1986.

Blackmur, R. P. *Form and Value in Modern Poetry.* New York: Doubleday, 1957.

Blake, David Haven. "Berryman, Celebrity, and the Culture of Confession." *American Literary History* 13, no. 4 (2001): 716–736.

Blasing, Mutlu Konuk. *Lyric Poetry: The Pain and the Pleasure of Words.* Princeton, NJ: Princeton University Press, 2007.

Blaumeries, Harry. *The New Bloomsday Book.* 1966. New York: Routledge, 1989.

Bloom, Harold. *The Anxiety of Influence: A Theory of Poetry.* 1973. New York: Oxford University Press, 1997.

————. "Introduction." In *Modern Critical Views: John Berryman*, edited by Harold Bloom, 1–4. New York: Chelsea House, 1989.

Bloom, James D. *The Stock of Available Reality: R. P. Blackmur and John Berryman.* Lewisburg, PA: Bucknell University Press, 1984.

Booker, M. Keith. *Ulysses, Capitalism, and Colonialism: Reading Joyce after the Cold War.* Westport, CT: Greenwood Press, 2000.

Bornstein, George. *Material Modernism: The Politics of the Page.* New York: Cambridge University Press, 2001.

Boswell, Matthew. "'Black Phones': Postmodern Poetics in the Holocaust Poetry of Sylvia Plath." *Critical Survey* 20, no. 2 (2008): 53–64.

Bradley, Matthew. "'Annotation Mapping' and What It Means: Developing the Gladstone Catalogue as a Resource for the History of Reading." *Literature Compass* 6, no. 2 (2009): 499–510. Accessed 31 March 2020, https://onlinelibrary.wiley.com/doi/abs/10.1111/j.1741-4113.2008.00610.x.

Brain, Tracy. "Hughes and Feminism." In *The Cambridge Companion to Ted Hughes*, edited by Terry Gifford, 94–106. New York: Cambridge University Press, 2011.

————. *The Other Sylvia Plath.* New York: Longman, 2001.

Brantley, Jessica. "The Prehistory of the Book." *PMLA* 142, no. 2 (March 2009): 632–639.

Breslin, James E. B. *From Modern to Contemporary: American Poetry, 1945–1965.* Chicago, IL: University of Chicago Press, 1984.

Brinnin, John Malcolm and Bill Read, eds. *The Modern Poets: An American-British Anthology.* New York: McGraw-Hill, 1963. Former Owner Berryman, Minnesota.

Britzolakis, Christina. "*Ariel* and Other Poems." In *The Cambridge Companion to Sylvia Plath*, edited by Jo Gill, 107–123. New York: Cambridge University Press, 2006.

———. *Sylvia Plath and the Theatre of Mourning.* New York: Oxford University Press, 1999.

Brooke-Rose, Christine. *A ZBC of Ezra Pound.* Berkeley: University of California Press, 1971.

Brooker, Jewel Spears, ed. *Approaches to Teaching Eliot's Poetry and Plays.* New York: Modern Language Association, 1988.

———. ed. *T.S. Eliot: The Contemporary Reviews.* New York: Cambridge University Press, 2004.

Brooks, Cleanth. *Modern Poetry and the Tradition.* Chapel Hill: University of North Carolina Press, 1939.

———. *The Well Wrought Urn: Studies in the Structure of Poetry.* New York: Harcourt Brace, 1947. Former Owner Plath, Smith.

———. *The Well Wrought Urn: Studies in the Structure of Poetry.* New York: Reynal & Hitchcock, 1947. Former Owner Berryman, Minnesota.

———. *The Well Wrought Urn: Studies in the Structure of Poetry.* New York: Harcourt, Brace and Company, 1954. Former Owner Plath, Smith.

———. Jr. and Robert Penn Warren. *Understanding Poetry: An Anthology for College Students.* 1938. New York: H. Holt and Company, 1946. Former Owner Plath, Smith.

Brown, Bill. *The Material Unconscious: American Amusement, Stephen Crane, and The Economies of Play.* Cambridge, MA: Harvard University Press, 1996.

———. "The Secret Life of Things (Virginia Woolf and the Matter of Modernism)." *Modernism/modernity* 6, no. 2 (1999): 1–28.

———. *A Sense of Things: The Object Matter of American Literature.* Chicago, IL: University of Chicago Press, 2003.

Bulson, Eric. *The Cambridge Introduction to James Joyce.* New York: Cambridge University Press, 2006.

Bundtzen, Lynda K. *The Other* Ariel. Amherst: University of Massachusetts Press, 2001.

———. *Plath's Incarnations: Woman and the Creative Process.* Ann Arbor: University of Michigan Press, 1978.

Burt, Stephen [Stephanie]. "My Name Is Henri: Contemporary Poets Discover John Berryman." In *Reading the Middle Generation Anew: Culture, Community, and Form in Twentieth-Century American Poetry*, edited by Eric Haralson, 233–252. Iowa City: University of Iowa Press, 2006.

Busch, Frederick. "Ralph the Duck." *The Children in the Woods.* New York: Ticknor and Fields, 1994.

Bush, Ronald. *The Genesis of Ezra Pound's Cantos.* Princeton, NJ: Princeton University Press, 1976.

———. "Modernism, Fascism, and the Composition of Ezra Pound's *Pisan Cantos.*" *Modernism/modernity* 2, no. 3 (1995): 69–87.

Butscher, Edward. "Edward Bustcher Collection of papers on Sylvia Plath." Mortimer Rare Book Collection, MRBC-MS-00002, Smith College Special Collections, Northampton, MA.

———. *Sylvia Plath: Method and Madness*. New York: Seabury Press, 1976.

———. ed. *Sylvia Plath: The Woman and the Work*. 1977. New York: Dodd, Mead & Company, 1985.

Buurma, Rachel Sagner and Laura Heffernan. "The Classroom in the Canon: T. S. Eliot's Modern English Literature Extension Course for Working People and *The Sacred Wood*." *PMLA* 133, no. 2 (2018): 264–281.

———. "The Common Reader and the Archival Classroom: Disciplinary History for the Twenty-First Century." *New Literary History* 43, no. 1 (Winter 2012): 113–135.

Camille, Michael. *The Image on the Edge: The Margins of Medieval Art*. London: Reaktion Books, Ltd., 1992.

Campbell, Joseph and Henry Morton Robinson. *A Skeleton Key to Finnegans Wake: Joyce's Masterwork Analyzed*. 1944. New York: Penguin Books, 1986.

Carlson, Craig. "Death and Life in the Poetry of Anne Sexton." Student Paper. Sent to the Author.

Carroll, Lewis. *Through the Looking-Glass and What Alice Found There*. 1872. New York: Random House, 1946.

Chametzky, Jules, John Felstiner, Hilene Flanzbaum, and Kathryn Hellerstein, eds. *Jewish-American Literature*: A *Norton Anthology*. New York: Norton, 2001.

Chase, Mary Ellen, Letter to Alfred Kazin, n.d. [Fall 1954], Alfred Kazin Collection of Papers, Berg Collection, New York Public Library, New York, NY.

———. "Mary Ellen Chase – 'With Feeling' on English 11." *Sophian*. Vol. II, No. 27. Smith College. January 21, 1954. Page 1.

Chen, Amy Hildreth. "Archival Bodies: Twentieth Century Literary Collections." PhD diss., Emory University, 2013.

———. "The Perils of Literary Celebrity: The Archive Stories of Ted Hughes and Sylvia Plath." *The Ted Hughes Society Journal* 2 (Winter 2011): 20–31.

Cheng, Vincent J. *Joyce, Race, and Empire*. New York: Cambridge University Press, 1995.

Chinitz, David E. *T. S. Eliot and the Cultural Divide*. Chicago, IL: University of Chicago Press, 2003.

Christie, Stuart. *Worlding Forster: The Passage from Pastoral*. New York: Routledge, 2005.

Christodoulides, Nephie. *Out of the Cradle Endlessly Rocking: Motherhood in Sylvia Plath's Work*. New York: Rodopi, 2005.

Churchill, Suzanne W. *The Little Magazine* Others *and the Renovation of Modern American Poetry*. Burlington, VT: Ashgate Press, 2006.

Clark, Heather. *The Grief of Influence: Sylvia Plath and Ted Hughes*. New York: Oxford University Press, 2011.

———. "P(l)athography: Sylvia Plath and Her Biographers." Lecture. 19 March 2018. The Center for the Humanities. The Graduate Center, City University of New York. New York, NY.

———. *The Ulster Renaissance: Poetry in Belfast 1962–1972*. New York: Oxford University Press, 2006.

Clarke, Graham. "Hearing Eliot: 'The Hollow Men' as Exemplary Text." In *Approaches to Teaching Eliot's Poetry and Plays*, edited by Jewel Spears Brooker, 94–96. New York: Modern Language Association, 1988.

Clifford, Clare Emily. "Suicides Have a Special Language." PhD diss., University of Alabama, 2005.

Cole, Jane Coil. "'To Terrify & Comfort': John Berryman's *Dream Songs* and the Quest of the Poetic Imagination." PhD diss., Drew University, 1982.

Cole, Sarah. *The Violet Hour: Modernism and Violence in England and Ireland.* 2012. New York: Oxford University Press, 2014.

Coleman, Philip. *John Berryman's Public Vision: Relocating the Scene of Disorder.* Dublin: University College Dublin Press, 2014.

———. "'What Am I Myself Here Doing?': Revisiting Henry in Dublin." *Thumbscrew* 15. Accessed 5 June 2007. www.bristol.ac.uk/thumbscrew/thum_rev. html#coleman.

Coleridge, Samuel Taylor. *A Book I Value: Selected Marginalia.* Edited by H. J. Jackson. Princeton, NJ: Princeton University Press, 2003.

———. *Coleridge's Poetry and Prose.* Edited by Nicholas Halmi, Paul Magnuson, and Raimonda Modiano. New York: Norton, 2004.

———. *The Collected Works of Samuel Taylor Coleridge, Volume 12: Marginalia: Part I: Abbt to Byfield.* Edited by George Whalley. Princeton, NJ: Princeton University Press, 1980.

———. *A Critical Edition of the Major Works.* Edited by H. J. Jackson. 1985. New York: Oxford University Press, 1992.

Collis, Stephen and Graham Lyons, eds. *Reading Duncan Reading: Robert Duncan and the Politics of Derivation.* Iowa City: University of Iowa Press, 2012.

Conarroe, Joel. *John Berryman: An Introduction to the Poetry.* New York: Columbia University Press, 1977.

Conklin, William R. "Pair Silent to the End." *The New York Times.* 20 June 1953, page 1.

Connors, Kathleen. Gallery Talk. *Eye Rhymes* Exhibition. *Sylvia Plath Seventieth Year Literary Symposium.* Bloomington: Indiana University, October 2002.

———. "Living Color: The Interactive Arts of Sylvia Plath." In *Eye Rhymes: Sylvia Plath's Art of the Visual*, edited by Kathleen Connors and Sally Bayley, 4–144. New York: Oxford University Press, 2007.

———. and Sally Bayley, eds. *Sylvia Plath's Art of the Visual.* Oxford: Oxford University Press, 2007.

Conrad, Joseph. *Heart of Darkness.* 1902. Edited by Paul B. Armstrong. New York: Norton, 2006.

Cookson, William. "Introduction." In Ezra Pound, *Selected Prose 1909–1965*, edited by William Cookson, 7–18. New York: New Directions, 1973.

Cooper, Brendan. "John Berryman Reconsidered: Cold War Politics in Dream Song 59." *Explicator* 66, no. 3 (Spring 2008): 139–142.

———. "'We Want Anti-Models': John Berryman's Eliotic Inheritance." *Journal of American Studies* 1 (2008): 1–18.

Cooper, John Xiros. *The Cambridge Introduction to T. S. Eliot.* New York: Cambridge University Press, 2006.

Creadick, Anna G. *Perfectly Average: The Pursuit of Normality in Postwar America.* Amherst: University of Massachusetts Press, 2010.

Crispi, Luca. "Storiella as She Was Wryt: Chapter II.2." In *How Joyce Wrote Finnegans Wake*, edited by Luca Crispi and Sam Slote, 214–249. Madison: University of Wisconsin Press, 2007.

Cross, Amanda. *The James Joyce Murder.* Thorndike: G. K. Hall, 1982.

Crowther, Gail and Peter K. Steinberg. *These Ghostly Archives: The Unearthing of Sylvia Plath*. Stroud: Fonthill Media, 2017.

Cuddy-Keane, Melba. *Virginia Woolf, the Intellectual, and the Public Sphere*. New York: Cambridge University Press, 2003.

Cummings, E. E. "i: six nonlectures." Cambridge, MA: Harvard University Press, 1954. Former Owner Plath, Smith.

Daiches, David. *English Literature*. Englewood Cliffs, NJ: Prentice-Hall, 1964.

———. *The Novel and the Modern World*. 1939. Chicago, IL: University of Chicago Press, 1960.

Davison, Neil R. *James Joyce, Ulysses, and the Construction of Jewish Identity*. 1996. New York: Oxford University Press, 1998.

Davison, Peter. *The Fading Smile: Poets in Boston, from Robert Frost to Robert Lowell to Sylvia Plath, 1955–1960*. 1994. New York: Norton, 1996.

Defries, Harry. *Conservative Party Attitudes to Jews: 1900–1950*. Portland, OR: Frank Cass Publishers, 2001.

De Gay, Jane. *Virginia Woolf's Novels and the Literary Past*. Edinburgh: Edinburgh University Press, 2006.

Derrida, Jacques. *Archive Fever*. 1995. Translated by Eric Prenowitz. Chicago: University of Chicago Press, 1996.

———. *The Post Card: From Socrates to Freud and Beyond*. Translated by Alan Bass. Chicago, IL: University of Chicago Press, 1987.

———. "This Is Not an Oral Footnote." In *Annotation and Its Texts*, edited by Stephen A. Barney, 192–206. New York: Oxford University Press, 1991.

Diepeveen, Leonard. *The Difficulties of Modernism*. New York: Routledge, 2003.

Dodson, Samuel Fisher. *Berryman's Henry: Living at the Intersection of Need and Art*. Amsterdam/New York: Rodopi, 2006.

"*Dollars…. and Sense*." *The Colgate Maroon* (Hamilton, NY). November 16, 1971. Page 4.

Donadio, Rachel. "The Closest Reader." *New York Times*, Late Edition, December 10, 2006. Page 12.

Donohue, Denis. "Berryman's Long Dream." In *Modern Critical Views: John Berryman*, edited by Harold Bloom, 21–34. New York: Chelsea House, 1989.

Donohue, Kate. Interview with the Author. Minneapolis, MN. June 17, 2007.

Dos Passos, John. *U. S. A.* New York: Modern Library, c. 1937. Former Owner Plath, Lilly.

Dostoevsky, Fyodor. *Crime and Punishment*. 1886. Translated by David Magarshack. 1951. Middlesex, Harmondsworth, 1956. Former Owners Sylvia Plath and Ted Hughes, Emory.

———. *The Possessed*. 1872. Translated by Constance Garnett. New York: Modern Library, c. 1930. Former Owner Sexton, Ransom Center.

Doyle, Laura. *Bordering on the Body: The Racial Matrix of Modern Fiction and Culture*. New York: Oxford University Press, 1994.

Drew, Elizabeth A. "*Lecture Notes*." Boxes 770, 770.1, and 771. Elizabeth A. Drew Papers. Smith College Archives, CA-MS-00056, Smith College Special Collections, Northampton, MA.

———. *The Novel: A Modern Guide to Fifteen English Masterpieces*. New York: Norton, 1963.

———. *Poetic Patterns: A Note on Versification*. Northampton, MA: Kraushar Press, 1956. Former Owner Plath, Lilly.

———. *T. S. Eliot: The Design of His Poetry*. New York: Charles Scribner's Sons, 1949.

———. *T. S. Eliot: The Design of His Poetry*. New York: Charles Scribner's Sons, 1950. Former Owner Plath, Smith.

———. and George Connor. *Discovering Modern Poetry*. New York: Holt, Rinehart and Winston, 1961.

———. and John L. Sweeney. *Directions in Modern Poetry*. New York: Norton, 1940.

Dunkerley, Hugh. "Hughes and Creative Writing." In *Ted Hughes in Context*, edited by Terry Gifford, 315–324. Cambridge: Cambridge University Press, 2018.

Dydo, Ulla E. *The Language That Rises: 1923–1934*. Evanston, IL: Northwestern University Press, 2003.

Earle, David M. "MySpace Modernism." *Modernism/modernity* 16, no. 3 (September 2009): 478–481.

Eliot, T. S. *The Annotated* Waste Land *with Eliot's Contemporary Prose*. Edited by Lawrence Rainey. 2005. New Haven, CT: Yale University Press, 2006.

———. *The Complete Poems and Plays*. New York: Harcourt, Brace & World, [1952]. Former Owner Plath, Smith.

———. *The Complete Poems and Plays 1909–1950*. New York: Harcourt, Brace and Co., c. 1952. Former Owner Sexton, Ransom Center.

———. *The Complete Poems and Plays 1909–1950*. 1952. New York: Harcourt, Brace & World, 1971.

———. "Introduction: 1928" (1929/1948), *New Selected Poems and Translations* by Ezra Pound, edited by Richard Sieburth. 1926. Norfolk, CT: New Directions, 2010.

———. *On Poetry and Poets*. New York: Farrar, Straus and Cudahy, 1957.

———. "Introduction: 1928" (1929/1948). In Ezra Pound, *New Selected Poems and Translations*, edited by Richard Sieburth, 361–372. Norfolk, CT: New Directions, 2010.

———. *The Letters of T. S. Eliot, Volume 2: 1923–1925*. Edited by Valerie Eliot and Hugh Haughton. 2009. New Haven, CT: Yale University Press, 2011.

———. *The Poems of T. S. Eliot, Volume I: Collected and Uncollected Poems*. Edited by Christopher Ricks and Jim McCue. Baltimore, MD: Johns Hopkins University Press, 2015.

———. "Ulysses, Order, and Myth." In *James Joyce: Two Decades of Criticism*, edited by Seon Manley, Eugène Jolas, and others, 198–202. New York: Vanguard Press, 1948.

———. *The Waste Land and Other Poems*. New York: Harcourt, Brace and Co., 1955. Former Owner Sexton, Ransom Center.

———. *The Waste Land: A Facsimile and Transcript of the Original Drafts Including the Annotations of Ezra Pound*. Edited by Valerie Eliot. New York: Harcourt, 1971.

Ellmann, Richard. "Ez and Old Billyum." In *New Approaches to Ezra Pound: A Co-Ordinated Investigation of Pound's Poetry and Ideas*, edited by Eva Hesse, 55–85. Berkeley: University of California Press, 1969.

———. *James Joyce*. 1959. New York: Oxford University Press, 1983.

———. *Yeats: The Man and the Masks*. New York: Macmillan, 1948.

Emre, Merve. *Paraliterary: The Making of Bad Readers in Postwar America*. Chicago, IL: University of Chicago Press, 2017.

Enemark, Richard D. Email to the Author. September 28, 2005.

———. Interview with the Author. 19 March 2008.

Erkkila, Betsy, ed. *Ezra Pound: The Contemporary Reviews*. New York: Cambridge University Press, 2011.

Feinstein, Elaine. *Ted Hughes: The Life of a Poet*. New York: Norton, 2001.

Faas, Ekbert. *Ted Hughes: The Unaccommodated Universe*. Santa Barbara: Black Sparrow Press, 1980.

Ferguson, Frances. "Coleridge and the Deluded Reader: 'The Rime of the Ancient Mariner.'" In *Coleridge's Poetry and Prose*, edited by Nicholas Halmi, Paul Magnuson, and Raimonda Modiano, 696–709. New York: Norton, 2004.

Ferretter, Luke. *Sylvia Plath's Fiction: A Critical Introduction*. Edinburgh: Edinburgh University Press, 2010.

Fielding, Penny. "Reading Rooms: M. R. James and the Library of Modernity." In *Gothic and Modernism: Essaying Dark Literary Modernity*, edited by John Paul Riquelme, 147–167. Baltimore, MD: Johns Hopkins University Press, 2008.

Fields, Beverly. "The Poetry of Anne Sexton." In *Poets in Progress*, edited by Edward Hungerford, 250–285. Evanston, IL: Northwestern University Press, 1967.

Filreis, Alan. *Counter-Revolution of the Word: The Conservative Attack on Modern Poetry, 1945–1960*. Chapel Hill: University of North Carolina Press, 2008.

Flanzbaum, Hilene. "The Imaginary Jew and the American Poet." *ELH* 65, no.1 (1998): 259–275.

Ford, Jane. "James Joyce's Trieste Library: Some Notes on Its Use." In *Joyce at Texas: Essays on the James Joyce Materials at the Humanities Research Center*, edited by Dave Oliphant and Thomas Zigal, 141–158. Austin: The Humanities Research Center, The University of Texas, 1983.

Forster, E. M. *Howards End*. 1910. New York: Modern Library, 1999.

———. "In My Library." 1949. In *A Bloomsbury Group Reader*, edited by S.P. Rosenbaum, 292–295. Oxford: Blackwell, 1993.

———. "Preface." Mulk Raj Anand, *Untouchable*. 1935. New York: Penguin Books, 1940.

Frank, Anne. *Diary of A Young Girl*. 1947. Translated by B. M. Mooyaart-Doubleday New York: Pocket Books, 1953. Two copies. Former Owner Berryman, Minnesota.

Frazer, Sir James George. *The Golden Bough: A Study in Magic and Religion*. New York: The Macmillan Company, 1952. Former Owner Plath, Smith.

Freedman, Mike. "Mussels, Muskrats, and Juncos: Instability in Sylvia Plath and Robert Frost." *The Massachusetts Review* 48, no. 3 (Fall 2007): 465–480, 493.

Froula, Christine. *A Guide to Ezra Pound's Selected Poems*. 1982. New York: New Directions, 1983.

———. *To Write Paradise: Style and Error in Pound's Cantos*. New Haven, CT: Yale University Press, 1984.

Furst, Arthur. *Anne Sexton: The Last Summer*. New York: St. Martin's Press, 2000.

Garber, Marjorie and Rebecca L. Walkowitz, eds. *Secret Agents: The Rosenberg Case, McCarthyism, and Fifties America*. New York: Routledge, 1995.

Gardner, Helen. *The Art of T. S. Eliot*. 1949. London: The Cresset Press, 1968.

Genette, Gerard. *Paratexts: Thresholds of Interpretation*. 1987. New York: Cambridge University Press, 1997.

George, Diana Hume. *Oedipus Anne: The Poetry of Anne Sexton*. Urbana: University of Illinois Press, 1987.

Gibbons, Luke. "'Have You No Homes to Go To?': James Joyce and the Politics of Paralysis." In *Semicolonial Joyce*, edited by Derek Attridge and Marjorie Howes, 150–171. New York: Cambridge University Press, 2000.

Gibian, George. "Traditional Symbolism in *Crime and Punishment*." In Feodor Dostoevsky, *Crime and Punishment*, edited by George Gibian, 526–543. 1964. New York: Norton, 1989.

Gifford, Don. *Ulysses Annotated*. 1974. Berkeley: University of California Press, 1988.

Gifford, Terry, ed. *The Cambridge Companion to Ted Hughes*. Cambridge: Cambridge University Press, 2011.

———. "Introduction." *Ted Hughes in Context*, edited by Terry Gifford, 1–9. New York: Palgrave Macmillan, 2015.

Gilbert, Sandra M. "In Yeats's House: The Death and Resurrection of Sylvia Plath." In *No Man's Land: The Place of the Woman Writer in the Twentieth Century: Volume 3: Letters from the Front*, edited by Sandra M. Gilbert and Susan Gubar, 266–318. New Haven: Yale University Press, 1994.

Gilbert, Stuart. *James Joyce's Ulysses: A Study*. New York: Alfred A. Knopf, 1931.

———. *James Joyce's Ulysses: A Study*. 1952. New York: Vintage Books, 1955. Former Owner Plath. University of Virginia Library, Charlottesville, VA.

Gill, Jo. *Anne Sexton's Confessional Poetics*. Gainesville: University Press of Florida, 2007.

———. "Anne Sexton and Confessional Poetics." *The Review of English Studies* 55, no. 220 (June 2004): 425–445.

———. *The Cambridge Introduction to Sylvia Plath*. New York: Cambridge University Press, 2008.

———. "Ted Hughes and Sylvia Plath." In *The Cambridge Companion to Ted Hughes*, edited by Terry Gifford, 53–66. Cambridge: Cambridge University Press, 2011.

———. "Textual Confessions: Narcissism in Anne Sexton's Early Poetry." *Twentieth Century Literature* 50, no. 1 (Spring 2004): 59–87.

———. "'This House / of Herself': Reading Place and Space in the Poetry of Anne Sexton." In *This Business of Words: Reassessing Anne Sexton*, edited by Amanda Golden, 17–37. Gainesville: University Press of Florida, 2016.

Gill, Joanna. "'My Sweeney, Mr. Eliot': Anne Sexton and the Impersonal Theory of Poetry." *Journal of Modern Literature* 27, no. 1/2 (Fall 2003): 36–56.

Gillespie, Diane F. "Introduction." In *The Library of Leonard and Virginia Woolf: A Short-Title Catalog*, edited by Julia King and Laila Miletic-Vejzovic, vii-xx. Pullman: Washington State University Press, 2003.

Gillespie, Michael Patrick. *James Joyce's Trieste Library: A Catalogue of the Materials at the Harry Ransom Humanities Research Center The University of Texas at Austin*. Austin, TX: The Harry Ransom Humanities Research Center, 1986.

———. "Kenner on Joyce." In *Re-Viewing Classics of Joyce Criticism*, edited by Janet Egleson Dunleavy, 142–154. Chicago: University of Illinois Press, 1991.

Golden, Amanda. "Anne Sexton's Modern Library." In *Collecting, Curating, and Researching Writers' Libraries: A Handbook*, edited by Richard W. Oram and Joseph Nicholson, 65–76. Lanham, MD: Rowman & Littlefield, 2014.

———. "'A Brief Note in the Margin:' Virginia Woolf and Annotating." In *Contradictory Woolf: Selected Papers from the Twenty-First Annual Conference on Virginia Woolf*, edited by Derek Ryan and Stella Bolaki, 209–214. Clemson, SC: Clemson University Digital Press, 2012.

———. "Introduction: Reassessing Anne Sexton." In *This Business of Words: Reassessing Anne Sexton*, edited by Amanda Golden, 1–16. Gainesville: University Press of Florida, 2016.

———. "John Berryman at Midcentury: Annotating Ezra Pound and Teaching Modernism." *Modernism/modernity* 21, no. 2 (April 2014): 507–528.

———. "Sylvia Plath's Teaching and the Shaping of Her Work." In *Sylvia Plath in Context*, edited by Tracy Brain, 255–263. Cambridge: Cambridge University Press, 2019.

———. "Sylvia Plath's Teaching Syllabus: A Chronology." *Plath Profiles: An Interdisciplinary Journal of Sylvia Plath Studies* 2 (August 2009): 209–220.

———. "Ted Hughes and the Midcentury American Academy." *The Ted Hughes Society Journal* 3, no. 1 (2013): 47–52.

———. "Ted Hughes, Isaac Bashevis Singer, and an Interview with Jules Chametzky." *The Ted Hughes Society Journal* 3, no.1 (2013): 59–66.

———. "Textbook Greek: Thoby Stephen in *Jacob's Room*." *Woolf Studies Annual* 23 (2017): 83–108.

———. "Virginia Woolf's Marginalia Manuscript." *Woolf Studies Annual* 18 (2012): 109–117.

Golding, Alan. "American Poet-Teachers and the Academy." In *A Concise Companion to Twentieth-Century American Poetry*, edited by Stephen Fredman, 55–74. Malden, MA: Blackwell, 2005.

———. *From Outlaw to Classic: Canons in American Poetry*. Madison: University of Wisconsin Press, 1995.

Gordon, David M. *Ezra Pound and James Laughlin Selected Letters*. New York: Norton, 1994.

Gordon, John. "Being Sylvia Being Ted Being Dylan: Plath's 'The Snowman on the Moor.'" *Journal of Modern Literature* 27, no. 1 (2003): 188–192.

Gordon, Lyndall. *T.S. Eliot: An Imperfect Life*. 1998. New York: Norton, 2000.

Gourley, James. "The same anew: James Joyce's Modernism and its influence on Sylvia Plath's *Bell Jar*." *College Literature* 45, no. 4 (Fall 2018): 695–723.

Graff, Gerald. *Professing Literature: An Institutional History*. Chicago, IL: University of Chicago Press, 1987.

Grafton, Anthony. *The Footnote: A Curious History*. Cambridge, MA: Harvard University Press, 1997.

Graves, Robert. *The White Goddess: A Historical Grammar of Poetic Myth*. 1948. New York: Farrar, Strauss and Giroux, 2001.

Graves, Robert Perceval. *Robert Graves and the White Goddess 1940–85*. London: Weidenfeld and Nicolson, 1995.

Greenblatt, Stephen. *Renaissance Self-Fashioning: From More to Shakespeare*. 1984. Chicago, IL: University of Chicago Press, 1984.

———. *Shakespearean Negotiations: The Circulation of Social Energy in Renaissance England*. Berkeley: University of California Press, 1988.

———. and Catherine Gallagher. *Practicing New Historicism*. Chicago, IL: University of Chicago Press, 2000.

Greetham, D. C. *The Margins of the Text*. Ann Arbor: University of Michigan Press, 1997.

———. *Textual Scholarship: An Introduction*. New York: Garland Publisher, 1994.

Grobe, Christopher. *The Art of Confession: The Performance of Self from Robert Lowell to Reality TV*. New York: New York University Press, 2017.

———. "The Breath of the Poem: Confessional Print/Performance circa 1959." *PMLA* 127, no. 2 (March 2012): 215–230.

Groszewski, Gillian. "Hughes and America." In *Ted Hughes in Context*, edited by Terry Gifford, 155–164. Cambridge: Cambridge University Press, 2018.

———. "'I Fear a Man of Frugal Speech': Ted Hughes and Emily Dickinson." In *Ted Hughes: From Cambridge to Collected*, edited by Mark Wormald, Neil Roberts, and Terry Gifford, 160–176. Basingstoke: Palgrave Macmillan, 2013.

Guillory, John. *Cultural Capital: The Problem of Literary Canon Formation*. 1993. Chicago, IL: University of Chicago Press, 1994.

Haffenden, John. *The Life of John Berryman*. 1982. Boston, MA: Routledge, 1983.

Haffenden / Berryman Collection. Rare Book & Manuscript Library, Columbia University Libraries, New York, NY.

Hall, James and Martin Steinmann, eds. *The Permanence of Yeats: Selected Criticism*. New York: Macmillan, 1950.

Halliday, E. M. *John Berryman and the Thirties: A Memoir*. Amherst: University of Massachusetts Press, 1987.

Halmi, Nicholas. *The Genealogy of the Romantic Symbol*. New York: Oxford University Press, 2008, 118.

Hamilton, Ian. *Robert Lowell: A Biography*. New York: Random House, 1982.

Hammer, Langdon. "Plath's Lives: Poetry Professionalism, and the Culture of the School." *Representations* 75 (Summer 2001): 61–88.

Hammill, Faye and Mark Hussey. *Modernism's Print Cultures*. New York: Bloomsbury, 2016.

Hargrove, Nancy D. *The Journey Toward* Ariel: *Sylvia Plath's Poems of 1956–1959*. Lund: Lund University Press, 1994.

Harvard Summer School Final Catalogue 1954, Official Register of Harvard University, LI, No. 4 (1954), Harvard University Archives, Cambridge, MA.

Hauptman, Robert. *Documentation: A History and Critique of Attribution, Commentary, Glosses, Marginalia, Notes, Bibliographies, Works-Cited Lists, and Citation Indexing and Analysis*. Jefferson, NC: McFarland & Company, Inc., 2008.

Hawthorne, Nathaniel. *Hawthorne's Short Stories*. Edited by Newton Arvin. New York: Vintage Books, 1955, Former Owner Plath, Smith.

Healey, Judith Kroll, Richard J. Kelly, and Bob Lundegaard. "Berryman as Teacher and Friend: Personal Reminiscences." In *John Berryman: Centenary Essays*, edited by Philip Coleman and Peter Campion, 13–28. New York: Peter Lang, 2017.

Hecht, Anthony. Correspondence and Teaching Files. Anthony Hecht Papers. MSS 926. Stuart A. Rose Manuscript, Archives, and Rare Book Library, Emory.

Helle, Anita. "Anne Sexton's Photographic Self-Fashioning." In *This Business of Words: Reassessing Anne Sexton*, edited by Amanda Golden, 38–72. Gainesville: University Press of Florida, 2016.

———. "Lessons from the Archive: Sylvia Plath and the Politics of Memory." *Feminist Studies* 31, no. 3 (Fall 2005): 631–652.

———. "A Plath Photograph Annotated: Point Shirley, 1936." *Virginia Woolf Miscellany* 71, no. 1 (Spring/Summer 2007): 10–12.

―――. ed. *The Unraveling Archive: Essays on Sylvia Plath.* Ann Arbor: University of Michigan Press, 2007.

―――. "Introduction: Archival Matters." In *The Unraveling Archive: Essays on Sylvia Plath,* edited by Anita Helle, 1–16. Ann Arbor: University of Michigan Press, 2007.

Henn, Thomas Rice. *T. e Lonely Tower: Studies in the Poetry of W. B. Yeats.* London: Methuen, 1950.

―――. *The Lonely Tower: Studies in the Poetry of W. B. Yeats.* 1950. New York: Pelligrini & Cudahy, 1952.

Herr, Cheryl. "Art and Life, Nature and Culture, *Ulysses.*" In *James Joyce's Ulysses: A Casebook,* edited by Derek Attridge, 55–82. New York: Oxford University Press, 2004.

Hicok, Bethany. *Degrees of Freedom: American Women Poets and the Women's College 1905–1955.* Lewisburg, PA: Bucknell University Press, 2008.

Highet, Gilbert. *The Art of Teaching.* New York: Vintage Books, 1954. Former Owner Plath, Lilly.

―――. *A Clerk of Oxenford: Essays on Literature and Life.* New York: Oxford University Press, 1954.

Holmes, John. *Writing Poetry.* Boston, MA: The Writer Inc., 1960. Former Owner Sexton, Ransom Center.

Homberger, Eric, ed. *Ezra Pound: The Critical Heritage.* Boston, MA: Routledge, 1972.

Hornbeak, Katherine Gee. "Lecture Notes for English 11-Notes, etc." c. 1954, box 6, folder 2, Katherine Gee Hornbeak papers, Smith College Archives, CA-MS-00154, Smith College Special Collections, Northampton, MA.

Howe, Irving. "The Plath Celebration: A Partial Dissent." In *Sylvia Plath: The Woman and the Work,* edited by Edward Butscher, 225–235. New York: Dodd, Mead & Company, 1977.

Howe, Susan. "Melville's Marginalia." In *The Nonconformist's Memorial.* 1989. New York: New Directions, 1993.

Hoy, Philip. *Interviews with Anthony Hecht.* London: Between the Lines, 2004.

Hughes, Laura. "In the Library of Jacques Derrida: Manuscript Materiality after the Archival Turn." *New Literary History* 49, no. 3 (Summer 2018): 403–424.

Hughes, Ted. *Birthday Letters.* New York: Farrar Straus Giroux, 1998.

―――. "Cambridge Was Our Courtship." In *Love Letters: 2000 Years of Romance,* edited by Andrea Clarke, 118–121. London: British Library, 2011.

―――. *Collected Poems.* Edited by Paul Keegan. London: Faber and Faber, 2005.

―――. *Crow: From the Life and Songs of the Crow.* New York: Harper and Row, 1971. Former Owner Sexton, Ransom Center, hardcover and paperback.

―――. *The Hawk in the Rain.* New York: Harper & Brothers Publishers, 1957. Former Owner Sexton, Ransom Center.

―――. Interview with Drue Heinz, 1995. In *The Paris Review Interviews, III,* edited by Philip Gourevitch, 270–304. New York: Picador, 2008.

―――. "Last Letter." In Melvyn Bragg, "Ted Hughes: The Final Poem." *New Statesman* (11 October 2010): 42–44.

―――. *Letters of Ted Hughes.* Edited by Christopher Reid. London: Faber and Faber, 2007.

―――. Letter, Ted Hughes to Frieda Hughes, ca. 1970s, box 1, folder 1, MSS 1014, Letters to Frieda Hughes, Stuart A. Rose Manuscript, Archives, and Rare Book Library. Emory University, Atlanta, GA.

———. Library of Ted Hughes. Stuart A. Rose Manuscript, Archives, and Rare Book Library. Emory University, Atlanta, GA.

———. "Notes on the Chronological Order of Sylvia Plath's Poems." *Tri-Quarterly* no. 7 (Fall 1966): 81–8.

———. Ted Hughes Papers, 1940–2002. MSS 644. Stuart A. Rose Manuscript, Archives, and Rare Book Library. Emory University, Atlanta, GA.

———. *Winter Pollen: Occasional Prose*. Edited by William Scammell. 1994. New York: Picador, 1995.

———. and Keith Sagar. *Poet and Critic: The Letters of Ted Hughes and Keith Sagar*. Edited by Keith Sagar. London: The British Library, 2012.

Hummel, Gary. "Anne Sexton, Acclaimed Poet, Reads Work," *The Colgate Maroon* (Hamilton, NY), 10 November 1965. Page 1.

Hungerford, Amy. *Making Literature Now*. Stanford, CA: Stanford University Press, 2016.

———. "On the Period Formerly Known as Contemporary." In *American Literary History* 20, no. 1–2 (Spring/Summer 2008): 410–419.

———. *Postmodern Belief: American Literature and Religion since 1960*. Princeton, NJ: Princeton University Press, 2010.

Hunter, Dianne M. "Family Phantoms: Fish, Watery Realms, and Death in Virginia Woolf, Sylvia Plath, and Ted Hughes." *Plath Profiles: An Interdisciplinary Journal of Sylvia Plath Studies* 2 (August 2009): 103–134.

———. "The Fisherman and His Wife as Uncanny Motif in Woolf and Plath." *Virginia Woolf Miscellany* 71, no. 1 (Spring/Summer 2007): 8–10.

Ibsen, Henrik. *Hedda Gabler*. 1891. New York: Dover, 2012.

Jackson, H. J. "Editing and Auditing Marginalia." In *Voice, Text, Hypertext: Emerging Practices in Textual Studies*, edited by Raimonda Modiano, Leroy F. Searle, and Peter L. Shillingsburg, 72–80. Seattle: University of Washington Press, 2004.

———. "'Marginal Frivolities': Readers' Notes as Evidence for the History of Reading." In *Owners, Annotators and the Signs of Reading*, edited by Robin Myers, Michael Harris, and Giles Mandelbrote, 137–152. London: The British Library, 2005.

———. *Marginalia: Readers Writing in Books*. New Haven, CT: Yale University Press, 2001.

Jaillant, Lise. *Cheap Modernism: Expanding Markets, Publishers' Series and the Avant-Garde*. Edinburgh: Edinburgh University Press, 2017.

———. *Modernism, Middlebrow and the Literary Canon: The Modern Library Series, 1917–1955*. London: Pickering and Chatto, 2014.

James, Emily. "The Modernist Inkblot." *Twentieth Century Literature* 63, no. 3 (September 2017): 299–328.

———. "Virginia Woolf and the Child Poet." *Modernist Cultures* 7, no. 2 (2012): 279–305.

James, Henry. *The Ambassadors*. New York: Harper and Brothers, [1948]. Former Owner Plath, Smith.

———. *The American*. New York: Rinehart and Co., 1949. Former Owner Plath, Lilly.

———. *Portrait of a Lady*. New York: Modern Library, [1951]. Former Owner Plath, Smith.

———. *Selected Fiction*. Edited by Leon Edel. New York: E. P. Dutton & Co, Inc., [c. 1953]. Former Owner Plath, University of Virginia Library, Charlottesville, VA.

————. *Selected Short Stories*. Edited by Quentin Anderson. New York: Rinehart & Co., Inc., [c. 1950]. Former Owner Plath, Smith.

James, William. *The Varieties of Religious Experience: A Study in Human Nature*. 1902. New York: The Modern Library, 1929. Former Owner Plath, Smith.

Javadizadeh, Kamran. "Anne Sexton's Institutional Voice." In *This Business of Words: Reassessing Anne Sexton*, edited by Amanda Golden, 73–103. Gainesville: University of Florida Press, 2016.

————. "Bedlam and Parnassus: Madness and Poetry in Postwar America." PhD. diss, Yale University, May 2008.

Jernigan, Adam T. "Paraliterary Labors in Sylvia Plath's *The Bell Jar*: Typists, Teachers, and The Pink-Collar Subtext." *Modern Fiction Studies* 60, no. 1 (Spring 2014): 1–27.

Johnson, Nora. *A Step Beyond Innocence*. 1961. New York: Dell Publishing, 1962.

Johnston, Maria. "'We Write Verse with Our Ears': Berryman's Music." In *"After Thirty Falls:" New Essays on John Berryman*, edited by Philip Coleman and Philip McGowan, 191–208. New York: Rodopi, 2007.

Jones, Christine Kenyon and Anna Snaith. "'Tilting at Universities': Woolf at King's College London." *Woolf Studies Annual* 16 (2010): 1–44.

Joyce, James. *Chamber Music*. New York: Columbia University Press, 1954, Former Owner Plath, Smith.

————. *The Dead*. Edited by Daniel R. Schwarz. New York: Bedford/St. Martin's, 1994.

————. *Dubliners*. 1914. New York: Modern Library, n.d. Former Owner Plath, Smith.

————. *Exiles*. 1918. New York: Viking Press, 1961. Former Owner Sexton, Ransom Center.

————. *Finnegans Wake*. 1939. New York: The Viking Press, 1939. Former Owner Alfred Young Fisher, Smith.

Fisher, Alfred Young Fisher Papers, Mortimer Rare Book Collection, MRBC-MS-0031, Smith College Special Collections, Northampton, MA.

————. *Finnegans Wake*. 1939. New York: Penguin Books, 1999.

————. *Finnegans Wake*. 1939. New York: Viking Press, 1945. Former Owner Berryman, Minnesota.

————. *Finnegans Wake*. 1939. London: Faber and Faber, 1950. Former Owner Plath, Smith.

————. *Finnegans Wake, Book II, Chapter 2: A Facsimile of Drafts, Typescripts & Proofs Volume I*. Edited by Michael Groden. New York: Garland Publishing, Inc., 1978.

————. *A First Draft Version of Finnegans Wake*. Edited by David Hayman. Austin: University of Texas Press, 1963.

————. *Letters of James Joyce*. Edited by Stuart Gilbert. New York: The Viking Press, 1957.

————. *The Portable James Joyce*. 1946. Edited by Harry Levin. New York: Viking Press, 1955. Former Owner Plath, Lilly.

————. *A Portrait of the Artist as a Young Man*. 1916. New York: New American Library, 1948. Former Owner Plath, Former Owner Hughes, Emory.

————. *A Portrait of the Artist as a Young Man*. 1916. New York: Viking, 1963. Former Owner Sexton, Ransom Center.

————. *Ulysses.* 1922. Paris: Shakespeare and Company, 1928. Former Owner Evelyn Waugh, Ransom Center.

————. *Ulysses.* New York: The Modern Library, 1942. Former Owner Fisher, Fisher Papers, Smith.

————. *Ulysses.* 1922. New York: Random House, 1946. Former Owner Plath, Smith.

————. *Ulysses.* 1922. New York: Random House. Enid Mark's Personal Copy. Owned by Eugene Mark.

————. *Ulysses.* 1922. New York: Random House, 1934. Former Owner Berryman, Minnesota.

Joyce, Stanislaus. *The Complete Dublin Diary of Stanislaus Joyce.* Edited by George H. Healey. 1962. Ithaca, NY: Cornell University Press, 1971.

————. *My Brother's Keeper: James Joyce's Early Years.* 1958. Cambridge: Da Capo Press, 2003.

Juhasz, Suzanne. *Naked and Fiery Forms: Modern American Poetry by Women, A New Tradition.* New York: Farrar, Straus & Giroux, 1976.

Kafka, Franz. *Selected Short Stories.* Translated by Willa and Edwin Muir. 1936. New York: Modern Library, 1952. Former Owner Sexton, Ransom Center.

Kalaidjian, Walter. *The Edge of Modernism: American Poetry and the Traumatic Past.* Baltimore, MD: Johns Hopkins University Press, 2006.

"Kaufman Rejects 11th-Hour Appeal." *The New York Times.* 20 June 1953. Page 6.

Kelly, Richard J. Interview with the Author. Minneapolis, MN. 19 June 2007.

————. *John Berryman: A Checklist.* Metuchen, NJ: Scarecrow Press, 1972.

————. *John Berryman's Personal Library: A Catalogue.* New York: Peter Lang, 1999.

————. and Alan K. Lathrop, eds. *Recovering Berryman: Essays on a Poet.* Ann Arbor: University of Michigan Press, 1993.

Kendall, Tim. *Sylvia Plath: A Critical Study.* New York: Faber & Faber, 2001.

Keniston, Ann. "The Holocaust Again: Sylvia Plath, Belatedness, and The Limits of The Lyric Figure." In *The Unraveling Archive: Essays on Sylvia Plath,* edited by Anita Helle, 139–158. Ann Arbor: University of Michigan Press, 2007.

————. *Overheard Voices: Address and Subjectivity in Postmodern American Poetry.* New York: Routledge, 2006.

Kenner, Hugh. *Dublin's Joyce.* 1956. New York: Columbia University Press, 1987.

————. *The Invisible Poet: T. S. Eliot.* New York: McDowell, Obolensky, 1959.

————. "The Portrait in Perspective." In *James Joyce: Two Decades of Criticism,* edited by Seon Manley, Eugène Jolas, and others, 132–174. New York: Vanguard Press, 1948.

————. *The Pound Era.* Berkeley: University of California Press, 1971.

Keynes, John Maynard. "On Reading Books." 1936. In *A Bloomsbury Group Reader,* edited by S. P. Rosenbaum, 286–291. Cambridge, MA: Blackwell, 1997.

Kindley, Evan. *Poet-Critics and the Administration of Culture.* Cambridge, MA: Harvard University Press, 2017.

King, Julia and Laila Miletic-Vejzovic, eds. *The Library of Leonard and Virginia Woolf: A Short-title Catalog.* Pullman: Washington State University Press, 2003.

Kinsella, Nancy Flanagan. Personal Correspondence. September 6, 2005.

————. Photocopies of annotated pages from Sexton's books.

Kirsch, Adam. *The Wounded Surgeon: Confession and Transformation in Six American Poets: Robert Lowell, Elizabeth Bishop, John Berryman, Randall Jarrell, Delmore Schwartz, and Sylvia Plath*. New York: Norton, 2005.

Knickerbocker, Scott. "'Bodied Forth in Words': Sylvia Plath's Ecopoetics." *College Literature* 36, no. 3 (Summer 2009): 1–27.

Konkol, Margaret. "Prototyping Mina Loy's Alphabet." *Feminist Modernist Studies* 1, no. 3 (October 2018): 294–317.

Kopp, Jane Baltzell. "'Gone, Very Gone Youth': Sylvia Plath at Cambridge, 1955–1957." In *Sylvia Plath: The Woman and the Work*, edited by Edward Butscher, 61–80. New York: Dodd, Mead & Company, 1977.

Koren, Yehuda and Eilat Negev. *A Lover of Unreason: The Life and Tragic Death of Assia Wevill*. London: Robson, 2006.

Kroll, Judith. *Chapters in a Mythology: The Poetry of Sylvia Plath*. New York: Harper & Row, 1976.

Krook, Dorothea. "Recollections of Sylvia Plath." In *Sylvia Plath: The Woman and the Work*, edited by Edward Butscher, 49–60. New York: Dodd, Mead & Company, 1977.

Kukil, Karen V. "The Frances Hooper Collection of Virginia Woolf Books and Manuscripts." *Humanities Collections* 1, no. 1 (1998): 7–24.

———. ed. *Selected Papers from the Thirteenth Annual Conference on Virginia Woolf*. Clemson, SC: Clemson University Press, 2005.

———. "True to Her Words." *Smith Alumnae Quarterly* (Spring 2001). Accessed 13 March 2005. http://backissues.saqonline.smith.edu/aarticle.epl?articleid=168.

———. and Lynda K. Bundtzen. "The Connection." Radio Broadcast. December 15, 2000. Accessed 2 February 2015. http://theconnection.wbur.org/2000/12/15/sylvia-plath.

———. and Stephen C. Enniss. *"No Other Appetite": Sylvia Plath, Ted Hughes, and the Blood Jet of Poetry*. New York: Grolier Club, 2005.

Kumin, Maxine. *Always Beginning: Essays on a Life in Poetry*. Port Townsend: Copper Canyon Press, 2000.

———. "A Friendship Remembered." In *Critical Essays on Anne Sexton*, edited by Linda Wagner-Martin, 233–239. Boston, MA: G.K. Hall & Co., 1989.

Lackey, Michael. "Worlding Forster: The Passage from Pastoral." *Modern Fiction Studies* 53, no. 1 (Spring 2007): 197–202.

Lameyer, Gordon. *Dear Sylvia*. Unpublished memoir. Box 147, Folders 3 and 4 (Parts One and Two). Hughes Papers.

———. "Letters from Sylvia." *Smith Alumnae Quarterly* 67, no. 2 (1975): 3–10.

———. "Sylvia at Smith." In *Sylvia Plath: The Woman and the Work*, edited by Edward Butscher, 32–41. New York: Dodd, Mead & Company, 1977.

Lange-Berndt, Petra. Introduction to *Materiality*. Edited by Petra Lange-Berndt, 12–23. Cambridge, MA: MIT Press, 2015.

Laughlin, James. *Byways*. 1993. Edited by Peter Glassgold. New York: New Directions, 2005.

Laughlin, IV, James, ed., *New Directions 1938*. Norfolk, CT: New Directions, 1938. Former Owner Berryman, Columbia.

Lawrence, D. H. *Complete Short Stories of D. H Lawrence*. London: Heinemann, 1955. Former Owner Plath, Smith.

———. *Lady Chatterley's Lover*. 1928. New York: Grove Press, 1959. Former Owner Berryman, Minnesota.

——. *The Man Who Died.* 1931. London: Heinemann, 1950. Former Owner Hughes, Emory.

——. *Sons and Lovers.* 1913. New York: Modern Library, 1922. Former Owner Plath, Smith.

——. *Studies in Classic American Literature.* 1923. Garden City, NY: Doubleday, 1951. Former Owner Plath, Smith.

——. *Women in Love.* 1920. London: Heinemann, 1954. Former Owner Plath, Smith.

Leavis, F. R. *How to Teach Reading: A Primer for Ezra Pound.* Cambridge: Gordon Frazer, The Minority Press, 1932. Former Owner Berryman, Minnesota.

Lee, Hermione. *Edith Wharton.* New York: Knopf, 2007.

——. *Virginia Woolf.* New York: Random House, 1996.

Leinwand, Theodore. "Berryman's Shakespeare / Shakespeare's Berryman." *The Hopkins Review* 2, no. 3 (Summer 2009): 374–403.

"Letter by Mrs. Rosenberg to the President." *The New York Times.* 20 June 1953. Page 7.

Levenson, Michael H. *A Genealogy of Modernism: A Study of English Literary Doctrine 1908–1922.* 1984. New York: Cambridge University Press, 1986.

——. *Modernism and the Fate of Individuality: Character and Novelistic Form from Conrad to Woolf.* New York: Cambridge University Press, 1991.

Levin, Harry. *James Joyce: A Critical Introduction.* Norfolk: New Directions, 1941.

——. "What Was Modernism?" In *Varieties of Literary Expression,* edited by Stanley Burnshaw, 307–330. New York: New York University Press, 1962.

Levine, Philip. *The Bread of Time: Toward an Autobiography.* 1993. Ann Arbor: University of Michigan Press, 2001.

——. "Mine Own John Berryman." In *Recovering Berryman: Essays on a Poet,* edited by Richard J. Kelly and Alan K. Lathrop, 17–42. Ann Arbor: University of Michigan Press, 1993.

Lewis, Wyndham. "Serial Story—Tarr." *The Egoist* 3, no. 4 (April 1, 1916)–4, no. 3 (April 1917). Former Owner Pound, Ransom Center.

Lifton, Robert Jay. *Death in Life: Survivors of Hiroshima.* New York: Random House, 1967.

Lindop, Grevel. "The White Goddess: Sources, Contexts, Meanings." In *Graves and The Goddess: Essays on Robert Graves's* The White Goddess, edited by Ian Firla and Grevel Lindop, 25–39. Selinsgrove, PA: Susquehanna University Presses, 2003.

Lipking, Lawrence. "The Marginal Gloss." *Critical Inquiry* 3, no. 4 (Summer 1977): 609–655.

Liu, Allen. "The Meaning of the Digital Humanities." *PMLA* 128, no. 2 (2013): 409–423.

Logan, William. "Berryman at Shakespeare." *New Criterion* 17, no. 9 (May 1999): 69.

Longenbach, James. *Modern Poetry after Modernism.* New York: Oxford University Press, 1997.

Love, Heather K. "Forced Exile: Walter Pater's Queer Modernism." In *Bad Modernisms,* edited by Douglas Mao and Rebecca L. Walkowitz, 19–43. Durham, NC: Duke University Press, 2006.

Lowell, Robert. *Collected Prose.* Edited by Robert Giroux. New York: Farrar, Straus and Giroux, 1987.

———. Correspondence. Robert Lowell Collection. Houghton Library, Harvard University. Cambridge, MA.

———. *The Letters of Robert Lowell*. Edited by Saskia Hamilton. New York: Farrar, Straus and Giroux, 2005.

———. *Life Studies and For the Union Dead*. 1956. New York: Farrar, Straus and Giroux, 1997.

Lowes, John Livingston. *The Road to Xanadu: A Study in the Ways of the Imagination*. 1927. Boston, MA: Houghton Mifflin, 1964.

Lurz, John. *The Death of the Book: Modernist Novels and the Time of Reading*. New York: Fordham University Press, 2016.

Maber, Peter. "So-called *black*': Reassessing John Berryman's Blackface Minstrelsy." *Arizona Quarterly* 64, no. 4 (Winter 2008): 129–149.

Macaulay, Robbie. "Voices of Victims." *New York Times* (New York, NY), September 10, 1967, Page 346.

MacDonald, Gail. *Learning to Be Modern: Pound, Eliot, and the American University*. New York: Oxford University Press, 1993.

———. "Through Schoolhouse Windows: Women, the Academy, and T. S. Eliot." In *Gender, Desire, and Sexuality in T. S. Eliot*, edited by Cassandra Laity and Nancy K. Gish, 175–194. New York: Cambridge University Press, 2004.

MacNeice, Louis. *Poetry of W. B. Yeats*. New York: Oxford University Press, 1941.

Malcolm, Janet. *The Silent Woman: Sylvia Plath and Ted Hughes*. New York: Norton, 1993.

Mancini, Jr., Joseph. *The Berryman Gestalt: Therapeutic Strategies in the Poetry of John Berryman*. New York: Garland Publishing, 1987.

Mao, Douglas. *Fateful Beauty: Aesthetic Environments, Juvenile Development, and Literature, 1860–1960*. Princeton, NJ: Princeton University Press, 2008.

———. *Solid Objects: Modernism and The Test of Production*. Princeton, NJ: Princeton University Press, 1998.

———. and Rebecca L. Walkowitz. "Introduction: Modernisms Bad and New." In *Bad Modernisms*, edited by Douglas Mao and Rebecca L. Walkowitz, 1–17. Durham, NC: Duke University Press, 2006.

———. "The New Modernist Studies." *PMLA* 123, no. 3 (May 2008): 737–748.

Mariani, Paul. *Dream Song: The Life of John Berryman*. 1989. New York: Paragon House, 1992.

———. *Lost Puritan: A Life of Robert Lowell*. New York: Norton, 1994.

———. "Lowell on Berryman on Lowell." In *Recovering Berryman: Essays on a Poet*, edited by Richard J. Kelly and Alan K. Lathrop, 57–76. Ann Arbor: University of Michigan Press, 1993.

Mark, Enid Epstein. "Notebooks." Classes of 1951–1960 records, Smith College Archives, CA-MS-01024, Smith College Special Collections, Northampton, MA.

"Maroon Names Three Associate Editors." *The Colgate Maroon*, 18 April 1972. Page 12.

Materer, Timothy. *Modernist Alchemy: Poetry and the Occult*. Ithaca, NY: Cornell University Press, 1995.

———. "Occultism as Source and Symptom in Sylvia Plath's 'Dialogue over a Ouija Board." *Twentieth Century Literature* 37, no. 2 (Summer 1991): 131–147.

Matovich, Richard M. *A Concordance to the Collected Poems of Sylvia Plath*. New York: Garland Publishing, Inc., 1986.

Mazzaro, Jerrome. "The Yeatsian Mask: John Berryman." In *Modern Critical Views: John Berryman*, edited by Harold Bloom, 111–132. New York: Chelsea House, 1989.

McClatchy, J. D. "Anne Sexton: Somehow to Endure." In *Sexton: Selected Criticism*, edited by Diana Hume George, 29–72. Chicago, IL: University of Chicago Press, 1988.

———. ed. *Anne Sexton: The Artist and Her Critics*. Bloomington: Indiana University Press, 1978.

McGann, Jerome. *The Textual Condition*. Princeton, NJ: Princeton University Press, 1991.

McGowan, Philip. *Anne Sexton and Middle Generation Poetry: The Geography of Grief*. Westport, CT: Praeger Publishers, 2004.

McGurl, Mark. *The Program Era: Postwar Fiction and the Rise of Creative Writing*. Cambridge, MA: Harvard University Press, 2009.

McHugh, Roland. *Annotations to Finnegans Wake*. 1980. Baltimore, MD: Johns Hopkins University Press, 1991.

Melody, Helen. "The Archive as an Extension of Self: What We Can Learn about Ted Hughes from Archival Collections." *The Ted Hughes Society Journal* 3 (2013): 42–46.

Melville, Herman. *Melville's Marginalia Online*. Boise State University. Accessed 15 February 2020. http://melvillesmarginalia.org/.

Mendelson, Edward. "How to Read Berryman's *Dream* Songs." In *Modern Critical Views: John Berryman*, edited by Harold Bloom, 53–70. New York: Chelsea House, 1989.

Meyers, Jeffery. *Manic Power: Robert Lowell and His Circle*. New York: Arbor House, 1987.

———. ed. *Robert Lowell: Interviews and Memoirs*. Ann Arbor: University Michigan Press, 1988.

Michailidou, Artemis. "Edna St. Vincent Millay and Anne Sexton: The Disruption of Domestic Bliss." *Journal of American Studies* 38 (2004): I, 67–88.

———. "Gender, Body, and Feminine Performance: Edna St. Vincent Millay's Impact on Anne Sexton." *Feminist Review* 78 (November 2004): 117–140.

Middlebrook, Diane Wood. *Anne Sexton: A Biography*. 1991. New York: Random House, 1992.

———. "Anne Sexton: The Making of 'The Awful Rowing Toward God.'" In *Rossetti to Sexton: Six Women Poets at Texas*, edited by Dave Oliphant, 223–235. Austin, TX: Harry Ransom Humanities Research Center, 1992.

———. "Becoming Anne Sexton." In *Anne Sexton: Telling the Tale*, edited by Steven E. Colburn, 7–21. Ann Arbor: University of Michigan Press, 1988.

———. Binder, 1987–1988 (disbound). Box 1, Folders 2–7, Audiotapes and Papers of Anne Sexton, 1956–1988. Schlesinger Library, Radcliffe Institute, Harvard University, Cambridge, MA.

———. "Circle of Women Artists: Tillie Olsen and Anne Sexton at the Radcliffe Institute." In *Listening to Silences: New Essays in Feminist Criticism*, edited by Elaine Hedges and Shelley Fisher Fishkin, 17–22. New York: Oxford University Press, 1994.

———. *Her Husband: Ted Hughes and Sylvia Plath—A Marriage*. New York: Viking, 2003.

———. "Housewife into Poet: The Apprenticeship of Anne Sexton." *The New England Quarterly* 56, no. 4 (December 1983): 483–503.

————. "'I Tapped My Own Head': The Apprenticeship of Anne Sexton." In *Coming to Light: American Women Poets in the Twentieth Century*, edited by Diane Wood Middlebrook and Marilyn Yalom, 195–213. Ann Arbor: University of Michigan Press, 1985.

————. "Plath, Hughes, and Three Caryatids." In *Eye Rhymes: Sylvia Plath's Art of the Visual*, edited by Kathleen Connors and Sally Bayley, 158–166. New York: Oxford University Press, 2007.

————. "Poet of Weird Abundance [Excerpts]." In *Critical Essays on Anne Sexton*, edited by Linda Wagner-Martin, 72–80. Boston, MA: G.K. Hall & Co., 1989.

Middleton, Peter. *Distant Reading: Performance, Readership, and Consumption in Contemporary Poetry*. Tuscaloosa: University of Alabama Press, 2005.

Miller, Cristanne. *Reading in Time: Emily Dickinson in the Nineteenth Century*. Amherst: University of Massachusetts Press, 2012.

Minarich, Chris. "Leftist Bernadette Devlin to Give Lecture Tonight." *The Colgate Maroon* (Hamilton, NY), 11 February 1971. Page 1.

Moffat, Wendy. *A Great Unrecorded History: A New Life of E. M. Forster*. New York: Farrar, Straus and Giroux, 2010.

Molesworth, Charles. *The Fierce Embrace: A Study of Contemporary American Poetry*. Columbia: University of Missouri Press, 1979.

Molière, *Eight Plays by Molière*. Translated by Morris Bishop. New York: Modern Library, 1957. Former Owner Hughes, Emory.

————. *Théatre choisi de Molière*. Paris: Garnier Frères: [1937?] Former Owner Hughes, Emory.

Monas, Sidney. Interview with the Author. Austin, TX. September 11, 2007.

Moore, Marianne. *Predilections*. New York: Viking Press, 1955. Former Owner Plath, Smith.

Moses, Kate. *Wintering: A Novel of Sylvia Plath*. New York: St. Martin's Press, 2003.

Munro, Alice. "The Love of a Good Woman." *The Love of a Good Woman: Stories*. New York: Random House, 1998.

Murphy, Richard. *The Kick: A Life among Writers*. 2002. London: Granta, 2003.

Musgrove, Sydney. *The Ancestry of "The White Goddess."* Auckland: University of Auckland, 1962.

Myers, Lucas. *Crow Steered Bergs Appeared: A Memoir of Ted Hughes and Sylvia Plath*. Sewanee, TN: Proctor's Hall Press, 2001.

————. *An Essential Self: Ted Hughes and Sylvia Plath*. Nottingham: Richard Hollis, 2011.

Nadel, Ira B. *Cambridge Introduction to Ezra Pound*. New York: Cambridge University Press, 2007.

————. "Introduction: Understanding Pound." In *The Cambridge Companion to Ezra Pound*, edited by Ira B. Nadel, 1–21. New York: Cambridge University Press, 1999.

Nelson, Cary. *Repression and Recovery: Modern American Poetry and the Politics of Cultural Memory, 1910–1945*. Madison: University of Wisconsin Press, 1989.

Nelson, Deborah. "Introduction—Twentieth-Century Poetry: Expanding Archives and Methods." *PMLA* 127, no. 2 (March 2012): 212–214.

————. *Pursuing Privacy in Cold War America*. New York: Columbia University Press, 2002.

Nodelman, Ellen Bartlett. Interview with the Author. Old Saybrook, CT. 4 September 2006.

———. and Amanda Golden. "Recollections of Mrs. Hughes's Student." *Plath Profiles* 5, Supplement (Fall 2012): 125–139. Accessed 17 February 2020. http://scholarworks.iu.edu/journals/index.php/plath/article/view/4353/3978.

Nordau, Max. *Degeneration.* 1892. London: University of Nebraska Press, 1993.

Northouse, Cameron and Thomas P. Walsh. *Sylvia Plath and Anne Sexton: A Reference Guide.* Boston, MA: G. K. Hall & Co., 1974.

Olwyn Hughes Papers, MSS 980, Stuart A. Rose Manuscript, Archives, and Rare Book Library, Emory University, Atlanta, GA.

O'Keefe, Paul. *Some Sort of Genius: A Life of Wyndham Lewis.* Berkeley, CA: Counterpoint, 2015.

Oram, Richard W. "Cultural Record Keepers: The Evelyn Waugh Library, Harry Ransom Humanities Research Center, University of Texas at Austin." *Libraries & the Cultural Record* 42, no. 3 (2007): 325–328.

Orgel, Stephen. *The Reader in the Book: A Study of Spaces and Traces.* New York: Oxford University Press, 2015.

Orr, Peter. "Sylvia Plath." In *The Poet Speaks: Interviews with Contemporary Poets Conducted by Hilary Morrish, Peter Orr, John Press, and Ian Scott-Kilvert.* New York: Barnes and Noble, 1966.

Paul, Catherine. *Poetry in the Museums of Modernism.* Ann Arbor: University of Michigan Press, 2002.

Peel, Robin. "From *Dogs* to *Crow*: Ted Hughes and a 'world lost' 1956–1970," *English* 55 (Summer 2006), 157–80.

———. "The Political Education of Sylvia Plath." In *The Unraveling Archive: Essays on Sylvia Plath,* edited by Anita Helle, 39–64. Ann Arbor: University of Michigan Press, 2007.

———. *Writing Back: Sylvia Plath and Cold War Culture.* Madison, NJ: Fairleigh Dickinson University Press, 2002.

Peiffer, Steven. Email Correspondence with the Author. 17 September 2007.

Perloff, Marjorie. *21st-Century Modernism: The "New" Poetics.* New York: Blackwell, 2002.

———. "The Contemporary of Our Grandchildren: Pound's Influence." In *Ezra Pound among The Poets,* edited by George Bornstein, 195–230. Chicago, IL: University of Chicago Press, 1985.

———. *The Dance of the Intellect: Studies in the Poetry of The Pound Tradition.* New York: Cambridge University Press, 1985.

———. "*Poètes Maudits* of the Genteel Tradition: Lowell and Berryman." *American Poetry Review* 12, no. 3 (May/June 1983): 32–38.

———. "The Two Ariels: The (Re)Making of the Sylvia Plath Canon." In *Poems in Their Place: The Intertextuality and Order of Poetic Collections,* edited by Neil Fraistat, 308–333. Chapel Hill: University of North Carolina Press, 1986.

Peters, H. F. *Rainer Maria Rilke: Masks and the Man.* Seattle: University of Washington Press, 1960. Former Owner Sexton, Ransom Center.

Phillips, Robert. *The Confessional Poets.* Carbondale: Southern Illinois University Press, 1973.

Plath, Sylvia. *Ariel.* Uncorrected Proof. London: Faber and Faber, 1965. Former Owner Sexton, Emory.

———. *Ariel.* 1965. New York: HarperCollins, 1999.

———. *Ariel: The Restored Edition*. New York: HarperCollins, 2004.

———. "Ariel and Other Poems" Typescript, Correspondence, Drafts of the *Ariel* poems, and Outline for *The Bell Jar*, Smith.

———. *The Bell Jar*. New York: Harper & Row, 1971.

———. *The Bell Jar*. 1971. New York: HarperCollins, 1999.

———. "Calendar, 1952," box 7, folder 5, Plath mss. II, Lilly.

———. "Calendar, Jan–Aug. 1953," box 7, folder 5, Plath mss. II, Lilly.

———. "Calendar, July 1954–June 1955," box 7, folder 6, Plath mss. II, Lilly.

———. "Cambridge, Newnham College; Teaching Year at Smith." Box 13, Folder 10, Plath mss. II, Lilly.

———. *Collected Poems*. 1981. Edited by Ted Hughes. New York: Harper Perennial, 1992.

———. Correspondence, Diaries, "Notebook from Newton Arvin's Course," and Library, Sylvia Plath Papers, Plath mss. II, 1932–1977, Lilly Library, Indiana University, Bloomington, IN.

———. *Johnny Panic and the Bible of Dreams: Short Stories, Prose, and Diary Excerpts*. 1977. New York: HarperCollins, 2000.

———. "Joyce notebook." Box 10, Folder 10, Plath mss. II, Lilly.

———. *Letters Home*. 1975. Edited by Aurelia Schober Plath. London: Faber and Faber, 1999.

———. *The Letters of Sylvia Plath: Volume 1: 1940–1956*. Edited by Peter K. Steinberg and Karen V. Kukil. New York: HarperCollins, 2017.

———. *The Letters of Sylvia Plath: Volume 2: 1956–1963*. Edited by Peter K. Steinberg and Karen V. Kukil. London: Faber and Faber, 2018.

———. "Modern Poetry Notebook." Box 12, Folder 1, Plath mss. II, Lilly.

———. "The Perfect Setup." *Seventeen* (October 1952): 76, 101–104.

———. "Progress reports: typescripts," 1 May 1962, box 5, folder 47, Plath Collection.

———. "Reading by Sylvia Plath, Poetry and Comments, Recorded Live, Springfield, MA, Introduction by Lee Anderson, 1958. Box 23, Folder 1, Smith.

———. "Religion 14 Notebook." Box 11, Folder 8, mss. II, Lilly.

———. "Smith Scrapbook." Folder 36, Plath mss. II oversize 8, LMC 1862, Pictures Filed in Folder 36, Lilly.

Sylvia Plath Collection, Mortimer Rare Book Collection, MRBC-MS-00045, Smith College Special Collections, Northampton, MA.

———. Sylvia Plath Papers, Box 872, Smith College Archives, CA-MS-00142, Smith College Special Collections, Northampton, MA.

———. "Transcript." 1955. Box 20, Folder 25, Plath Collection, Smith.

———. "Two Lovers and a Beachcomber by the Real Sea." 14 April 1955. Box 14, Folder 271, Plath Collection, Smith.

———. "Two Lovers and a Beachcomber by the Real Sea." [1956–1957]. Typescript. Box 14, Folder 271, Plath Collection, Smith.

———. "Two Lovers and a Beachcomber by the Real Sea." *Granta* 61 (1957), page 5. Box 14, Folder 271, Plath Collection, Smith.

———. *The Unabridged Journals of Sylvia Plath 1950–1962: Transcribed from the Original Manuscripts at Smith College*. Edited by Karen V. Kukil. New York: Random House, 2000.

———. "20th Century, Miss Drew: Holograph. Notes for English 211 at Smith College." Box 20, Folder 17, Plath Collection, Smith.

Plotz, John, et al. "An Interview with John Berryman." In *Berryman's Understanding: Reflections on the Poetry of John Berryman,* edited by Harry Thomas, 3–17. Boston, MA: Northeastern University Press, 1988.

"Poet will Teach Here Next Spring." *The Colgate News* (Hamilton, NY), October 29, 1971. Page 10

Poirier, Richard. *The Renewal of Literature: Emersonian Reflections.* New York: Random House, 1987.

Pollak, Vivian R. "Moore, Plath, Hughes, and 'The Literary Life." *American Literary History* 17, no. 1 (2005): 95–117.

Pollard, Clare. "Her Kind: Anne Sexton, the Cold War and the Idea of the Housewife." *Critical Quarterly* 48, no. 3 (Autumn 2006): 1–24.

Pound, Ezra. *ABC of Reading.* London: George Routledge and Sons, 1934. Former Owner Pound, Ransom Center.

———. *ABC of Reading.* 1934. New York: New Directions, 1960.

———. *Cantos LII-LXXI* (Norfolk, CT: New Directions, 1940. Former Owner Berryman, Minnesota.

———. *The Cantos of Ezra Pound.* 1973. New York: New Directions, 1986.

———. *Certain Noble Plays of Japan: From The Manuscripts of Ernest Fenollosa, Chosen and Finished by Ezra Pound.* Translated by Ernest Fenollosa. Churchtown, Dundrum: The Cuala Press, 1916. Former Owner Berryman, Minnesota.

———. *The Classic Anthology Defined by Confucius.* Cambridge, MA: Harvard University Press, 1954. Former Owner Berryman, Minnesota.

———. *A Draft of XXX Cantos.* New York: Farrar & Rinehart, 1935. Former Owner Berryman, Minnesota.

———. *Eleven New Cantos: XXXI-XLI.* New York: Farrar & Rinehart, 1934. Former Owner Berryman, Minnesota.

———. "A Few Don'ts by an Imagiste." *Poetry* 1, no. 6 (March 1913): 200–6.

———. *The Fifth Decad of Cantos.* Norfolk, CT: New Directions, 1937. Former Owner Berryman, Minnesota.

———. "Foreword." *Selected Cantos.* 1934. New York: New Directions, 1970. 1.

———. *Homage to Sextus Propertius.* London: Faber and Faber, 1934. Former Owner Berryman, Minnesota.

———. *Hugh Selwyn Mauberley.* The Ovid Press, 1920. Former Owner Berryman, Minnesota.

———. "I Gather the Limbs of Osiris," 1911–1912. In *Selected Prose 1909–1965,* edited by William Cookson, 19–43. 1950. New York: New Directions, 1973.

———. *The Letters of Ezra Pound: 1907–1941.* New York: Harcourt Brace, 1950. Former Owner Berryman, Minnesota.

———. *Make it New: essays by Ezra Pound.* London: Faber and Faber, 1934. Former Owner Pound, Ransom Center.

———. *Patria Mia: A Discussion of the Arts and Their Use and Future in America.* Chicago, IL: Ralph Fletcher Seymour, 1950. Former Owner Berryman, Minnesota.

———. *Personae.* New York: Boni and Liveright, 1926. Former Owner Berryman, Minnesota.

———. *Personae: The Shorter Poems.* 1926. New York: New Directions, 1990. page 111.

———. *The Pisan Cantos.* New York: New Directions. 1948. Former Owner Plath, Lilly.

―――. *The Pisan Cantos*. New York: New Directions, 1948. Former Owner Berryman, Minnesota.

―――. *Selected Poems*. Edited by T. S. Eliot. London: Faber and Faber, 1934. Former Owner Berryman, Minnesota.

―――. *Selected Prose 1909–1965*. Edited by William Cookson. New York: New Directions, 1973.

―――. *Selected Letters 1907–1941*. Edited by D. D. Paige. New York: New Directions, 1971.

―――. "Three Cantos I." *Poetry* X, no. 3 (June 1917): 113–121.

―――. and James Joyce. *Pound / Joyce: The Letters of Ezra Pound to James Joyce*. 1965. Edited by Forrest Read. New York: New Directions, 1967.

―――. and James Laughlin, *Ezra Pound and James Laughlin Selected Letters*. Edited by David M. Gordon. New York: Norton, 1994.

―――. and William Carlos Williams. *Pound / Williams: Selected Letters of Ezra Pound and William Carlos Williams*. Edited by Hugh Witemeyer. New York: New Directions, 1996.

The President's Report to the Board of Trustees. October 21, 1961. Smith College, Northampton, MA. Smith College Archives, Smith College Special Collections.

Raine, Craig. *T. S. Eliot*. New York: Oxford University Press, 2006. Kindle edition.

Raine, Kathleen. *Death-in-life and Life-in-Death: "Cuchulain Comforted" and "News for the Delphic Oracle."* Dublin: The Dolmen Press, 1974.

Rainey, Lawrence. *Institutions of Modernism: Literary Elites and Public Culture*. New Haven, CT: Yale University Press, 1998.

―――. "Pound or Eliot: Whose Era." In *The Cambridge Companion to Modernist Poetry*, edited by Alex Davis and Lee M. Jenkins, 87–113. New York: Cambridge University Press, 2007.

―――. *Revisiting* The Waste Land. New Haven, CT: Yale University Press, 2005.

Rákóczi, Basil Ivan. *The Painted Caravan: A Penetration into the Secrets of The Tarot Cards*. The Hague: L.J.C Boucher, 1954. Former Owner Plath, Smith.

Ramazani, Jahan. *A Transnational Poetics*. Chicago, IL: University of Chicago Press, 2009.

Reeves, Gareth. "Songs of the Self: Berryman's Whitman." *Romanticism* 14, no. 1 (2008): 47–56.

Regan, Stephen. "Contemporary and Post-War Poetry." In *T. S. Eliot in Context*, edited by Jason Harding, 359–369. New York: Cambridge University Press, 2011.

Reiman, Donald H. *The Study of Modern Manuscripts: Public, Confidential, and Private*. Baltimore, MD: Johns Hopkins University Press, 1993.

Reiss, Timothy J. *The Discourse of Modernism*. Ithaca, NY: Cornell University Press, 1982.

Richards, I. A. *Practical Criticism: A Study of Literary Judgment*. 1929. New York: Harcourt, Brace, & World, 1962.

―――. *Selected Letters of I. A. Richards, CH*. Edited by John Constable. New York: Oxford University Press, 1990.

"Richards Diagrams Estimate of Poetry." *Sophian*, Smith College. March 4, 1954. Page 1.

Riesman, David. *The Lonely Crowd: A Study of the Changing American Character*. Garden City, NY: Doubleday & Company, Inc., 1953. Former Owner Plath, Smith.

Rifkin, Libbie. *Career Moves: Olson, Creeley, Zukofsky, Berrigan, and the American Avant-Garde*. Madison: University of Wisconsin Press, 2000.

Rilke, Rainer Maria. *Letters to a Young Poet.* Translated by M. D. Herder Norton. 1934. New York: Norton, 2004.

Rimbaud, Arthur. *Une Saison en Enfer & Le Bateau Ivre. A Season in Hell & The Drunken Boat.* Translated by Louise Varèse. Norfolk, CT: J. Laughlin, 1961. Former Owner Sexton, Ransom Center.

Robbins, Bruce. "Helplessness and Heartlessness: Irving Howe, James Bond, and the Rosenbergs." In *Secret Agents: The Rosenberg Case, McCarthyism, and Fifties America,* edited by Marjorie Garber and Rebecca L. Walkowitz, 142–154. New York: Routledge, 1995.

Roberts, Neil. "Class, War, and the Laureateship." In *The Cambridge Companion to Ted Hughes,* edited by Terry Gifford, 150–161. New York: Cambridge University Press, 2011.

———. *Ted Hughes: A Literary Life.* New York: Palgrave Macmillan, 2006.

———. "Ted Hughes and Cambridge." In *Ted Hughes: From Cambridge to Collected,* edited by Mark Wormald, Neil Roberts, and Terry Gifford, 17–32. Houndmills, Basingstoke: Palgrave, 2013.

Rollyson, Carl. *American Isis: The Life and Art of Sylvia Plath.* New York: St. Martin's Press, 2013.

Rooney, Brian. "Anne Sexton: Once a Charming Hostess." *The Colgate Maroon* (Hamilton, NY), March 7, 1972. Page 11.

Rose, Jacqueline. *The Haunting of Sylvia Plath.* Cambridge, MA: Harvard University Press, 1992.

———. *On Not Being Able to Sleep: Psychoanalysis and the Modern World.* Princeton, NJ: Princeton University Press, 2003.

Rosenthal, M. L. *The New Poets: American and British Poetry since World War II.* New York: Oxford University Press, 1967.

Rosner, Victoria. *Modernism and the Architecture of Private Life.* New York: Columbia University Press, 2005.

Ross, Ralph, John Berryman, and Allen Tate. *The Arts of Reading.* New York: Thomas Y. Crowell Company, 1960.

Russo, John Paul. *I. A. Richards: His Life and Work.* Baltimore, MD: Johns Hopkins University Press, 1989.

Saint-Amour, Paul K. "Introduction: Weak Theory, Weak Modernism." *Modernism/modernity* 25, no. 3 (September 2018): 437–459.

———. *Tense Future: Modernism, Total War, Encyclopedic Form.* New York: Oxford University Press, 2015.

Saldívar, Toni. *Sylvia Plath: Confessing the Fictive Self.* New York: Peter Lang Publishing, 1992.

Salvio, Paula M. *Anne Sexton: Teacher of Weird Abundance.* Albany, NY: State University of New York Press, 2007.

———. "Teacher of 'Weird Abundance': Portraits of the Pedagogical Tactics of Anne Sexton." *Cultural Studies* 13, no. 4 (1999): 639–660.

Sansone, Claudio. "John Berryman's 'Poundian Inheritance' and the Epic of 'Synchrisis.'" In *John Berryman: Centenary Essays,* edited by Philip Coleman and Peter Campion, 47–64. New York: Peter Lang, 2017.

Scholes, Robert E. *Paradoxy of Modernism.* New Haven, CT: Yale University Press, 2006.

Schuchard, Ronald. *Eliot's Dark Angel: Intersections of Life and Art.* New York: Oxford University Press, 1999.

———. "Hughes and Eliot: Possession." *Fixed Stars Govern a Life: Transforming Poetics and Memory with Emory's Ted Hughes Archive.* Emory Across Academe, No. 6. The Academic Exchange, 2006.

———. "'The Man Who Suffers and the Mind which Creates.' In *The Waste Land.*" T. S. Eliot International Summer School. University of London School for Advanced Studies. London, UK. July 2011.

Sennett, Richard. *The Fall of Public Man.* 1974. New York: Norton, 1992.

Sexton, Anne. *All My Pretty Ones.* 1961. Boston, MA: Houghton Mifflin, 1962.

———. *Anne Sexton: A Self-Portrait in Letters.* 1977. Edited by Linda Gray Sexton and Lois Ames. Boston, MA: Houghton Mifflin, 1991.

———. Audiotapes and Papers of Anne Sexton, 1956–1988. Schlesinger Library, Radcliffe Institute, Harvard University, Cambridge, MA.

———. "The Call," box 9, folder 4, Sexton Papers.

———. "Classroom at Boston University." In *Robert Lowell: Interviews and Memoirs,* edited by Jeffrey Meyers, 178–180. Ann Arbor: University of Michigan Press, 1988.

———. *The Complete Poems.* 1981. New York: Houghton Mifflin, 1999.

———. Correspondence and Poem Worksheets, Anne Sexton Papers, Harry Ransom Center, The University of Texas at Austin, Austin, TX.

———. "Eighteen Days Without You," "[1967]," box 6, folder 6, Sexton Papers.

———. "Lecture Materials for Colgate University Course," Box 16, Folder 5, Sexton Papers.

———. Letter, Anne Sexton to Bruce Berlind. 1 December 1971. Colgate University Special Collections and Archives. Hamilton, NY.

———. Library. Harry Ransom Center, The University of Texas at Austin, Austin, TX.

———. *No Evil Star: Selected Essays, Interview, and Prose.* Edited by Steven E. Colburn. Ann Arbor: University of Michigan Press, 1985.

———. "Presentations 1968–1974 nd." Box 16, Folder 4, Sexton Papers.

———. *To Bedlam and Part Way Back.* Boston, MA: Houghton Mifflin, 1960.

———. *Words for Doctor Y.: Uncollected Poems with Three Stories.* Edited by Linda Gray Sexton. Boston, MA: Houghton Mifflin, 1978.

Sexton, Linda Gray. Conversation with the Author. 17 June, 2013.

———. *Half in Love: Surviving the Legacy of Suicide.* Berkeley, CA: Counterpoint Press, 2011. Kindle edition.

———. *Searching for Mercy Street.* New York: Little, Brown and Co., 1994.

Seymour-Smith, Martin. *Robert Graves: His Life and Work.* 1982. London: Bloomsbury, 1995.

Shelton, Jen. Issy's Footnote: Disruptive Narrative and the Discursive Structure of Incest in *Finnegans Wake. ELH* 66, no. 1 (Spring 1999): 203–221.

———. *Joyce and the Narrative Structure of Incest.* Gainesville: University Press of Florida, 2006.

Silver, Brenda R. "Textual Criticism as Feminist Practice: Or, Who's Afraid of Virginia Woolf Part II." In *Representing Modernist Texts: Editing as Interpretation,* edited by George Bornstein, 193–222. Ann Arbor: University of Michigan Press, 1991.

———. *Virginia Woolf's Reading Notebooks.* Princeton, NJ: Princeton University Press, 1983.

Simpson, Eileen. *The Maze.* New York: Simon and Schuster, 1975.

———. *Poets in Their Youth.* 1982. New York: Farrar, Straus, and Giroux, 1990.

Skorczewski, Dawn M. *An Accident of Hope: The Therapy Tapes of Anne Sexton.* New York: Routledge, 2012.

Smith, Caleb. "Detention without Subjects: Prisons and the Poetics of Living Dead." *Texas Studies in Language and Literature* 50, no. 3 (2008): 243–267.

Smith College Bulletin: The Catalogue Number 1952–1953. Northampton, MA. Smith College Archives, Smith College Special Collections.

Smith College Bulletin: The Catalogue Number: 1957–1958. Northampton, MA. Smith College Archives, Smith College Special Collections.

Smith, Ernest J. "John Berryman's 'Programmatic' for the *Dream Songs* and an Instance of Revision." *Journal of Modern Literature* 23, no. 3–4 (Summer 2000): 429–439.

Snodgrass, W. D. Conversation. Lowell, MA. 26 April 2007.

Southam, B. C. *A Guide to the Selected Poems of T. S. Eliot.* New York: Harcourt Brace, 1968.

Spivack, Kathleen. "In Memory of Anne Sexton." In *Critical Essays on Anne Sexton*, edited by Linda Wagner-Martin, 231–233. Boston. MA: G.K. Hall & Co., 1989.

———. "Robert Lowell: A Memoir." In *Robert Lowell: Interviews and Memoirs*, edited by Jeffrey Meyers, 349–359. Ann Arbor: University of Michigan Press, 1988.

———. *With Robert Lowell and His Circle: Sylvia Plath, Anne Sexton, Elizabeth Bishop, Stanley Kunitz, & Others.* Boston, MA: Northeastern University Press, 2012.

Steedman, Carolyn. *Dust: The Archive and Cultural History.* New Brunswick: Rutgers University Press, 2001.

Steinberg, Milton. *A Partisan Guide to the Jewish Problem.* B'nai B'rith Hillel Foundations in American Universities. Cornwall, NY: The Cornwall Press, Inc., 1945.

Steinberg, Peter K. *Great Writers: Sylvia Plath.* Philadelphia, PA: Chelsea House Publishers, 2004.

Steiner, Nancy Hunter. *A Closer Look at Ariel: A Memory of Sylvia Plath.* New York: Harper & Row, 1973.

Stevens, Wallace. *The Collected Poems of Wallace Stevens.* New York: A. A. Knopf, 1955. Former Owner Plath, Smith.

Stevenson, Anne. *Bitter Fame: A Life of Sylvia Plath.* 1989. Boston, MA: Houghton Mifflin, 1998.

Stevenson, Robert Louis. "The Strange Case of Dr. Jekyll and Mr. Hyde." In *The Norton Anthology of English Literature: Volume E: The Victorian Age*, edited by Stephen Greenblatt, Carol T. Christ, Alfred David, Barbara K. Lewalski, Lawrence Lipking, George M. Logan, Deirdre Shauna Lynch, Katharine Eisaman Maus, James Noggle, Jahan Ramazani, Catherine Robson, James Simpson, Jon Stallworthy, and Jack Stillinger, 1677–1719. New York: Norton, 2012.

Stitt, Peter. "The Art of Poetry: An Interview with John Berryman." In *Berryman's Understanding: Reflections on the Poetry of John Berryman*, edited by Harry Thomas, 18–44. Boston, MA: Northeastern University Press, 1988.

———. "John Berryman: His Teaching, His Scholarship, His Poetry." In *Recovering Berryman: Essays on a Poet*, edited by Richard J. Kelly and Alan K. Lathrop, 43–56. Ann Arbor: University of Michigan Press, 1993.

Stock, Noel. *The Life of Ezra Pound: An Expanded Edition.* 1970. San Francisco, CA: North Point Press, 1982.

Strangeways, Al. *Sylvia Plath: The Shaping of Shadows.* Madison, NJ: Fairleigh Dickinson University Press, 1998.

Switaj, Elizabeth. "Joyce, Berlitz, and the Teaching of English as a Foreign Language." *Joyce Studies in Italy* 12 (2012): 153–165.

Synge, John M. *Collected Plays: The Shadow of the Glen, Riders to the Sea, The Tinker's Wedding, The Well of the Saints, The Playboy of the Western World, Deirdre of the Sorrows.* Harmondsworth, Middlesex: Penguin, 1952. Former Owner Plath, Smith.

Taylor, Richard. "The Texts of *The Cantos.*" In *The Cambridge Companion to Ezra Pound*, edited by Ira B. Nadel, 161–186. New York: Cambridge University Press, 1999.

Terrell, Carroll F. *A Companion to The Cantos of Ezra Pound.* Berkeley: University of California Press, 1980.

Thomas, Harry, ed. *Berryman's Understanding: Reflections on the Poetry of John Berryman.* Boston, MA: Northeastern University Press, 1988.

Thoreau, Henry David. *Walden and On the Duty of Civil Disobedience.* 1854. New York Rinehart & Company, 1957. Former owner Hughes, Emory

Thornbury, Charles. "A Reckoning with Ghostly Voices (1935–36)." In *Recovering Berryman: Essays on a Poet*, edited by Richard J. Kelly and Alan K. Lathrop, 77–112. Ann Arbor: University of Michigan Press, 1993.

Tindall, William York. *A Reader's Guide to James Joyce.* 1959. Syracuse, NY: Syracuse University Press, 1995.

Tintner, Adeline R. *Henry James's Legacy: The Afterlife of His Figure and Fiction.* Baton Rouge: Louisiana State University Press, 1998.

Trachtman, Ilana, prod. and dir. *Biography: Sylvia Plath.* Working Dog Productions, A&E *Biography* Series, December 27, 2004.

Travisano, Thomas. *Midcentury Quartet: Bishop, Lowell, Jarrell, Berryman, and the Making of a Postmodern Aesthetic.* Charlottesville: University Press of Virginia, 1999.

Treseler, Heather. "Making Poems, Making History: An Interview with Maxine Kumin." *Notre Dame Review* 39 (2015): 135–146.

Trinidad, David. "Anne Sexton Visits Court Green." *TriQuarterly Online.* Monday January 10, 2011. Accessed 8 August 2019. https://www.triquarterly.org/issues/issue-139/anne-sexton-visits-court-green.

———. "Two Sweet Ladies." *American Poetry Review* 35, no. 6 (November/December 2006): 21–29.

Trotter, David. "The Modernist Novel." In *The Cambridge Companion to Modernism*, edited by Michael Levenson, 69–98. New York: Cambridge University Press, 1999.

———. "T. S. Eliot and Cinema." *Modernism/modernity* 13, no. 2 (2006): 237–365.

Troupes, David. "Hughes and Intertextuality." In *Ted Hughes in Context*, edited by Terry Gifford, 40–53. New York: Palgrave Macmillan, 2015.

Tryphonopoulos, Demetres P. and Stephen J. Adams, eds. *The Ezra Pound Encyclopedia.* Westport, CT: Greenwood Press, 2005.

Twitchell, James B. *The Living Dead: A Study of the Vampire in Romantic Literature.* Durham, NC: Duke University Press, 1981.

Tytell, John. *Ezra Pound: The Solitary Volcano.* New York: Doubleday, 1987.

Untermeyer, Louis, ed. *Modern American and Modern British Poetry.* 1919. New York: Harcourt Brace, 1955, Former Owner Plath, Berg.

Van Doren, Mark. "John Berryman: 1914–1972." In *The Essays of Mark Van Doren (1924–1972)*, edited by William Claire, 160–162. Westport, CT: Greenwood Press, 1980.

Van Dyne, Susan R. "The Problem of Biography." In *The Cambridge Companion to Sylvia Plath*, edited by Jo Gill, 3–20. New York: Cambridge University Press, 2006.

———. *Revising Life: Sylvia Plath's Ariel Poems.* Chapel Hill: University of North Carolina Press, 1994.

Van Hulle, Dirk. *Modern Manuscripts: The Extended Mind and Creative Undoing from Darwin to Beckett and Beyond.* New York: Bloomsbury, 2014.

Van Mierlo, Wim. "Reading Joyce in and out of the Archive." *Joyce Studies Annual* 13 (Summer 2002): 32–63.

Van O'Connor, William and Edward Stone, eds. *A Casebook on Ezra Pound.* New York: Thomas Y. Crowell Company, 1959.

Vendler, Helen. *Coming of Age as a Poet: Milton, Eliot, Plath, Keats.* Cambridge, MA: Harvard University Press, 2003.

———. *The Given and the Made: Strategies of Poetic Redefinition.* Cambridge, MA: Harvard University Press, 1995.

———. *Last Looks, Last Books: Stevens, Plath, Lowell, Bishop, Merrill.* Princeton, NJ: Princeton University Press, 2010.

———. "Lowell in the Classroom." In *Robert Lowell: Interviews and Memoirs*, edited by Jeffrey Meyers, 288–297. Ann Arbor: University of Michigan Press, 1988.

———. Mellon Lecture. Email to the author. 14 June 2007.

———. *Our Secret Discipline: Yeats and Lyric Form.* Cambridge, MA: Harvard University Press, 2007.

———. *Poets Thinking: Pope Whitman Dickinson Yeats.* Cambridge, MA: Harvard University Press, 2004.

Vickery, John B. *Robert Graves and the White Goddess.* Lincoln: University of Nebraska Press, 1972.

Wagner-Martin, Linda, ed. *Critical Essays on Anne Sexton.* Boston, MA: G.K. Hall & Co., 1989.

———. "Plath and contemporary American Poetry." In *The Cambridge Companion to Sylvia Plath*, edited by Jo Gill, 52–62. New York: Cambridge University Press, 2006.

———. "Review of Sylvia Plath: The Shaping of Shadows." *American Literature* 71, no. 1 (1999): 192–193.

Wagner-Martin, Linda. *The Bell Jar A Novel of the Fifties.* New York: Twayne Publishers, 1992.

———. *Sylvia Plath: A Literary Life.* New York: St. Martin's Press, 1999.

Wagner-Martin, Linda W. *Sylvia Plath: A Biography.* New York: St. Martin's Griffin, 1987.

Webster, Jean. *Daddy-Long-Legs.* 1912. New York: Random House, 2011.

Webster, John and Cyril Tourneur. *Four Plays*, ed. Eric Bentley. New York: Hill and Wang, Inc., 1956. Former Owner Plath, Smith.

Webster, Noah. *Webster's New Collegiate Dictionary.* Springfield, MA: G. & C. Merriam Co., c. 1949. Former Owner Plath, Smith.

Weissbort, Daniel. "Sylvia Plath and Translation." In *Theme and Vision: Plath and Ronsard*, edited by Anthony Rudolph, 1–15. London: The Menard Press, 1995.

Werner, Marta. *Emily Dickinson's Open Folios: Scenes of Reading, Surfaces of Writing*. Ann Arbor: University of Michigan Press, 1995.

Weston, Jessie Laidlay. *From Ritual to Romance*. 1920. Garden City, NY: Doubleday, 1957. Former Owner Plath, Former Owner Hughes, Emory.

White, Gillian. *Lyric Shame: The "Lyric" Subject of Contemporary American Poetry*. Cambridge, MA: Harvard University Press, 2014.

White, Hayden. *The Content of the Form: Narrative Discourse and Historical Representation*. Baltimore, MD: Johns Hopkins University Press, 1987.

Whittier-Ferguson, John. *Framing Pieces: Designs of the Gloss in Joyce, Woolf, and Pound*. New York: Oxford University Press, 1996.

Williams, C. K. Email to the author. 10 March 2008.

Williams, David Park. "The Background of the Pisan Cantos." *Poetry* (January 1949). In *A Casebook on Ezra Pound*, edited by William Van O'Connor and Edward Stone, 39–43. New York: Thomas Y. Crowell Company, 1959.

Williams, Polly C. "Sexton in the Classroom." In *Anne Sexton: The Artist and Her Critics*, edited by J. D. McClatchy, 96–101. Bloomington: Indiana University Press, 1978.

Williams, Raymond. *Culture and Materialism*. 1980. New York: Verso, 2005.

———. *Politics of Modernism*. 1989. New York: Verso, 2007.

Williams, William Carlos. *Imaginations*. 1938. Edited by Webster Schott. New York: New Directions, 1971.

Wilson, Andrew. *Mad Girl's Love Song: Sylvia and Life before Ted*. London: Simon & Schuster, 2013.

Wilson, Edmund. *Axel's Castle: A Study in the Imaginative Literature of 1870–1930*. 1931. New York: Charles Scribner's Sons, 1950. Former Owner Plath, Smith.

Winder, Elizabeth. *Pain, Parties, Work: Sylvia Plath in New York, Summer 1953*. New York: HarperCollins, 2013.

Wojahn, David. "'In All Them Time Henry Could Not Make Good': Reintroducing John Berryman." *Blackbird* 4, no. 2 (Fall 2005). Accessed December 12, 2008. http://www.blackbird.vcu.edu/v4n2/nonfiction/wojahn_d/berryman.htm

Wollaeger, Mark A. "Introduction" and "Between Stephen and Jim: Portraits of Joyce as a Young Man." In *James Joyce's Portrait of the Artist as a Young Man: A Casebook*, edited by Mark A. Wollaeger, 3–26, 343–356. New York: Oxford University Press, 2003.

"Women of Talent." *Newsweek* LVIII, no. 17 (October 23, 1961): 94–98.

Woodward, Lydia. Interview with the Author. 10 November 2005.

Woolf, Virginia. *The Common Reader: First Series Annotated Edition*. Edited by Andrew McNeillie. 1925. New York: Harcourt Brace, 1984.

———. "The Love of Reading." *A Bloomsbury Group Reader*. Edited by S. P. Rosenbaum, 415–418. Oxford: Blackwell, 1993.

———. *Orlando: A Biography*. 1928. New York: Penguin Books, 1946. Former Owner Plath, Special Collections, Ekstrom Library, University of Louisville, Louisville, KY.

———. *The Pargiters: The Novel-Essay Portion of* The Years. Edited by Mitchell A. Leaska. New York: Harcourt Brace, 1977.

————. *A Room of One's Own*. 1929. Edited by Susan Gubar. New York: Harcourt, 2005.

————. *Three Guineas*. 1938. New York: Harcourt, Inc., 1966.

————. *To the Lighthouse*. New York: Harcourt, Brace, & Co., 1927. Former Owner Plath, Former Owner Hughes, Emory.

————. *To the Lighthouse*. 1927. New York: Oxford University Press, 2008.

————. *The Waves*. 1931. New York: Harcourt Brace, 1959.

————. *A Writer's Diary*. 1953. London: Hogarth Press, 1954. Former Owner Plath, Former Owner Hughes, Emory.

————. "(writing in the margin)." University of Sussex Library. Sussex, UK.

————. *The Years*. 1937. Edited by Eleanor McNees. New York: Harcourt, 2008.

Yeats, William Butler. *Celtic Twilight: Men and Women, Dhouls and Faeries*. London: Lawrence and Bullen, 1893. Former Owner Berryman, Minnesota.

————. *The Collected Poems of W. B. Yeats*. New York: Macmillan, 1952. Former Owner Plath, Smith.

————. *A Vision*. London: T. Werner Laurie Ltd., 1925. Former Owner Berryman, Minnesota.

————. *A Vision*. London: MacMillan & Co., Ltd., 1937. Former Owner Berryman, Minnesota.

Yorsz, Stanley. "The Confessions of A Poetess." *The Colgate Maroon* (Hamilton, NY), February 15, 1972. Page 10.

Index

Note: Page numbers followed by 'n' refer to endnotes.